Idaho

Idaho

Wendy J. Pabich, Ph.D.

The Countryman Press ✳ Woodstock, Vermont

FIRST EDITION

We welcome your comments and suggestions. Please contact Explorer's Guide Editor, The Countryman Press, P.O. Box 748, Woodstock, Vermont 05091, or e-mail countrymanpress@wwnorton.com.

First Edition

ISBN 978-0-88150-744-7

Cover photo © Laurence Parent Photography
Interior photos by the author unless otherwise specified
Book design by Bodenweber Design
Page composition by PerfecType, Nashville, TN
Maps by Mapping Specialists Ltd., © 2008 The Countryman Press

Published by The Countryman Press, P.O. Box 748, Woodstock, Vermont 05091
Distributed by W.W. Norton & Company, Inc., 500 Fifth Avenue, New York, NY 10110

Printed in the United States of America

10 9 8 7 6 5 4 3 2 1

This book is dedicated to my beloved and sorely missed grandparents, Irene G. Lord (1915–2004) and Chester M. Lord (1919–2006), who, I learned somewhere along the way, carefully tracked and mapped all my worldly travels—to the Far East, Patagonia, and the Himalaya, throughout the western United States, and to many points in between; and to Molly (1994–2006), my beautiful, bounding black-lab best friend, who was my finest traveling companion for many a year. They all would have liked to have participated—in some way—in the journey of traveling for and researching and writing this book.

EXPLORE WITH US!

Welcome to the first edition of *Idaho: An Explorer's Guide*. For those of you adventurers looking to get off the beaten path, breathe some crisp mountain air, and stretch your legs (and perhaps push your physical limits), Idaho is your kind of place. Some lesser informed friends may inquire, "Why are you going to *Iowa*?" to which you can just respond with a wry and knowing smile, all the while dreaming of *Idaho's* dramatically rugged mountain ranges stacked one after another, its rushing crystalline rivers, its days upon days of sun (yes, Sun Valley is aptly named), and a deep, dark night sky bursting with stars. Or perhaps you'll be envisioning your time in our funky little mountain towns that brim with creative energy, happy people, warm beds, and fabulous food. Personally, I'd be fantasizing about the arcing turns I was going to rip through a powdery backcountry tree stash, spraying up face shot after face shot until burning quads and lungs demanded that I stop, followed by the hard-won beer shared with friends at the end of the day. It's pretty simple.

In your travels around and through our fabulous playground, this book should provide you with some insights to help you see Idaho as the locals do—a little historical context here, some local lore there, an outrageous story to top it off. Further, this book will point you in the direction of the coolest spots around—showing you where to play, eat, and sleep. In Idaho, just as often as not, exploration is not of the mild kind—we do some serious backcountry travel here. For those of you really interested in seeing this country, this book provides a host of information from which you might begin planning a serious adventure. This book is a compilation of resources, and as much as possible, I've referred to other more localized and detailed guides—entire books dedicated to hiking, mountain biking, or fishing in all or certain parts of the state, as well as Web resources that provide nuts and bolts about where and how to reserve a campsite, outline hiking routes, or offer more detailed information about historical spots along the way. In addition, for all outdoor activities, it is generally best to talk with the local experts about where the alpine wildflowers are blooming, which are the best and safest places to ski in the backcountry, and how the rivers are running.

With this in mind, for each region I've included listings of local ski, boating, and outdoor shops, avalanche centers, Forest Service offices, and more. Please consult with these resources in planning your outdoor trip. And please do follow the backcountry adage: Know before you go! This means if you want to go backcountry skiing, you'd better understand snow and avalanches and how to use a beacon, probe, and shovel, and you'd best have the proper clothing and equipment. If the rivers are calling your name, be sure you are skilled enough to handle the waters you choose to boat. If it is solace you seek, please know how to read a map. In all cases, if you're not sure that you know, hire a guide! Idaho has hundreds of licensed outdoor outfitters running backcountry skiing, mountaineering, river rafting and kayaking, hiking, horseback riding, and hunting trips through all sorts of terrain and for explorers of all abilities. These folks are generally highly skilled outdoorspeople who are more than happy to share their knowledge about the backcountry, help you have a safe trip, regale you with crazy outdoor lore, and pamper you with wonderful camp cuisine. It's a great way to go!

WHAT'S WHERE

This compendium of Idaho facts and figures, geology, geography, and lore will give you some insight into those things that become part of the psyche when you spend enough time in a place. This A-to-Z list is by no means complete, but it highlights some of Idaho's great spots and activities, outlines some of the natural history that so defines this state, and provides some tips and information to help you travel safely throughout this wild country.

LODGING

For those areas where it was possible, I focused lodging descriptions on those privately owned and quainter bed & breakfasts, hotels, lodges, and other places to stay. While not my cup of tea, chain hotels are often the only option when you are looking for a place to sleep on your way in and out of some backcountry adventure or another. For some of Idaho's more remote spots, where the options are slim, I've listed some chain hotels; a shower and a warm bed can be good.

RESTAURANTS

With the exception of a few finer dining spots in the resort areas, throughout Idaho dining attire is generally casual. In fact, a man walking around most towns wearing a suit will garner some odd looks (no joke). As with lodging, some of our great little cultural meccas have plenty of fabulous dining, but once you hit the long, winding road between destinations, don't expect much. In fact, if you're smart, you'll bring a cooler of food and drinks on longer road trips.

PRICES AND HOURS OF OPERATION

Prices and opening times at restaurants and lodgings often shift like the sands of time, particularly in Idaho. In fact, in the resort town of Ketchum, we have our very own "Ketchum Time," which essentially means you can show up when you show up. Prices and hours are provided throughout this book more as a barometer than exact figures. If you really need to know, give a call to the hotel or restaurant before you show up.

We would appreciate any comments or corrections so that our next edition will be as complete as possible. Please write to Explorer's Guide Editor, The Countryman Press, P.O. Box 748, Woodstock, VT 05091, or e-mail countryman press@wwnorton.com.

ACKNOWLEDGMENTS

In addition to being the product of more than a little slave labor, this book would not have been possible were it not for the many friends, acquaintances, and strangers who were often eager to share stories, insights, descriptions, and interpretations about the places in Idaho that mean so much to each of them. Such warm reception came from country-store owners who know more local juice than anyone, Forest Service rangers willing to give up valuable tips on backcountry gems, friends sharing boisterous adventure banter, and old-salts-around-town who know more than they think they know.

A slew of folks provided excellent assistance with some of the more tedious research, including John Foster, Leslie Lindsley, and Britt Udesen. Matt Furber gets special thanks for also lending some wordsmithing. I cannot thank each of them enough for their contributions.

Great words of wisdom came from Willy Felton, Jen King, and Pam Street. Matt Furber (again) and Chris Pilaro, two photographically talented friends, stepped up with beautiful pictures of Idaho's goods. Heartfelt thanks go to Mitzi and Stu Felton for taking in a forlorn and unknown friend-of-their-nephew rather than letting me sleep by the side of the road, turning what might have been an "interesting" experience into a fabulous weekend.

My parents, Dick and Diane Pabich, deserve credit for taking me at an early age to places near and far, instilling in me a pesky travel bug that clearly won't go away—no matter how far I venture.

Best and last of all, countless appreciation goes to James Foster for being a fun, adventurous coexplorer and photographer and an awesome supporter, for cooking me dinners, providing moral support and all other good things, and generally putting up with me in the final weeks prior to my deadline.

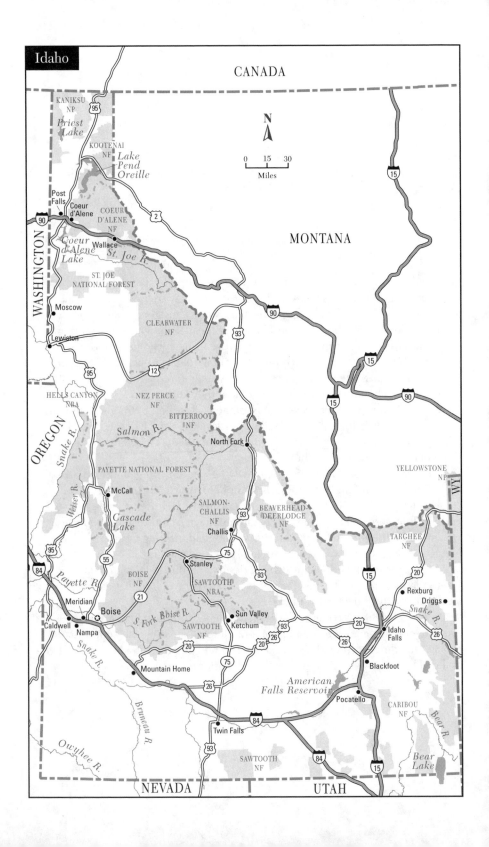

CONTENTS

INTRODUCTION

I am a relative newcomer to Idaho. Drawn to its wide-open spaces, jagged peaks, crystalline rivers, and a community of adventurous souls, a handful of years ago I made sleepy little Hailey, Idaho, my home. Nestled beneath Carbonate Mountain in the Wood River Valley, this quaint western town stills displays evidence of its history as a mining center. The craftsman-style houses are generally small and manageable, the gridded streets make sense, neighbors are truly neighbors. It was this small-town appeal, so much a part of my New England history, that made me feel instantly at home here. Yet there are some discernable differences. Volvos are replaced with Ford F150s. Biodiesel is the new compost. Skis, snow shovels, climbing gear, kayaks, snowmobiles, avalanche beacons, and mountain bikes outnumber sailboats, tennis racquets, beach chairs, and play structures, ten to one. Free spirits are encouraged, economic success tolerated. Artists, musicians, writers, adventurers, risk-takers, yogis, and skiers abound. Tibetan prayer flags wave freely. The sun shines daily. Bluebird skies are the norm. Dogs and people run free.

Like many before me, I was lured by the sense of adventure that Idaho's geography, geology, and physical environment offer. As one of the least-populated states in the Lower 48, Idaho represents a frontier where you can disappear into the mountains for weeks on end—on foot or on ski or however you may choose—to intimately connect with the earth, guided only by your own ingenuity, intuition, and emotions, and experience freedom like no other. It is a place where you can make your own way. For me, it was a place to take my hard-won academic credentials and experience as an environmental scientist and hydrologist and find quick welcome as a water expert in an alpine desert region facing incredible growth and development pressures. All the while, I've been alpine and backcountry and Nordic and skate skiing, hiking and mountain biking and yurting and camping and river rafting like a fiend. Not to be missed along the way has been the discovery of Idaho's people and way of life—the farmers and the ranchers and the old-school explorers, the towns, the farming and animal husbandry, the music and art festivals, the mining history, and, throughout all, the shared sense of independence.

As a scientist and an artist, I have long been compelled by the fractal patterns, strength, beauty, and changeability of Mother Nature and have spent endless time observing her in action. Growing up by the Atlantic Ocean, I came to know the sea in the intimate way that is made possible only by being in and around it and by looking, touching, tasting, and feeling. It is this kinesthetic sense that allows me to recognize the nuances in light and wave, sky and scent, beach form and season that portend an arriving northeaster or give evidence of its passing, to discern whether I am walking on a winter or a summer beach, and to read the seas' whispers about whether the fishing is good or whether it is time to go home. Yet in my first couple visits to Idaho, in late summer, I didn't feel this connection to the landscape. I remember finding the vast openness both compelling and disquieting—it seemed that there was a paucity of tree cover, the hills were brown and dry, it was hot. Where was the water? Where was the green?

Since those days, I have spent countless hours in Idaho's outdoors: Backpacking through the chalky white peaks of the Boulder–White Clouds and swimming in crystalline blue alpine lakes. Walking with my dog in nearby canyons in sub zero temperatures, watching the alpenglow illuminate snow-covered peaks, listening to the Styrofoam squeak of frigid snow beneath my feet, and feeling cold, dry air permeate through my corduroys to literally freeze the fat on my butt. Sometimes drifting, sometimes churning though deep alpine desert canyons by kayak and by raft. Skiing everywhere and everyhow—some days slogging up a ridgeline with telemark skis and skins, everywhere surrounded by white, save the boughs of conifers peeking out beneath a blanket of new snow; other days, feeling my face aglow as the sun baked my skin and too soon exposed muddy southern slopes; and still others, skating along through stands of pine and along willow-lined streams enjoying the exertion and the wind on my face. And some days just quietly hiking near verdant wetlands and sage-strewn hills.

During these explorations, I began to understand that this landscape, too, demands an intimate understanding, that the nuances of the ocean are also to be found in the sage and scree by those with a discerning eye, nose, tongue, and skin. I now feel the messages in the landscape: how the dense stands of Douglas fir distinguish north slopes from their sage-covered south-facing counterparts (and how they guard their powder stashes in winter); where to find boundless patches of alpine wildflowers secreted away only for those willing to hike; the way the scent of cottonwoods heralds the spring and what it means that the desert smells like rain. Throughout this book, I hope to share some of what this beautiful place means to me.

Idaho is all about the country. Dramatic landscapes seem endless, and the opportunities for recreation and contemplation in these places are correspondingly boundless. Scattered across this landscape are little gems of civilization— small towns filled with art and theater, music, and fine food. Lodging ranges from the fabulous (and pricey) guest ranches, lodges, and destination resorts that satisfy even the most discerning to warm beds that can be found along the way when you've had enough camping. People are friendly and laid-back; smiles abound. And, while great amenities and funky urban charm are to be found in some of these enclaves, most often there are many, many road miles between coffee shop–laden villages. Take note: If you are looking for conveniences, you might be coming to the wrong place. Idaho is not a shopper's paradise; you are not likely to find that cute little blouse you were looking for, and your chances of showing up in a random town and finding a quaint bed & breakfast are slim. Camping and traveling on the cheap are ways of life here. That being said, come and have fun!

WHAT'S WHERE IN IDAHO

AGRICULTURE

Agriculture has only recently been supplanted by manufacturing as the most important sector in Idaho's economy. Idaho has long been known as the Potato State, producing more potatoes (primarily Russet Burbank) each year than any other state. Hay, wheat, and barley are also important export crops, and cattle and dairy goods are among the state's leading agricultural products, with dairy cows producing about 10 billion pounds of milk annually. The majority of Idaho's agricultural production occurs in southern Idaho, in a patchwork of contiguous, hexagonally packed irrigated circles of verdant green, straw yellow, and every tone in between, stretching across the vast semicircle of alluvial sediment of the 10,800-square-mile Snake River Plain. These vast fields of beans, peas, potatoes, alfalfa, sugar beets, wheat, and barley depend upon irrigation supplied by the underlying Snake River Aquifer,

Matt Furber

which is thought to contain as much as 1 billion acre-feet of water, making it one of the world's largest aquifers.

AIRLINES

The air carriers that service Idaho's various airports include **Alaska Airlines** (800-426-0333), **Delta/Skywest Airlines** (800-221-1212), **Express Jet** (888-958-9538), **Frontier Airlines** (800-432-1359), **Horizon Air** (800-547-9308), **Northwest Airlines** (800-225-2525), **Southwest Airlines** (800-435-9792), **United/United Express** (800-241-6522), and **US Airways** (800-428-4322).

AIRPORTS

Idaho has six primary airports: **Boise Air Terminal** (Gowen Field; 208-383-3110; www.cityofboise.org/departments/airport/); **Friedman Memorial Airport** in Hailey (Ketchum and Sun Valley; 208-788-4956; www.flysunairport.com); **Idaho Falls Regional Airport** (Fanning Field; 208-612-8221; www.ci.idaho-falls.id.us/main/index2.asp?PageId=1050); **Lewiston–Nez Perce County Airport** (208-746-7962; www.lcairport.net/); **Magic Valley Regional Airport** in Twin Falls (Joslin Field; 208-733-5215; www.tfid.org/airport/); and **Pocatello Regional Airport** (208-234-6154; www.pocatello.us/Airport/Airport.htm). The state also has many regional, county, and municipal airports. For more listings, see http://www.airnav.com/airports/us/ID. If you are jetting about Idaho, you might want to look into relatively cheap commuter flights between Boise and Spokane, Washington.

AMTRAK

Amtrak (800-872-7245; www.amtrak

.com) operates one long-distance train through Idaho, the *Empire Builder*, with daily service from Chicago and Minneapolis to Seattle and Portland via **Sandpoint**.

AREA CODE

Idaho has but one area code: 208. We are rural. Case closed.

AVALANCHE ADVISORY CENTERS

Avalanche awareness is requisite to backcountry travel in Idaho's mountainous terrain during winter conditions. Avalanche advisories and education are available from three avalanche centers in the state: **Idaho Panhandle National Forests Avalanche Center** (Coeur d' Alene; 208-765-7323; www.fs.fed.us/ipnf/visit/conditions/backcountry/index.html); **Payette Avalanche Center** (McCall;

WARNING

WHEN YOU PASS BEYOND THIS SKI AREA BOUNDARY YOU ARE LEAVING THE AREA OF SKI PATROL SERVICES. THERE ARE NO AVALANCHE HAZARD REDUCTION MEASURES, TRAIL GROOMING, OR SIGNAGE.

YOU ARE ENTERING A HIGH RISK AREA WHICH HAS MANY HAZARDS INCLUDING BUT NOT LIMITED TO AVALANCHES, CLIFFS, AND HIDDEN OBSTACLES. YOU ARE AT RISK FROM THESE NATURAL HAZARDS. YOU ARE RESPONSIBLE FOR YOUR DECISIONS AND ACTION, YOUR OWN RESCUE, FOR THE COST OF YOUR RESCUE AND YOU WAVE ALL CLAIMS FOR INJURY. YOUR LIFT TICKET FURTHER DEFINES YOUR RESPONSIBILITIES.

208-634-0409; www.payetteavalanche
.org); and **Sawtooth National Forest Avalanche Center** (Ketchum–
Sun Valley; 208-622-8027; www
.avalanche.org/~svavctr/). Avalanche
training is also offered by many of the
winter outfitters and guiding operations in the state. For more information on avalanche safety and
education, contact the **American
Avalanche Association** (www
.americanavalancheassociation.org) or
Avalanche.org (www.avalanche.org).
Please play safely.

BEARS
Idaho is home to healthy populations
of black and grizzly bears. There are
at least 300 to 400 grizzlies living in
the northwestern Rockies. Idaho's
populations are found in the Cabinet-
Yaak, Selkirk, and Greater Yellowstone ecosystems. As many as 20,000
black bears inhabit Idaho, living primarily in the state's northern forested
regions. For tips on safe behavior in
bear country, visit **Idaho Panhandle
National Forest**'s Web site (http://
www.fs.fed.us/ipnf/visit/brochures/
bears/index.html).

BICYCLING
There is a decent road-biking scene
centered in Boise, but because there
are relatively few roads in Idaho, for
the most part the best riding is on the
trails. See Mountain Biking.

BIRD-WATCHING
One of the top birding destinations in
the state is the 600,000-acre **Snake
River Birds of Prey National Conservation Area** (208-384-3300; www
.birdsofprey.blm.gov), a large tract of
chaparral and sagebrush that runs
along the Snake River from just south
of Boise to the Mountain Home and

Bruneau areas. This conservation area
was set aside in 1993 to protect one of
the world's densest populations of
birds of prey, including falcons,
eagles, hawks, and owls. It is an area
worth checking out; see Part 2, Southwestern Idaho: Class V Adventure,
Chapter 6, The Bruneau and Owyhee
Rivers: Cowboy Country, To Do—
Wildlife Viewing). With so much
ruggedly wild terrain in the state,
birds (and other wildlife) are abundant. If you get out onto a trail, you
might be lucky enough to spot a bald
eagle, great blue heron, sage grouse,
or any number of the more than 400
bird species that can be found here.
Two field guides that come highly recommended are *The Idaho Bird Guide*
by Dan Svingen and Kas Dumroese
(Backeddy Books, 2004), which provides information on Idaho's major
ecoregions, top birding destinations,
and "Idaho Rarities," and *Field Guide
to Birds—Western Region* by Donald
and Lillian Stokes (Little, Brown and
Co., 1996). This book is well organized by bird group for ease of identification in the field.

BOATING
Idaho's larger lakes and reservoirs
attract a fair number of sailors, flatwater canoers and kayakers, and motorheads. Some of the more popular
destinations include Lucky Peak
Reservoir and Lake Lowell near
Boise, C. J. Strike Reservoir near
Mountain Home, Payette and Cascade lakes near McCall, Priest Lake
and Lakes Pend Oreille and Coeur
d'Alene in the north, Redfish Lake
near Stanley, and flatwater spots on
the Snake River near Lewiston. A
handful of sailing organizations can
provide information on boating facilities, sailboat rentals, yacht clubs, and

sailing regattas, including the notorious Spud Cup in Sandpoint. Check out **Coeur d'Alene Sailing Association** (www.ussailing.net/csa), **Lewis-Clark Sailing Association** (www.lcsailing.org), **Sandpoint Sailing Association** (www.sandpointsailing.com), and **Southern Idaho Sailing Association** (www.idahosailing.org). **Idaho Division of Tourism Development** (208-334-2470; www.visitidaho.org) also provides a wealth of information on boating opportunities throughout the state. See also Whitewater Kayaking and Rafting.

BUGS AND SNAKES

For the most part, higher elevations help create relatively bug-free experiences in Idaho's backcountry. At lower elevations and around water, mosquitos can be an issue. West Nile virus just recently migrated to Idaho, so remember to bring insect repellent. Bees are a concern, and for those with allergies, help can be far away (don't forget to bring your epipen!). Idaho has a few nasty spiders, including black widows, brown recluses, and hobo spiders. Of course, for the avid fly fishermen and women who flock to Idaho's churning rivers, our prolific riparian bug hatches are a glorious sight!

For the less squeamish, Idaho's Mormon cricket provides an interesting bug tale. These two-inch-long black katydids live a boom-and-bust lifecycle, and in some years, prodigious insect booms have ruined crops and blanketed roadways in southern Idaho with a carpet of carapaces—a truly creepy sight (and sound!). The insect earned its name in 1848, when in throngs it besieged crops planted by early Mormon pioneers in Utah; it is told that the crops were saved only by concerted prayer that brought flocks of seagulls to eat the crickets, thereby saving crops and lives.

Below 5,000 feet, rattlesnakes can be found in arid desert areas and in some of Idaho's major river basins, including the Salmon and Snake River basins. Be aware when hiking on lower-elevation trails (even during day excursions on river trips) during the warmer months.

BUREAU OF LAND MANAGEMENT (BLM)

BLM has 12 field offices administering 11.9 million acres of public land throughout Idaho—22 percent of the state's federal acreage. In addition, the agency manages almost 40 million acres of subsurface mineral resources on federal, tribal, and private lands and manages grazing allotments and timber sales on its lands. See BLM's Web site (www.blm.gov/id/st/en/prog/recreation.html) for comprehensive information on recreational activities on BLM land in Idaho.

BUS SERVICE

Bus service throughout the state is provided by **Greyhound Bus Service** (1-800-231-2222; www.greyhound.com), **Northwestern Stage Lines** (208-336-3300; http://66.193.141.11), **Salt Lake Express** (800-356-9796; www.saltlakeexpress.com), and **Sun Valley Express** (877-622-8267; https://secure.sunvalleyexpress.com). See Idaho's **Division of Tourism Development** (208-334-2470; www.visitidaho.org/about/transportation.aspx) for the location of the state's nine bus stations and their schedules.

CABIN RENTALS

The U.S. Forest Service operates more than 50 rustic cabins in some gorgeous spots throughout Idaho, providing access for hiking, skiing, mountain biking, horseback riding, and other recreational activities on public lands. Cabins are available for rent for up to a week at a time for short money and can be reserved via **Recreation One-Stop** (877-444-6777; www.reacreation.gov). **Idaho Department of Parks and Recreation** (208-334-4199; http://parksand recreation.idaho.gov) also operates a system of cabins and yurts throughout the state. They are a sweet way to ease into the wilds!

CAMPGROUNDS

In Idaho, there are far more places to camp than lodges to sleep in. With more than 66 percent of Idaho's land owned by the federal or state government, opportunities for dispersed camping on public lands are virtually limitless. The U.S. Forest Service (USFS) is the largest owner of these lands, followed by the U.S. Bureau of Land Management (BLM; see separate entry above). For information on established campgrounds on public lands, visit the **Public Lands Information Center** (505-345-9498 or 877-851-8946; www.publiclands.org). This site lists 551 public-land camping areas in Idaho. It also provides information on educational programs offered on public lands throughout the state, including courses on Leave No Trace camping practices (see entry below). Another resource is the federal government's **Recreation One-Stop** Web site (www.recreation .gov), which provides information on 161 public campgrounds in Idaho. For information and rules governing dispersed camping, contact the appropriate USFS or BLM office for the area in which you're interested. Idaho is part of the **USDA Forest Service Intermountain Region** (www.fs.fed .us/r4), and contact information for each of the 13 national forests in Idaho can be found on their Web site.

A guide to recreational activities, including camping in designated and nondesignated campsites in each of the 12 **BLM management districts** in Idaho, can be found on the BLM Web site (www.blm.gov/id/st/en/prog/recreation.1.html).

CAR RENTALS

Cars are available for rent at most of the airports throughout Idaho from many of the major rental companies, including **Avis** (800-831-2847; www.avis.com), **Budget** (800-527-0700; www.budget.com), **Enterprise** (800-736-8227; www.enterprise.com/car_rental/home), **Hertz** (800-654-3131; wwww.hertz.com), and **Thrifty** (800-367-2277; www.thrifty.com).

CHAMBERS OF COMMERCE

Local and regional chambers of commerce are listed in each chapter under Guidance. For many of the smaller, remote towns in Idaho, chamber organizations are often small and may not have public offices. It is best to call ahead or check out listed Web sites.

CITIES

Idaho has 12 incorporated cities with populations greater than 20,000, of which Boise is both the largest (with a population of roughly 193,000) and the state capital. Other principal cities are Nampa, Pocatello, Idaho Falls, and Meridian. Here's a note of interest: In Idaho, a city may be formed when residents of any unincorporated contiguous area containing not less than 125 qualified electors present a petition signed by the majority of the electors to the board of county commissioners asking that they be incorporated as a city. This means that we have some *very* small "cities."

CLIMATE

Idaho is a study in extremes. Annual temperature patterns depend on both latitude and altitude and result in temperatures ranging from -60 degrees F to 118 degrees F. The southern part of the state is characterized by hot, dry, high-desert summer days and cool nights, while more northern locales are cooler and wetter. Summers are short. Winter in the mountains is often very cold and snowy, but also can be filled with stunning days with bluebird skies. Average annual precipitation ranges from 12 inches in the south to about 25 inches in the north. It is best to come prepared for a range of weather; this is critically important if you plan to venture into the wilderness or even drive Idaho's remote highways.

COFFEE

It seems that many of the outdoorsy folks who make Idaho home are also coffee snobs who insist on only the best beans—regardless of how lightly they might be trying to travel. Fortunately, we in Idaho are not at a loss for good brew, and great coffeehouses

abound. We also have a few local coffee companies, including Moxie Java and White Cloud Coffee.

CONSERVATION GROUPS

Idaho has a plethora of conservation groups. Some of the larger organizations include the **Conservation Fund** (208-726-4419; www.conservationfund.org), **Greater Yellowstone Coalition** (208-522-7927; www.greateryellowstone.org), **Idaho Conservation League** (208-345-6933; www.wildidaho.org), **Idaho Rivers United** (208-343-7481; www.idahorivers.org), the **Nature Conservancy** (208-788-8988; www.nature.org), **Winter Wildlands Alliance** (208-336-4203; www.winterwildlands.org), and **Yellowstone to Yukon Conservation Initiative** (Y2Y; 406-570-0152; www.y2y.net). This is just a smattering of the conservation groups hard at work in Idaho; many other dynamic organizations operate locally.

COUNTIES

Idaho has 44 counties, from Ada County to Washington County. With just over 300,000 residents, Ada County (home to Boise) is the most populous county in the state. By contrast, rural Camas County has fewer than 1,000 residents in about the same number of square miles. Not surprisingly, Idaho County, smack-dab in the middle of Idaho's great Clearwater region, is the state's largest county, spanning more than 8,500 square miles. With 407 square miles to its name, Payette County is the state's smallest.

DRIVING

Idaho is a road-tripper's paradise. With land area twice that of the six New England States combined and miles and miles of scenic roads winding around and through stunning alpine terrain, glowing yellow meadows, sage-strewn ranches, verdant green irrigated farmland, and scenic little western outposts, there is no end to back road driving possibilities. Most of Idaho is very remote, with long stretches of road between any signs of civilization.

I would be remiss if I didn't issue a few words of caution about driving in Idaho. Given its remoteness and the rugged terrain, you would be wise to ensure that your vehicle is in good working order and you have adequate food and water, the necessary tools to change a flat tire or wire up a dangling muffler, and road safety supplies such as flares and a flashlight. I also recommend bringing a first-aid kit, warm clothes, a down sleeping bag, and tire chains, especially when traveling in winter. Know when you go that help could be far away, roads can be really rough, cell phones don't work in many places (satellite phones can come in handy), and it can be a long while between cars. Also be aware that you are very likely to encounter wildlife while driving at night on remote roads; there are some places that you would be best not to drive at night. Further, unless you can deal with an endless diet of gas-station burritos, bring your own food when you set out from a bigger town. If you are questioning whether you need to gas up, gas up. Expect to pee in the bushes here and there.

Lastly, it is a really bad idea to speed in little Idaho towns. Speed limits near these towns drop in zones from highway speeds to 45 miles per hour, then 35, then 25, and the like, and small-town cops will be waiting to snag out-of-staters with fat fines. Not fun.

EMERGENCIES

Dial 9-1-1 statewide in case of emergency. Phone numbers and addresses for regional medical facilities are provided under Medical Emergencies for each region in this guidebook. It is a good idea to be prepared for emergencies when traveling throughout Idaho. Much of the state is remote, and help is not always easily accessible. I have been pulled out of a snow-filled ditch by a state plow on a desolate road leading out of Stanley in the dead of winter only moments after sliding into it. I have also had the pleasure of being taken by ambulance from this same region to the hospital in Ketchum to be treated for bee sting–induced anaphylactic shock, after an ungodly long discussion, an unnecessary paper work session, and phone calls to extinct phone numbers by emergency medical technicians that scared me more than the bee did. Just be aware that you may be on your own. **Air Saint Luke's** (208-706-1000; www.stlukesonline.org/specialties_and_services/ASL/) or **Saint Alphonsus Life Flight** (208-367-3996; www.sarmc.org/bodysarmc3.cfm?id=32) both offer heli-transport to a major medical center for wilderness and other emergencies. Given the remoteness of this state and our predilection for adventure, many locals buy this service ($50 per year).

EVENTS

There is no shortage of things to do, people to see, and events to attend in Idaho. **Idaho Division of Tourism Development** (www.visitidaho.org) is a great resource providing up-to-date information on cultural events, fairs and festivals, film fests, historic events, rodeos, sporting events, winter celebrations, and even Lewis and Clark–related events. In addition, select events are listed under Special Events throughout this book.

FACTS AND FIGURES

Here are a few numbers to put the state in perspective. Population: 1,466,465, according to the 2006 U.S. Census estimate). Statehood: July 3, 1890; Idaho is the 43rd state. Nickname: Gem State. Motto: Esto Perpetua ("It is perpetual"). State bird: mountain bluebird (*Sialia currucoides*). State flower: syringa (*Philadelphus lewisii*), also known as Lewis's mock orange. State tree: western white pine (*Pinus monticola*). Abbreviation: ID. For more statistics, see also Geography.

FARMER'S MARKETS

Given Idaho's agricultural bounty, it is no surprise that great farmer's markets can be found throughout the state. Organic produce is becoming easier to find at these markets, and artists are also increasingly represented. **Rural Roots** (http://www.ruralroots.org/FMD/FMDListing.asp) is a great source of information on Idaho's farmer's markets. See also the entries under To See in each chapter.

FISHING

Idaho has more than 10 blue-ribbon wild trout streams, including the renowned Henrys Fork, Silver Creek (of Ernest Hemingway fame), and St. Joe rivers, which attract anglers from around the globe and provide fodder for many a local fish tale. Nestled in our rugged mountains are more than 1,500 high alpine lakes with great trout fishing; numerous large lakes and reservoirs provide additional fishing opportunities. Most Idaho fishing waters are open to the public with

free access; fly-fishing men and women are often seen scattered along and in the most popular rivers, each in their own Zen world. Secret spots will not be given up easily. Consult **Idaho Fish and Game** (208-334-3700; www.fishandgame.idaho.gov/fish/) for information on obtaining fishing licenses and fishing and angling guides containing general information on most of the state's fisheries. *Fly Fisher's Guide to Idaho* by locals Ken Retallic and Rocky Barber (Wilderness Adventures Press, 2002) is a favorite guidebook to the great fishing spots of Idaho.

Like many areas, Idaho is having trouble with the proliferating New Zealand mud snail, which first showed up in the Snake River in 1987. Because they can outcompete native species for food, these critters can wreak havoc on local ecosystems and can ruin your favorite fisheries!

Anglers are asked to take special precautions, including thoroughly cleaning and rinsing equipment before leaving a fishing site, drying all equipment (including boats) for at least 48 hours prior to using it again, removing any visible vegetation from all equipment (fishing gear, clothes, boat, trailer, etc.) that has been in the water, and staying on the lookout for snails and mussels on your equipment to help quell the spread of this prolific snail. These organisms multiply so quickly, it is thought that one snail theoretically could be responsible for producing a population of 3.7 million within two years.

FORESTED LANDS

Idaho is truly a wild place, boasting 20,458,000 acres of national forestlands, covering almost 40 percent of the state's land area. With 9.3 million acres of inventoried roadless areas,

Idaho has the most roadless acreage of the Lower 48. At 2.3 million acres, the Frank Church–River of No Return Wilderness Area is the second-largest area of protected wilderness in the continental United States. The **U.S. Forest Service** (www.roadless .fs.fed.ud/states/id/state3.shtml) provides great maps to inventoried roadless areas throughout the state. as well as Web sites for each of the **13 national forests** (www.fs.fed .us/recreation/map/state_list.shtml).

GEOGRAPHY

Idaho is 479 miles long by 305 miles wide and encompasses 83,574 square miles; this makes it the 14th-largest state in the United States. With 823 square miles covered by water, Idaho has no shortage of stunning alpine lakes, ponds, rivers, streams, and creeks, nor does it suffer from flatness. Borah Peak, at 12,662 feet above sea level, is the highest point in Idaho, while portions of the Snake River, near Lewiston in the northwestern part of the state, are only 710 feet above sea level. Flatlanders should take note that the mean elevation is 5,000 feet above sea level; some people experience windedness and fatigue prior to acclimatization to altitude. Idaho lies entirely west of the Continental Divide, which forms its eastern boundary for some distance near Yellowstone National Park. Idaho's landscape is widely varied; explorers can find mountains, canyons, alpine meadows, verdant wetlands, fertile lowlands, and arid plains.

GEOLOGY

Idaho is a geologically active and diverse landscape. Evidence of recent geologic activity abounds: Uneroded cinder cones, craters, and lava fields cover vast portions of southern Idaho, including Craters of the Moon National Monument. More than 500 cirques, carved by advancing glaciers, are found throughout Idaho's high mountain regions. The pronounced Idaho Batholith, a composite mass of granitic plutons covering approximately 15,400 square miles in central Idaho, attests to a history of oceanic plate subduction, followed by crustal melting and resultant orogenic uplift and isostatic rebound. The 400-mile-long, crescent-shaped Snake River Plain sweeps across the southern part of the state as a legacy of the crustal movement across the Yellowstone hot spot. Along with this geologic history comes stunning alpine peaks, incising rivers, rare minerals and gemstones, hot springs, and a wealth of beauty that is better experienced than described. Geology buffs should be sure to bring a copy of *Roadside Geology of Idaho* by David D. Alt and Donald W. Hyndman (Mountain Press Publishing Company, 1989) when cruising throughout the Gem State.

GOLF

Idaho has 115 golf courses, including five awarding-winning courses in Sun Valley, Coeur d'Alene, Worley, and Eagle, as well as a Jack Nicklaus–designed course (the Idaho Club) currently under construction in Sandpoint. For a complete listing of the state's golf courses, see **GolfLink** (www.golflink.com/golf-courses/ state.asp?state=ID). See also the entries under To Do in each chapter.

GUEST RANCHES

With its snowcapped alpine peaks, rushing streams, Douglas firs, and open meadows, Idaho has got to be one of the most romantic spots on the planet; a vacation at a guest ranch nestled in this geography seems to fulfill many childhood fantasies. A couple Web sites that are helpful in locating guest ranches throughout Idaho are www.duderanches.com/ cgi-bin/duderanch/search.cgi?State =Idaho and www.infohub.com/ Lodgings/guest_ranch/usa_idaho _guest_ranches.html. The **Idaho Outfitters and Guides Association** (208-342-1438; www.ioga.com) also has a comprehensive listing of guest ranches affiliated with guiding operations to help facilitate a backcountry adventure, staged from the luxury of a warm bed and cozy hearth.

GUIDES AND OUTFITTERS

Idaho Outfitters and Guides Association (208-342-1438; www.ioga.org) represents the majority of the state's full-time outfitters and guides, listing more than 250 outfitters that can take you on guided hunting, fishing, river running, trail riding, hiking, biking, climbing, skiing, snowmobiling, and guest-ranch trips. **Idaho Outfitters and Guides Licensing Board** (208-327-7380; www.oglb.idaho.gov) in Boise is the state's official licensing body, and it maintains a list of all licensed outfitters throughout the state. Its Web site allows you to search for guides by region and activity.

HIGHWAYS

Idaho's network of highways tends to follow river valleys (often trending southeast–northwest), sometimes making the crow's route between points more attractive. Idaho's primary highways are these: I-84 runs through southwestern Idaho from the Salt Lake, Utah, area to Idaho's bor-

der with Oregon near Payette. I-15 runs north–south through eastern Idaho and through Idaho Falls and Pocatello. I-90 skims east–west across Idaho's panhandle. US 95 runs north–south in western Idaho. US 93 and ID 75 run north–south right down the middle of the state. **Idaho Department of Transportation** (www.itd .idaho.gov/byways/) is a great resource for information on Idaho's numerous Scenic Historic and Backcountry Byways. If you are planning a driving trip through Idaho, see *Idaho's Scenic Highways: A Mile-by-Mile Road Guide* by K. E. Rivers (Great Vacations! Inc., 1997). Also see Wandering Around in each chapter.

HIKING

A series of books, encyclopedic in length, could be written about hiking opportunities in Idaho. If you are looking to spend a few days (or the remainder of your life) hiking though-out Idaho, your best bet is to pick up one or more of the detailed hiking guides written about the areas you plan to visit. For a great guide to hiking some of the wilder and more remote spots throughout Idaho, see *Hiking Idaho* by Ralph and Jackie Maughan (2nd edition, the Globe Pequot Press, 2001). For more serious climbers, another great resource is *Exploring Idaho's Mountains: A Guide for Climbers, Scramblers, and Hikers* by Tom Lopez (The Mountaineers Books, 1990). Margaret Fuller also has a handful of great trail guides, including *Trails of the Frank Church–River of No Return Wilderness*, *Trails of Western Idaho*, *Trails of Eastern Idaho*, and *Trails of the Sawtooth and White Cloud Mountains* (Trail Guide Books, 2002). The **U.S. Forest Service** (www.fs.fed.us/r4)

can provide a wealth of information on hiking, camping, and other recreational opportunities in each of the 13 national forests within Idaho. Calling the individual national forest offices can often be highly fruitful if you can speak to a ranger working in the district in which you're interested. They know more about popular hiking and camping spots, wildlife, maps, and possible issues (such as wildfires or road washouts) than anyone and are usually happy to help. See also Hiking under To Do in each chapter.

HISTORY

Idaho's history is a tale of Native Americans, then explorers and miners, followed by farmers and timber barons. In prehistoric times (15,000–6,000 BC), Idaho's Native American inhabitants were big-game hunters who made a living hunting mastodons, woolly mammoths, and other large game, as well as fishing and gathering wild plants. Warming of the planet during the Archaic Period (6,000 BC–AD 500) led to the demise of large mammals and an increase in river volumes. Native peoples adapted by adopting a diet that included fish and mussels. In the Late Period (AD 500–1805), descendants of the Archaic tribes interbred with desert people. The descendents of these tribes are the modern-day Shoshone, Nez Perce, and Paiute Indians. Idaho was the last state to be discovered by European settlers when Lewis and Clark traversed its rugged terrain in 1805. The area remained largely unsettled by whites until gold was discovered in the Clearwater and Salmon River canyons. In 1890, Idaho was admitted into the Union, becoming the 43rd state. Select tidbits of Idaho's history are woven throughout this book, and a few historical attractions are listed under To See in each chapter. For history fans, a fantastic resource is *Idaho for the Curious—A Guide* by Cort Conley (Backeddy Books, 1982). The **Idaho State Historical Society** (208-334-2682; www .idahohistory.net), formed in 1907 as a state agency, is another important resource. The society, located in Boise, oversees historic sites at four locations in the state—Pierce, Franklin, Hansen, and Boise—in conjunction with local groups.

HORSEBACK RIDING

Idaho is the Wild West, and horseback riding is part of the culture. With its vast expanses of wildlands, opportunities for trail riding are virtually limitless. Horseback-riding enthusiasts enjoy staying at many of the working guest ranches throughout Idaho, where trail rides are generally part of the program (see entries under Lodging in each chapter). A plethora of outfitters are also available to take visitors on daily trail rides and the more adventurous on multiday pack trips into remote mountainous spots. For a list of ranches and outfitters, contact **Idaho Division of Tourism Development** (800-334-2470; www.visitidaho.org) and **Idaho Outfitters and Guides Association** (208-342-1438; www.ioga.org). See also entries under To Do in each chapter.

HOT SPRINGS

Thanks to a stationary hot spot, now located under Yellowstone National Park, and the heat generated beneath the Great Idaho Batholith (see Geology, above), abundant volcanic and geothermal activity has produced hundreds of natural hot springs in Idaho, more than in any other state in the country. The National Geophysical Data Center of NOAA lists 232 thermal springs in Idaho. It is a favorite pastime of many a local to seek out these natural baths to soothe sore muscles après-ski and to camp and soak their way around the state. Very few hot springs in Idaho have been commercially developed, so most often you need to know where to go and may need to hike to get there. Nudity and beer are not unexpected. Two great resources for hot-springs fanatics are *Hiking: Hotsprings in the Pacific Northwest* by Evie Liton (The Globe Pequot Press, 2001) and the *Complete Guide to Idaho Hot Springs* by Doug Roloff (The Writers' Collective, 2002). These books will tell you how to find some of these hidden gems, as well as all you need to know about hot-spring etiquette and safety. Just know that hot springing can be a way of life.

HUNTING

Idaho has a rich heritage of hunting. From the first Native Americans thought to live in Idaho and identified as big-game hunters to the provisioners of the Lewis and Clark Expedition, which brought the first white people to Idaho in 1805, to the gold miners who flocked to Idaho in search of riches in the mid- to late 1800s and hunted to feed their families, to present-day private hunters and hunting guides seeking birds and game for food or trophy, hunting has always been a part of Idaho life. It is a premier place to hunt big game ranging from elk, deer, antelope, and bighorn sheep to mountain goats, black bears, and cougars; upland game including sage grouse, chukars, and pheasants; and birds such as Canada geese and ducks. Single- or multiday guided hunting trips can be arranged by a slew of licensed hunting outfitters, and many backcountry lodges support hunting excursions into the deep wilds of Idaho (see entries under Lodging in each chapter). For a comprehensive listing of licensed guides and backcountry lodges and ranches affiliated with licensed outfitters, contact **Idaho Outfitters and Guides Association** (208-342-1438; www.ioga .org). Bird hunters may enjoy *Wingshooter's Guide to Idaho: Upland Birds and Waterfowl* by Ken Retallic and Rocky Barber (Wilderness Adventures Press, 1997). Contact **Idaho Fish and Game** (208-334-3700; www.fishandgame.idaho.gov)

for information on hunting licenses, fees, and regulations.

IDAHO CENTENNIAL TRAIL

The Idaho State Centennial Trail stretches the entire length of the state, running approximately 1,200 miles from Idaho's southern border with Nevada north to the Canadian border and passing through three out of the four regions demarcated in this book. The trail wanders through a variety of terrain, including dry, sage-strewn high desert; rugged mountains; and vast tracts of contiguous deep wilderness. Various portions of this multiuse trail are available for hiking, cross-country skiing, horseback riding, mountain biking, and motorized uses. For more information, check with **Idaho Department of Parks and Recreation** (208-335-4199; www.idahoparks.org); its Web site has a great map of the trail

system, including links to scores of maps detailing the topography on and around the length of the trail.

INDIAN RESERVATIONS

Idaho has four Indian reservations—**Coeur d'Alene** (208-686-1800; www.cdatribe-nsn.gov), **Fort Hall** (800-806-9229; www.shoshonebannock tribes.com/), **Nez Perce** (208-843-2253; www.nezperce.org), and **Duck Valley** (208-759-3100; www.shopai tribes.org)—representing four federally recognized Indian tribes: the Coeur d'Alene, Shoshone-Bannock, and Nez Perce tribes of Idaho and the Shoshone-Paiute Tribe of Nevada, respectively. The Kootenai Tribe of Idaho is also federally recognized and was deeded 12.5 acres of land in Bonners Ferry in 1975 after declaring war on the United States. The original inhabitants of the area that is now Idaho also included the Blackfeet, Palouse, Kalispel, and Spokane Salish tribes. Many of these reservations encompass beautiful stretches of Idaho country and offer opportunities for fishing, white-water rafting, and other outdoor adventures. Please note that Indian reservations constitute the land of sovereign nations, and all activities on those lands are governed by these sovereignties rather than by the U.S. government; therefore, you need to check with each reservation for its rules on camping, fishing, hunting, and boating permit requirements and the like.

KAYAKING

See Boating and White-water Kayaking and Rafting.

LAKES

With 823 square miles of the state covered by water, 2,000-plus named lakes, and thousands of unnamed ones, water babies will not be disappointed in Idaho. Northern Idaho is bejeweled with three of the state's largest and most beautiful lakes: Coeur d'Alene, Pend Oreille, and Priest lakes. The first two are said to be among the most beautiful lakes in the world!

LEAVE NO TRACE

Leave No Trace (303-442-8222 or 800-332-4100; www.lnt.org) is an international nonprofit organization dedicated to promoting and inspiring responsible outdoor recreation through education, research, and partnership. The Leave No Trace educational program promotes seven principles designed to foster conservation of natural resources by outdoor users: planning ahead and preparing, traveling and camping on durable surfaces, practicing proper waste disposal, leaving what you find, minimizing campfire impacts, respecting wildlife, and being considerate of other visitors. It is a good idea to familiarize yourself with these practices to ensure that you are a responsible outdoor enthusiast.

LEWIS AND CLARK TRAIL

In 1803, President Thomas Jefferson dispatched Meriwether Lewis and William Clark to find a water route to the Pacific and explore the uncharted West. The latter part of their two-year journey took them over Lemhi Pass from Montana into Idaho, across northern Idaho, and ultimately to the mouth of the Columbia River at the Pacific Ocean. The Lewis and Clark Backcountry Byway follows the portion of the trail running north along the Montana–Idaho border; the Northwest Scenic Passage Byway fol-

lows U.S. 12 and ID 13 across northern Idaho, along the Lochsa and Clearwater rivers to their confluence with the Snake River. For more information on this popular historical route, see **Idaho Department of Transportation**'s Scenic, Historic, and Back County Byways Web site (www.itd.idaho.gov/byways/index.htm). See also entries under Wandering Around in each chapter.

LODGING

The lodging entries in this book generally focus on unique places to stay, including bed & breakfasts, guest lodges, and resorts, rather than typical hotels or motels. **Idaho Division of Tourism Development** (208-334-2470; www.visitidaho.org) has an extensive guide to lodging options throughout the state.

MAPS

The *Idaho Atlas and Gazatteer* (DeLorme; available at www.delorme.com) is an essential compendium of detailed topographic maps covering the entire state. It includes back roads, federal and state lands, and information on outdoor recreational activities. **U.S. Geological Survey** (http://store.usgs.gov) 7.5-minute topographic maps are available through the USGS Web site, which also lists by state the local stores carrying these maps.

MICROBREWERIES

With more than 5,000 barley producers in the state, it is not surprising that

Idaho does not lack for good suds. **BrewPubZone** (www.brew pubszone.com) lists 36 brewpubs in Idaho, and the **North American Brewers' Association** (www.north americanbrewers.org) has made Idaho its home. The organization hosts the annual Mountain Brewers' Beer Fest in Idaho Falls each summer (see Special Events in part IV, Southeastern Idaho: The Simple Pleasures, chapter 9, Teton Basin, Swan Valley, and Henrys Fork Country: Gateway to Yellowstone), as well as the North American Beer Awards, which judges more than 700 beers.

MINING
In the mid- to late 1800s, Idaho was ablaze with a frenzy of mining activity. Idaho's dramatic geologic history of crustal deformation, igneous activity, and regional metamorphism (see Geology, above) produced vast quantities of copper, gold, lead, silver, zinc, and other precious mineral ores. Discovery of gold ore in the Pend Oreille River in 1852 catalyzed a frantic rush to the region that ultimately resulted in rich placer discoveries in Pierce, Elk City, Orofino, Boise Basin, Florence, Warren, and other locations throughout the state. Other strategically important basic and noble metals have been mined in Idaho, many of which were used to support the World Wars I and II military efforts. Further, an unusual variety of gemstones, crystals, and silicified woods are found throughout our hills. Idaho now ranks as the ninth most important gold-producing state in the United States, and it is perhaps number one in importance for total mineral resources. Today, the ghostly remains of mining activities and the boomtowns that supported them dot

Idaho's landscape (see entries under To See in each chapter).

MOUNTAINS
Idaho's rugged alpine landscape—which includes snowcapped peaks and jagged skylines, glacial tarns and cirques often filled with the bluest of waters, alpine meadows strewn with the colors of delicate flowers—is breathtaking. Idaho's 80 recognized mountain ranges provide for dramatic geography. More than 50 peaks higher than 10,000 feet rise in stark contrast to the country's deepest gorge—the Snake River Gorge, along Idaho's western boundary, which plummets 8,000 feet from He Devil Peak on the east rim to the river valley below. Undulating folds of crust form a succession of mountain chains across Central Idaho. A litany of names spills forth: The Smoky, Pioneer, Boulder, and White Cloud mountains tower above the Wood River Valley. The jagged Sawtooth Mountains give rise to the mighty Salmon River farther north. The Lost River, Lemhi, and Beaverhead mountains are parallel wrinkles on the map. The Salmon River, Clearwater, and Selkirk mountains dominate the landscape of northern Idaho and its panhandle. These mountains are some of the most remote and beautiful in the continental United States. They are here for the exploring, but please be aware of and follow mountain safety precautions. A great guide for mountain-goers of all ilk is *Idaho: A Climbing Guide* by Tom Lopez (The Mountaineers Books, 2000).

MUSEUMS
Idaho is proud of its history and, despite its rural character, has more than its share of museums. A few of

Chris Pilaro

the more prominent museums include the **Boise Art Museum** (208-345-8330; www.boiseart museum.org) in Boise, which is nationally recognized for excellence in the visual arts; the **Discovery Center of Idaho** (208-343-9895; www .scidaho.org), also in Boise, where you can see science in action; the **Herrett Center for Arts and Science** (208-732-6655; http://herrett.csi.edu) in Twin Falls, which houses a fabulous collection of anthropological artifacts; and the **Museum of Idaho** (208-522-1400; www.museumofidaho.org) in Idaho Falls, which is dedicated to the state's natural and cultural history. Even the smallest of enclaves seems to have its own museum (some of them bizarre, but all interesting) to showcase its local mining, Indian, or pioneer history. For a complete listing of museums, contact **Idaho Division of Tourism Development** (208-334-2470; www.visitidaho.org). See also entries under To See in each chapter.

MUSIC

Sprawling on a blanket atop soft grass, watching the light shift on mountains beyond, bare toes wiggling, a glass of wine in hand, and your being resonating to the strum of acoustic guitar and rhythmic thumping of drums—this is the stuff of mountain concerts. Idaho has a remarkable outdoor summer music scene, including symphonies, music festivals, and local concert series that bring renowned musicians to the state (see Cultural Offerings in each chapter). Whether you favor bluegrass, jazz, country, rock, alternative, or classical music, you are likely to find a venue that suits you. One relatively new annual event of note is the **Targhee Fest** (www.grand targhee.com/summer/music-festivals/ targhee-fest.php) at Grand Targhee

Resort near Driggs, a three-day camp, groove, and hang fest with a great lineup of acoustic-based Americana, folk, blues, and roots music. Other music festivals, series, and events are highlighted throughout this book under Special Events.

NATIONAL MONUMENTS

Idaho's unique geology has provided for what are now several national monuments: At City of Rocks National Reserve in Almo, granite pinnacles and monoliths more than 60 stories tall and 2.5 billion years old offer exceptional rock climbing. Craters of the Moon National Monument and Preserve in Arco, Carey, and Rupert has been described as a "weird and scenic landscape," with its vast ocean of lava flows, cinder cones, and sagebrush. Hagerman Fossil Beds National Monument in Hagerman boasts the largest concentrations of Hagerman Horse (*Equus simplicidens*) fossils in North America, along with more than 220 species of plant and animal fossils marking the world's richest late Pliocene fossil deposit. Minidoka Internment National Monument in Jerome marks the site of one of the Japanese internment camps of World War II. See entries under Wilder Places in each chapter.

NATIONAL PARKS

A portion of America's first national park, Yellowstone, is located in eastern Idaho. Made famous by its spectacular geysers and hot springs, the park is also home to a variety of wildlife, including grizzly bears, bison, elk, and wolves. This park is a secret gem in the winter. The Nez Perce National Historical Park in northern Idaho is a moving tribute to the Nimiipuu, or Nez Perce, who have inhabited the rivers, canyons, and prairies of the inland Northwest for eons. See entries under Wilder Places in each chapter.

NATIONAL TRAILS

Both the California National Historic Trail and the Oregon National Historic Trail traverse southern Idaho, marking the path of gold seekers heading west and fur traders, missionaries, and more gold diggers heading to the Pacific, respectively. The Lewis and Clark National Trail, which runs north along Idaho's border with Montana and then west across Idaho's panhandle, marks the famous 1803–1805 route of Meriwether Lewis and William Clark and their Corps of Discovery as they journeyed west from Illinois to find a water route to the Pacific Ocean. See entries under Historic Sites in each chapter.

PUBLIC LANDS

Most of Idaho belongs to the public. The federal government owns about 64 percent of the 53 million acres of land in Idaho, and the state and other public agencies own an additional 10 percent. It is this heritage that has protected the vast open spaces and the mountains, canyons, grasslands, forests, deserts, and rivers that make Idaho wild and stunningly beautiful. Some 39 percent of this federal land is owned by the U.S. Forest Service, with varying degrees of protection, while about 22 percent is under the care of the U.S. Bureau of Land Management, managed as working lands that produce minerals, timber, and livestock.

REST AREAS

Idaho is a vast land with many miles between towns and rest stops. **Idaho**

Department of Transportation provides a database of state rest areas (http://itd.idaho.gov/highways/ops/maintenance/RestSearch.asp).

RIVERS

Idaho receives 100 million acre-feet of water annually in the form of rain and snow, supplying 16,000 miles of rivers and streams. It is the proud home of the Middle Fork and Main Stem of the Salmon, Lochsa, Payette, Selway, Clearwater, and Snake rivers, among other gems. The rugged Salmon River, hailed the "River of No Return" by early explorers, winds 425 miles through the mountains of central Idaho, carving a gorge deeper than the Grand Canyon. Many of these rivers are federally designated Wild and Scenic; a mere taste of these crystalline rivers teeming with fish, churning rapids, glowing white beaches, abundant wildlife, and towering old-growth cedars confirms their spectacular wildness. It is no wonder that Idaho has earned the title the "White-water State," attracting countless white-water thrill-seekers each summer, and is a world-renowned retreat for fly fishermen and women.

Despite their remoteness, Idaho's rivers are not escaping the perils of human activity. The mighty Snake and Salmon rivers, both historic spawning grounds for anadromous chinook salmon, sockeye salmon, and steelhead trout, are facing reduced flows due to increased diversions for development, industry, and power production. Less water means warmer temperatures, reduction in the quantity and quality of habitat and spawning grounds, and generally bad news for fish. Numerous environmental groups are hard at work to remove dams, restore habitat, and reduce water diversions. See also White-water Kayaking and Rafting.

ROAD REPORTS

Idaho Transportation Department (www.511.idaho.gov) alerts travelers to construction delays, road closures, and other highway concerns. Its Web site also provides winter road closure information for the state's mountain passes. It is critically important to follow the weather, snow, and avalanche conditions when traveling on Idaho's remote highways during the winter. See also Driving, above.

ROCK CLIMBING

While rock climbing is a relatively quiet endeavor, rock climbers are increasingly taking note of Idaho's impressive climbing terrain. City of Rocks National Reserve is known internationally for its technical rock climbing; see Dave Bingham's bible, *City of Rocks Idaho: A Climber's Guide* (7th edition, Falcon Distribution, 2004). Adjacent Castle Rocks, Idaho's newest state park, is gaining notice; see Dave Bingham's *Castle Rocks Idaho* (Falcon Distribution, 2004). A slew of other climbing options are found in all regions of the state. A great resource for rock-climbing route descriptions throughout Idaho is www.rockclimbing.com. See entries under To Do in each chapter.

RODEOS

Idaho hosts numerous rodeo events, ranging from national events such as the annual Dodge National Circuit Finals in Pocatello to many county and community rodeos throughout the summer months. The Mackay Rodeo, in the stunning Big Lost River Valley, is a wild, local favorite. A listing of rodeos can be found on www .visitidaho.org. Please note that rodeos are not for the faint of heart. See entries under Special Events in each chapter.

SAND DUNES

There is something compelling about a sand dune rising out of the desert, its form revealed by starkly beautiful, dusky shadows. The Bruneau Sand Dune, in southwestern Idaho, is said to be the tallest single-structure sand dune in North America, towering 470 feet above desert lakes. It is a peaceful place to relax and watch the stars. For a little rowdier experience, you might visit Saint Anthony Sand Dunes, whose 400-foot-high rollers covering more than 11,000 acres attract many an off-road vehicle. While the scenery is cool, the scene might not be that cool. See entries under Wilder Places in each chapter.

SKIING AND SNOW SPORTS

Where to begin? Charging the powder, getting lost in the quiet of a back-country glade, skinning your way between Douglas firs to a frozen peak above—this is why many of us live here. Idaho is a winter wonderland, with 17 alpine resorts, 46 Nordic ski centers, virtually limitless backcountry skiing terrain (some serviced by comfy yurts), and more than 7,200 miles of groomed snowmobile trails. Winter carnivals, ice skating, and snowshoeing are all part of the scene. Many of the special spots and fun local events are mentioned throughout the book. See www.idahowinter .org for a full listing of resorts and activities in Idaho.

STATE PARKS

In 2008, Idaho celebrated the centennial of its first state park, Heyburn

James Foster

State Park in Plummer. Idaho has 30 state parks, scattered evenly throughout the state in a variety of ecosystems. From the exposed granite spires that rise from the desert at Castle Rocks State Park in southern Idaho to the quiet shores of Lake Pend Oreille (Idaho's largest lake) at Farragut State Park, these parks offer a plethora of opportunities to rock climb, ski, mountain bike, hike, fish, camp, and play (see entries under Wilder Places in each chapter). The parks department operates a system of cabins and yurts throughout the state (see Cabin Rentals, above). Contact **Idaho Parks and Recreation** (208-334-4199; http://parksandrecreation.idaho .gov) for information on recreational activities, maps and directions, fees, and reserving cabins and yurts.

TIME ZONES
By some bizarre legislative act, Idaho was divided into two time zones. The larger, southern portion of the state follows Mountain Standard Time, and the Panhandle observes Pacific Standard Time. The division roughly follows the course of the Salmon River. In fact, the bridge on US 95 over the Salmon River just north of Riggins has been dubbed the "time zone bridge," literally and figuratively transporting people from one reality to another— that is, North Idaho is its own country.

TRAVEL INFORMATION
A good resource for statewide travel information, including getting to and around Idaho, is Idaho's **Division of Tourism Development** (208-334-2470; www.visitidaho.org). The Web site provides a comprehensive list of **visitor information centers** (www .visitidaho.org/thingstodo/visitor -centers.aspx) throughout the state.

WATER
Idaho is the definition of the arid West. If you've read *Cadillac Desert: The American West and Its Disappearing Water* by Marc Reisner (Penguin Group, 1993), you'll understand it when they say, "Whiskey is for drinkin', water is for fightin' over" (Mark Twain). As with many other western states, Idaho's legacy of water scarcity continues. As a high-alpine desert, the state doesn't get a lot of precipitation; Idaho's mean annual precipitation is about 27 inches, but it is delivered in a complex precipitation pattern with northern areas often receiving 40–50 inches per year, while many portions of the southern part of the state, including the agricultural belt of the Snake River Plain, receive less than 10 inches annually. Increased development pressure, albeit lagging somewhat behind that occurring in other western states, is bringing a heightened concern about Idaho's traditionally clean and abundant (relative to consumptive use) water supply. Recent years of drought and climate change are adding to the level of discomfort, while environmental assaults such as the injection of liquid nuclear wastes into the Snake River Aquifer by Idaho National Laboratory are a continuing worry. Idaho is just now moving into the final stages of the 20-year Snake River Adjudication effort, in which an independent court, with the Idaho Department of Water Resources acting as an expert to the court, is attempting to unravel the tangled mess of water rights that determine who gets what water and in what quantities throughout much of the state. While the adjudication may result in codifying previously sketchy water uses, it is unlikely to have much

impact in maintaining annual consumptive water use at levels lower than the amount of water naturally recharged into the groundwater system each year. In north Idaho, the Spokane Valley–Rathdrum Prairie aquifer, which underlies 325 square miles of northern Idaho and eastern Washington and provides drinking water for more than 450,000 residents, is also coming under increasing pressure. The Idaho State Legislature has authorized the Northern Idaho Adjudication to evaluate and codify water rights in the Coeur d' Alene–Spokane (which feeds the Spokane Valley–Rathdrum Prairie aquifer), Palouse, Kootenai, and Clark Fork–Pend Oreille river basins. As of this writing, the process has not yet commenced.

WEATHER

For comprehensive weather information, visit the **National Weather Service**'s Web site (www.weather.gov/view/states.php?state=ID&map=on).

Here you can find current weather conditions, weather forecasts and alerts, wildfire data, climate information, and the like.

WHITE-WATER KAYAKING AND RAFTING

With more than 3,000 white-water river miles, Idaho is *the* white-water state. You can't get much better than a weeklong trip on the Middle Fork of the Salmon: lots of churning water, pristine wilderness, hot springs, historical mining claims, and several lodges—including the Middle Fork Lodge and the Flying B Ranch. For the more serious boater, Loon Creek and Big Creek (part of the Middle Fork), the Payette system, and the petrifying North Fork offer enough nail-biters to challenge the best. The Lochsa, which flows at near-perfect levels over Memorial Day, is likened by locals to a journey to Mecca. The Jarbridge, Bruneau, and Owyhee rivers offer more obscure but equally satisfying journeys. For the bible to

Idaho's paddling experiences, see *Idaho—the Whitewater State; a Guidebook* by Grant Amaral (Bookcrafters, 1990). A good resource for arranging shuttles for river trips is www.riverconnections.com. See entries under To Do in each chapter.

WILDFIRE
The West has a history of dramatic, raging wildfires—fires that whip themselves up into a furor, storming through vast, thick stands of stately conifers and tangled underbrush, consuming hundreds of thousands of acres of western forested land each year. Shocking as it may seem each year to those who bear witness, Mother Nature and history are only repeating themselves. Idaho's most

notorious and destructive fire occurred in 1910: The Big Burn, as it is called, ravaged almost 3 million acres in the Bitterroot Mountains of Idaho and Montana and killed 85 people (see McCall Smokejumper Camp in Southwestern Idaho: Class V Adventure, Chapter 4, McCall and the Payette River Mountain Region: Sun and Fun, To See—Historic Sites). The process continues. Months of hot, dry weather, stacked upon several years of drought cycle, coalesced in 2007, bringing one of the worst fire years since the Big Burn; by the end of August, nearly 840,000 acres in Idaho had been devastated. Some recent scientific reports suggest that there is a correlation between climate change—particularly, early spring snowmelt—and increased incidence of wildfires. Fire suppression has long been a contentious issue: On the one hand, by not allowing Mother Nature to do her housecleaning, controlling wildfire leads to increased forest density and, hence, fuel density; on the other hand, uncontrolled fire risks lives and property and mars our beautiful landscapes. It is a conundrum at best, likely to worsen as we continue to put pressure on our natural resources. If you encounter burned areas in your explorations, please stay away; charred soils are fragile and prone to erosion, and scorched trees are at risk of falling (in other words, they can be widowmakers).

WILDFLOWERS
You know it is May Day in Idaho's Smoky Mountains when you are greeted at every turn on the trail by a symphony of wild color—warm red Indian paintbrush, delicate lilac-colored phlox, bursts of yellow bells and arrowleaf balsamroot—forming a

rock garden that one could only hope to emulate in a backyard. Spring bloom in the mountains is not to be missed, and it can turn a bad day sunny in a moment. Locals may often point you to a favorite secret stash of alpine mystery. See *Idaho Mountain Wildflowers: A Photographic Compendium* by A. Scott Earle (Farcountry Press, 2001) for a beautiful armchair rendition of Idaho's wild beauties and *Sagebrush Country: A Wildflower Sanctuary* by Ronald J. Taylor (Mountain Press Publishing Company, 1992) if you want to learn your botany. *Along Mountain Trails (and in Boggy Meadows): A Guide to Northern Rocky Mountain Wildflowers and Berries* by Doreen Marsh Dorward and Sally Randall Swanson (Boggy Meadows Press, 1993) is a great guidebook to take along with you on the trail. **Idaho Native Plant Society** (www.idahonativeplants.org) is another important resource if you have a serious interest in the botany of native Idaho plants.

WILDLIFE

With its vast expanses of unadulterated wilderness, Idaho has an abundance of wildlife. More than 3,200 species can be found across the state, including mule deer, coyotes, foxes, chipmunks, squirrels, Clark's nutcrackers, juncos, and chickadees, as well as more elusive species such as black bears, gray wolves, mountain lions, bobcats, beavers, moose, bighorn sheep, elk, sandhill cranes, and golden eagles. Witnessing these wild animals in their natural setting is an amazing experience that can be earned by getting into the backcountry, taking your time, and staying still and quiet. Generally, animals are most active during the early morning

and evening, so these are good times to keep your eyes peeled. Riparian and wetland zones, with their lush vegetation and water supply, are important wildlife areas, as are transitional zones between one ecotone and another—for example, between a meadow and a forest. These are good spots to look for wildlife. Bare branches of snags—as dead trees are called—are great places to look for birds of prey, and woodpeckers can often be seen hard at work excavating nesting holes. For those interested in getting into the backcountry and reading the signs of animals in the wild, a great book to bring along is the pocket-sized *Scats and Tracks of the Rocky Mountains* by James C. Halfpenny, Ph.D. (The Globe Pequot Press, 2001), which provides illustrations of animals native to this region, their prints and scat, range, and brief descriptions of their habitat, behavior, and other signs. Even for those who are not interested in venturing deep into the wilderness, wildlife often can be viewed from more accessible spots, including the highways in some of Idaho's remoter regions (see Wildlife Viewing under To See in each chapter). Other helpful guides are *Idaho: Wildlife Viewing Guide* by Aimee L. Pope (Watchable Wildlife Series; Adventure Publications, 2003) and the more regional *Audubon Guide to the National Wildlife Refuges: Rocky Mountains: Idaho, Colorado, Montana, Utah, Wyoming* by John Grassy and Theodore Roosevelt IV (Saint Martin's Griffin, 2000).

WILDLIFE REFUGES

Idaho has six designated national wildlife refuges—Bear Lake, Camas, Deer Flat, Grays Lake, Kootenai, and Minidoka—and Oxford Slough

Chris Pilaro

Waterfowl Production Area. Detailed information about each reserve can be found on the **U.S. Fish and Wildlife Service** Web site (http://www.fws .gov/refuges/profiles/ByState.cfm ?state=ID). See also Wilder Places in each chapter.

WINERIES

Idaho's Snake River Valley was recently designated as an American Viticultural Area (AVA) by the U.S. Alcohol and Tobacco Tax and Trade Bureau in recognition of the region's unique grape-growing conditions capable of producing excellent wines. Though the industry is fledgling—growing approximately 45 varieties of grapes on 1,200 acres of vineyards—new wineries continue to emerge (Idaho currently has about 18 wineries), and the industry continues to garner national and international awards and recognition. A good source of information for mapping out a wine tour is **Idaho Wineries and Vineyards** (www.idahowine.org). See Winery Tours under To See in each chapter.

Northern Idaho: A Hidden Jewel

COEUR D'ALENE, PEND OREILLE,
AND PRIEST LAKES: LAKE COUNTRY

MOSCOW AND THE PALOUSE: HEART
OF THE ARTS

THE CLEARWATER REGION: BIG
FISH, BIG TREES, BIG WHITEWATER

INTRODUCTION

Northern Idaho is typified by churning, clear rivers and placid lakes that emanate from thick, luxuriant forests and ultimately pour into the Snake River. The region, where the Intermountain West meets the Pacific Northwest, comprises the largest inland temperate rain forest in North America. Beneath these expansive forests lie deep deposits of now-lithified Precambrian sediments. Deposited prior to the arrival of organisms with exoskeletons—some 543 million years ago or more—these formations contain no fossils to help geologists discern their history. Thought to be tens of thousands of feet thick at a minimum, these deep sedimentary bands pose a bit of a quandary for geologists. Some posit that sediments were deposited in what was at one time an ocean basin; others believe the sediment catch is a giant meteorite crater. In much more recent geologic history—10,000–100,000 years ago—several glacial advances and retreats scraped the area, carving out a seemingly endless number of lakes sprinkled across the landscape, including the sparkling jewels of Pend Oreille (pronounced "pon-da-RAY"), Coeur d'Alene (pronounced "core-da-LANE"), and Priest lakes.

Long and skinny, Idaho's northernmost territory is aptly named the Panhandle, for it stretches over 100 miles from Coeur d'Alene north to the Canadian border but is only 46 miles wide along the northern boundary. This configuration was, in part, an accident of history. In 1864, when the Montana Territory was carved out of the Idaho Territory, all lands west of the Continental Divide were to go to Idaho. During the survey for the new territory, however, the Bitterroot Mountain range north of Lost Trail Pass near North Fork, Idaho, was mistaken for the Continental Divide and designated as the boundary between the two territories. In reality, the Continental Divide veers east through present-day Glacier National Park in Montana. The mistake was realized late in the game, and the boundary demarking the thin Panhandle was left unchanged. Although Idaho lost parts of present-day Montana west of the Continental Divide, including the mineral wealth of Butte, the enclaves of Missoula and Kalispell, Flathead Lake, and the western half of Glacier National Park, Idaho travelers still enjoy a wealth of natural beauty, including the state's largest lakes, the Kootenai National Wildlife Refuge, and the 2.5 million-acre Idaho Panhandle National Forest.

In late 1864, the seat of the Territorial government was moved from Lewiston to Boise; northern Idaho has maintained a sticky political reputation ever since.

Beginning with proletariat uprisings by Idaho miners in the 1880s and, later, participation in the national unionizing efforts of the Wobblies (as members of the Industrial Workers of the World, or IWW, are known), northern Idaho garnered a reputation as a place "difficult to govern." Twice, efforts have failed to make the northern part of present-day Idaho its own state. During the second attempt, in 1901, the failed proposal attempted to make the Panhandle and Eastern Washington the "State of Lincoln." Northern Idaho today remains distinctly separate from the rest of the state; roughly 21 percent of Idaho's population dubs its home "North Idaho."

Despite political and social challenges, this region has become a popular outdoors destination. Jewel-like lakes provide for a plethora of water sports, from sailing and kayaking to fishing and waterskiing; lush green mountains call to the hiker; and the panoramic views of Schweitzer Mountain Resort near Sandpoint and vast expanses of backcountry powder beckon the winter enthusiast. Creature comforts and a dose of culture can be found in Coeur d'Alene's vibrant downtown and waterfront, as well as in some of the other important cities in the region, including Lewiston, Moscow (home of the University of Idaho), Sandpoint, Post Falls, Hayden, and the smaller towns of St. Maries and Bonners Ferry. These and the other many small towns in northern Idaho boast plenty of "mom-and-pop" shopping; museums focused on the region's mining, forestry, and railroad history; and near-endless opportunities for hiking and camping. In the consciousness of Idahoans, the Panhandle region is oft thought of as a separate state. True to form, the Panhandle keeps its own time, observing Pacific standard time, while the rest of the state keeps Mountain standard time.

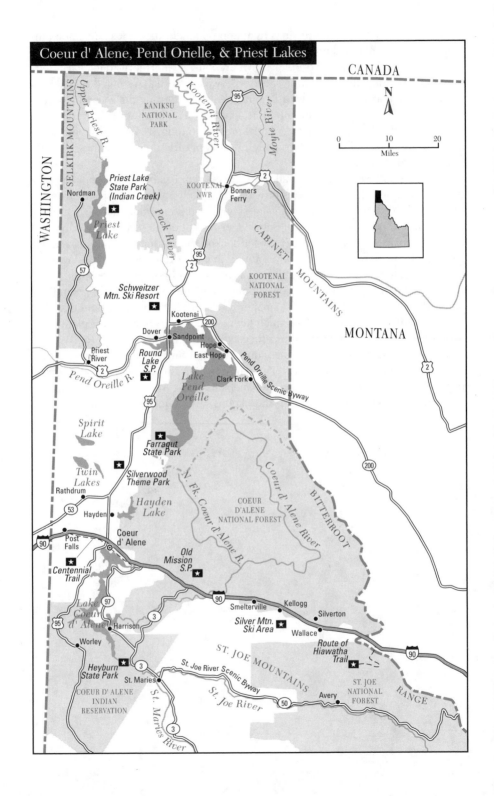

Coeur d' Alene, Pend Orielle, & Priest Lakes

COEUR D'ALENE, PEND OREILLE, AND PRIEST LAKES: LAKE COUNTRY

These three large, deep glacial lakes are considered Idaho's jewels, and some say they are among the most beautiful lakes in the world. Coeur d'Alene gained its name during the 1790s when French-speaking trappers traveling through the Panhandle and trading with Native folk dubbed them the "Coeur d'Alene." The name translates as "heart of awl" or "point of the awl" (the awl being a sharp leather-working tool), a reference to the shrewd trading skills of the local Schee-Schu-Umsh Indians.

Coeur d'Alene, once known for logging and mining, is now one of Idaho's key tourism centers. This destination resort area bustles with water sports (including lots of power boating), golf, lakeside bicycling, a 3,000-foot-long boardwalk, large marinas, and exclusive resorts. Sisters Lake Pend Oreille and Priest Lake are much more low-key. Lake Pend Oreille (French for "hangs from ears"—an early comment on the large shell earrings worn by the Natives) glows with the vibrance of the funky, artsy town of Sandpoint; serene Priest Lake is yet further removed—nestled within thick cedar forests and dotted with remote cabins and rustic resorts.

GUIDANCE

Bonners Ferry Chamber of Commerce (208-267-5922; www.bonnersferry chamber.com), 7198 US 95, Bonners Ferry 83805.

Coeur d'Alene Area Chamber of Commerce (208-664-3194 or 877-782-9232; www.cdachamber.com), 1621 N. Third St., P.O. Box 850, Coeur d'Alene 83816.

Greater Sandpoint Chamber of Commerce (800-800-2106 or 208-263-0887; www.sandpointchamber.org), 900 N. Fifth Ave., P.O. Box 928, Sandpoint 83864.

Harrison Chamber of Commerce (208-689-3669; www.harrisonidaho.org), P.O. Box 222, Harrison 83833.

Historic Silver Valley Chamber of Commerce (208-784-0821; www.silver valleychamber.com), 10 Station Ave., Kellogg 83837.

Priest Lake Chamber of Commerce (208-443-3191 or 888-774-3785; www .priestlake.org), P.O. Box 174, Coolin 83821.

By car
I-90 bisects the panhandle from east to west, with Post Falls (just east of Spokane, Washington) and Coeur d'Alene on its western end and Mullan on its eastern end just west of Lookout Pass, Montana. From Coeur d'Alene, **ID 97** loops south along the lake's east shore to **ID 3**, a north–south byway connecting with St. Maries to the south and I-90 to the north at Cataldo. Farther west, **US 95** bisects the panhandle from south to north, passing through Moscow in the south and Sandpoint (on Lake Pend Oreille) and Bonners Ferry to the north. **US 2,** another east–west route, takes you from the city of Priest River (just east of Newport, Washington) east through Sandpoint to Hope and Clark Fork near the Montana border. From Priest River, you can venture north on **ID 57** to reach Priest Lake.

By air
Coeur d'Alene Airport (COE; 208-446-1860; www.cdaairport.com), 10375 Sensor Ave., Hayden 83835, accepts private flights.

Priest Lake has a couple small airstrips that accept private flights.

Sandpoint Airport (208-263-9102), 2 miles from downtown Sandpoint, accepts private flights.

Spokane International Airport (509-455-6455; www.spokaneairports.net) is the closest commercial airport, about 35 miles west of Coeur d'Alene via I-90 and 90 miles southwest of the Priest River–Sandpoint area.

See also Airports in What's Where.

By train
Amtrak (800-872-7245; www.amtrak.com) has one stop in Idaho, in Sandpoint's historic depot on Railroad Avenue just off Bridge Street, where the *Empire Builder,* with daily service from Chicago and Minneapolis to Seattle and Port-land, stops.

MEDICAL EMERGENCIES
Bonner General Hospital (208-263-1441; www.bonnergen.org), 520 N. Third Ave., Sandpoint, is the primary health-care facility for the larger Sandpoint area.

Deaconess Medical Center (509-458-5800; www.deaconessmedicalcenter.org), 800 W. Fifth Ave., Spokane, is a nearby major medical facility.

Holy Family Hospital (509-482-0111; www.holy-family.org), 5633 N. Lidger-wood St., Spokane, is another nearby major medical facility.

Kootenai Medical Center (208-666-2000; www.kmc.org), 2003 Lincoln Way, Coeur d'Alene, is the primary health-care facility in the Coeur d'Alene region.

Northwest Medstar (800-422-2440 or 509-532-7990; www.nwmedstar.org) transports patients with medical emergencies from both the panhandle's local hospitals to major medical care hospitals in Spokane.

Sacred Heart Medical Center (509-474-3131; www.shmc.org), 101 W. Eighth Ave., Spokane, is another nearby major medical facility.

Bonners Ferry, on US 95 a few miles south of the Canadian border. Located in the Kootenai River Valley and surrounded by three forested mountain ranges, Bonners Ferry was named for Edwin Bonner, who in 1834 journeyed from New York to the Pacific Northwest to capitalize on frontier business opportunities. In 1864, he began operating a ferry service to shuttle miners across the Koonenai River. He didn't stick around very long, but the town bearing his name has. Today, Bonners Ferry is considered the "International Gateway to Idaho." The area has easy access to numerous trails and back roads that lead to pristine high-altitude alpine lakes, rivers, and streams and forested areas teeming with wildlife. Several spectacular falls, including the Copper Falls geological area, Snow Creek Falls, and Smith Creek Falls, are worth checking out.

Clark Fork, on ID 200 (Pend Oreille Scenic Byway) near the Montana border. Named for William Clark, in recognition of his leadership of the famed 1804 expedition with Meriwether Lewis, Clark Fork rests on the east side of Lake Pend Oreille at the confluence of the Clark Fork River and Lightning Creek. The Cabinet Gorge dam and the Cabinet Gorge fish hatchery are just upstream.

Coeur d'Alene, off I-90 at US 95. With 35,000 people, Coeur d'Alene is the largest city in the region and the Kootenai County seat. Coeur d'Alene's economy caters to visitors, who come for outstanding outdoor recreation, distinctive regional shops, casual and gourmet dining, and luxury hotels. The city's attractions include the North Idaho Museum, the City Park and Beach, the Coeur d'Alene Summer Theater, Lake City Playhouse, and the Centennial and Mineral Ridge trails. It is also home to North Idaho College, located on the grounds of the old Fort Sherman, a key military installation from 1878 to 1901. Lakeside resorts and businesses offer tours and toys for the lake, including all you'll need to water ski, Jet Ski, or sail. The Boardwalk at the Coeur d'Alene Resort, the longest floating boardwalk in the world, is a nice place to take an evening stroll and watch the sunset.

Hayden and Hayden Lake, off US 95 just north of Coeur d'Alene. The small enclaves of Hayden and adjacent Hayden Lake (home to fewer than 10,000 people combined) are nestled beside the tranquil Hayden Lake itself, which lies north of Coeur d'Alene Lake. Despite the beautiful serenity of the smaller lake, the place has some very controversial history. From the 1970s until 2001, a 20-acre rural compound near Hayden Lake functioned as the headquarters of the neo-Nazi Aryan Nations. In September 2000, an Idaho jury awarded the Southern Poverty Law Center a $6.3 million judgment against the organization and punitive and compensatory damages to Victoria Keenan and her son, Jason, who were attacked by Aryan Nations guards in 1991. As a result of the judgment, the former Aryan Nations leader, Richard Butler, turned over the property on the lake to the Keenans, who in turn sold it to a philanthropist who donated the property to North Idaho College. The site has since been designated as a "peace park."

Hope and East Hope, on ID 200 about 12 miles southeast of Sandpoint. If you drive around the perimeter of Lake Pend Oreille, you'll encounter these tiny hamlets perched on its shores. There is not much around here except deep pine forests and beautiful lake views. Hope, which possesses a deep Idaho railroad history, was once a bustling hub on the Northern Pacific Mainline and home to many Chinese immigrants who helped build the railroad.

Post Falls, off I-90 just west of Coeur d'Alene. Named for Frederick Post, who built a sawmill here along the Spokane River in 1800, this fast-growing city has a few interesting spots, including a spectacular 40-foot waterfall cascading into the Spokane River at Falls Park. Pictographs at Treaty Rock are said to constitute the original signed treaty between Frederick Post and Coeur d'Alene Chief Seltice that allowed Post to use the falls to power his mill. Q'emiln (pronounced "ka-mee-lon") Riverside Park, just off South Spokane Street, provides easy access to day hikes, a swimming beach, picnic tables, and a boat launch. Cavanaugh Templin's Resort offers daily cruises on their *River Queen* through Labor Day. For those looking to shop, this place is outlet mall heaven, with more than 75 discount stores located at Prime Outlets and Post Falls Factory Outlet Stores.

Sandpoint, at the junction of US 2 and US 95. The vibrant, eclectic enclave of Sandpoint is perched on the north shore of Lake Pend Oreille, less than an hour north of Coeur d'Alene. For quite some time, Sandpoint has been quietly collecting a diverse, artsy community (population about 6,835), drawn to the region for its fabulous natural amenities that include the lake itself, the beautiful Cabinet Mountains to the east, and and the Selkirk Mountains to the west, which stretch north deep into British Columbia. Sandpoint is a gateway to alpine skiing at Schweitzer Mountain, loads of backcountry skiing, and fishing and boating

SANDPOINT'S FUNKY SCENE

Matt Furber

NORTHERN PACIFIC RAILROAD DEPOT MUSEUM IN WALLACE

galore. Only recently has the outside world (spurred by some national and international press) come to recognize what 6,000 Sandpointers knew all along: this is a really cool little place. Along with the local creative juices comes the flair that makes for a great little town: funky coffee shops, welcoming eateries that tantalize not only your taste buds but also your sense of aesthetics (with eclectic surroundings filled with velvet chairs, compelling oil paintings by local artists, and serene gardens splashed with color), plenty of live music, and a lively buzz that makes you want to stay. Rumor has it that many a repeat visitor has become a local.

St. Maries, on ID 3 southeast of Coeur d'Alene. Located at the confluence of the St. Maries and St. Joe rivers and at the eastern edge of the Coeur d'Alene Indian Reservation, St. Maries was originally developed as a steamboat stop. Today, it continues as a distribution center for raw logs—albeit, with the downturn of the timber industry, a flagging one. The town is a jumping-off point for river adventures on the Wild and Scenic St. Joe River (see To Do—White-water Kayaking and Rafting) and is a gateway to recreational activities—including plenty of hiking and camping—within St. Joe National Forest. The town itself has several boat ramps and boating parks.

Wallace, off I-90 about 10 miles west of the Montana border. Bursting with history, the entire town of Wallace is listed on the National Register of Historic Places. In 1885, the discovery of galena ore in the nearby Coeur d'Alene Mountains and the opening of the Bunker Hill Mine catalyzed the largest silver rush in U.S. history, attracting the usual slew of prospectors, conmen, and women of ill repute. Within five years, 90 mines had sprung up in the region, producing $5 billion worth of metal over the next 100 years; the region was dubbed "Silver Valley." Wallace was the heart of the Silver Valley mining district, and today it boasts one of the best regional collections of turn-of-the-20th-century architecture, with buildings dating back to 1890. A handful of museums provide an interesting window on Wallace's boomtown history, including the Northern Pacific Railroad Depot Museum, the Sierra Silver Mine Tour, the Wallace District Mining Museum, and the Oasis Bordello Museum. Some interesting artifacts, including old miners' cabins, can be seen by strolling about town.

✳ Wandering Around

International Selkirk Loop (www.selkirkloop.org), 280 paved miles starting from Priest River and looping counterclockwise through British Columbia and Washington back to Priest River. This scenic drive heads east on US 2 to Sandpoint, then north on US 95 through Bonners Ferry to ID 1, which continues north to the Canadian border. Inside southern British Columbia, the route heads north and west on BC 21 and BC 3A, skimming alongside **Kootenay Lake**, and then turns south on BC 6 through the 7,000-foot peaks of the **Selkirk Mountain Range** into Washington on WA 31 and WA 20 along the **Pend Oreille River** to US 2 east back to Priest River. A number of small towns along the route provide lodging and other amenities. A diversity of habitat types range from dense forests to grasslands, alpine terrain, and lush riparian areas; visitors are likely to see a wide variety of bird and wildlife species (see To See—Wildlife Viewing).

Lake Coeur d'Alene Scenic Byway (www.idahobyways.gov), 36 paved miles on ID 97 and ID 3 from I-90 east of Coeur d'Alene to Cataldo back on I-90. This route winds along the lake's eastern shore, south through Harrison, and then north along the river. Along the way, visitors enjoy the **Mineral Ridge** interpretative trail, which provides spectacular views of Wolf Lodge Bay on Lake Coeur d'Alene; **Beauty Bay Recreation Area**, a day-use area with picnic tables and bird-watching opportunities; and **Thomas Lake Wildlife Refuge**, home to the largest population of nesting ospreys in the western United States.

Pend Oreille Scenic Byway (www.idahobyways.gov), 33 paved miles on ID 200 from Sandpoint to the border with Montana. Open year-round. Pend Oreille Scenic Byway meanders eastward along the southeastern shore of Lake Pend Oreille. The route traverses wide tracts of farmland and river delta and provides spectacular mountain and lake views. Special attractions along the way include the **Pend Oreille Geologic View Site**, the **Denton Slough Wildfowl Area**, and **Cabinet Gorge Fish Hatchery**.

St. Joe River Scenic Byway (www.idahobyways.gov), 89 paved miles on Forest Service (FS) road 50 and FS 218 from St. Maries to the Montana border. First half of route open year-round; second half, only after snowmelt. The St. Joe River Scenic Byway runs east from St. Maries for 75 miles along the scenic St. Joe River, then heads north for 14 miles to the Montana state line. Special attractions along the way include the **Marble Creek Interpretive Site**, which honors the difficult work of loggers who moved white pine logs from Marble Creek to mills along St. Joe River; Historic **Avery**, featuring a museum dedicated to railroad and pioneer history; and spectacular views of the Bitterroot Mountains. Numerous developed and undeveloped campsites are available along the way.

Wild Horse Trail Scenic Byway (www.idahobyways.gov), 89 paved miles on US 2, US 95, and ID 1 from the Washington state line to the Canadian border. This is the Idaho leg of the International Selkirk Loop (see above).

✳ To See

ART TOURS
Artists' Studio Tour (800-800-2106; www.arttourdrive.org), Sandpoint. The local art community hosts a tour several times during the summer when you can visit local studios and see working artists in action. Artists on the tour welcome visitors all year by appointment.

Arts Alliance (208-255-5273; www.artsalliance.info), in Sandpoint. The town and its surrounds have a thriving art scene. Sandpoint is home to numerous working artists and a slew of galleries. Interesting artwork can be found on coffee-shop and wine-bar walls and as murals on building exteriors. The Arts Alliance is a great source of information about galleries, art classes, and special art events offered throughout the region. See also Cultural Offerings—Art Galleries.

ArtWalk (208-292-1629; www.artsincda.com), downtown Coeur d'Alene. Held 5–8 on the second Fri. each month Apr.–Dec. During this event, art galleries host opening receptions with live music, snacks, and artists presenting new works.

BOAT TOURS
Heyburn State Park Cruises (208-686-1308), 1291 Chatcolet Rd., Plummer 83851. Operates summer and fall. Reservations required. Cruises onboard the *Idaho*, an 87-passenger boat operated by the park, include weekly catered brunch cruises, a monthly catered dinner cruise, interpretive cruises, a Fourth of July jaunt, and special brunch cruises on Mother's Day and Father's Day.

Lake Coeur d'Alene Cruises (208-765-4000; www.cdaresort.com), at City Park at Independence Point, Coeur d'Alene. Apr.–Oct. A variety of popular boat tours cruise around Coeur d'Alene Lake.

Lake Pend Oreille Cruises (208-255-LAKE; www.lakependoreillecruises .com), Sandpoint. May–Oct.; dinner cruise 5:30–8, $35 per person. Locals call the gourmet dinner cruise on Lake Pend Oreille a "must-do." A classic old 1966 vintage boat, initially operated as a ferry, takes diners on a tour near bald eagle nesting habitat. Other tours include wine tasting and eagle-watching, a fall foliage island tour, and daily and afternoon cruises around Lake Pend Oreille.

Priest Lake Excursions (253-377-9301; www.laketour.com), at Priest Lake. May–Sept. $200 for two-hour tour with up to four people. Motorheads might enjoy a ride on Priest Lake aboard a 21-foot Thunder Jet. The outfitter offers transportation and boat tours for up to six people; most tours are two hours long.

River Cove Dinner Cruises (208-773-9190 or 877-773-9190; www.theriver cove.com), operating out of Post Falls. May–Oct. A variety of tours cruise the Spokane and St. Joe rivers.

Westcoast River Queen (208-773-1611), operating out of Post Falls. May–Oct. A variety of tours can be taken around Coeur d'Alene Lake, Lake Pend Oreille, the Spokane River, and St. Joe River.

FARMER'S MARKETS

Summer farmers' markets are plentiful in northern Idaho. Fresh produce, garden starts, handcrafts, flowers, food, and music can be found at the following:

Boundary County Farmer's Market, intersection of US 95 and Kootenai Street, Bonners Ferry. Open 8–1 Sat. May–Sept.

Downtown Coeur d'Alene Farmers' Market, at Sherman and Fifth streets, Coeur d'Alene. Open 4–7 Wed. May–Sept.

Hope Farmers' Market, at the Hope Memorial Community Center, ID 200 and Centennial Road, Hope. Open 3–6 Fri. June–Sept.

Kootenai County Farmers' Market, at US 95 and Prairie Avenue, Hayden. Open 4–7 Wed. and 8–1 Sat. May–Oct.

Priest River Farmers' Market, on High and Treat streets, Priest River. Open 9–2 Sat. May–Oct.

Sandpoint Farmers' Market (208-290-3088; www.sandpointfarmersmarket .com), in Farmin Park at Third and Main streets, Sandpoint. Open 3–5:30 Wed. and 9–1 Sat. Apr.–Oct. **St. Maries Farmers' Market**, on Main Street, St. Maries. Open 2:30–5:30 Fri. May–Sept.

FOR FAMILIES

Silverwood Theme Park (208-683-3400; www.silverwoodthemepark.com), on US 95, 15 miles north of Coeur d'Alene. Open 11–close (hours vary) May–Sept. $37 for adults, $20 for children. Kids (large and small) might enjoy a side trip to the largest theme park in the Northwest. It offers world-class wooden roller coasters, steam locomotive tours, magic and ice shows, and theme restaurants.

Triple Play and Raptor Reef Water Park (www.3Play.com), at US 95 and Orchard Avenue, Hayden. Open 10–10 Sun.–Thurs., 10–12 Fri.–Sat. $6.50 and up per attraction. An indoor water park—"Raptor Reef"—features a wave pool, a children's lagoon and two-story play structure, a Jacuzzi, and three large waterslides (one of which measures just under 400 feet). The park also offers bowling, bumper boats, go-carts, indoor and outdoor miniature golf, laser tag, a climbing wall, and an arcade.

Wild Waters Water Park (208-667-6491; www.WildWatersWaterPark.com), 2119 N. Government Way, Coeur d'Alene. Open 11–6 daily. $13 and up. Here you'll find 14 waterslides, a water tube ride, two pools, two giant hot tubs, a snack bar, arcades, a large covered pavilion, a grassy picnic area, and a special 12 and under children's section.

Old Mission at Cataldo State Park (208-682-3814; http://parksandrecreation
.idaho.gov), off I-90 in Cataldo. Open 9–5 daily. Free. Sacred Heart Mission,
Idaho's oldest standing building, was constructed between 1850 and 1853 by
Catholic missionaries and Coeur d'Alene Indians and is listed on the National
Register of Historic Places. Also on-site are the restored Parish House, a historic
cemetery, and an interpretive exhibit that provides a glimpse of the complex
relationship between the missionaries and the Indians. The trailhead to the Trail
of the Coeur d'Alenes is within the park (see To Do—Bicycling).

MUSEUMS

Bonner County Historical Society (208-263-2344; www.bonnercountyhistory
.org), 611 S. Ella Ave., Sandpoint. Open 10–4 Tues.–Sat. $2 for adults, $1 for
children, $5 family. The facility houses an impressive historical archive of news-
papers, photographs, and documents, plus exhibitions and a research library.

Fort Sherman Museum (208-664-3448; www.museumni.org), on North Idaho
College Campus on West Garden Avenue, Coeur d'Alene. Open 1–4:45
Tues.–Sat. May–Sept. $3 adults, $1 children. This powder house operated by the
Museum of North Idaho is dedicated to General William Tecumseh Sherman,
who commissioned a territorial fort on this site in the 1870s in order to protect
local railroad and telegraph interests and make way for settlement of the region.
The general named the bunker Fort Coeur d'Alene, but it was later renamed in
his honor.

Museum of North Idaho (208-664-3448; www.museumni.org), just east of City
Park at 115 Northwest Blvd., Coeur d'Alene. Open 11–5 Tues.–Sat. Apr. 1–Oct.
31. $3 adults, $1 children. Numerous exhibits are dedicated to the history of the
Coeur d'Alene region, including logging, mining, agriculture, railroads, and
Native American histories.

MUSEUM OF NORTH IDAHO IN COEUR D'ALENE

Northern Pacific Railroad Depot Museum (208-752-0111), 219 Sixth St., Wallace. Open 10–3 Mon.–Sat. Apr. and Sept.–Oct.; 9–7 Mon.–Sat. June–Aug. $2 adults, $1 children. This museum is housed in a turn-of-the-20th-century chateau-style depot constructed of brick imported from China and concrete panels made of mine tailings. While not at its original location, the depot, like all buildings in town, is listed on the National Register of Historic Places.

Oasis Bordello Museum (208-753-0801), 605 Cedar St., Wallace. Open 9:30–5:30 daily Apr.–Oct. $5. This Wallace museum offers up its share of bawdy history to visitors. Here, you can see the ghost remains of one of five brothels that operated freely on Wallace's Main Street, this one until quite recently. Constructed in 1895, the bordello operated for almost a century as a hotel and saloon, servicing the lonely men of Wallace, who outnumbered women 200 to 1. The museum showcases clothing, makeup, toiletries, and personal effects of the last occupants of the place, who seemed to have abandoned it in a hurry.

Wallace District Mining Museum (208-556-1592), 509 Bank St., Wallace. Open 9–6 daily July–Aug. $2 adults, $0.50 children. Exhibits include a variety of artifacts, photographs, and commissioned paintings related to the mining history

CRANE HOUSE MUSEUM IN HARRISON

of Silver Valley, depicting the living conditions of those who flocked to the area
in search of riches.

SCENIC FLIGHTS

Brooks Seaplane Service (208-664-2842), in Coeur d'Alene; takeoffs and land-
ings on the water. Taking wing via a scenic flight provides a bird's-eye view of
northern Idaho's impressive landscape—its rushing rivers, glinting lakes, thick
alpine forests, and crenulated ridgelines—and some insight into why Idaho has
earned a reputation as the final frontier in the Lower 48. A 20-minute Coeur
d'Alene Lake Loop flies over Chain Lakes, Coeur d'Alene and Fernan lakes,
Coeur d'Alene and St. Joe rivers, and Beauty Bay. Longer flights (and group
rates) can include other surrounding lakes in Northern Idaho.

TOURS

Sierra Silver Mine Tour (208-752-5151; www.silverminetour.org), 420 Fifth
St., Wallace. Tours 10–4 daily May–Sept. $10.50 adults, $8 children. Hard hats
required in the mine. A walking tour heads into an underground silver-mining
drift, and a trolley tour takes in historically important spots about town.

WILDLIFE VIEWING

David Thompson Game Preserve, off ID 200 near Hope, on the Hope
Peninsula. Locals joke that this place is located "beyond Hope." Here, the Sam
Owen Campground provides more than 80 prized campsites and fabulous
wildlife-viewing opportunities. Visitors are likely to see abundant grazing white-
tailed deer and resting bald eagles. The area also has a beach and a boat ramp.

Farragut State Park (208-683-2425; http://parksandrecreation.idaho.gov), on
southern shore of Lake Pend Oreille 30 miles north of Coeur d'Alene. This
4,000-acre accessible wildlife-viewing spot, once the world's second-largest naval
training station, is home to white-tailed deer, squirrels, black bears, coyotes, and
mountain lions. Frequently sighted birds in its coniferous forest include owls,
hummingbirds, hawks, woodpeckers, ducks, and Idaho's state bird, the mountain
bluebird.

Kootenai National Wildlife Refuge (www.fws.gov/kootenai), along the Kootenai River 20 miles south of the Canadian border and 5 miles west of Bonners
Ferry. Open daily year-round. This 2,774-acre reserve is a fabulous spot to watch
wildlife. Established in 1965, this protected area spans a wide variety of habitat
types—including wetlands, meadows, riparian forests, and cultivated agricultural
fields—and provides an important resting spot for migrating waterfowl. More
than 300 species of wildlife inhabit the refuge. Visitors can wander around on
footpaths within the reserve or take a 4.5-mile automobile tour around the main
wetland areas to see open and tree-lined ponds, cattail and bulrush marshes, and
flowing creeks. Dense coniferous tree stands and riparian forests flank the western edge of the refuge.

Two Nation Birding Vacation (www.twonationbirdingvacation.com), on the
International Selkirk Loop (see Wandering Around). A coalition including the
Kootenai National Wildlife Refuge, the Creston Valley Wildlife Management

Area, and the International Selkirk Loop promote this eco-tourism experience, which highlights numerous birding locations along the route. Two weeks is recommended to complete the counterclockwise loop, although the tour can be shortened and done in either direction.

✳ To Do

BICYCLING

Centennial Trail, 23 paved miles from east of Coeur d'Alene to the Washington border. Completed in 1995, the path winds along the Spokane River from Blue Creek Bay, 6 miles east of Coeur d'Alene, through Post Falls to the Washington border. At the border the route merges with the **Spokane River Centennial Trail**, which runs another 22.5 miles through Riverfront Park to Nine Mile Falls west of Spokane.

Route of the Hiawatha (208-744-1301; www.ridethehiawatha.com), 15 miles paved miles from the Montana border to Pearson. Tickets—and bicycle, helmet, and light (required) rentals—available at **Lookout Pass Ski Area** lodge (208-744-1301; www.skilookout.com). This trail starts at Lookout Pass, on I-90 12 miles east of Wallace, and follows the former Olympian Hiawatha railroad route, all at a 2 percent downhill grade. Traversing a stunning alpine landscape, including panoramic views of the Bitterroot Mountains, this stretch has been called the "crown jewel" of rail-to-trail mountain biking routes. Along the way, riders cross over seven high steel trestles and through 10 tunnels, including the 1.7-mile-long St. Paul or "Taft Tunnel," which runs under the state line. Signs along the trail describe the history of the railroad, forest fires, mining, and early Forest Service activity in the area.

Trail of the Coeur d'Alenes, 72 paved miles from Plummer to Mullan. This is considered one of the most spectacular trails in the western United States, spanning the Idaho Panhandle from Plummer off US 95 through Idaho's historic Silver Valley and along scenic rivers and lakes. The trail crosses 40 bridges and passes through 13 towns, ending at Mullan off I-90. This rail-to-trail conduit was originally used by the Coeur d'Alene Indians as a path and later became a mining rail line that operated from 1887 until 1992.

Rentals
Blades N' Wheels (208-777-2636), 108 W. 17th Ave., Post Falls. Rent bikes and gear here.

Pedal Pushers Bike Rental and Repair (208-689-3436; www.bikenorthidaho .com), 101 N. Coeur d'Alene Ave., Harrison. This shop rents bikes from both their storefront in Harrison and at **Heyburn State Park** (208-686-1308) on the south end of Coeur d'Alene Lake. From both spots, you can easily jump on the Trail of the Coeur d'Alenes. Their Harrison shop also serves up some great espresso!

Sweet Bicycles (208-266-0530), off ID 200, Clark Fork. Rent bikes and gear here.

Two Wheeler & Ski Dealer (208-772-8179), 9551 N. US 95, Hayden Lake. Rent bikes and gear here, too.

Vertical Earth (208-667-5503; www.verticalearth.com), 206 N. Third Ave.,
Coeur d'Alene. Bikes and gear can be rented here.

BOATING
Coeur d'Alene Lake's beach at the North Idaho College campus is a nice place to launch a kayak on the lake.

The **North Fork of the Coeur d'Alene,** the **lower St. Joe,** and the **Spokane and Pack rivers** offer many floatable miles of mellower waters suitable for canoeing, kayaking, and inner tubing.

Outfitters
Kayak Coeur d'Alene (208-676-1533 or 877-676-1533; www.KayakCoeur DAlene.com), 307 E. Locust Ave., Coeur d'Alene. For those who prefer muscle power, this place runs guided kayak tours around the lake. Three-hour kayak tours around Coeur d'Alene Lake, morning, afternoon, and sunset, are offered every day during the summer. If you don't need instruction or a guide, the company also rents kayaks and gear.

IT'S EASY TO LAUNCH A CANOE OR KAYAK ON LAKE COEUR D'ALENE.

Rentals

Outdoor Pursuits (208-667-1381 or 208-769-5941), on the beach in front of Rosenberry Drive, Coeur d'Alene. North Idaho College's beachfront shop rents kayaks, canoes, sailboats, and white-water rafting gear.

Vacation Sports Rentals (208-665-0686), Coeur d'Alene. If you want to pilot your own boat, you can rent boats and Jet Skis here for full or half days.

Water Adventures (208-689-3693; www.harrisonboatrentals.com), 200 N. Coeur d'Alene Ave., Ste. C, Harrison. On the southern end of the lake, this place rents kayaks and motorboats.

FISHING

As the only inland western state with ocean-run salmon and steelhead, and with consistent hatchery releases and numerous world-class wild trout, Idaho boasts some exciting fishing. This region is no different, and its landscape glitters with high-alpine lakes and rushing streams. In fact, one-third of Idaho's record-breaking fish have come out of the panhandle region. Contact **Idaho Fish and Game** (208-334-3700; www.fishandgame.idaho.gov) for information on fishing rules and licenses.

Coeur d'Alene Lake, famous for its large chinook salmon and cutthroat trout, is rumored to have produced a 42-pound chinook (most are 3 to 7 pounds). Large- and smallmouth bass, kokanee trout, northern pike, rainbow trout, and mackinaw are also abundant.

Lake Pend Oreille yielded a world-record 37-pound Kamloops trout; the lake is also full of trout, crappie, perch, largemouth bass, bullheads, channel catfish, bluegills, sunfish, northern pike, and tiger muskies.

Hayden Lake, once home to the neo-Nazi Aryan Nations organization, is famous for producing a 39.9-pound pike—a state record proving that the big fish of Northern Idaho don't discriminate. Early-spring northern pike can be found in Fernan, Twin, Spirit, and Hayden lakes.

Kootenai, Pend Oreille, Priest, and Clark Fork rivers (above the railroad bridge) offer good year-round river fishing, as do the slack waters of the **St. Joe and St. Maries rivers**. The St. Joe River, in particular, is known for its great fly-fishing and unrivaled beauty.

Outfitters

Idaho Outfitters and Guides Association (208-342-1438; www.ioga.org) has a list of area fishing outfitters. While most fishing areas are accessible to the public, the best way to fetch the big catch may still be to hire a fishing guide. Numerous outfitters run guided trips on area rivers and lakes.

Diamond Charters (208-265-2565 or 800-4-TROUT-6; www.diamondcharters .com), Hope.

Joe Roope's Castaway Fly Fishing Shop (800-410-3133; www.castawayfly fishingshop.com), Coeur d'Alene.

River Odysseys West (ROW; 208-765-0841; www.rowadventures.com), Coeur d'Alene.

St. Joe Outfitters & Guides (208-245-4002; www.stjoeoutfitters.com), St. Maries.

Tom Loder's Panhandle Outfitters (509-922-8289; www.panhandle -outfitters.com), Valleyford, Washington.

Western Waters (877-822-8282; www.WesternWaters.com), Superior, Montana.

Rentals

Fins & Feathers Tackle Shop and Guide Service (208-667-9304; www.fins1 .com), 1816 Sherman Ave., Coeur d'Alene. You might also want to check out this local fly-fishing shop for gear and advice.

Northwest Outfitters (208-772-1497; www.nwoutfitters.com), 402 Canfield Ave., Coeur d'Alene. Another local fly-fishing shop has gear and advice.

GOLF

It's not Scotland, but golf is green and plentiful in Northern Idaho. Dozens of golf courses, ranging from small public nine-hole courses to competition-grade 18-hole courses, dot the landscape. You can find a more complete list of Northern Idaho golf courses by contacting **North Idaho Golf** (877-782-9232; www .cdagolf.org).

Avondale (208-772-5963; www.avondalegolfcourse.com), Hayden Lake. $53. This scenic 18-hole course is by the lake's Gold Coast.

Circling Raven (800-523-2464; www.circlingraven.com), on US 95 south of Coeur d'Alene. Apr.–Oct. $150 and up for play-and-stay packages. This award-winning 18-hole course was voted by *Golf* Magazine as one of the top 10 new golf courses for 2004.

Coeur d'Alene Resort Golf Course (208-667-4653 or 800-935-6283; www .cdaresort.com/golf/), 900 Floating Green Dr., Coeur d'Alene. $199 and up for golf-and-lodging packages. Complete with its famous floating green, this 18-hole course was rated by *Golf Digest* as one of the nation's top golf courses.

The Highlands (208-773-3673 or 888-900-3673; www.thehighlandsgc.com), Post Falls. $20 for 9 holes, $30 for 18 holes. Also popular is this public 18-hole course overlooking the falls; the course has a new fairway and green added in 2007.

StoneRidge (208-952-2948; www.stoneridgeidaho.com), off ID 41 just outside Blanchard. Apr.–Oct. Starting at $27 for 9 holes, $40 for 18 holes. This 18-hole course is 30 minutes northwest of Coeur d'Alene.

Twin Lakes Village Golf Course (208-607-1311; www.golftwinlakes.com), off ID 41 just north of Rathdrum. $18 for 9 holes, $30 for 18 holes. This is a public 18-hole course.

HIKING

Northern Idaho provides endless opportunities to put your hiking boots to the test. While the region has no national parks or designated wilderness areas (i.e., all this beautiful land is relatively unprotected!), there are millions of acres of national forestland. The Idaho Panhandle National Forests, which include the

Coeur d'Alene and St. Joe national forests and portions of the Kaniksu National Forest, encompass some of Idaho's most scenic mountain ranges. With the Selkirk, Cabinet, Coeur d'Alene, and Bitterroot mountains, Idaho's three largest lakes (Coeur d'Alene, Priest, and Pend Oreille), some key rivers (Coeur d'Alene, St. Joe, Kootenai, Pend Oreille, Moyie, and Priest), 425 species of wildlife, and 73 species of fish, the Panhandle is a naturalist's paradise. **Idaho Panhandle National Forests** (www.fs.fed.us/ipnf/rec/activities/trails/list.html) provide a host of information about hiking, camping, and mountain biking opportunities in the region. Individual Forest Service ranger stations also are also a good source of information; links to individual ranger station Web sites can be found on the Panhandle National Forests Web site. Ranger stations in the region include the following:

Forest Supervisors Office (208-765-7223), 3815 Schreiber Way, Coeur d'Alene.

Bonners Ferry Ranger District (208-267-5561), 6286 Main St., Bonners Ferry.

Coeur d'Alene River Ranger District (208-769-3000), 2502 E. Sherman Ave., Coeur d'Alene.

Priest Lake Ranger District (208-443-2512), 32203 ID 57, Priest River.

St. Joe Ranger District (208-245-2531), 222 S. Seventh St., Ste. 1, St. Maries.

Sandpoint Ranger District (208-263-5111), 1500 US 2, Ste. 110, Sandpoint.

For shorter hikes, try some of these interpretive trails in the area:

Hanna Flat Ceder Grove Trail, about 1 mile; off ID 57 just east of Priest Lake. This popular hike winds through 16 acres of protected old-growth cedar trees ranging from 200 to 800 years old! The grove contains eight tree, 10 shrub, and more than a dozen other plant species.

Mineral Ridge Trail, 3.3 miles; near Coeur d'Alene Resort via ID 97 at Beauty Bay. This hike climbs 735 feet (to elevation 2,875 feet) and provides similarly beautiful views of the lake. Twenty-two numbered stations identify natural features along the way.

Pulaski Trail, 2 miles; 1 mile south of Wallace. The interpretive trail tells the story of early U.S. Forest Service Ranger Edward Pulaski, who saved his crew from a 1910 wildfire. The pulaski, a special handheld wildfire-fighting implement that combines an ax and a mattock in one tool, is named for Edward Pulaski.

Tubbs Hill, 2 miles; near Coeur d'Alene Resort. This self-guided walk provides excellent views of the lake and forest and historical points along the way.

HORSEBACK RIDING

A great way to see the backcountry is to take to the saddle. Several area outfitters offer one-day and multiday pack trips into the Cabinet and Selkirk mountains:

Idaho Outdoor Experience (208-266-1216; www.idahooutdoorexperience .com), on Cabinet Gorge Road, Clark Fork.

Rider Ranch (208-667-3373; www.RiderRanch.com), 6219 S. Wolf Lodge Rd., Coeur d'Alene. They offer shorter day rides, dinner rides, hayrides, children's parties, and activities for families and large groups.

Western Pleasure Guest Ranch (208-263-9066 or 888-863-9066; www .westernpleasureranch.com), 1413 Upper Gold Creek Rd., Sandpoint.

ICE SKATING

Northern Idaho typically relies on the wiles of Mother Nature to provide skating opportunities. The ice on many of the smaller lakes in the area, including **Fernan, Spirit, and Twin lakes**, is often thick enough for safe skating. During very cold winters, some of the larger lakes, including **Hayden Lake**, also have good skating ice.

When temperatures stay below freezing long enough, there is good skating to be had on **Sand Creek,** below the Cedar Street Bridge, in Sandpoint. The city also typically clears an ice skating area at **City Beach** near the mouth of Sand Creek.

MOUNTAIN BIKING

Bernard Peak Loop Mountain Bike Route (Coeur d'Alene Ranger District, 208-769-3000; www.fs.fed.us/ipnf), 18.5 gravel miles, just north of Coeur d'Alene. Take US 95 north to Athol and ID 54 east 4 miles to Goodhope Road; head south about 1 mile to Twete Road and go left to the road-end trailhead. This single- and double-track gravel road offers views of the southern end of Lake Pend Oreille.

Canfield Mountain Bike Trail 1562 (Coeur d'Alene Ranger District, 208-769-3000; www.fs.fed.us/ipnf), more than 32 miles of nonmotorized trails; accessed from FS 1562, an old logging road. From I-90 in Coeur d'Alene, take exit 14 (15th Street), head north 1.1 miles to Nettleton Gulch Road, turn right, and go 2.2 miles to parking area. The entire system (including trails for both motorized and nonmotorized uses) is a mix of smooth, maintained logging roads and single-track (with grades up to 35 percent) adjacent to Hayden Lake.

Mount Coeur d'Alene Mountain Bike Loop (Coeur d'Alene Ranger District, 208-769-3000; www.fs.fed.us/ipnf), 8.1 gravel miles, near Coeur d'Alene. Drive east on I-90 from Coeur d'Alene to ID 97 south to Road 438; go left 0.75 mile to Beauty Creek Campground and trailhead. This road provides views of Coeur d'Alene Lake.

Schweitzer Mountain Resort trails (208-263-9555; www.schweitzer.com), west of US 95 north of Sandpoint. Helmets required on all Schweitzer trails; equipment rentals available on-site. Downhill mountain bikers looking for a lift can take the Great Escape quad chairlift to the top of Schweitzer Peak; aerobic junkies can challenge themselves with the 2,400-foot elevation gain on the network of trails.

Silver Mountain Resort trails (877-230-2193; www.silvermt.com), 610 Bunker Ave., Kellogg. Located just east of Coeur d'Alene, this ski resort also offers a gondola ride to the top of the mountain and a trail system with some 30 miles of double- and single-track terrain for intermediate and advanced riders. Easier trails are also available—the 2.8-mile **Silver Mountain Nature Trail** can be accessed from the base of the mountain, and the 14.8-mile (one-way) **Silver Mountain–Big Creek Banzai Biking Trail** is also nearby. This multiuse trail traverses varied terrain and is often shared with horseback riders and hikers.

Priest Lake trails (Priest Lake Ranger District, 208-443-2512; www.fs.fed .us/ipnf/priestlake/), off ID 57 west of Priest Lake. Some easier mountain biking along the lake takes riders through timber and across brushy hillsides and provides beautiful views of the lake. The multiuse **Upper Priest Lake Navigation Trail** is an excellent 9.4-mile single-track mountain bike trail that runs through an old-growth forest near the lake.

Recommended Reading
Stephen Stuebner's *Mountain Biking Idaho* (Falcon Publishing, 1999) is a good source for these and other rides in the panhandle.

SKIING
Consistent snow in Northern Idaho makes for a powder hound's heaven. The region offers enough developed ski resorts, groomed Nordic trails, and backcountry adventures to keep every winter sports enthusiast happy.

Alpine Skiing
Lookout Pass Ski and Recreation (208-744-1301; www.skilookout.com), just off I-90 at Wallace, near the Montana border. This is a good, mellow place for skiers new to the sport. The resort offers 1,150 feet of vertical, 540 acres of skiable terrain, 23 named runs, two gladed areas, and 400 inches of snow annually.

Schweitzer Mountain Resort (208-263-9555 or 800-831-8810; www .schweitzer.com), 11 miles northwest of Sandpoint. Nestled high in the Selkirk Mountains, 50 miles south of Canada, this is the premier ski area in the panhandle. As the locals know, Schweitzer has been doling out thick stashes of fresh powder for more than 30 years. Not unlike Lake Tahoe, panoramic summit views take in Lake Pend Oreille and snowcapped peaks that stretch all around— from Idaho into Canada, Montana, and Washington. Twenty-nine thousand acres and big bowls, gladed tree skiing, steeps, moguls, cruisers, and some easy pitches make this place fun for everyone! The resort also maintains a half-pipe and boasts 85 trails on 2,900 skiable acres, 2,400 feet of vertical, and 300 inches of snow annually.

Silver Mountain (877-230-2193; http://silvermt.com), 610 Bunker Ave., Kellogg. Just east of Coeur d'Alene, Silver Mountain is famous for its powder (about 300 inches per year) and for having the world's longest single-stage gondola. The resort boasts two mountains with 2,000 feet of vertical, 1,600 acres of skiable terrain, 67 named trails, a terrain park, and extensive glade and off-piste skiing. Yippee!!

Nordic Skiing
Cross-country skiing provides amazing winter access to wild country across northern Idaho. The well-maintained trail systems of Northern Idaho's state parks are popular for Nordic skiing. A $25 Annual Passport from the **Idaho**

State Department of Parks & Recreation (208-769-1511; www.idahoparks .org) will get you in to cross-country ski at Farragut, Priest Lake, Round Lake, and Winchester Lake state parks. Passes are available at any state park.

Centennial Trail, 23 miles from east end of Coeur d'Alene Lake through Post Falls to the Washington state line (plus another 22.5 miles to Spokane). This popular bike path also operates as a popular Nordic escape in winter (see Bicycling).

Nordic Sports Center at Priest Lake (208-443-2525; www.priestlake.org/ nordski/), at Priest Lake Golf Course, mile 27.8 on ID 57. During winter a blanket of snow transforms the golf course into some of the finest groomed skiing in the region.

Schweitzer Mountain Resort (208-263-9555 or 800-831-8810; www .schweitzer.com), 11 miles northwest of Sandpoint. The resort also offers 32 kilometers of trails and hosts two fun annual Nordic races: the Cougar Gulch 10K/5K and the Great Scott 10K/5K.

Backcountry Skiing

The powder-laden cirques and peaks of the Selkirk and Cabinet mountains provide bountiful backcountry skiing opportunities. Many choice slopes can be accessed via Forest Service roads, but it is a tough slog in to some of the best peaks, so a snowmobile is often preferred. The **Sandpoint Ranger District office** (208-263-5111), in the Federal Building on ID 2, 1500 Ste. 2, Sandpoint, provides maps for the area. Backcountry access to the Selkirks can be gained off the 280-mile **International Selkirk Loop** (208-267-0822 or 888-823-2626; www.selkirkloop.org); see Wandering Around. Other favored spots include the following:

Cabinet Mountains' Trestle Creek, off ID 200 near Hope.

Schweitzer Mountain Resort (208-263-9555 or 800-831-8810; www .schweitzer.com), 11 miles northwest of Sandpoint. The resort also offers liftserve access to extensive backcountry skiing just outside the resort boundaries.

Selkirks hot spots include numerous pitches off Upper Pack River Road, off US 95 north of Sandpoint; Jeru Creek Road, 8.5 miles up Pack River Road; and French Creek, nearby.

Avalanche Safety

Idaho Panhandle National Forests Avalanche Center (208-765-7323; www .fs.fed.us/ipnf/visit/conditions/backcountry) provides information on snow and avalanche conditions. Avalanche advisories are updated each weekend and, unless otherwise noted, are relevant for a three-day period. The center also offers free refresher **avalanche awareness classes** (not the full-meal-deal avy course). Please be aware of the risks associated with backcountry skiing, and know before you go: know and understand snow and avalanches; bring and know how to use a beacon, probe, and shovel; and bring proper equipment and clothing and plenty of water and food.

Outfitters

If you're not sure that you know enough (or just want to have an awesome guided experience into secret powder stashes!), you may want to employ the services of backcountry professionals like the following:

Peak Adventures (208-682-3200; www.peaksnowcats.com), Cataldo. They offer snowcat and guiding services in the St. Joe Mountains 26 miles east of Coeur d'Alene. Prices are $275 per day, including lunch and snacks. For an additional $145, you can have a gourmet dinner and a warm bed in a cozy yurt.

Selkirk Powder Company (208-263-6959; www.selkirkpowderco.com), out of Schweitzer Mountain Resort. This crew offers daily guided tours right from the resort and guided snowcat skiing in the broader Selkirk Mountain Range.

WHITE-WATER KAYAKING AND RAFTING

While the whitewater in the panhandle isn't as intense as it is in other parts of the state—including the Clearwater and Lochsa to the south—there are rapids to be found.

Clark Fork River, along ID 200. This river has some great class III boating, and Albertson Gorge on the Montana side of the Clark Fork is renowned for warm water and intermediate rapids.

Lower Priest River, about 6 hours from the put-in off ID 57, about 3 miles north of the town of Priest River. Advanced boaters enjoy a stretch of this Wild and Scenic–designated river.

Moyie and St. Joe rivers offer adrenaline-packed boating through spectacularly forested canyons. The 120-mile St. Joe River is a working river, replete with tugboats pulling rafts, or "booms," of logs to lumber mills. Also known as the "highest navigable river" in the world, it offers boaters a series of class II and III rapids.

Outfitters

A couple outfitters offer white-water trips in this region, including the following:

River Odysseys West (ROW) Adventures (208-765-0841 or 800-451-6034; www.rowadventures.com), Coeur d'Alene.

St. Joe Outfitter and Guides (208-245-4002; www.stjoeoutfitters.com), St. Maries.

Western Waters (877-822-8282; www.WesternWaters.com), Superior, Montana.

Wiley Waters (888-502-1900; www.RiverRafting.net), Post Falls. They offer trips on the Clark Fork and other rivers.

✳ Wilder Places

With some 80 percent of its land area covered in forest, Northern Idaho is the epitome of wild. While there are no designated wilderness areas in the lakes region, there are vast tracts of de facto wilderness—some in the form of national forest, some in state preserves, and a limited amount in privately held wildlands.

Idaho Panhandle National Forests (www.fs.fed.us/ipnf/rec/activities/trails/list.html), which include the Coeur d'Alene and St. Joe national forests and portions of the Kaniksu National Forest, comprise some 2.5 million acres, the vast majority of which is in Northern Idaho's Panhandle. Smaller portions of the forests extend into eastern Washington and western Montana. Graced by the

majestic peaks of the Selkirk, Cabinet, Coeur d'Alene, and Bitterroot mountains;
scoured-out glacial cirques; and pristine, crystalline, high-alpine lakes, this landscape is stunning. Vast forests, primarily white pine, western red cedar, Douglas
fir, and ponderosa pine (but also some ancient cedar groves) stretch out in
swaths of green in all directions. Eagles and ospreys thrive, and abundant
wildlife, including elk, white-tailed deer, black bears, and several endangered
species, make their homes here. Northern Idaho provides the only remaining
habitat in the Lower 48 for the woodland caribou, and a small number of grizzlies populate the most remote corners of the forest. If you are looking for a
road less traveled—for hiking, camping, fishing, or Nordic skiing—this might be
your spot.

LAKES

Coeur d'Alene Lake, 30 miles long, between 1 and 3 miles wide, with a maximum depth of 209 feet. Fed principally by St. Joe's and Coeur d'Alene rivers,
the lake's outflow forms the Spokane River to the west. While Coeur d'Alene
Lake was formed by glacial scour, today its water level is controlled by the Post

LAKE PEND OREILLE'S WILD SHORELINE

Falls Dam. Historically, because there were few roads and no highways around the lake, steamboats were a primary means of transportation, carrying mail, freight, and people across the lake and up the rivers and supporting a thriving lumber business, with as many as 72 major sawmills in the region. Steamboat traffic peaked in 1915 as the automobile gained popularity. In recent times, several relict steamboats and a handful of antique cars have been found at the bottom of the lake by divers. Since the late 1800s, the lake has been recognized for its beauty and its recreational opportunities. With promotion by the steamboat and railroad companies, the area became a popular tourist destination. Today's visitors enjoy the area's abundant wildlife; of particular interest is Wolf Lodge Bay, at the north end of the lake, a prime winter nesting area for eagles. Despite the lake's beauty, mining, logging, and urban development have left a legacy of heavy metals and nutrient contamination, particularly in the Coeur d'Alene River and adjacent floodplains. The U.S. Environmental Protection Agency and state, local, and tribal governments are currently working to reduce exposure to contaminants.

Lake Pend Oreille, 43 miles long, 15 miles across at its widest point, and about 1,100 feet deep (the fifth-deepest lake in the United States). Its shoreline is a resting and nesting area for bald eagles, herons, hawks, kestrels, and ospreys. The 4,000-acre Farragut State Park along the southern tip of the lake is home to elk, deer, bears, and moose. Lake Pend Oreille has an interesting geologic history: 10,000–15,000 years ago, the area was covered by a massive inland sea— Lake Missoula—which formed when huge glaciers protruding down the Purcell Trench from Canada south through the Kootenai Valley created a 2,500-foot-high ice wall that dammed the Clark Fork River. The resulting inland sea stretched an estimated 2,900 square miles—roughly the size of Lakes Erie and Ontario combined—and retained approximately 500 cubic miles of water. In a catastrophic collapse of the dam, the entire volume of Lake Missoula was drained in less than 48 hours, releasing a 2,000-foot-high wall of water that raged through the Clark Fork landscape. Maximum flow rates are estimated to have been about 9.5 cubic miles per hour (386 million cubic feet per second), producing water velocities on the order of 30–50 miles per hour. Impressively, the very deep remnant Lake Pend Oreille was one of the features left behind by this catastrophic flood.

Priest Lake, 23,000 acres and 19 miles long. Relatively pristine, tucked beneath the majestic Selkirk Mountains, and surrounded by the deep wilderness of the Kanisku National Forest, Priest Lake is a stunning cobalt blue. Home to only about 650 permanent residents, the lake and its environs provide a quiet respite for residents and visitors alike. To the north, Priest Lake is connected to the smaller, and more isolated, 3-mile-long Upper Priest Lake by a gentle but spectacular 2-mile-long river; the only entry is by boat or on foot. Seven islands that pepper Priest Lake make for great exploration. Visitors enjoy an area teeming with wildlife, including black bears, blue herons, white-tailed deer, moose, woodland caribou, cougars, and the occasional grizzly (which come, perhaps, in search of the renowned huckleberries), plus a lake full of hefty mackinaw trout. The lake gained its moniker when Father Pierre Jean De Smet visited the region in

1846, naming it for J. P. Roothann, a Jesuit teacher; the name was later reduced to his occupation.

OPEN SPACES

Coeur d'Alene Indian Reservation (208-686-1800; www.cdatribe-nsn.gov), Plummer. Established in 1873, the reservation occupies 345,000 acres along the western edge of the northern Rocky Mountains and the rolling hills of the Palouse, encompassing the southern third of Couer d'Alene Lake and the St. Joe River. This is a fraction of the tribe's original land holdings, which initially included all of Coeur d'Alene Lake but were reduced over time by a series of treaty agreements. The tribe operates a 6,000-acre farm producing wheat, peas, lentils, barley and canola and manages 180,000 acres of timberland. In 2000, the U.S. Supreme Court upheld tribal ownership of these resources. The Trail of the Coeur d'Alenes (see To Do—Bicycling), which runs through the reservation, was funded with settlement and damage monies from railroad and mining companies.

Kootenai Indian Reservation (208-267-3519; www.kootenai.org). The Kootenai Tribe sturgeon fish hatchery and the Kootenai Wildlife Refuge near Bonners Ferry are worth touring.

PARKS

Coeur d'Alene City Park, west end of Front Street, Coeur d'Alene. The City of Coeur d'Alene maintains some significant greenery, managing more than 394 acres of public lands, including 17 developed parks. The most popular of these is this fairly expansive 16.5-acre, lushly green lakeside park. This is a great spot for a picnic or a romp in the park's Fort Sherman playground (see To See—Museums). Just to the east is Tubbs Hill, a 120-acre, heavily wooded knoll jutting out into the lake that is crisscrossed by a network of footpaths (see To Do—Hiking). It is a favorite promenade for residents and visitors alike and a great spot to watch the sun sink over the lake.

Coeur d'Alene Parkway State Park (208-699-2224; www.parksandrecreation .idaho.gov), along north shore of Coeur d'Alene Lake. The parkway provides access to more than 0.5 mile of public shoreline, with picnic tables, an exercise course, and restrooms.

Farragut State Park (208-683-2425; http://parksandrecreation.idaho.gov), south end of Lake Pend Oreille. See To See—Wildlife Viewing.

Heyburn State Park (208-686-1308), south end of Lake Coeur d'Alene. The park operates cruises on the lake (see To See—Boat Tours).

Old Mission at Cataldo State Park (208-682-3814; http://parksandrecreation .idaho.gov), off I-90 in Cataldo. Established in 1851 and now a museum with walking paths between the scattered buildings (see To See—Museums), this historical site is a great place to picnic and stretch your legs.

Priest Lake State Park (http://parksandrecreation.idaho.gov), several units around the lakeshore—Indian Creek, Lionhead, Dickensheet, Reeder Bay. Good camping can be found at both the north and south ends of the lake, including boat-in or hike-in-only spots on the islands and the upper lake.

Round Lake State Park (208-263-3489; http://parksandrecreation.idaho.gov, off US 95 south of Sandpoint. This serene 58-acre lake surrounded by 142 acres of forest attracts canoeists and fishermen and women. The park offers hiking, picnicking, biking, and camping.

✴ Lodging

Accommodations in Northern Idaho run the gamut from roughing it under the stars to snuggling beneath luxurious, cozy comforters in a top-notch resort. Some options are listed below; for other options, check out **Majestic North Idaho** (www.northidaho .org) or the **North Idaho Vacation and Travel Guide** (www.fyinorth idaho.com).

BED & BREAKFASTS AND INNS

Coeur d'Alene

Katie's Wild Rose Inn (208-765-9474 or 800-371-4345; www.katies wildroseinn.com), 7974 E. Coeur d'Alene Lake Dr., Coeur d'Alene 83814. Here you'll find an exquisite view from Coeur d'Alene Lake's north shore, adjacent to the Centennial Trail bike path. Two of the four guest rooms have a private bath, one with an in-room Jacuzzi; the other two share a bath. $110 to $235.

Roosevelt Bed & Breakfast Inn (800-290-3358; www.therooseveltinn .com), 105 E. Wallace St., Coeur d'Alene 83814. Conveniently located just off the main drag and not far from the lake, this property—a renovated schoolhouse, built in 1905—is on the National Register of Historic Places. If you like doilies and frill, you will enjoy this spot. $89 and up offseason; $119 and up high season.

Harrison

Osprey Inn (208-689-9502; www .ospreyinn.com), 134 Frederick Ave.,

Harrison 83833. Built in 1915 as a boardinghouse for lumberjacks, the Osprey now offers five guest rooms each with a private bath. Perched on the shores of Coeur d'Alene Lake, the inn provides a convenient place to hang your hat, and its porch is a great perch from which to watch the sun melt into the lake at dusk. $73.50 and up.

Hayden

Clark House (208-772-3470 or 800-765-4593; www.clarkhouse.com), 5250 E. Hayden Lake Rd., Hayden Lake 83835. This upscale bed & breakfast is housed in a beautifully restored mansion. At the time it was built in 1910, the Clark House was the most expensive home in Idaho and was filled with fine European furnishings, crystal chandeliers, and Oriental rugs. Over time, the mansion fell into disrepair and was almost razed. Saved from ruin in 1989 by the current owners, the property was lovingly restored to a bed & breakfast with nine finely appointed guest rooms and a formal dining room, where a gourmet menu of delectables including roast halibut with pecan-scallop mousse, leg of lamb with herb apple butter, and roast pork tenderloin are served up. $125 and up.

Sandpoint

Church Street House Bed & Breakfast (208-255-7094; www .churchstreethouse.com), 401 Church St., Sandpoint 83864. Two guest rooms with breakfast are provided in this arts and crafts bungalow house listed on the National Register of Historic Places. $100 and up off-season; $110 and up high season.

Coit House Bed and Breakfast (866-265-2648; www.coithouse.com), 502 N. Fourth Ave., Sandpoint 83864. This beautifully appointed, renovated Victorian is conveniently located near downtown Sandpoint. A mixture of antiques and an eclectic artsy flair make this a place you might want to call home. Add the owners' great hospitality and fabulous cooking (think fresh eggs, Belgian waffles, and locally roasted coffee), and you might be a goner; massage services can be arranged too. $99 and up.

Paradise Valley Inn (208-267-4180 or 888-447-4180; www.paradisevalley inn.com), off US 95 between Bonners Ferry and Sandpoint, 83805. Perched atop a ridgeline providing spectacular views of the expansive Kootenai Valley, this 18-acre inn offers five bed & breakfast rooms in the lodge, all with private baths, and one Garden Cabin that sleeps two. Rooms $99 and up; cabin $125.

Sand Creek Inn (208-255-2821; www.innatsandcreek.com), 105 S. First Ave., Sandpoint 83864. Recently renovated, this upscale inn offers three suites, crisply appointed with a European flair, and a fabulous restaurant downstairs. Not only will you be well rested and well fed, but you'll find yourself smack in the heart of Sandpoint at this great spot. $95 and up in off-season; $125 and up most holidays.

GUEST RANCHES

Sandpoint
Western Pleasure Guest Ranch (208-263-9066 or 888-863-9066; www

.westernpleasureranch.com), 1413 Upper Gold Creek Rd., Sandpoint 83864; about 16 miles northeast of town. This fourth-generation cattle ranch has operated on the same land since 1940. Today it provides a full-service, all-inclusive fabulous guest ranch experience, with three home-cooked, family-style meals daily, trail riding on one of the ranch's 43 horses, and sleigh rides, snowshoeing, and some cross-country skiing during the winter. Secluded on 960 acres of sprawling pine-timbered land and open pastures, with breathtaking

ROOSEVELT BED & BREAKFAST INN, COEUR D'ALENE

views of the Selkirk and Cabinet mountains, this is a great place to just relax. You can't beat kicking back on the wraparound porch, sipping a cold drink, taking in the view, and chatting with the owners and other guests. This is a really nice family experience; in fact, many of the lodge's guests are return customers. Most people stay at the ranch for about five days, although stays of three to seven days are possible. $125 and up off-season; $200 and up in summer.

LODGES

Harrison

Red Horse Mountain Lodge (888-689-9680; www.redhorsemountain .com), 11077 E. Blue Lake Rd., Harrison 83833. This rustically beautiful 600-acre guest lodge is nestled against the Idaho Panhandle National Forests. The resort offers an inviting lodge and cabin accommodations, dining, a pool and hot tub, and a plethora of activities including horseback riding, mountain biking, yoga, kayaking, archery, fly-fishing, and more. Inclusive packages $249 and up in shoulder seasons; $299 and up in summer.

Sandpoint

Caribou Mountain Lodge (208-255-2333; www.cariboumountain lodge.com), 10 miles north of Sandpoint, 83840; accessible only by a 7-mile ski in. Nestled at 5,000 feet between the Caribou and Berry Creek drainages, the lodge sits atop a ridgeline and offers spectacular views, cozy accommodations for up to 10 people, and access to a wide variety of backcountry terrain. Backcountry ski hounds enjoy open bowls and gladed trees for less experienced skiers and trees and steep chutes for experts.

Entire lodge $900 for three-day weekend or four days midweek; $1,500 for full week.

Selkirk Lodge and White Pine Lodge (877-487-4643 or 800-RED-LION; www.schweitzer.com), both at Schweitzer Mountain Resort, 11 miles from Sandpoint, 83864. Visitors looking to stay hillside near Schweitzer might want to check out these European-style lodges. Together these two properties offer 82 rooms, including suites, efficiency kitchenettes, and Jacuzzi rooms, plus more than 50 condominium units. Rooms $145 and up; condos $230 and up.

MOTELS

Coeur d'Alene

Bates Motel (208-667-1411), 2018 E. Sherman Ave., Coeur d'Alene 83814. If you are on a tight budget, traveling alone, and have a sense of humor, try this place (think *Psycho*). Rooms are affordable and neat and have only one bed. The place is rumored to be haunted. $40.

RESORTS

Coeur d'Alene

Coeur d'Alene Resort (800-688-5253 or 208-765-4000; www.cdaresort .com), 115 S. Second St., Coeur d' Alene 83814. If you've just come in from the woods and are in need of some pampering, this resort is certainly cushy (and pricey). This place has the works: luxurious accommodations, excellent cuisine, spa treatments, a stunning lakeside location, and year-round recreational and cultural activities. Even if you aren't staying here, it's a nice place to have a drink, watch the sunset, and, if your timing is right, catch some live entertainment outside on the promenade. Packages $258 and up.

✴ Where to Eat

DINING OUT

Coeur d'Alene

Anthony's Midtown Bistro (208-765-7723), 315 E. Walnut Ave. The menu is limited, but the food at this tapas bar is spectacular and the cocktails are the talk of the town.

Coeur d'Alene Resort (208-765-4321 or 800-688-5253; www.cdaresort .com), 115 S. Second St. A handful of restaurants are located at the resort, including **Bonsai Bistro,** 111 Sherman Ave., which serves fine Asian cuisine prepared in an open kitchen; **Beverly's Restaurant**, the resort's signature five-star, award-winning restaurant, which boasts a $1.5 million wine cellar; and **the Cedars Floating Restaurant**, which offers a wide selection of fresh seafood, aged steaks, prime rib, and pasta dishes.

Sandpoint

Sand Creek Grill (208-255-5736; www.sandcreekgrill.com), 105 S. First Ave. This wonderful spot is housed in the restored 1906 Fidelity Trust Bank Building. Its colorful flower garden and warm patio surroundings offer beautiful water views during the warmer months. During the winter, fireplaces and cozy interior finishes provide the perfect ambience for the restaurant's innovative menu of Inland Northwest cuisine with a distinct global influence. Favorite meals include aged, corn-fed, Midwestern beef and Caribbean rubbed scallops over linguine. **Dulce**, the wine bar, has an extensive wine list and serves sushi. Reservations are recommended.

Bonner's Ferry

Jill's Café (208-267-1950), 7211 Main St. This local favorite serves all-American lunch fare featuring fresh homemade soups, salads and sandwiches, western barbecue burgers, fabulous desserts, and espresso.

Mugsy's Tavern & Grill (208-267-8059), 7161 Main St. Burgers, sandwiches, steaks, and pasta are accompanied by a large selection of wines and microbrews. Mondays are dedicated to vegetarian fare.

Coeur d'Alene

Coeur d'Alene has plenty of restaurants, running the gamut from super-casual to fancy-pants. Listed below are some of the more popular spots, although you might want to just stroll down downtown Sherman Avenue and see what strikes you.

Angelo's Ristoranté (208-765-2850; www.AngelosRistorante.net), 846 B Fourth St. Great Roman-style Italian food is made from fresh, often organic ingredients. With an extensive wine selection, outdoor seating, and tasty food, this place is a local favorite.

Iron Horse Bar and Grill (208-667-7314), 407 E. Sherman Ave. Steak, seafood, pasta, burgers, salads, and the like are served with a DJ on Thurs. nights and live music on Fri. and Sat.

The Moon Time (208-667-2331), 1602 E. Sherman Ave., Ste. 116. If you are looking for some hearty casual food, you might want to check out this fun pub with great beers and a menu that includes items like Mediterranean lamb burger, pork verde soup, and sweet sesame spinach salad. The pub serves microbrews for a dollar a pop on Thurs. nights after 9, along with live music.

The Wine Cellar (208-664-9463; www.coeurdalenewinecellar.com), 313 Sherman Ave. This is a cozy spot, complete with loungy couches, exposed bricks, and revolving artwork. True to its name, the Wine Cellar has a great selection of retail wines and offers tasty Mediterranean cuisine with live blues and jazz. It's a great spot to hang out and drink a glass of wine at the end of the day.

The Wolf Lodge Steakhouse (208-664-6665; www.wolflodgerestaurants .com), 11741 E. Frontage Rd. This has been a Coeur d'Alene favorite for more than 25 years. Open-flame cooking over a tamarack fire makes for some tasty steaks and other classic steakhouse fare.

Hope

The Floating Restaurant (208-264-5311; www.hopefloatingrestaurant .com), on ID 200. Open Apr.–Oct. This place does, in fact, float on Lake Pend Oreille. The restaurant features fresh fish, local beef, fresh pasta dishes, and homemade breads and desserts. They serve a full bar with an award-winning wine list and boast panoramic views of the lake.

Hope Market Café (208-264-0506), 620 Wellington Pl. Open for breakfast, lunch, and dinner. Here you'll find fabulous, eclectic bistro fare, pizzas, and some of the finest beer and wine in the West. Plus, the café has outdoor seating and live music. Their menu includes deli sandwiches, soups, salads, and delectable homemade desserts, including pastries, cakes, cookies, and chocolates. The adjoining specialty foods market sells an extensive array of gourmet foods, fine wines, ales, and artisan cheeses.

Priest River

Trinity at Willow Bay (208-265-8854; www.trinityatwillowbay.com), 520 Willow Bay Rd. This is the sister restaurant to Sandpoint's Café Trinity, and it serves up similar Southern-inspired casual food—but here, it's on the water! The menu includes sandwiches, chowders, gumbos, and more. Deckside dining provides for spectacular sunsets and panoramic views.

Sandpoint

Café Trinity (208-255-7558; www .cafetrinitysandpoint.com), 115 N. First St. This spot comes highly recommended. With delectables like warm Caesar salad, burgers, barbecued pulled pork, and crab cakes, there is something for everyone on Trinity's Southern-inspired menu.

Cricket's Original BBQ (208-265-9600), 212 N. Fourth Ave. If you are on the run, this little food shacks serves up some tasty sandwiches; try the turkey and cranberry sandwich or Philly steak and cheese (and the pizza place next door serves a good slice). Outside picnic tables also provide a nice respite.

DiLuna's (208-263-0846), 207 Cedar St. Breakfast is served all day, in addition to hand-cut steaks, homemade soups, and vegetarian cuisine. Twice a month, the restaurant hosts dinner concerts featuring acoustical musicians from around the nation.

Eichardt's (208-263-4005), 212 Cedar St. If you want to see what Sandpoint is all about, this is the spot. This traditional dining pub has great food, even better beer (more than a dozen beers on tap), a warm atmosphere, and fabulous live music. The locals will all tell you that this is the best place in town. With an eclectic set of local patrons, great food, and live music, including open mic night, what's not to like?

Ivanos Ristorante (208-263-0211; www.ivanossandpoint.com), 102 S. First Ave. This is another local favorite. The Sandpoint dining crowd comes for the casual atmosphere and finest food, wine, service, and hospitality around. They offer a great martini bar and half-menu.

Jalapeno's Mexican Restaurant (208-263-2995), 314 N. Second Ave. This spot serves traditional and unusual Mexican specialties in a comfortable setting in the heart of Sandpoint that includes a lounge and outdoor seating.

Mick Duff's Brewing Company (208-255-4351; www.mickduffs.com), 312 N. First Ave. Stop in for great local brew (made by local brewmaster Mickey Mahoney) and tasty pub fare. The Huge Porter Brownie dessert is a temptation for even the most disciplined diner (how can you pass up Knot Tree Porter over chocolate?). Plus, the place has its own kind of funkiness, complete with unexpected velvet chairs in the sitting area.

Oishii Sushi (208-263-1406; www.oishiisandpoint.com), 115 N. First St., Ste. C. This is quickly becoming known as Sandpoint's hottest fusion sushi and saketini bar. With soft lighting, modern art adorning the walls, and deliciously fresh sushi, what more could you want?

Panhandler Pies Restaurant & Bakery (208-263-2912; www.panhandlerpies.com), 120 S. First Ave. Hearty fare includes full pancake or bacon and egg breakfasts; Rueben sandwiches, chicken pot pie, and

burgers for lunch; and chicken fried streak and pot roast for dinner. You might want to stop in just for a fat slice of homemade pie!

Second Avenue Pizza (208-263-9231), 215 S. Second Ave. According to some locals, this place serves "the best pizza in the world." Certainly the pizza is tasty and huge! Be prepared to walk away with a doggie bag.

Spuds Rotisserie & Grill (208-265-4311; www.spudsonline.com), 102 N. First Ave. Open for lunch and dinner. Regional American food includes grilled steaks, marinated tri-tip, rotisserie chicken, fresh seafood, and Southwest specials, plus The Butler Did It take-home dinners. This yacht club–themed restaurant features a large deck overlooking Sand Creek and a streetside patio.

Stage Right Cellars (208-265-8116; www.stagerightcellars.com), 302 N. First Ave. Here's a great selection of wine, beer, and cigars. You can buy a bottle to go or sit and share a glass with friends at one of the bar tables or couches, listening to a pickup jazz ensemble during Jazz Night and checking out the latest art adorning the walls.

Wallace
The Historic Jameson Restaurant Saloon & Inn (208-556-6000; www.jamesonrestaurant.com), 304 Sixth St. Built in 1890 as a pool hall, the building is recognized as a regional landmark by the National Trust for Historic Preservation. A step back in time, the restaurant serves a great surf-and-turf menu that includes prime rib, shrimp scampi, chicken fried steak, and fish-and-chips, plus hearty baked potatoes, salads, and big chocolate desserts.

COFFEEHOUSES

Sandpoint

Monarch Mountain Coffee (208-265-9382 or 800-599-6702; www.monarchmountaincoffee.com), 208 N. Fourth Ave. This great local coffee joint is complete with walls adorned by local art—landscapes and coffeescapes—old oak tables, and great espresso and lattes. If you are looking for a place to kick back, read the *New York Times* or a great book, or even plug in your laptop (God forbid), this is a great spot.

✳ Cultural Offerings

ART GALLERIES

Art Works Gallery (208-263-2642; www.sandpointartworks.com), 214 N. First Ave., Sandpoint. This cooperative fine art gallery operated by 60 regional artists features work in a wide variety of materials, from wood to crystal, and of varying media, from sculpture to painting. An extensive gift shop has frequent demonstrations and receptions; this place was voted Sandpoint's Favorite Gallery.

Autumn's Loft (208-255-8272; www.freemanlakeart.com), 1213 US 2, Priest River. The loft features rustic home furnishings, nature photography, functional art by local artisans, handcrafted slab wood furniture, custom frames and furniture, and fine art.

Common Knowledge Bookstore and Teahouse (208-263-0178; www.commonknowledgeid.com), 823 Main St., Sandpoint. This spot also shows some great local art.

En"tree" Gallery (208-443-2001; www.entreegallery.com), 1755 Reeder Bay Rd., Priest River. This place spells its name En"tree" in homage to the forests around Priest Lake, and it features work from some 100 nationally recognized local and regional artists.

Hallans Gallery (208-263-4704; www.rosshallcollection.com), 323 N. First Ave., Sandpoint. Striking black-and-white vintage photography by Ross Hall and Dick Himes is showcased here.

Hen's Tooth Studio Gallery (208-263-3665), 323 N. First Ave., Sandpoint. This place has some great fish images.

Wallace District Arts Center (208-752-8381), 610 Bank St., Wallace. This fine arts gallery housed in the historic Coeur d'Alene Hardware Company building features exhibits by local and regional artists and also offers art courses.

MUSIC

MusicWalk (www.artsincda.org/MusicWalk.html), downtown Coeur d'Alene. Coeur d'Alene offers monthly MusicWalks throughout the year, 5–midnight on fourth Fri. each month Jan.–Mar. and June–Aug. The event features live music—jazz, rock, classical, and pop—at various venues around town, fine dining, and a chance to gather with friends.

Coeur d'Alene Symphony (208-765-3833; www.cdasymphony.org), Schuler Performing Arts Center, Boswell Hall, North Idaho College campus, Coeur d'Alene. Ten or so shows each year include productions like their Autumn Classic, a Christmas Showcase, and a Family Concert. A free Labor Day Concert in the Park is held outdoors.

Opera Plus! (208-664-2827; www.operaplus.org), Coeur d'Alene. Free public performances, concerts, an annual fully staged opera, and outreach and education bring opera to a variety of audiences. Venues vary by production.

THEATER

Coeur d'Alene Summer Theatre (208-769-7780; www.nic.edu/summer theatre.com), Schuler Performing Arts Center, Boswell Hall, North Idaho College campus, Coeur d' Alene. Idaho's oldest performing arts organization brings a string of fabulous Broadway musicals to Northern Idaho for a 12-week summer season each year. Recent productions have included *A Chorus Line, Peter Pan, Pippin*, and *The King and I. USA Today* recently named the theater one of the top 10 regional theaters in the United States.

Panida Theatre (208-263-9191 or 208-255-7801; www.panida.org), 300 N. First Ave., Sandpoint. This is a fabulous place to find a little culture. The theater building, with its Spanish Mission style architecture, is a western icon in its own right and on the National Register of Historic Places. Opened in 1927 as a vaudeville and movie house, the theater's enduring mission, reflected in its name—synthesized from the words PANhandle and IDAho—is to feature performers and performances for Panhandle audiences. In 1985, the Sandpoint community restored the Panida building to its former glory, and it now functions as a community-owned cultural center for cinema, theater, and music.

Sixth Street Melodrama (208-752-8871), 212 Sixth St., Wallace. Melodramas and musical variety shows are produced year-round in another of Wallace's former brothels. Audience participation is encouraged. Recent productions have included *Nightmare at Dream* and *Tied to the Tracks*.

Song Bird Theatre–Performing and Fine Arts Center (208-664-3672), 315 N. Fourth St., Coeur d' Alene. An array of live theater performances are offered throughout the year, including mystery dinner theater on Sat. nights, concerts, recitals, drama, dance, and more.

✱ Special Events

January: **Sandpoint Winter Carnival** (208-263-0887 or 800-800-2106; www.sandpoint.org/wintercarnival/), Sandpoint. Celebrating its 35th year in 2007–2008, the Sandpoint Winter Carnival rocks the town each Jan. with live music, a torchlight parade, cook-offs, a pizza-eating contest, and the K-9 Keg Pull.

Snowshoe Softball Tournaments (www.priestlake.org), Priest Lake. Each winter Priest Lake hosts a spirited softball tournament, played (yes) on showshoes. This has become a favorite local pastime. The finals are held in Feb.

February: **U.S. Pacific Coast Championship Sled Dog Races** (208-443-3191; www.priestlake.org), Priest Lake. For more than 35 years, this annual dogsled race has been held at Priest Lake, attracting 75–100 teams from across the United States and Canada. Teams come from as far away as Alaska to compete in events that include sprints, long-distance races, and a triathlon.

April: **Artist Showcase** (208-765-1437), Kootenai County Fairgrounds, Coeur d'Alene. Third weekend in Apr. Sponsored by the Couer d'Alene

Art Association, this juried show features fine arts by more than 40 local artists.

Loggers Day (888-774-3785), Nordman; end of ID 57 at northwest end of Priest Lake. Held on the cusp of spring each year, this event pulls some Grizzly Adams types out of the woods for ax throwing, log cutting, and tug of war in the mud. Loggers Day provides a window into authentic Idaho.

May: **Coeur d'Alene Marathon** (www.cdamarathon.org), Coeur d'Alene. Memorial Day weekend. Along with the marathon, there's a half marathon and a 5K; note that the course elevation is at approximately 2,300 feet. This is a nice way to experience this country.

Depot Day (http://wallace-id.com/), Wallace. Each spring, Wallace celebrates the coming of spring and the railroad that helped the town earn its title as "the Silver Capital of the World." The Classic Car Show features sleek engines from across the Inland Northwest, plus there's a model-train exhibit, live music, food, and events for kids.

Lost in the '50s Weekend (http://sandpoint.org/lostin50s/), downtown Sandpoint. Each year, hundreds of vintage cars are on parade, live '50s music and dancers fill the streets, and Sandpointers come out to play. This is billed as Sandpoint's biggest party of the year!

June: **A Plein Air** (Timber Stand Gallery, 208-263-7748; www.timber stand.com), Sandpoint. Local galleries sponsor this paint outdoors weekend featuring more than 20 regional artists.

Car d'Lane (208-667-5986), Coeur d'Alene. This classic car show for '78

models and older cruises through town for two days. Fri. night features a car cruise, while Sat. is packed with a Car Show and Shine, an evening street dance, and a collector car auction.

Ironman Coeur d'Alene (208-664-3194 or 877-782-9232; www.iron mancda.com), Coeur d'Alene. This favorite event features a 2.4-mile swim, a 112-mile bike ride, and a 26.2-mile run along Coeur d'Alene and Hayden lakes.

July: **Coeur d'Alene Garden Club Tour** (208-772-3148), Coeur d'Alene. Tickets available at local garden centers. This renowned garden tour features a handful of the area's spectacular estate and other gardens each year.

Fourth of July in Northern Idaho is Norman Rockwellesque. Fireworks can be seen at Luby and Cavanaugh bays on **Priest Lake**; **Coeur d'Alene** hosts a grand parade, a boat parade, and fireworks; and **Sandpoint** has not just its own Independence Day Celebration, but also a replica Statue of Liberty at Sandpoint City Park.

Pend Oreille Valley Lavender Festival (Le Clerc Creek Lavenders lavender farm, 509-447-6451; www .lavendercreek.net), 13401 LeClerc Rd. N.; just north of Cusick, Washington, about 60 miles west of Sandpoint. This weekend celebration of the luxurious lavender blooms that dot the Pend Oreille River offers live classical music, a juried arts and crafts fair, food and produce by local growers, and self-guided garden tours.

River City Rod Run Show (208-777-1712; www.hotrodcafe.com), Post Falls. This three-day celebration fea-

WHAT? THE STATUE OF LIBERTY AT SANDPOINT CITY PARK?

tures more than 900 hot rods, bands, flame throwing, fireworks, a Miss Hot Rod contest, a demolition derby, and food and beverages.

Sandpoint Wooden Boat Festival (http://sandpoint.org/boatfestival/), Sandpoint. For four days, this event showcases beautifully gleaming classic wooden boats in a boat show, boat parade, parties, and movie showings.

August: The first weekend in August is a busy time in downtown Coeur d'Alene. Three events are held concurrently, attracting more than 40,000 attendees, so plan ahead!

Art on the Green (208-667-9346; www.artonthegreen.org), North Idaho College Campus, Coeur d'Alene. First weekend in Aug. Celebrate local artists.

Downtown Street Fair (208-667-4040; www.CDADowntown.com), Coeur d'Alene. First weekend in Aug. Fine arts and crafts from regional artists are showcased alongside food and entertainment with more than 200 vendors.

Festival at Sandpoint (208-265-4554; www.festivalsandpoint.com), Memorial Field, Sandpoint. About $149 for Early Bird season passes for entire concert series. Held each year since 1983, this 10-day, internationally renowned outdoor concert series features a wide range of live musical performances, including orchestral, pops, folk music, blues, and more in a relaxed atmosphere. Bring a picnic basket and a bottle of wine and kick back!

Lake Pend Oreille Long Bridge Swim (http://sandpoint.org/long bridgeswim), Sandpoint. This event held each summer has gained notoriety as the Northwest's premier open-

water swim: 1.76 miles across Lake Pend Oreille in 65- to 70-degree water.

North Idaho Fair and Rodeo (208-765-4969; www.NorthIdahoFair.com), Kootenai County Multi-Use Events Center, 4056 N. Government Way, Coeur d'Alene. This classic western fair features rodeo events, a draft horse and pull show, motocross, a demolition derby, home arts and livestock contests, and more.

Taste of the Coeur d'Alenes, Coeur d'Alene. First weekend in Aug. Gastronomic delights can be found at 25 booths, along with collectible art by regional artists. Live jazz, big band, Dixieland, and blues music also rocks the streets.

September: **Coeur d'Alene Lake Balloonfest** (877-782-9232; www .cdaballoonfest.com), multiple locations throughout Coeur d'Alene and Post Falls. Labor Day weekend. This annual event features sunrise balloon launches, a spectacular Night Glow Extravaganza of choreographed music and glowing hot air balloons, live entertainment, an antique and classic car show, and more.

Dry Rot Wooden Boat Brunch and Parade (www.priestlake.org), in Reeder Bay, Priest Lake. An annual event on the lake.

October: **Autoberfest Annual Classic & Antique Car Show** (www .priestlake.org), Priest Lake. Another event where you can see yet more shiny, pristine antique cars.

November: **Holiday Light Show Parade** (208-667-5986; www.CDA Downtown.com), Coeur d'Alene. Fri. after Thanksgiving. The annual event ushers in the holiday season.

November and December: **Coeur d'Alene Resort Holiday Light Show**, Coeur d'Alene. More than a million lights sparkle across Lake Coeur d'Alene, more than 225 holiday displays deck the boardwalk at the resort, and what is purported to be the world's tallest living Christmas tree is on view.

Journey to the North Pole Cruises (208-664-7280 or 800-684-0512 ext. 7811), Coeur d'Alene Resort Boardwalk, Coeur d'Alene. Free. Passengers board cruise boats of the Lake Coeur d'Alene Fun Fleet to visit the "North Pole," featuring a magical toyland, a Victorian village, and holiday lights galore.

MOSCOW AND THE PALOUSE:
HEART OF THE ARTS

One of the few punctuations in Idaho's rugged mountainscape is the vast Columbia Plateau, 200,000 square miles of lava-flow highland stretching from Washington's Cascade Range west to Idaho's Northern Rocky Mountains and arching south to include the Snake River Plain in southern Idaho. The Palouse feels a world apart from much of Idaho's ruggedly alpine terrain. Instead, the vistas here are pastoral: endless, undulating hills splay out in all directions forming the Palouse—variously said to have been derived from the Sehaptin language of the Nez Perce to mean "something sticking down the water" and perhaps to have evolved to imply "village" (although the etymology remains a bit murky). A thick blanket—as much as 150 feet of it in some places—of fertile loess (wind-blown dust of Pleistocene age) carpets the underlying lava, making way for rich agriculture. Vast fields of dryland wheat now paint the Palouse landscape.

Perched atop this plateau, and seemingly rising out of a sea of cultivars, is the semiurban enclave of Moscow (population greater than 20,000), home to Idaho's land grant institution: the University of Idaho and its almost 12,000 students. (Just 8 miles west in Washington is its sister college town, Pullman, home of Washington State University.) Moscow was first permanently settled in 1871 by farmers and miners, who named the town Paradise Valley after nearby Paradise Creek. The name was short-lived, and in 1875 it was changed to Moscow. Word on the street is that the first farmers informally dubbed the area Hog Heaven in tribute to the abundant camas bulbs that kept their pigs fat and happy. Today, like any good college town, Moscow has a progressive scene filled with hip coffee shops, brewpubs and restaurants, used bookstores, performance theater, great galleries, and summers filled with live outdoor music. If you are in the area and need a cultural fix, you might want to check out the town!

GUIDANCE

Moscow Chamber of Commerce (208-882-1800 or 800-380-1801; www .moscowchamber.com), 411 S. Main St., Moscow 83843.

North Central Idaho Travel Association (877-364-3246; www.northcentral idaho.info), Lewiston 83501.

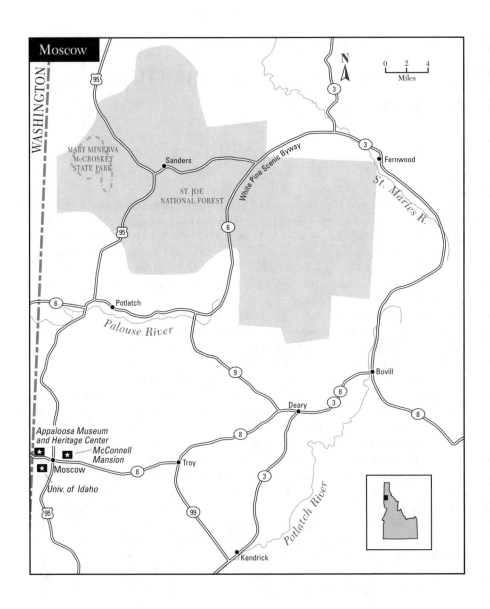

By car

Moscow is on **US 95**, which runs north along with western edge of Idaho from Lewiston all the way to the Canadian border. Smaller highways thread the Palouse: **ID 8** heads east from Moscow through Deary and Bovill to Elk River, and **ID 6** runs east from Palouse, Washington, through Potlatch to ID 3.

By air

Pullman-Moscow Regional Airport (509-338-3223; www.pullman-wa.gov), Pullman, Washington. This nearby airport serves the region with Horizon Air flights.

Spokane International Airport (509-455-6455; www.spokaneairports.net), Spokane, Washington; 85 miles west. Cheaper flights might be found in Spokane, with Alaska Airlines, Delta/Skywest Airlines, Express Jet, Frontier Airlines, Horizon Air, Northwest Airlines, Southwest Airlines, United/United Express, and US Airways.

MEDICAL EMERGENCIES

Gritman Medical Center (208-882-4511 or 800-526-CARE; www.gritman .org), 700 S. Main St., Moscow. This community hospital is the major medical facility in this area.

Pullman Regional Hospital (509-332-2541; www.pullmanhospital.org), on Washington State University campus, 835 SE Bishop Blvd., Pullman, Washington. This is a Level III Trauma Center for the Palouse region.

✳ Wandering Around

White Pine Scenic Byway, 82 paved miles on ID 3 near I-90 at Cataldo south to Santa and on ID 6 southwest to Potlatch. This byway passes through timber country, alongside numerous lakes and marshlands. The route starts at the Old Mission at Cataldo (see To See—Historical Sites in chapter 1, Coeur d'Alene, Pend Oreille, and Priest Lakes: Lake Country), Idaho's oldest standing building, and meanders through the lumber-mill town of St. Maries to historic Potlatch, established in 1905 when Frederick Weyerhauser opened the world's largest white-pine mill. Along the way, visitors enjoy the recreational opportunities of **Laird Park**, which includes camping, swimming, horseback riding, and gold panning (for real!); the Hughes House Museum, a historic men's club; and St. Joe National Forest, home to the country's largest stand of white pine.

✳ To See

ART TOURS

Moscow Artwalk (208-883-7036; http://moscow-arts.org), Moscow. Mid-June–mid-Sept. The Moscow Arts and Cultural Alliance organizes an artwalk featuring a wide variety of media and styles displayed at galleries and shops throughout town and live music at several venues.

MOSCOW'S CITY HALL

FARMER'S MARKETS

Moscow Farmer's Market (208-882-7036), Friendship Square, Fourth and Main streets, Moscow. Held 8–12 Sat. May–Oct. Beautiful, locally grown fresh fruit, vegetables, flowers, and more, plus live music by local musicians.

FOR FAMILIES

Palouse Discovery Science Center (509-332-6869; ww.palousescience.org), 2371 NE Hopkins Court, Pullman, Washington; 8 miles west of Moscow. Open 10–3 Wed.–Sat. Free. "Hands-on, minds-on" science for kids is promoted through educational programs, exhibits, teaching collections, and hands-on learning activities.

GARDENS

University of Idaho Arboretum and Botanical Garden (208-885-5978; www.uidaho.edu/arboretum), 1200 W. Palouse River Dr., Moscow. Just south of the President's Residence on Nez Perce Drive, this 63-acre arboretum is filled with hundreds of North Temperate Zone tree species and shrubs; additional thematic gardens showcasing Asian, European, and Easter species; a xeriscape garden; and numerous water features. Not surprisingly, all this vegetation attracts a

UNIVERSITY OF IDAHO ARBORETUM IN MOSCOW CONTAINS HUNDREDS OF TREE SPECIES, INCLUDING ASPEN.

Chris Pilaro

significant population of resident and migratory birds, including songbirds and raptors. A 1.4-mile trail system, complete with granite benches, winds throughout the property, allowing visitors to amble, observe, and contemplate. Just north of the President's Residence is the **Charles Houston Shattuck Arboretum**, a 14-acre grove of mature American beech, California incense-cedar, Canadian hemlock, and other trees. Nestled within them is a giant sequoia. Private tours can be arranged.

HISTORIC SITES

Fort Russell Neighborhood Historic District (www.moscow.id.us), between Monroe and Jefferson streets and D and Second streets, Moscow. Encompassing roughly 10 city blocks in downtown Moscow, this area is the proud home of a diversity of 19th-century architecture, including Queen Anne, stick, and Gothic Revival structures. The entire neighborhood is on the National Register of Historic Places. A map of the area is available from the city Web site.

McConnell Mansion (208-882-1004; http://users.moscow.com/lchs/mansion .html), 327 E. Second Ave., Moscow. Open 1–4 Tues.–Sat. $2 suggested donation. Built in 1886, this house was home to Poker Bill (aka William J. McConnell), who sold produce to miners during the Boise Basin gold rush, led vigilantes to capture horse rustlers, and later ranched, taught, and served in the Oregon legislature. In Moscow, he earned the title of "Merchant Prince of Idaho" with a prosperous mercantile business and later served as state senator and governor. Despite his accomplishments, he fell into relative obscurity after going bust in the Depression of 1893. The main floor of this Victorian gem has been restored to conditions representative of circa 1890–1930. The Historical Society's changing exhibits explore Latah County history.

University of Idaho (208-885-6424; www.uidaho.edu), 875 Perimeter Dr., Moscow. The anchor of this community, UI was founded as a land-grant institution in 1889, essentially as a bribe to prevent ruling factions in North Idaho from seceding from Idaho Territory. Idaho received statehood a year later. UI enrolls about 12,000 students and offers more than 140 undergraduate degree programs, as well as Education Specialist, MS, JD, and PhD degrees. The campus spans 1,585 acres with more than 250 buildings, an arboretum (see Gardens) several farms, and a public golf course. If nothing else, with its tree-lined paths and wide lawns, it is a nice place to take a stroll.

MUSEUMS

Appaloosa Museum (208-882-5578; www.appaloosamuseum.org), 5070 ID 8 W., Moscow. Open 8–5 Mon.–Fri. year-round, 9–3 Sat. in summer. $4 per family, $2 per person suggested donation. This museum honors the rich history of this beautifully spotted horse, bred and revered by the native Nez Perce people, through artifacts, photos, and paintings demonstrating the history of the horse in art and literature and documenting the relationship between the Appaloosa and the Nez Perce. An Appaloosa viewing corral is open during summer months.

IDAHO'S RURAL CHARM

WINERY TOURS

Camas Prairie Winery (208-882-0214 or 800-616-0214; www.camasprarie winery.com), 110 S. Main St., Moscow. Open 12–7 Mon.–Sat. If you are looking for an afternoon glass of wine, this independent winery offers wine tasting and tours.

✳ To Do

Recreational opportunities in the Palouse are generally of the mellower variety. A slew of area parks and trails provide great opportunities to swim, boat, hike, camp, and just relax. About a dozen parks, suitable for picnicing and tamer recreation, are located within Moscow's city limits, and the Potlatch River provides great fishing.

BICYCLING

Palouse Recreational Trail system, 26 paved miles. Beginning in the city are these paved biking pathways, including a trail running from Moscow to Pullman and another connecting the UI campus with downtown Moscow.

GOLF

Elks Golf Course (208-882-3015), Moscow. This private par 72 course has nine holes.

Palouse Ridge Golf Club, at Washington State University, Pullman. Construction is underway on this new 18-hole course.

University of Idaho Golf Course (208-885-6171; www.auxserv.uidaho.edu/golf), 1215 Nez Perce Dr., Moscow. This public par 72 course has 18 holes.

ICE SKATING

Palouse Ice Rink (208-882-7188; www.palouseicerink.com), Latah County Fair Grounds, Moscow. This covered venue offers skating lessons, free skating, ice hockey, and more.

SKIING

Nordic

Palouse Divide Nordic Area (http://palousedividenordic.org), off ID 6 near Emida. $7.50 daily pass, $25 annual pass; available as part of Idaho Parks and Recreation Park N' Ski Pass system. The Nordic ski center features nine trails, with mostly gently sloping terrain, and despite its fairly low elevation (3,600 feet), it seems to sustain a relatively deep snowpack—5–7 feet in good winters. Some trails are groomed.

✳ Wilder Places

PARKS

Mary Minerva McCroskey State Park (208-699-2224; www.parksand recreation.idaho.gov), off US 95 south of Plummer. This 5,300-acre park is dedicated to frontier women in acknowledgment of their hardships. The park features an 18-mile skyline drive on unimproved roads through Palouse country, 32 miles of multipurpose trails, and camping and picnic areas.

✳ Lodging

BED & BREAKFASTS

Moscow

The Ivy Bed & Breakfast (208-883-0748), 902 E. B St., Moscow 83843. Located in the lovely, historic Old Fort Russell area, the home itself is a French cottage offering three guest rooms. $55–85.

Mary Jane's Farm (208-882-6819; www.maryjanesfarm.com), 1000 Wild Iris La., Moscow 83843. May 1–July 15, Mary Jane offers a beautifully decked-out wall tent (with a "Farmgirl" wall-tent shower house) and a farm-fresh homemade breakfast on her expansive, community-oriented organic farm. The farm has a historic schoolhouse and runs the Pay Dirt Farm School, which offers farm apprenticeships and short courses on organic cooking, organic gardening, food preservation, biofuels, and more. This is a really neat outfit. Wall tents $139 Mon.–Thurs., $169 Fri.–Sun.

HOTELS AND MOTELS

Moscow

Best Western University Inn (208-882-0550; www.uinnmoscow.com), 1516 Pullman Rd., Moscow 83843. Rooms $79–99, suites $150–50.

Hillcrest Motel (208-882-7579 or 800-368-6564), 706 N. Main St., Moscow 83843. $32–84.

Palouse Inn (208-882-5511 or 888-882-5511; www.palouseinn.com), 101 Baker St., Moscow 83843. $31–110.

Super 8 Moscow (208-883-1503 or 800-800-8000; www.super8.com), 175 Peterson Dr, Moscow 83843. $56–110.

✳ Where to Eat

DINING OUT

Moscow
Moscow's main drag (aka Main Street) has quite a few restaurants. You might want to stroll down the street and see if something catches your eye.

The Red Door (208-882-7830; www.red-door-restaurant.com), 215 S. Main St. Great slow-cook cuisine is served in a warm atmosphere. Fresh ingredients and dishes such as arugula salad with goat cheese and mango, Lonehawk Farm's elk, black rasperry and port wine reduction sauce, wild rice and sautéed spinach, and a great wine list make this a happy spot. Reservations accepted for parties of five or more.

West of Paris (208-882-4279), 403 S. Main St. This upscale French restaurant serves fine multicourse meals with menu items like roast duckling and filet mignon made of the best ingredients—local meats and vegetables and imported essential French ingredients. They also have a nice

EATERIES ON MOSCOW'S MAIN DRAG

Matt Furber

wine list that includes both French and Northwest wines.

EATING OUT

Moscow

La Casa Lopez (208-833-0536), 415 S. Main St. If you're up for Mexican, this is a local favorite, despite its divey appearance; the food and margaritas are quite good. They have outside seating as well.

Moscow Food Co-op (208-882-8537; www.moscowfood.coop), 121 E. Fifth St. For wholesome sandwiches, check out the deli counter here.

One World Café (208-883-3537; one-world-cafe.biz), 533 S. Main St. You might want to try their great java and light breakfast or lunch.

Wheatberries Bake Shop (208-882-4618; www.wheatberriesbakeshop .com), 531 S. Main St., Ste. B. If you just want a pick-me-up of baked goodies and joe, this is a good spot.

Bucer's Coffee House Pub (208-882-5216), 201 S. Main St. For an iconoclastic coffeehouse experience, check out this spot named for Martin Bucer, an influential German reformer of the 1500s. With warmly worn wooden tables, bookshelves, and late-night coffee, here you might feel like you've walked into an intellectual Oxford gathering spot. They serve light food, too.

✳ Cultural Offerings

ART GALLERIES

University of Idaho Prichard Art Gallery (208-883-3586; www.webs .uidaho.edu/prichard/), 414 S. Main St., Moscow. Open 10–8 Tues.–Sat., 10–3 Sun.; 1–7 Tues.–Fri., 9–4 Sat. in summer. This gallery is Moscow's premier art center and exhibits works by some of the nation's finest artists. A wide genre of work is represented, including traditional painting and sculpture and edgier ceramics, photography, glass, crafts, folk, computer, and installation art.

WSU Art Gallery (509-335-1910; www.wsu.edu/artmuse), in Washington State University's Fine Arts Center, Wilson Road and Stadium Way, Pullman, Washington. Open 12–4 Tues.–Sat in summer. Free. This is the largest fine arts facility in the Inland Northwest. The gallery offers changing exhibits of traditional and contemporary art forms by regional, national, and international artists. They also offer educational lectures and docent tours.

DANCE

Festival Dance Academy at the University of Idaho (208-883-3267; www.festivaldance.org), Moscow. UI sponsors dance companies and touring Broadway shows—from the likes of St. Petersburg Ballet to Momix—and also houses a dance academy.

MUSIC

Fresh Aire Concerts, East City Park, Moscow. Held 6:30–7:30 Thurs. in summer. Free. Bring some wine and cheese and a blanket and kick back with some friends for some outdoor music!

Idaho-Washington Concert Chorale (208-882-3749; www .iwchorale.org), various churches in the region. Additional musical entertainment is this series of chorus events.

Washington-Idaho Sympony (509-332-3408; www.washingtonidaho symphony.org), several venues in the area. Symphony buffs might enjoy attending a performance of this well-established symphony, which brings live classical music to the Palouse region through five to six performances by accomplished regional musicians each year.

THEATER

Theatrical opportunities abound in Moscow and its twin town, Pullman, Washington.

Idaho Repertory Theatre (208-885-7212; www.class.uidaho.edu/irt/), at **University of Idaho's Hartung Theatre** (208-885-7986), Sixth and Rayburn streets, Moscow. Recent productions have included a *Midsummer's Night Dream, Doubt: A Parable, The Clean House*, and *Oleanna*.

Moscow Community Theater (208-882-4731), at **Kenworthy Performing Arts Centre** (208-882-4127; www.kenworthy.org), 508 S. Main St., Moscow. This circa 1908 theater on the National Register of Historical Places is home to the theater's dramas, comedies, and musicals. The Kenworthy also offers films, concerts, and other public events.

Washington State University Theatre (509-335-7447), Daggy Hall 320, P.O. Box 642432, Pullman, Washington 99164. Student and other live theater productions have included *Titus Andronicus, Passion, The Exonerated*, and *Sylvia*.

✱ Entertainment

COLLEGE SPORTS

University of Idaho Vanguards (188-88-UIDAHO; www.auxserv .uidaho.edu/tickets), Moscow. If you're interested in watching some college football, basketball, or volleyball, you might want to catch a UI Vanguards game during the academic year.

✱ Special Events

February: **Lionel Hampton International Jazz Festival** (208-885-7212; www.jazz.uidaho.edu), Moscow. This festival invites elementary through college students to meet, listen to, learn from, and play with some of the world's great jazz musicians, including Ella Fitzgerald, Diana Krall, and Winton Marsalis. Since its modest inception in 1967, this jazz festival has attracted lots of star power, from jazz greats to rising stars. Thousands of students make this annual pilgrimage to four days of concerts and workshops; listeners are welcome too.

May: **Renaissance Fair** (208-882-5860; http//moscowrenfair.org), Moscow. In a tribute to spring, this fair features arts and crafts by Northwestern artists, international cuisine, and live music and entertainment.

June: **Studio Tour of the Palouse** (208-883-7036; http://moscow-arts .org), Moscow. Passbooks $10; available at Moscow City Hall and Moscow Farmer's Market. The Moscow Arts Commission and Moscow Artwalk sponsor a tour of the working studios of local artists.

July: **Rendezvous in the Park** (208-882-1178; www.moscowmusic.com/ rendezvous), East City Park, Moscow. This popular annual summer music festival features three nights of outdoor concerts with nationally acclaimed musicians and a fourth performance at the Lionel Hampton School of Music at the UI campus. It includes several concerts for kids, too.

August: **Annual Lentil Festival** (509-334-3565; www.lentilfest.com),

Reaney Park, Pullman, Washington. The Palouse region produces one-third of the nation's lentils, and thus, Moscow and Pullman have something to celebrate! Since 1989, this annual event has been attracting an increasing amount of attention with its Lentil Cook-Off, a street fair, live music, a Microbrewery Tasting Tent, free lentil chili served from a 220-gallon pot ("so big we have to stir it with an oar"), a Grand Parade, and athletic events such as the 100K Tour de Lentil bike ride.

September: **Latah County Fair** (208-883-5722), 1021 Harold St., Moscow. This traditional county fair features, like most others, pigs and bunnies, strange large vegetables, and local arts and crafts—a fun place to take kids.

THE CLEARWATER REGION: BIG FISH, BIG TREES, BIG WHITEWATER

The Clearwater wilds of Northern Idaho are as remote and rugged as they come. The vast forested area of the Clearwater Mountains and the Clearwater and Lochsa rivers stretches across the middle of the Panhandle to the Bitterroot Mountains at Idaho's border with Montana, encompassing the Nez Perce Indian Reservation, the 1.8 million-acre Clearwater National Forest, 1.6 million-acre Bitterroot National Forest (part of which spans into Montana), and 2.2 million-acre Nez Perce National Forest. Nearly half the area within the Nez Perce National Forest is designated wilderness—the Selway-Bitterroot, Gospel Hump, and Frank Church–River of No Return wilderness areas. Considered Idaho's "Big Wild," this region, with its churning whitewater, alpine lakes, and rugged peaks, provides fabulous habitat for migratory and resident fish, elk, moose, black bears, cougars, gray wolves, white-tailed and mule deer, mountain goats, and many species of smaller mammals.

This area is also rich in history. It is the ancestral homeland of the Nez Perce Indians; Lewis and Clark passed through here on their search for a Northwest Passage (now US 12—the Northwest Passage Scenic Byway); and Idaho's first gold rush occurred here. The area is replete with mining camps, old timber towns, and numerous museums and interpretive exhibits that share Native and explorer histories. Amenities are relatively slim, and most visitors are either looking to get out into the great wilds or to explore the region's history.

GUIDANCE

Grangeville Chamber of Commerce (208-983-0460; www.grangevilleidaho.com), US 95 at Pine Street, Grangeville 83530.

Kamiah Chamber of Commerce (208-935-2290; www.kamiahchamber.com), 518 Main St., Kamiah 83536.

Kooskia Chamber of Commerce (208-926-4362; www.kooskia.com), P.O. Box 310, Kooskia 83539.

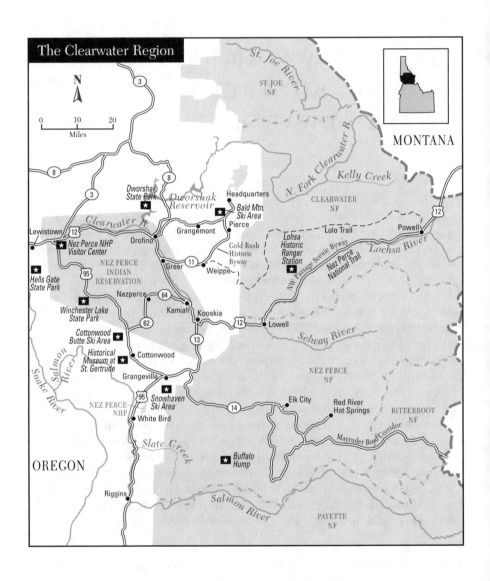

The Clearwater Region

N

0   10   20
Miles

MONTANA

St. Joe River

ST. JOE
NF

N. Fork Clearwater R.

Kelly Creek

CLEARWATER
NF

Dworshak
State Park

Dworshak
Reservoir

Headquarters

Bald Mtn.
Ski Area

Pierce

Lolo Trail

Powell

Clearwater R.

Lewistown

Grangemont

Orofino

Lohsa
Historic
Ranger
Station

Lochsa River

Nez Perce NHP
Visitor Center

Gold Rush
Historic
Byway

Greer

Weippe

NW Passage Scenic Byway

Nez Perce
National Trail

NEZ PERCE
INDIAN
RESERVATION

Hells Gate
State Park

Nezperce

Kamiah

Kooskia

Winchester Lake
State Park

Lowell

Selway River

Cottonwood
Butte Ski Area

Historical
Museum at
St. Gertrude

Cottonwood

Salmon River

Grangeville

NEZ PERCE
NF

Snowhaven
Ski Area

Elk City

Red River
Hot Springs

BITTERROOT
NF

NEZ PERCE
NHP

White Bird

Mayruder Road Corridor

Snake River

OREGON

Slate Creek

Buffalo
Hump

Riggins

Salmon River

PAYETTE
NF

Lewiston Chamber of Commerce (208-743-3531 or 800-473-3543; www .lewistonchamber.org), 111 Main St., Ste. 120, Lewiston 83501.

Nez Perce Tribe (208-843-7400; www.nezperce.org), P.O. Box 305, Lapwai 83540.

Orofino Chamber of Commerce (208-476-4335; www.orofino.com), P.O. Box 2346, Orofino 83544.

GETTING THERE

By car
The main connectors through the Clearwater region are **US 95**, which runs north–south along Idaho's border with Washington and Oregon, from near Boise north to Grangeville, Lewiston, and beyond; and **US 12**, which follows the Lochsa River from the Montana border west through the Clearwater Mountains to Kooskia, Kamiah, Orofino, Lewiston, and beyond. Smaller highways lead into the great wilds: **ID 13** connects US 95 and US 12 between Grangeville and Kooskia; **ID 14** heads east from ID 13 to Elk City; **ID 11** winds its way east from US 12 through Weippe and Pierce to Headquarters.

By air
Boise Air Terminal (Gowen Field; 208-383-3110; www.cityofboise.org/ departments/airport/), about 270 miles south of Lewiston via US 95. Many air travelers coming to the Clearwater region fly in and out of Boise.

Lewiston–Nez Perce County Regional Airport (www.lcairport.net), Lewiston. Regional air travelers may fly into Lewiston.

Spokane International Airport (509-455-6455; www.spokaneairports.net), just over 100 miles north of Lewiston (about a two-hour drive) via US 195. Spokane is the closest commercial airport; it is serviced by Alaska Airlines, Delta/Skywest Airlines, Express Jet, Frontier Airlines, Horizon Air, Northwest Airlines, Southwest Airlines, United/United Express, and US Airways.

MEDICAL EMERGENCIES
St. Joseph Regional Medical Center (208-743-2511; www.sjrmc.org), 608 Fifth Ave., Lewiston. This is the nearest major medical facility in the region.

Tri-State Memorial Hospital (509-758-5511; www.tristatehospital.org) is in neighboring Clarkston, Washington.

Northwest Medstar (509-532-7990 or 800-422-2440; www.nwmedstar.org) transports patients needing more acute care to major medical care hospitals in Spokane, which include **Deaconess Medical Center** (509-458-5800; www .deaconessmedicalcenter.org), 800 W. Fifth Ave.; **Holy Family Hospital** (509-482-0111; www.holy-family.org), 5633 N. Lidgerwood St.; and **Sacred Heart Medical Center** (509-474-3131; www.shmc.org), 101 W. Eighth Ave.

✷ Cities and Villages

Grangeville, perched on the edge of the sprawling Camas Prairie and surrounded by five wilderness areas and four national forests, is in an idyllic setting.

During late spring and early summer, the 200,000-acre undulating Camas Prairie is transformed into a shimmering sea of purplish blue, bedecked by countless delicate bluebells interspersed with splashes of yellow buttercups. The prairie, particularly beautiful at sunset, is part of the ancestral Nez Perce homeland, a traditional gathering place where Indians came to gather camas bulbs, a staple of the indigenous diet. Today the prairie produces about 100 bushels of wheat per acre to sustain Grangeville's largely agricultural economy. Visitors enjoy great wildlife-viewing opportunities and the region's deep history. Grangeville acts as a hub for rafters and kayakers headed for adventures on any of the five nearby rivers.

Kamiah and Kooskia on US 12 along the Clearwater River. These are two of the oldest towns on the Clearwater. Kamiah was the winter home of the Nez Perce Indians, where they fished for steelhead and collected kame hemp to make mats or ropes. The outer bark of this plant was called the "Kamiah"; this is thought to be the derivation of the place name. Three sites in Kamiah are part of the Nez Perce National Historical Park (see To See—Historical Sites).

Perched at the confluence of the Middle and South forks of the Clearwater River, the area around Kooskia was originally called Koos-Koos-Kia, or "clearwater," by the Nez Perce in reference to the river's transparent quality. In 1895, 104 acres were set aside for the townsite of Stuart and the town was platted in 1897; the name was changed to Kooskia in 1902. The town is splayed out in two spurs along the Middle and South forks of the river; the spurs are separated by a large hogback that extends from Mount Stuart. Farming and ranching, logging, lumber production, and tourism sustain the economy here.

Lewiston, near the junction of US 12 and US 95. Located at the confluence of the Snake and Clearwater rivers, Lewiston is set in a narrow valley (elevation 738 feet) beneath the rolling hills of the Palouse that rise to 2,000 feet to the north. Idaho's oldest city, and yet another gold boomtown, Lewiston became the state capital in 1863 but retained this title for only one year before the capital was relocated to Boise. Today, residents and visitors enjoy theater and art offerings, a 25-mile-long greenbelt, and proximity to great recreational spots, including nearby Hells Canyon. Lewiston is home to Lewis-Clark State College.

Orofino, on US 12 at the confluence of the Clearwater and the North Fork of the Clearwater rivers. This is where Lewis and Clark recovered from the difficult chore of crossing the rugged mountains from Montana and took to the river to complete their journey seaward. Here, at what is now dubbed Canoe Camp, they built five dugout canoes. The townsite of Orofino was established in 1898 and later incorporated as a city in 1905, with a population of 207. The name Orofino is taken from the two-word name Oro fino (Spanish for "fine gold") of a nearby mining camp that had burned down; the post office compressed it into a single name in 1905.

White Bird on US 95 between Grangeville and Riggins. White Bird, a stop on the trail of the Nez Perce, is tiny (population 150). It was here, on the expansive White Bird Battlefield (see To See—Historic Sites—Nez Perce National Historical Park), that the first battle of the Nez Perce War was fought, on June 17, 1877.

Gold Rush Historic Byway (208-464-2222; www.idahobyways.gov/byways/
gold-rush.aspx), 42.5 paved miles on ID 11 from Greer at US 12 east to River
Spike Camp Headquarters. As this scenic road winds deep into the dense Clearwater National Forest, you will see panoramic views of the Clearwater Valley and
pass through historic **Weippe**, near where, in 1805, the Nez Perce offered food
to starving members of the Lewis and Clark party. You'll also go through the town
of **Pierce**, where gold was first discovered in Idaho, and ultimately arrive in the
River Spike Camp Headquarters—an old Potlatch company town. Built by
the Civilian Conservation Corps, this scenic road is used by campers, fly-fishers,
and loggers alike. The trip is a deep immersion into the wilds of Idaho on a primitive but manageable road where wildlife is frequently spotted.

Lolo Trail (www.fs.fed.us/r1/clearwater/lolo_trail.htm), 100 miles on primitive
Forest Service roads (FR) 100 and 500 from Kamiah to Lolo Pass. More adventurous explorers may want to follow this more rugged route, which follows the
ridgeline north of US 12.

Magruder Corridor Road (www.fs.fed.us/r1/nezperce/maps/brochures/
magruder.pdf), 101 miles from Red River Guard Station east of Elk City to
Darby, Montana. This is the only road that runs through the vast, undeveloped
areas of the 1.2 million-acre Selway-Bitterroot and the 2.3 million-acre Frank
Church River of No Return wilderness areas. The route was constructed by the
Civilian Conservation Corp in the 1930s and in 1980 was grandfathered into the
largest contiguous roadless area in the Lower 48, when Congress passed the
Central Idaho Wilderness Act. The route is named for Elk City merchant Lloyd
Magruder, who in 1863 was murdered along the way for his gold. His murderers
were tried and hanged in the first legal hanging in Idaho Territory. This rough,
winding, steep route requires approximately eight–10 hours of driving and is
only passable mid-July through early Oct., but the spectacular views and wilderness access are worth the drive. There are six primitive campsites along the way,
but a developed water supply is available only at mile 17.3.

Nez Perce National Historical Trail (www.fs.fed.us/npnht), 1,170 miles from
near Wallowa Lake, Oregon, to the Bears Paw Battlefield near Chinook, Montana. The Nez Perce Nimíipuu (pronounced "nee-me-poo") National Historic
Trail follows the 1877 flight of the Nez Perce as they fled from U.S. Army Gen-
erals Howard, Sturgis, and Miles during the Nez Perce War. The Nez Perce
were forced to leave their ancestral homelands by white settlers, and as they
were en route to a reservation east of Lewiston, conflict broke out between the
Nez Perce and white settlers; the U.S. Army was summoned. Led by Chiefs
Joseph, White Bird, Ollokot, Looking Glass, and Lean Elk, nearly 750 Nez Perce
and 1,500 horses fled more than 1,170 miles through the mountains, looking to
escape to Canada. After eluding capture for months, most of the band was over-
taken near the Bear Paw Mountains in Montana, just south of the Canadian border. The Nez Perce National Historic Trail follows this route from Oregon to
Montana, in Idaho passing through Lewiston and Kooskia, with a spur south to
Grangeville, and then east from Kooskia along the Lochsa River on US 12
through Lowell and Powell to the Montana border at Lolo Pass.

Northwest Passage Scenic Byway (www.idahobyways.gov), 176 paved miles on US 12 from Lewiston to Lolo Pass. Tracing the Idaho portion of the Nez Perce National Historic Trail, the Northwest Passage Scenic Byway follows US 12 northeast along the interconnected river corridors of the Clearwater River, Middle Fork of the Clearwater, and Lochsa River to Lolo Pass at Idaho's border with Montana. The trip backtracks along the historic route that Lewis and Clark took on their quest to find a water route from Missouri to Oregon—the hypothesized Northwest Passage. You'll find various points of interest along the way—among them the Lewis and Clark Discovery Center in Lewiston (see To See—Historic Sites), the Nez Perce National Historic Park in Spaulding (see To See—Historic Sites), a canoe camp and dam in Orofino, and a mammoth exhibit in Grangeville (yes, the remains of several wooly mammoth were found in this area). The route is bounded on both sides by national forest—the Clearwater National Forest to the north and the Nez Perce National Forest to the south; the land becomes increasingly wooded and lush as you move east toward Montana. Developed campgrounds can be found along the way at Lewiston, Orofino, Kamiah, Kooskia, Grangeville, and Lowell, and Forest Service and BLM campsites dot the Clearwater and Lochsa river corridors. In addition to its rich history

LOWELL, ON NORTHWEST PASSAGE SCENIC BYWAY, GATEWAY TO RIVER COUNTRY

as the route of the famous Lewis and Clark Expedition, the portion of this road along the Lochsa River is also a thoroughfare for boaters looking for whitewater (see To Do—White-water Kayaking and Rafting).

A **side loop of the byway** spurs south at Kooskia, running another 27 miles to Grangeville bordering the southeastern corner of the Nez Perce Indian Reservation and not far from the sprawling Camas Prairie. The prairie, the easternmost distal point of the Columbia Plateau, is splashed with an impressive and sprawling bluish purple carpet of camas lilies in the spring. Camas root was a staple food for the Nez Perce, who for thousands of years gathered on this prairie and harvested roots.

This byway segment is also part of the larger **Lewis and Clark National Historic Trail** (www.nps.gov/lecl), which stretches through 11 states—from Illinois to Washington—and more than 3,700 miles along the route traversed by Meriwether Lewis and William Clark in their search for the Northwest Passage—the "most direct and practicable water communication across [the] continent." A map of the entire length of the trail and the parks, museums, and interpretive sights along the way is available on the Web site. The Forest Service puts out a guide (www.fs.fed.us/r1/clearwater/VisitorInfo/Assets/pdfs/hwy12_corridor.pdf) to sights along US 12.

✳ To See

HISTORIC SITES

Bernard DeVoto Memorial Cedar Grove (Clearwater National Forest, 208-476-8276; www.fs.fed.us/r1/clearwater), on US 12 on the Idaho side of Lolo Pass. In this grove, the ashes of author and historian Bernard DeVoto were spread. As a scholar of the Lewis and Clark Expedition, he camped frequently in this grove of old-growth cedar trees—some as old as 2,000 years—that loom above a carpet of sword fern, foam flower, maidenhair fern, bracken fern, and dogwood. An interpretive trail loops through the site and leads to picnic tables by the river.

Camas Prairie, on US 95 some 30 miles southeast of Lewiston. An expansive, black-soil plateau, Camas Prairie stretches 300 miles, encompassing the towns of Grangeville, Cottonwood, Nez Perce, Craigmont, and Winchester. It represents the easternmost remnant of the great Columbia River basalt field. Surrounded by rolling, timbered hills, the 200,000-acre Camas Prairie is named for the camas lily (*Camassia quamash*), which blooms in a sprawling carpet of delicate blue blooms like "lakes of fine clear water" (as noted by Meriwether Lewis). The large flowers have six identical tepals and bright yellow anthers; the root of the camas was a staple food of the Nez Perce, who traditionally gathered here to collect these roots from the prairie using a *tookas* (digging stick). The tuber is prepared by removing the black outer skin and baking the inner white bulb underground for several days. The root is said to taste similar to sweet potatoes and is eaten fresh, dried, or ground into a cereal. When the Lewis and Clark Expedition arrived here in 1806, the Nez Perce fed camas root to the ravenous crew. The prairie is one of the sites of the Nez Perce National Historical Park (see below). Today, in addition to camas, the prairie is partially draped in undulating wheat and canola fields. In winter, snow converts this plateau into a sparkling winter wonderland. The vista is particularly beautiful at sunset.

Colgate Licks, along US 12, 25 miles west of Lolo Pass. A 1-mile nature trail loop takes visitors to the Colgate Licks, a naturally occurring mineral deposit, or "lick," where (if you are lucky) you may spy some game animals coming for salt. The licks are named for George Colgate, who was the cook for an ill-fated hunting party that was trapped by deep snows. Colgate died and was buried at the site; other members of the party survived.

Lewis-Clark State College Center for Arts and History (208-792-2243; www.lcsc.edu/museum), 415 Main St/, Lewiston. Housed in a historic building—listed on the National Register of Historic Places—in downtown Lewiston, the Center for Arts and History provides programs in performing, visual, and literary arts and educational opportunities for learners of all ages. The Center Gallery is the second-largest exhibit gallery in the state, displaying works from regional, national, and international artists. The center also offers Meet the Author events; Confluence Grape & Grain, an annual wine- and beer-tasting event; a Holiday Tea; and a fine gift store.

Nez Perce National Historical Park (208-843-7001; www.nps.gov/nepe), 38 interpretive sites and museums in Idaho, Montana, Washington, and Oregon. The Inland Northwest and its rivers, prairies, and canyons have long been the homelands of the Nez Perce. Nez Perce National Historical Park tells the story of the Nez Perce and their vibrant culture. A visitor guide to the park is available online. Two sites are presented in more detail below:

Spalding Visitor Center (www.nps.gov/archive/nepe/spalding1.htm), on US 95, 10 miles east of Lewiston, at the confluence of the Clearwater River and Lapwai Creek. The Spalding Visitor Center is home to the park headquarters. Situated on a 99-acre site, the facility includes historic buildings and cemeteries, a museum collection, an arboretum, archaeological artifacts, an introductory film, and other interpretive resources related to the history of the Nez Perce. An interpretive tour focusing on Nez Perce history, social traditions, and contemporary life, with a Nez Perce guide, can be arranged through the visitor center. Three other park sites are located nearby.

White Bird Battlefield (www.fs.fed.us/npnht/tour/whitebird.shtml), on US 95, 15 miles south of Grangeville. Located on the Nez Perce National Historic Trail, the White Bird Battlefield commemorates the first battle between the Nez Perce and the U.S. Army in the Nez Perce War. In the mid-1800s, the ancestral homeland of the Nez Perce Nation was under siege by settlers and miners looking to capitalize on their vast mineral, timber, and agricultural resources. In 1855, the Nez Perce signed the Treaty of 1855, which set aside 7.7 million acres as a reservation for the Nez Perce Nation. By 1863, the U.S. government was unable and unwilling to control the continued onslaught onto Nez Perce territory and negotiated a second treaty that reduced the reservation to one-tenth its initial size. Those Nez Perce who did not acknowledge this second treaty were labeled "nontreaty." It was here in 1877 at White Bird that the United States began its historic crackdown on "nontreaty" Nez Perce. Despite being outnum-

ROLLING HILLS NEAR WHITEBIRD, SITE OF A HISTORIC NEZ PERCE BATTLEFIELD

bered two to one, the Nez Perce had a vastly more intimate knowledge of the land and prevailed, killing 34 U.S. Cavalry soldiers and wounding four; only three Nez Perce were wounded.

MUSEUMS

Clearwater Historical Museum (208-476-5033; www.clearwatermuseum.org), 315 College Ave., Orofino. This museum houses a collection of more than 4,500 historical photographs, artifacts, and tools documenting the history of the Nez Perce and other Native Americans, as well as gold mining, the logging industry, Chinese immigrants, and pioneers. The collection includes Orofino newspapers from 1899, pioneer homestead artifacts, antique guns, and turn-of-the-20th-century medicinal and barber tools.

Historical Museum at St. Gertrude (208-962-2050; www.historicalmuseum atstgertrude.com), 465 Keuterville Rd., Cottonwood; on US 95 just north of Grangeville. Open 9:30–4 Tues.–Sat., 1:30–4:30 Sun. May–Sept. $5 for adults, $2 for students, free for children under 7. This is one of the oldest continuously operated museums in the Northwest. Nestled on the eastern slope of Cottonwood Butte, with stunning vistas of the Camas Prairie, this modern

7,200-square-foot facility houses some 70,000 artifacts (12,000 of which are on display) documenting the rich history of North Idaho. Exhibits and collections focus on the history of the Nez Perce, mining, religion, medicine, education, and other facets of Idaho's past. The museum is part of **St. Gertrude's Monastery**, home to the Benedictine Sisters since the 1920s. This twin-towered Romanesque structure was built from locally quarried stone and is on the Historic Register.

Lewis and Clark Discovery Center at **Hells Gate State Park** (208-799-5015 or 866-634-3246; www.idahoparks.org/parks/hellsgate.aspx), off US 12, 4 miles south of Lewiston; take a right on Snake River Avenue and follow signs for the state park. Perched on the banks of the Snake River, the center houses a series of exhibits, sculptures, and film presentations designed to document the Corps of Discovery and their 1805–06 expedition through Nez Perce territory. Hells Gate State Park provides access to the Hells Canyon National Recreation Area; Hells Canyon is North America's deepest river gorge.

Lochsa Historical Ranger Station Museum (208-926-4274), on US 12 about 50 miles east of Kooskia. Free. This museum on US 12 (the Nez Perce National Historic Trail) stands as a tribute to those who fought during the great "Pete King" fire, which burned for 44 days during the summer of 1934. The station was saved from ruin by 200 firefighters who fought off the massive fire that ultimately burned 375 square miles. A self-guided tour with historical photos takes visitors through the museum and around the grounds.

WILDLIFE VIEWING

The Clearwater region has abundant wildlife, and those who get out there to fish or hike are likely to view critters. It is not uncommon, however, to see wildlife along the roadway corridors.

Dworshak National Fish Hatchery (208-476-4591; www.dworshak.fws.gov), below Dworshak Dam (see Wilder Places—Parks) north of Orofino. The hatchery has one of the largest steelhead trout and spring chinook salmon hatcheries in the world, plus visitor displays, viewing balconies, and a self-guided tour.

US 12, which runs from Lewiston to Montana along the Lochsa River, is a beautiful wildlife-viewing corridor, full of mountain goats, elk, and deer. Visitors are also likely to see wildlife along the **Lolo Motorway** section of the Nez Perce National Historical Trail and the **Magruder Corridor Road** (see Wandering Around).

Outfitters

Some licensed guiding operations will take visitors on wildlife-viewing treks. The **Idaho Outfitters and Guides Association** (208-342-1438; www.ioga.org) maintains a full list of licensed guides.

✳ To Do

FISHING

The Clearwater region is known for its exceptionally clean and fast-running streams and rivers and a number of trail-accessible, high-alpine lakes. Most lakes, streams, and rivers in the area have native or stocked fish. Chinook and kokanee salmon, mountain whitefish, rainbow and brook trout, and bass are important fisheries. For fishing regulations and licenses, contact **Idaho Fish and Game** (208-334-3700; http://fishandgame.idaho.gov).

The **Clearwater River** is considered one of the top steelhead streams in the Northwest, producing fish that weigh in at more than 20 pounds and measure as many as 45 inches long. These anadromous trout make a biannual pilgrimage from the Pacific Ocean to the tributaries of the Snake River to spawn. Fall and spring steelhead runs attract anglers from near and far.

Some of the more popular fishing rivers include the **North Fork of the Clearwater River, Kelly Creek, Weitas Creek, Cayuse Creek, White Sand Creek,** and the **Lochsa River.**

Outfitters
More than a dozen guide services offer fishing trips in the Clearwater region. Contact the **Idaho Outfitters and Guides Association** (208-342-1438; www.ioga.org) for a full list of fishing guides.

HIKING
The Clearwater region offers opportunities for hiking too numerous to list here. People have been known to disappear for months into these great wilds (knowingly or unknowingly!). A great resource for information on camping in these and other national forests is the **U.S. National Forests Campground Guide** (www.forestcamping.com). Individual forests also provide information:

Bitterroot National Forest (www.fs.fed.us/r1/bitterroot/).

Clearwater National Forest (www.fs.fed.us/r1/clearwater/). Your best bet in planning a hiking trip into the Clearwater is to consult the online trail guide listing more than 200 trails within the forest. Individual ranger districts are generally very helpful and can provide information of trails and conditions, as well as camping, fishing, and hunting opportunities. Contact them directly: **Palouse Ranger District** (208-875-1131), 1700 ID 6, Potlatch; **North Fork Ranger District** (208-476-4541), 12730 ID 12, Orofino; **Lochsa Ranger District** (208-926-4274), on Route 1, Kooskia; and **Powell Ranger District** (208-924-3113), 44999 Lolo Creek Rd., Lolo, Montana.

Nez Perce National Forest (www.fs.fed.us/r1/nezperce/). For hikes and other recreational opportunities within the Nez Perce National Forest and its wilderness areas, consult their brochures on the Gospel Hump Wilderness Area, the Selway River Corridor, and other areas. Individual ranger districts within the Nez Perce National Forest include the **Salmon River Ranger District/Slate Creek Ranger Station** (208-839-2211), on HC 01, Whitebird; **Clearwater Ranger District** (208-983-1950), 1005 ID 13, Grangeville; **Red River Ranger District/Elk City Ranger Station** (208-842-2245), Elk City; and **Moose Creek Ranger District/Fenn Ranger Station** (208-926-4258), 813 Selway Rd., Kooskia.

Recommended Reading
Ralph and Jackie Maughan's *Hiking Idaho*, 2nd edition (Falcon, 2001), is another great resource.

HIKING TRAIL NEAR LOCHSA RIVER

HOT SPRINGS

Jerry Johnson Hot Springs, on US 12 at Mile 151, about 53 miles east of Lowell. Jerry Johnson Hot Springs is a favorite spot to soak. Weary boaters and campers and other hot springs enthusiasts often make this easy 1-mile hike along a little tributary stream to a series of hot pots. The pools vary in temperature, with the cooler ones closer to the creek. Clothing is optional. The springs are accessible by cross-country skis and snowshoes in the winter.

Red River Hot Springs, on County Road (CR) 234, 25 miles east of Elk City. Day-use fee for mineral hot springs $4 for adults, $3 for children 12 and under. The Forest Service Red River Campground next door offers 40 sites and running water. There's also a lodge (see Lodging—Resorts).

MOUNTAIN BIKING

There is some great mountain biking to be found in the Clearwater region. Many of the Forest Service roads offer double-track access to some spectacular country. Contact individual ranger district offices (see Hiking) for information on mountain biking in your particular area of interest.

Clearwater and Snake River National Recreation Trail (aka Lewiston Levees), 17 paved miles in Lewiston. For those just looking to spin, this trail atop the 18-foot levees bordering the Clearwater and Snake rivers is typically free of snow year-round. It's the lowest point in Idaho—700 feet above sea level.

Coolwater Ridge Epic Jungle Ride, 17.7 miles off US 12 near Lowell. Knobby-tire warriors seeking a gut-busting ride might look to this six- to eight-hour grind on mixed gravel road, double track, and single track that provides stellar views of the Selway-Bitterroot Wilderness.

Fish Creek Loops (www.grangevilleidaho.com/todo/hiking-biking.htm), 6.6-mile, single-track loop 7 miles south of Grangeville. This is one of the more well-known rides, suitable for beginners. Cruise through moderate forested terrain in the Nez Perce National Forest with great views of the Gospel Hump Wilderness.

Lolo Trail (www.fs.fed.us/r1/clearwater/lolo_trail.htm), 100 miles on FR 100 and FR 500 from Kamiah to Lolo Pass. This favored multistage ride generally runs about five days with camping.

Outfitters
Western Spirit (800-845-2453; www.westernspirit.com), Moab, Utah. You might want to hire an outfitter like this to carry your bags.

Rentals
For gear and recommendations from the locals, you may want to check in with a bike shop in the area:

Follett's Mountain Sports (208-743-4200), 714 D St., Lewiston.

TnT Bicycles (208-798-8717), 620 Main St., Lewiston.

Recommended Reading
For more information on these and other rides, see Stephen Steubner's *Mountain Biking Idaho* (Falcon Publishing, 1990).

SKIING
Bald Mountain Ski Area (208-464-2311 or 208-464-2269; www.skibald mountain.com), off ID 11 north of Pierce. This hill dubs itself the "Best Little Ski Hill in Idaho." And little it is, with 684 feet of vertical, 140 acres of variable terrain, 100 inches of snow annually, one rope tow, and one T-bar. It's perfect for beginners.

Cottonwood Butte Ski Area (208-926-3624), on Radar Road 5 miles west of Cottonwood. This ski resort is slightly higher than Snowhaven, offering 845 feet of vertical on seven runs, a T-bar and rope tow, and nice views of Camas Prairie.

Fish Creek Meadows Park n' Ski (208-983-1950; www.visitidaho.org), on Grangeville-Salmon Road (FR 221) 7 miles south of Grangeville (1 mile from Snowhaven). Permits available from Rae Brothers Sporting Goods on Main Street, Grangeville, or online. Here you'll find 10 miles of groomed, double-track Nordic trails. For backcountry enthusiasts, there is a marked but ungroomed ski track back to Snowhaven. The area includes a small ski-in warming hut with a woodstove and spectacular views of the Gospel Hump Wilderness and the Seven Devils Mountains.

Snowhaven Ski Area (208-983-3866), on Grangeville-Salmon Road (FR 221) 7 miles south of Grangeville. This is one of the few developed ski areas in the Clearwater region. With but one T-bar and a rope tow, 400 feet of vertical drop, and 40 acres of terrain, Snowhaven is a far cry from Sun Valley, but it's a great place for beginners. The area offers night skiing, tubing, and ski lessons.

WHITE-WATER KAYAKING AND RAFTING

The Clearwater region is renowned for wilderness paddling. Among the favored white-water rivers are the Selway, Lochsa, and Clearwater rivers. Both the Lochsa and the Selway, designated Wild and Scenic Rivers, provide access by boat to some otherwise inaccessible and stunning backcountry.

The **Lochsa River** draws local kayakers for an annual Memorial Day pilgrimmage to the technical course of big holes, big waves, and big boulders—mostly class III–IV. With roadside access for much of the lower Lochsa, it can be a fun white-water rodeo scene, with onlookers parked at strategic pullouts to watch, jeer, cheer, and drink beer. Great camping is easily accessible along US 12.

The **North Fork Clearwater River** is a beautiful, often-overlooked river. Boating on this river ranges from class II to VI, with several sections that are unrunnable and others that throw experts all they can handle. Favored day stretches on the North Fork Clearwater are the Quartz Creek Run, which goes from Quartz Creek to Aquarius Campground; the Bungalow Run, which goes from Weitas Creek Campground to Quartz Creek; and Black Canyon, which goes from Hidden Creek Campground to Kelly Creek Campground. Good camping is found along the way.

The **Selway River** is tightly regulated by a Forest Service policy that allows only one launch per day and permits less than 1,300 boaters per year to float this magnificent wilderness river. The fortunate few that earn a spot on a Selway trip will experience a protected canyon running through the heart of the Selway-Bitterroot Wilderness, a crystalline river teeming with fish (and class IV–V rapids), beautiful white beaches, abundant wildlife, and towering old-growth cedars.

Outfitters

Quite a few outfitters offer day and overnight trips on these rivers; **Idaho Outfitters and Guides Association** (208-342-1438; www.ioga.org) maintains a complete listing of licensed raft guides.

American River Touring Association (ARTA; 209-962-7873; www.arta.org), Groveland, California.

Ken Masoner's Whitewater Adventures (208-939-4374; www.selway.net), Boise.

Lewis and Clark Trail Adventures (406-728-7609 or 800-366-6246; www.trailadventures.com), Missoula, Montana.

River Odysseys West (ROW), Inc. (208-765-0841 or 800-451-6034; www.rowadventures.com), Coeur d'Alene.

Three Rivers Rafting (208-926-4430 or 888-926-4430; www.threeriversrafting.com), Kooskia.

WHITE-WATER KAYAKING IS A HUGE DRAW IN THE CLEARWATER REGION.

✳ **Wilder Places**

PARKS

Dworshak State Park (208-476-5994; www.parksandrecreation.idaho.gov), on the western shore of the reservoir behind **Dworshak Dam** (208-476-1255; www.nww.usace.army.mil/corpsoutdoors/dwa), off P1, 24 miles north of Orofino. The park's three units—Freeman Creek, Three Meadows Group Camp, and Big Eddy Lodge and Marina—offer hiking, camping, fishing, and boating. A boat ramp allows for easy launching most of the year. Built by the U.S. Army Corps of Engineers on the North Fork of the Clearwater River, Dworshak Dam stands 717 feet high and creates the 54-mile-long Dworshak Reservoir. The facility includes a visitors center at the top of the dam.

Hells Gate State Park (208-799-5015 or 866-634-3246; www.idahoparks .org/parks/hellsgate.aspx), off US 12, 4 miles south of Lewiston; take a right on Snake River Road and follow signs to the state park. Open 9–5 daily. $4 per vehicle. Hells Gate State Park provides access to Hells Canyon National Recreation Area and the deepest gorge in North America. In Idaho's "banana belt" (so dubbed due to low elevation—733 feet above sea level—and a long season of warm weather), visitors to this park enjoy shady campsites along the shores of the Snake River, group-use areas, miles of hiking, biking, and horseback trails, and access to Hells Canyon via Jet Boat trips that leave from the park's docks. The Hells Canyon area provides a glimpse into Idaho's pioneer past, with relict homesteads, prospector cabins, and petroglyphs. The geology is also spectacular—check out the massive, twisted columns of black basalt throughout the park!

Nez Perce National Historical Park (208-843-7001; www.nps.gov/nepe), 38 interpretive sites and museums in Idaho, Montana, Washington, and Oregon. See To See—Historical Sites.

Winchester Lake State Park (208-924-7563; http://parksandrecreation.idaho .gov), off US 95 west of Craigmont. Winchester is a quiet, 103-acre lake surrounded by a ponderosa pine and Douglas fir forest at the base of the Craig Mountains. Visitors to the park enjoy wildlife viewing, fishing, canoeing, camping (69 campsites and four yurts), hiking, and cross-country skiing. The park also offers interpretive walks and talks, and the Wolf Education and Research Center is located 1 mile from the park entrance.

WILDERNESS AREAS

With more than 9 million acres of roadless, undeveloped national forestland, Idaho has more wilderness than any other state in the Lower 48. And this region, which encompasses crazy, big wilderness, constitutes the core of Idaho's "Big Wild": three massive national forests—the 1.8 million-acre Clearwater National Forest, 1.6 million-acre Bitterroot National Forest (part of which spans into Montana), and 2.2 million-acre Nez Perce National Forest—and three designated wilderness areas—the Selway-Bitterroot, Gospel Hump, and Frank Church–River of No Return. Considered to be among the most intact forested lands in the country, Idaho's wilderness provides fabulous habitat for migratory and resident fish, elk, moose, bighorn sheep, black bears, cougars, white-tailed and mule deer, mountain goats, and many smaller mammal species. Rare species including the gray wolf, grizzly bear, Canada lynx, and steelhead and bull trout also make their homes here.

Frank Church–River of No Return Wilderness, 2.3 million acres; see Central Idaho: An Explorer's Nirvana, Wilder Places—Wilderness Areas. Abutting the southern boundary of the Selway-Bitterroot Wilderness, the Frank Church spans into Central Idaho.

Gospel-Hump Wilderness, 206,706 acres; **Red River Ranger District/Elk City Ranger Station** (208-842-2245), Elk City, or **Salmon River Ranger District/Slate Creek Ranger Station** (208-839-2211), on HC 01, Whitebird. Named for Gospel Peak (elevation 8,345 feet), which appears particularly magical enshrouded in snow and clouds, the wilderness also contains Buffalo Hump (elevation 8,926 feet), whose prominent intrusive into the granite Idaho Batholith resembles the hump of a buffalo. This wilderness area, which was designated in 1978, is remarkable for its relief—with elevations soaring from 1,970 feet at the Salmon River to 8,926 feet at the summit of Buffalo Hump. The weather varies correspondingly, with summertime temperatures nearing 100 degrees Fahrenheit along the Salmon River and typical alpine weather and snows in the peaks. Characterized by a gentle, heavily forested landscape in the north to steep, sparsely vegetated, glacial terrain in the south, the Gospel Hump Wilderness is truly a treasure. Backpackers and people traveling with livestock do not need permits to travel in the wilderness, but permits are required to float,

RECREATIONAL OPPORTUNITIES ABOUND IN THE CLEARWATER NATIONAL FOREST.

Jet-Boat, or kayak the Salmon River above Vinegar Creek June 20–Sept. 7 (see Central Idaho: An Explorer's Nirvana, To Do—White-water Kayaking and Rafting). In-season hunting and fishing are permitted.

Selway-Bitterroot Wilderness, almost 1.1 million acres in Idaho (about 250,000 acres in Montana); **Moose Creek Ranger District/Fenn Ranger Station** (208-926-4258), 813 Selway Rd., Kooskia. Declared a wilderness area by Congress in 1964, the Selway-Bitterroot is the third-largest wilderness area in the Lower 48 (Death Valley and the Frank Church–River of No Return wilderness areas rank one and two, respectively). Separated from the Frank Church by only the unimproved Magruder Corridor Road (see Wandering Around), this is arguably the most significant wilderness area in the continental United States. Characterized by raw granite peaks, steep-walled canyons, dense coniferous forests, delicate wildflowers, crystalline alpine lakes and rivers—including the Wild and Scenic Selway River—and abundant wildlife (black bears, mountain lions, moose, deer, and large herds of elk), this is divine country. For those looking for solace, this infrequently traveled landscape might be your calling. Hundreds of miles of trails traverse this landscape.

✳ Lodging

BED & BREAKFASTS

Elk City

Blackwood Manor Bed & Breakfast (208-842-2591; www.blackwood manor.com), 501 Elk Creek Rd., Elk City 83525. In the mountains just outside Elk City, this 5,000-square-foot English Tudor home sits on 56 acres with a working farm. Appointed with heavily carved antique furniture, tapestries, and canopied beds and warmed with fireplaces and an English pub, this place might make you feel as if you've stepped back in time. $75 and up.

Kooskia to Lowell

Bear Hollow B&B (208-926-7146), on US 12 at Milepost 81, Kooskia 83539. Three guest rooms—the Papa Bear, Mama Bear, and Cub Bear—are accompanied by a hot tub and a large gift shop. $100 and up.

Dream's B&B (208-926-7540), on US 12 at Milepost 86, Kooskia 83539. This B&B on 18.5 acres has two guest rooms with private baths, both separate from the main house and facing the Middle Fork Clearwater River, and a hot tub. Rates include a full three-course country breakfast. $70 and up.

Reflections Inn (208-926-0855 or 888-926-0855), on US 12 between Mileposts 84 and 85, 11 miles east of Kooskia, 83539. Located on 10 acres, this B&B offers seven guest rooms, each with a queen bed, private bath, private entrance, and hot tub, and all come with a full breakfast. $79 and up.

Lewiston

Carriage House Inn (208-746-9526 or 800-501-4506), 504 Sixth Ave., Lewiston 83501. This is a particularly nice bed & breakfast. Located in an old neighborhood by the Lewis-Clark State College, this inn offers several unique guest rooms with luxurious amenities that include a four-poster bed, a sun porch, or a Roman tub. $80 and up.

CABINS

Kooskia to Lowell

Forest Service Cabin and Lookout Rental Directory (www.fs.fed.us/r1/recreation_r1/cabin_dir.shtml). If you are looking for more rustic accommodations, the Bitterroot, Clearwater, and Nez Perce national forests all maintain a handful of remote cabins and now-defunct lookout towers that can be rented. For more information, contact the ranger district offices listed in To Do—Hiking. $30 and up.

HOTELS AND MOTELS

Lewiston

Howard Johnson Express Inn (208-743-9526 or 800-634-7669), 1716 Main St., Lewiston 83501. Sixty-six units. $55 and up.

Red Lion Hotel (208-799-1000 or 800-232-6730; www.redlionlewiston.com), 621 21st St., Lewiston 83501. The 183 guest rooms include 43 minisuites, plus there are two heated

pools, a Jacuzzi, and a health club. $99 and up.

Riverview Inn (208-746-3311 or 800-806-7666), 1325 Main St., Lewiston 83501. Check out these cheaper digs. $38 and up.

Sacajawea Select Inn (208-746-1393 or 800-333-1393), 1824 Main St., Lewiston 83501. Ninety units. $40 and up.

Super 8 (208-743-8808 or 800-800-8000), 3120 North-South Hwy., Lewiston 83501. Sixty-two units. $29 and up.

LODGES

Powell Junction

Lochsa Lodge (208-942-3405; www.lochsalodge.com), on US 12 at Milepost 163, Lolo, Montana 59847. Located on the upper Lochsa River near the Selway-Bitterroot Wilderness boundary, the lodge offers motel-style rooms and log cabins. The business started in 1929, but the lodge was

LOCHSA LODGE

rebuilt after it burned to the ground in 2001. It is open year-round, and in the winter it is a great place to cross-country ski and soak in hot springs. $40–85.

RESORTS

Elk City

Red River Hot Springs (208-842-2587), on CR 234, 25 miles east of Elk City, 83525. Rustic cabins and modern lodge rooms, a mineral hot springs pool and hot tubs, and a restaurant are located here. The hot springs are also open to the public for day use (see To Do—Hot Springs). $85 and up.

Kooskia to Lowell

Three Rivers Resort (208-926-4430; www.threeriversresort.com), on US 12 in Lowell, 83539. Located at the confluence of the Lochsa and Selway rivers, this place is a good spot to gear up for a river trip. The resort offers cabins, motel rooms, and a campground, as well as a heated swimming pool and Jacuzzis, a meeting room, a restaurant (Lochsa Louie's), a gift shop, and groceries. Idaho Fish and Game licenses and some sporting goods are available in the convenience store. Cabins $125 and up; rooms $59 and up.

✳ Where to Eat

EATING OUT

Options for city dining are few and far between in the rural Clearwater; however, in Lewiston you can find some good micro-brewed beer and a variety of American fare.

Lewiston

Bojacks Boiler Pit (208-746-9523), 311 Main St. Prime rib, steak, and seafood entrées are offered for dinner.

THREE RIVERS RESORT IN LOWELL, CONFLUENCE OF LOCHSA, SELWAY, AND CLEARWATER RIVERS

DINING OPTIONS ALONG US 12 ARE LIMITED.

El Sombrero (208-746-0658), 629 Bryden Ave. Mexican fare.

Jonathan's (208-746-3438), 1516 Main St. Steak and seafood are served for lunch and dinner.

M.J. Barleyhoppers Brewery & Sports Pub (208-746-5300), in the Red Lion Hotel, 621 21st St. A half dozen microbrews are made here and served along with 65 other beers on tap; burgers and sandwiches are on the menu.

Steelhead Irish Pub (208-754-8181), 452 Center St. Come here for some good pub food and brew.

Thai Taste (208-746-6192), 1410 21st St. For ethnic fare, try this place, which has garnered some good reviews for lunch and dinner.

Zany's Hollywood Grill (208-746-8131), 2006 19th Ave. Located in the Lewiston Mall complex, this spot has some funky decor and is chock full of random kitsch. The menu is standard American fare: burgers, fish-and-chips, pastas, ribs, salads, and sandwiches, plus a soda fountain.

COFFEEHOUSES

Lewiston
Coffee Cow, LLC (208-798-4488), 1441 G St. Check out this spot for a cup of java.

Hot Shot Espresso (208-746-6379), 607 Bryden Ave. Another coffee place.

✳ Special Events

July: **Grangeville Border Days** (208-983-1372; www.grangeville borderdays.org), Grangeville. Fourth of July. First held in 1912, the Grangeville Border Days is Idaho's oldest rodeo event. This celebration features traditional rodeo events, art shows, live music, fireworks, and more.

August: **Chief Looking Glass Pow-Wow** (208-926-4362), Kamiah. Third weekend in Aug. This event, open to the public, is organized by the descendents of Chief Lookingglass to honor this famous Nez Perce warrior and hunter through traditional dance and music. Powwow participants wear resplendently colorful traditional garb. Dance contests and traditional friendship dinners are offered. Vendors offer Native American arts, crafts, and beadwork.

1860s Days Celebration (208-435-4406; www.pierce-weippechamber .com/1860days.html), Pierce and Weippe. These two communities organize this event to celebrate the founding of the first gold-rush town in Idaho. The event features live music,

a cook-off, games, a softball tournament, and more.

Idaho County Fair (208-983-2667; www.idahocounty.org), Idaho County Fairgrounds, Cottonwood. Check out this traditional fair, too.

Nez Perce County Fair (208-743-3302; www.co.nezperce.id.us), Nez Perce County Fair Grounds, 1229 Burrell Ave., Lewiston. This fair is dubbed "Big Wheels and Pig Squeals" for 2008.

September: **Lewis County Fair** (208-937-2311 or 208-937-9227), Nez Perce. Traditional county fairs like this one—replete with 4-H livestock, horticulture, fine arts, home economics, and entertainment—are abundant in Idaho.

November: **Snake Clearwater Steelhead Derby** (208-743-3531; www .lewistonchamber.org/derby/), Lewiston. $25 for adults, $10 for kids. This weeklong derby is the largest steelhead derby in the Pacific Northwest, offering more than $15,000 in cash and prizes for daily and overall heaviest fish.

Southwestern Idaho: Class V Adventure

McCALL AND THE PAYETTE RIVER
MOUNTAIN REGION: SUN AND FUN

BOISE: LIFE IN THE BIG CITY

THE BRUNEAU AND OWYHEE
RIVERS: COWBOY COUNTRY

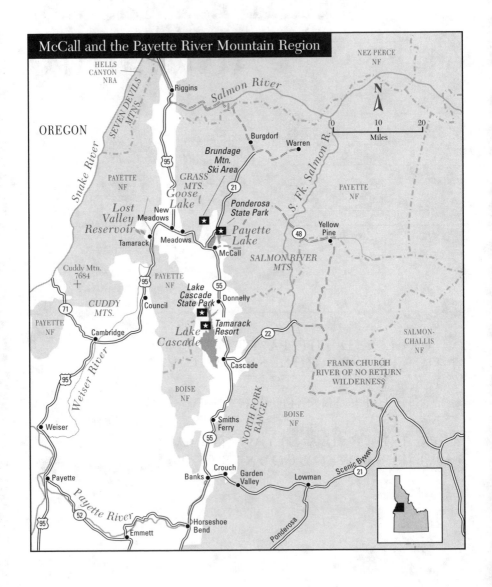

McCall and the Payette River Mountain Region

McCALL AND THE PAYETTE RIVER MOUNTAIN REGION: SUN AND FUN

The Payette River mountain region is stunning, rife with crystal waters, starry skies, ponderosa pines, and towering peaks. It runs from the Oregon border—the Snake River—on the west to the Middle Fork Salmon River in the east, from Horseshoe Bend, on the North Fork Payette River, in the south to Riggins, on the Salmon River, in the north. In the heart of this region, a series of small towns are strung like pearls along the North Fork Payette River and its surrounding meadowed valley. The valley, remarkably wide in spots, is thought to be a dropped fault block, typical of Basin and Range geology. Rugged mountains, as high as 9,393-foot-high He Devil Mountain, stretch north–south on either side of the valley: the North Fork Range and the Salmon River Mountains to the south and east, and the Cuddy Mountains, Grass Mountains, and Seven Devils Mountains to the west.

Surrounded by millions of acres of forest—2.3 million acres in the Payette National Forest, 2.6 million acres in the Boise National Forest, and 2.3 million acres in the Frank Church–River of No Return Wilderness Area—this region beckons the adventurer. Opportunities abound for great alpine, Nordic, and backcountry skiing, as well as fishing, hiking, swimming, white-water boating, and mountain biking (and more). To complete the picture, McCall offers the charm of a still-small ski-town, with great restaurants, funky coffee joints, some warm digs in which to rest your weary bones, and an artsy flair. Still relatively undiscovered, this region sings of charm.

GUIDANCE

Cascade Chamber of Commerce (208-382-3833; www.cascadechamber.com), 113 Main St., Cascade 83611.

Garden Valley Chamber of Commerce (208-462-5003; www.gvchamber.org), on ID 21 east of ID 55.

Greater Donnelly Area Chamber of Commerce (208-325-3545; www.donnellychamber.org).

Horseshoe Bend Chamber of Commerce (www.horseshoebendchamber
.com), at the junction of ID 52 and ID 55.

McCall Chamber of Commerce (208-634-7631 or 800-260-5130; www.mccall
chamber.org), on ID 55 about 12 miles east of US 95.

Payette Chamber of Commerce (208-642-2362; www.payettechamber.com),
2 N. Main St., Payette 83661.

Payette River Mountains Visitor Association (www.payetterivermountains
.com).

Salmon River Chamber of Commerce (208-628-3778; www.rigginsidaho.com),
on US 95 in Riggins.

Weiser Chamber of Commerce (208-414-0452; www.weiserchamber.com),
309 State St., Weiser 83672.

GETTING THERE
By car
McCall, the center of this region, is about 100 miles north of Boise. From the
Boise area, take **I-84** west to exit 46 (South Eagle Road/ID 55) toward Eagle
and McCall. Turn slightly right (east) onto East State Street/ID 44, then turn left
(north) on **ID 55** and travel about 100 miles to McCall. From points north, take
US 95 south to New Meadow, then take a left on ID 55 toward McCall.

During the summer, travelers from the east can take **US 93** south from
Salmon to Challis, then **ID 75** west to Stanley, and in Stanley pick up **ID 21**
west to Lowman, over Banner Summit. Banner Summit, elevation 7,056 feet,
often closes during the winter due to avalanche danger; mountain pass information and closures is provided by **Idaho Department of Transportation**
(http://511.idaho.gov). In Lowman, turn right onto **ID 17**, to Banks, and then
turn right onto ID 55 to Donnelly and McCall.

By air
Boise Air Terminal (Gowen Field; 208-383-3110; www.cityofboise.org/
departments/airport/), about 100 miles south of McCall. This is the hub used by
most air travelers coming to the McCall region.

McCall Municipal Airport (208-634-1488; http://www.mccall.id.us/government/
departments/airport/airport.html) provides services for small private aircraft.

McCall Air (208-992-6559 or 800-634-3917; www.mccallaviation.com), McCall
Municipal Airport. This backcountry air-charter outfit offers flight service
between Boise and McCall and other regional city-to-city flights (see also To
See—Scenic Flights).

Salmon Air (208-756-6211 or 800-448-3413; www.salmonair.com), McCall
Municipal Airport. Another backcountry air-charter outfit that offers flight service between Boise and McCall and other regional city-to-city flights.

MEDICAL EMERGENCIES
Cascade Medical Center (208-382-4242), 402 Old State Hwy., Cascade. Part-
ners with St. Alphonus Regional Medical Center in Boise.

McCall Memorial Hospital (208-634-2221 or 888-236-4643; www.mccallhosp .org), 1000 State St., McCall. Perhaps the largest medical facility in the region, McCall Memorial Hospital also operates a handful of clinics throughout the region, including these:

Council Mountain Medical Clinic (208-253-4915), 101 Council Ave., Ste. C, Council.

Donnelly Medical Clinic (208-634-2225), 454 W. Roseberry, Ste. 103, Donnelly.

Integrative Medicine Clinic (208-634-1400), 203 Hewitt St., McCall.

Meadows Valley Medical Clinic (208-347-2146), 320 Virginia St., New Meadows.

Payette Lakes Medical Clinic (208-634-2225), 211 Forest St., McCall.

Salmon River Medical Clinic (208-628-3666), 214 N. Main St., Riggins.

More life-threatening emergencies might be diverted to major medical facilities in Boise (see Boise: Life in the Big City—Medical Emergencies).

✳ Cities and Villages

Banks, on ID 55 at the confluence of the Main and North forks of the Payette River Banks, is River Central, and during the summer, this tiny little town is abuzz with the banter of river rats, some taking out from the gnarly North Fork Payette and others gearing up for a put-in and a little tamer adventure on the class III Main Payette stretch. At Banks, there is a good little breakfast joint and a rustic convenient store.

Burgdorf, northeast of McCall. This place was founded in the 1870s by gold-prospector Frederick Burgdorf, who—unsuccessful in his search for treasure—instead discovered a hot springs here. On the site, he built a pool with hotels, cabins, and barns. Many of these buildings remain today, and visitors can pay to use the hot pool and rent cabins (see To Do—Hot Springs). Nearby Crystal Mountain is interesting; there you can, aptly enough, find crystals.

Cascade, on ID 55 on the south shore of Lake Cascade. Cascade is a little larger (population about 1,000) than some of the other little hamlets scattered about this region. Historically, the town of Cascade's economic base was tied to the timber industry. With changes in the structure of the timber economy (greater automation and efficiency, falling lumber prices, stiff competition from Canada), a slew of lumber mills in the Pacific Northwest have closed in recent decades, including the Boise Cascade Mill in Cascade. The mill was closed in the early 2000s, and approximately 400 workers lost their jobs. (Pictures of the old mill can be seen at Mill Park next to the marina in McCall.) The region is reinventing itself as a recreational destination, and Cascade is a gateway to sailing, fishing, and waterskiing on Cascade Reservoir. Plenty of camping can also be found around the reservoir.

Council and **Cambridge,** on US 95 south of New Meadwos. These are a couple of cool little outposts on the way to Hells Canyon on the Snake River. Council, in particular is a really pretty little spot in former timber country that attracts some wayward recreationalists.

Crouch, off ID 17 at the confluence of the Middle Fork and South Fork of the Payette River. Nestled in a little cove, this hamlet provides for an interesting Idaho respite. A number of hot springs exist in the area, and there is great road-side camping off Middle Fork Road, which runs north out of Crouch along the Middle Fork of the Payette. This area attracts some low-key kayakers drawn to several solid class III–IV sections of the South Fork of the Payette River. In town, you'll find the infamous Long Horn Bar where cowboys and kayakers alike gather to imbibe, eat ranch-size meals, and listen to local music on warm sum-mer nights. Crouch also has a golf club and a decent food market.

Donnelly, on ID 55 on the northern end of Lake Cascade. This cute little town, population 151, is a gateway to recreational activities on Lake Cascade, with lots of camping and boating access nearby. More recently, it has become the entrance to Tamarack Resort, to the west. Surrounded by pastureland, ranching is still an important local industry in little Donnelly, but with the arrival of Tama-rack Resort, this area is likely to see some change in the near future. Donnelly has a handful of great little spots to eat, including a pizza place, a funky bakery, and a couple coffee shops. The historic village of Roseberry and the Valley County Museum are located just east of Donnelly (see To See—Museums).

Garden Valley, on ID 21 at the confluence of the Middle Fork and South Fork of the Payette River, near Crouch. This home to the great outdoor Starlight Mountain Theatre (see Cultural Offerings—Theater) has a local hot springs. It's a good spot to gas up on a long road trip. Food is available, but it is of the fried (and somewhat nasty) variety: deep-fried cheese sticks, the deep-fried potato slices known as JoJos (yes, I had to ask what these are), fried eggs rolls. There is good cross-country skiing in the area during the winter.

Horseshoe Bend, junction of ID 52 and ID 55. Located ashore a giant sweep-ing bend of the Payette River, this town was originally settled by gold prospec-tors staging to search for gold at higher elevations after snowmelt. Today, about 770 people call this place home; it is said to be morphing into a bedroom com-munity to Boise. A kayak play wave called the "Gutter," formed by diversions in the river associated with a hydroelectric project, draws some attention from white-water kayakers. Horseshoe Bend is also where you pick up the Thunder Mountain Line (see To See—Train Excursions) scenic and theatrical railroad rides.

McCall, on ID 55 east of New Meadows. With a population of about 2,500, McCall is the center of action in this region. A longtime regional resort commu-nity (following its history as a logging center), more recently the city of McCall has been attracting an increasingly eclectic crew of transplants of all stripes, each looking for his or her own Private Idaho, drawn to McCall's small-town appeal, incredible recreational access, and tranquil beauty. Plus, the place is becoming increasingly funkified with great coffee shops, restaurants, and art exhibits reflective of the slew of artsy folks and hard-core outdoor types that continue to populate this place. Summer brings outdoor concert series; long, sunny, water-sport-filled days; hiking; and mountain biking. Winter, of course, is all about the

MCCALL'S WINTER WONDERLAND IN THE PAYETTES

pow (the locals' affectionate term for the region's excellent powder snow). With the kicked-back, old-school ski resort of Brundage at its backdoor, great back-country terrain, and plenty of fluffy white stuff, McCall is a gateway for winter fun—plus, under a thick carpet of snow that blankets trees and houses and virtu-ally fills in the roads, McCall approaches a winter wonderland like few other places.

New Meadows, junction of US 95 and ID 55 northwest of McCall. Named for the verdant, sweeping meadows of the Meadow Valley, this small community (population 553) is gaining popularity as a vacation spot north of Boise. It has a new golf course (see To Do—Golf) and is proximate to the 80-mile Weiser River Trail (see To Do—Mountain Biking).

Riggins, on US 95 about 47 miles north of McCall. Riggins has a year-round population of only 400. In the warm months, however, tiny little Riggins swells with a sea of white-water and steelhead fishing fanatics into a vibrant river com-munity. The take-out for weeklong white-water raft and kayak trips on the Main Salmon River is 14 miles east of Riggins, and the put-in for a day trip on the Main is just north of Riggins. Check out the roses around town in the summer months!

Yellow Pine, nestled high in the Salmon River Mountains east of McCall. At elevation 4,765 feet, this town is somewhat difficult to get to via a tough 55 miles of partly dirt roads: east from Cascade out Warm Lake Road, then north along the South Fork Salmon River from Knox or north along Johnson Creek from Landmark Ranger Station; a similar drive east from McCall goes out Lick Creek Road to East Fork Road. Yellow Pine is a blast from the past. With only 40 residents, dirt streets, a country store, a little red schoolhouse, a fun local bar and restaurant (if you want them to open for breakfast in the morning, you might want to tell them the night before you'll be coming), and a collection of rustic cabins, this place will thrust you straight back into Idaho's mining days—or perhaps into current-day backcountry Alaska. It is a place where the locals make the laws and proudly fly the American flag. In fact, the nearby Secesh River gained its name during the Civil War, when a group of anti-abolitionists, called Seseches (secessionists or rebels) threatened to secede from the Union. (The Yankee Fork River outside Stanley, by contrast, earned its name for the abolitionist miners working in that region.) Today, Yellow Pine attracts a slew of boaters, drawn to the great class III–V boating on the South Fork of the Salmon River (see To Do—White-water Kayaking and Rafting). Yellow Pine is also known locally for its annual summer Harmonica Contest (see Special Events—August).

✳ Wandering Around

Payette River Scenic Byway (ID 55; 208-334-8214; www.idahobyways.gov), about 112 miles north from ID 44 near Boise through Horseshoe Bend and McCall to New Meadows at US 95. The section north of Horseshoe Bend, where the road hugs the churning, world-class Main and North forks of the Payette River for a 25-mile stretch and winds up and through a narrow, Douglas fir–lined and stunningly beautiful canyon, provides a great vantage point to watch boaters navigating the class IV–V rapids from Banks to Smiths Ferry on the North Fork (see To Do—White-water Kayaking and Rafting). Please drive carefully while you are gawking away; this portion of the road has been known to be fairly distracting for drivers. As you continue up the canyon, several funky wooden bridge crossings provide great views directly up- and downstream. The scene is particularly beautiful in winter when the Douglas firs are cloaked in white and the contours of the river have been narrowed and smoothed by a stencil of snow. As you emerge from this canyon, the vista splays open into a wide, flat, meadow-filled, idyllic valley that speaks of peace. Aptly called Long Valley, this dale is the gateway to the lake region of Cascade and Payette lakes. The byway continues north alongside the shore of Cascade Lake (where you can see Tamarack Resort on the western shore), through Donnelly, on to McCall on Payette Lake, and then north to New Meadows.

Ponderosa Pine Scenic Byway (ID 21; 208-334-8214; www.idahobyways.gov), about 131 miles from Boise north through Lowman and east over Banner Summit to Stanley. Banner Summit is quite often closed in winter due to avalanche danger, making this route often impassable; check with **Idaho Transportation Department**'s advisory (www.511.idaho.gov) for information on mountain pass closures and other road condition information. A solitary and beautiful drive along part of this byway begins in Lowman. The first part of the ride is alongside the South Fork of the Payette River; after the turnoff to Grandjean, the road leaves the river but takes you between two of Idaho's stunning wilderness areas: the Sawtooth Wilderness to the south, and the Salmon-Challis National Forest and the continguous Frank Church–River of No Return Wilderness to the north. The road takes you up and over Banner Summit, which at 7,056 feet is one of Idaho's highest passes, into the awe-inspiring Stanley Basin, where your first vision of the classicly rugged and remote Sawtooth Mountains might make your jaw drop.

US 95 35 miles from New Meadows north to Riggins; descriptive brochures and maps available from **Payette National Forest** (208-634-0400; www.fs.fed.us/r4/payette/), 800 W. Lakeside Ave., McCall. This route takes you through some beautiful, wide-open, windblown meadows in Meadow Valley and up a short pass, all the while hugging the breathtaking Little Salmon River, which is full of class III–IV and the occasional class V rapids. Drive carefully as your eyes wander to the boiling, churning water and associated drop-offs alongside. (US 95

PAYETTE RIVER SCENIC BYWAY IN WINTER

also runs 76 miles from Weiser north to New Meadows, on a long climb out of the Snake River canyon and through yet more beautiful scenery—rolling farmland littered with leaning old barns, timber stands, and several towns that can only be described as "real Idaho," Cambridge and Council among them.)

Warren Auto Tour, 42 miles from McCall north to Warren along Warren Wagon Road; descriptive brochures and maps available from **Payette National Forest** (208-634-0400; www.fs.fed.us/r4/payette/), 800 W. Lakeside Ave., McCall. Historical, geological, and natural history highlights include the area's significant mining history and related influences of Native Americans, Chinese, and other miners and settlers.

Working Forest Auto Tours, two scenic loops on Forest Service roads, each about 35 miles, outside New Meadows; descriptive brochures and maps available from **Payette National Forest** (208-634-0400; www.fs.fed.us/r4/payette/), 800 W. Lakeside Ave., McCall. Roads open during summer. These educational tours detail historical and current forest management practices. You will see historic homesteads, wildlife habitat, hot springs, and examples of active forest and range management.

✳ To See

FARMER'S MARKETS
McCall Farmers Market (208-634-3078), next to Gravity Sports, 503 Pine St., McCall. Open 10–2 Wed. June–Oct. This is a great place to buy some wholesome fruit, veggies, and baked goods!

HISTORICAL SITES
McCall Smokejumper Base (Payette National Forest office, 208-634-0390; www.mccallsmokejumpers.org), 605 S. Mission St., McCall Municipal Airport. Tours can be arranged, as the firefighting season permits, by calling ahead. The McCall Smokejumper Base has a long and intriguing history of bringing the most bad-ass of the bad-ass backcountry parachuting firefighters to McCall to fight wildfires in the Payette and other national forests. The story starts with a raging wildfire in the summer of 1910 (the Big Burn) that blackened 3 million acres of forest in the Bitterroot Range of Idaho and Montana and claimed 85 lives. By the middle of that very hot, dry summer, lightning and railroad-car sparks had ignited as many as 90 wildfires in the region; in late Aug., an anomalous cold front, complete with 75-mile-per-hour winds, melded these individual fires into one furious inferno. Witnesses to the fire described it as "one great conflagration," "a roaring furnace, a threatening hell." Following what has been referred to by *Popular Mechanics* as One of the Worst 101 Disasters in the Last 101 Years, the U.S. Forest Service began ramping up its firefighting capabilities, beginning to use aircraft for fire detection in 1917 and then for parachute drops of water and foam in the 1920s. By 1940, the U.S. Forest Service began its Parachute Project, and the concept of smoke jumping was born. McCall's Smokejumper Base was formed in 1943 and remains as one of only four smokejumper bases in the West. Today, about 70 seasonal smokejumpers return to McCall

each summer to fight the wildfires that rage each year through remote and rugged backcountry terrain.

Recommended Reading
If you are interested in learning more about the Big Burn, pick up a copy of *Year of the Fires: The Story of the Great Fires of 1910* (Penguin, 2002) by Stephen J. Pyne. For a gripping treatise on the human condition in disaster zones, including western wildfires, see *Fire* (Harper Perennial, 2002) by Sebastian Junger. Young adults might like *The Big Burn* (First Harcourt, 2003) by Jeanette Ingold.

MUSEUMS
Central Idaho Cultural Center and Museum (208-634-4497), 1001 State St., McCall. Open 11–4 Wed.–Sat. or by appointment. $2 for adults, $1 for youths and seniors, free for children under 12. This museum site, which includes eight historic buildings constructed by the Civilian Conservation Corps in 1936–37, was at one time the summer home for Idaho's governor and later the headquarters for the Southern Idaho Timber Protective Association. Presently, the facility houses a regional museum and archive dedicated to the area's mining, logging, forest management, fire suppression, and recreational history. The center also sponsors cultural and educational seminars.

Valley County Museum (208-325-8628), East Roseberry Rd., Donnelly. Located at the former townsite of Roseberry, this museum and the town are essentially one and the same. A collection of buildings from the turn of the 20th century include the original Methodist Church of Roseberry, the Roseberry General Store and gas station, the Larkin and Grover Miller homes, and the Barrenger House.

WILDLIFE VIEWING
McCall Fish Hatchery (208-634-2690), 300 Mather Rd., McCall. Open 8–5 daily year-round. The McCall Fish Hatchery is operated by Idaho Department of Fish and Game as a birthing center for the anadramous chinook salmon as part of a federal mitigation program to compensate for fish losses resulting from four dams on the Lower Snake River (an ill-conceived concept all around!). At a **satellite facility** on the South Fork of the Salmon River, near Warm Lake (open daylight hours mid-June–mid-Sept.), adult chinook salmon are trapped and spawned and their eggs are transported to the McCall Hatchery for incubation and rearing. About a million summer chinook salmon smolts are reared and released each year from this facility. The hatchery also raises about a half million catchable rainbow trout and cutthroats, for stocking about 250 alpine lakes throughout the state and releasing into local waters. Visitors can check out the incubation and rearing facilities and two outside raceways. At the satellite facility, you can see a weir, fish ladder and trap, two raceway holding ponds, and a fish spawning area.

McCall Fish Net Pens, on East Lake Street next to Sports Marina, McCall. Open daylight hours daily. These fish-rearing pens were constructed in 1991 to raise thousands of trout in the spring and summer to be released into Payette

Lake in the fall. The outfit is a joint project between the Payette National Forest, Idaho Department of Fish and Game, Trout Unlimited, and the local stakeholder group, Payette Lakes Net Pen Association. The swarming, mulling fish are quite a sight!

SCENIC FLIGHTS

If you're not afraid of small planes, taking a scenic backcountry flight is one of the coolest ways to view and understand the Idaho's grand topography. Viewed from a distance, the drama of the crust's orogenic history becomes clear—thrust-up mountain ranges stacked up linearly one after another, their surfaces worn by wind and water, dendritic patterns of incised channels fingering their way in between in a fractal pattern similar to one you might observe in a rumpled piece of fabric splayed across your dining room table. Several outfitters in the region offer scenic flights in the area, including over the Frank Church–River of No Return Wilderness Area:

Arnold Aviation (208-382-4844), Cascade.

G&S Aviation (208-325-4432; www.gsaviation.com), Donnelly.

McCall Air (208-992-6559 or 800-634-3917; www.mccallaviation.com), McCall Municipal Airport. Backcountry transport to backcountry lodges and for river trips, hunting, and fishing.

Salmon Air (208-756-6211 or 800-448-3413; www.salmonair.com), McCall Municipal Airport. Backcountry transport for river trips, for hunting and fishing, and to backcountry lodges.

Thunder Mountain Air (208-633-3218; www.thundermountainair.com), around McCall.

TRAIN EXCURSIONS

Thunder Mountain Line (208-793-4425; www.thundermountainline.com). If you are looking for a kitschy, fun thing to do, a ride on the Thunder Mountain Line might be it. Initially scoped out as a possible railroad route to support gold mining in the region, the historical Thunder Mountain Line was eventually built between 1910 and 1913 to support the timber industry—and continued to do so until quite recently. Today the historic railway runs a handful of scenic tours, the most notable of which is the Horseshoe Bend Express, which travels from Horseshoe Bend along the mesmerizing Payette River and the Old Wagon Road route to Banks. Live entertainment is provided on this 2.5-hour voyage. Check for special scheduled events, including a mystery dinner ride and a Wild West Show with a mock train robbery and shoot-out.

✳ To Do

FISHING

Payette River has great stream fishing on all stretches. Fly-fishing is clearly what's hot here. Ice fishing is also popular during the winter.

Reservoirs and alpine lakes around the McCall and Cascade area are abundant; dunkers can find some good spots to cast a line. Cutthroat trout, rainbow trout, brook trout, whitefish, sturgeon, and mackinaw abound, some of them quite large. Crystal-clear, high-alpine lakes, including Lake Louie, Marshall Lake, Loon Lake, Tule Lake, Payette Lake, Cascade Reservoir, Warm Lake, Horsethief, Goose Lake, Hazard Lake, Little Payette Lake, and Browns Pond, dot the landscape. Some hiking (from a short walk to a day's slog) is required to get to most of these lakes; the solitary escape into the mountains is part of the allure. Many of the high mountain lakes are stocked with hatchery fish (sadly enough) dropped by airplane.

Salmon and Little Salmon rivers near Riggins are meccas for steelhead fishing, with strong spring and fall runs.

Outfitters

Exodus Wilderness Adventures (800-992-3484; www.riverescape.com), Riggins. They offer one-day to multiday fishing trips in the area.

McCall Angler (208-634-4004; www.mccallanglers.com), 305 E. Park St., McCall. Check them out for gear, fly-fishing lessons, guided fishing tours, and perhaps some local secrets.

Northwest Voyageurs (800-727-9977; www.voyageurs.com), on US 95 in Pollack (10 miles south of Riggins). They also offer one-day to multiday fishing trips in the area.

Ron Howell's Fly Fish McCall (208-634-1324; www.flyfishmccall.com), McCall. They also offer one-day to multiday fishing trips in the area.

Wapiti Meadow Ranch (208-633-3217; www.wapitimeadowranch.com), Cascade. They offer weeklong backcountry fly-fishing adventures and fly-fishing lessons.

Recommended Reading

For a great guide to hike-and-fish options around McCall, check out *Hiking and Angling in McCall* (Lizard Prints Publishers, 2000) by Roger Phillips, which details 32 trails leading to 28 mountain lakes and eight streams and rivers in the Payette National Forest area near McCall.

GOLF

Cascade Municipal Course (208-382-4835), Cascade. Nine holes along the shore of Lake Cascade.

Council Mountain Golf Course (208-253-6908), Council. Nine holes.

Jug Mountain Ranch Golf Course (208-634-5072; www.jugmountainranch .com), McCall. 18 holes.

McCall Golf Course (208-634-7200; www.mccallgolfclub.com), McCall. Its 27 holes and greens are nestled in a sea of conifers.

Meadow Creek Golf Course (208-347-2555; www.meadowcreekresort.com), New Meadows. 18 holes near McCall.

Osprey Meadow Golf Course (208-325-GOLF; www.tamarackidaho.com), Tamarack Resort. This 18-hole course was designed by Robert Trent Jones Jr. The resort was rated America's Best New Public Golf Course $75 and Over by *Golf Digest* in 2006.

Terrace Lakes Resort (208-462-3250; www.terracelakes.com), near Crouch. 18 holes.

Whitetail Club Golf Course (800-657-6464; www.whitetailclub), McCall. An 18-hole destination golf course designed by Roger Packard and Andy North.

HIKING

Hells Canyon National Recreation Area (208-628-3916), office in Riggins, and **Hells Canyon Wilderness Area,** which includes the dramatic Seven Devils Mountain Range, offer incredible hiking and mountaineering opportunities west of McCall. A Hells Canyon National Recreation Area map and a map with scenic spots to check out as you drive around the recreation area are available. Rattlesnakes are common in the canyon and particularly active from May to Sept.; the Forest Service recommends that anyone entering the area carry a snake-bite kit.

Seven Devils Range's elevation differentials offer the longest hiking season in Idaho, with some early season hiking (early Mar.) possible at lower elevations around the Snake River. Three main trailheads provide access to the Seven Devils region, some of the most spectacular hiking within the wilderness area. Campgrounds at each trailhead have fire pits and toilets, but potable water is only available in season at Upper Pittsburg Landing. A high-clearance four-wheel-drive vehicle is required for the Black Lake and Windy Saddle roads, while a passenger car will do for the Upper Pittsburg Landing drive. Many of these trails are accessible only July–mid-Oct., usually due to snow.

Black Lake trailhead: from US 95 about 54 miles northwest of Council, take FR 112 (you'll need a Payette National Forest map to locate this access road).

Upper Pittsburg Landing trailhead: From US 95 at Whitebird (see Northern Idaho: A Hidden Jewel, the Clearwater Region: Big Fish, Big Trees, Big Whitewater), take FR 493 for 19 miles. This trailhead provides access to the **Snake River National Recreation Trail** (NRT), which winds south along the Snake River for 29 miles to Hells Canyon Dam.

Windy Saddle trailhead: From US 95 near Riggins, take FR 15 for 17 miles. From Windy Saddle, you can get onto the 27-mile **Seven Devils Loop Trail** that encircles the major peaks in the Seven Devils range. From this trail, you can pick up one of a series of side trails leading to the numerous high-alpine lakes dotting this landscape and to the bases of some the peaks themselves.

Idaho State Centennial Trail West. This 300-mile side spur of the 1,200-mile Idaho State Centennial Trail, which runs from the Idaho–Nevada border north to Canada, runs through the Salmon River Mountains east of McCall and north along the western boundary of the Gospel Hump Wilderness Area. For more information on the Idaho State Centennial Trail, see What's Where in Idaho.

Salmon River Mountains and the **Frank Church–River of No Return Wilderness Area**. Some great hiking, climbing, and mountaineering is accessible from the eastern part of this region. For more information on these areas, see Central Idaho: An Explorer's Nirvana, Salmon-Challis and Beyond: Mountains and Rivers Galore.

Weiser River Trail (208-887-2068 or 208-861-8614; www.weiserrivertail.org), 84 miles from Weiser to Rubicon, near New Meadows. The brainchild of the nonprofit Friends of the Weiser River Trail, this new recreational trail runs along the former Pacific and Idaho Northern railroad grade, passing through the towns of Midvale, Cambridge, and Council. The entire right-of-way was deeded to Friends of the Weiser River Trail by the railroad, and the group continues to work on developing access and facilities at the trailheads. Unlike rail-to-trail projects in more urban areas, this trail runs through open country and provides access to acres upon acres of riparian habitat, thick forests, rolling hills, and open canyons. Deer, elk, herons, and wild turkeys can be seen along the way. The rail-trail is popular for hiking, mountain biking, and horseback riding. Friends of the Wieser River Trail are looking for volunteers to help with this great public project, so don't be shy!

Recommended Reading

See Tom Lopez's *Exploring Idaho's Mountains: A Guide for Climbers, Scramblers & Hikers* (The Mountaineers, 1990) for routes in Hells Canyon and other areas, such as the West Mountains, the Cuddy and Hitt mountains along the Oregon border to the south, and the western part of the Sawtooth Mountain range farther east. For a good guide to trails within the Seven Devils area, check out Fred Barstad's *Hiking Hells Canyon and Idaho's Seven Devils Mountains* (Falcon, 2001) or *Hiking Idaho's Seven Devils: The complete guide to every trail, lake and peak in Idaho's Seven Devils Wilderness* by Gary D. Jones (CHJ Publishing, 2003).

HORSEBACK RIDING

Elk Springs Outfitters (208-634-5999) offers mule rides in the Payette Lake area.

4D Longhorn Guest Ranch (208-584-3118; www.4dranches.com), 450 High Valley Rd., Cascade. This working ranch offers part- to full-day guided horseback tours out of Smiths Ferry.

Northwest Voyagers (800-727-9977; www.voyageurs.com), on US 95 in Pollack (10 miles south of Riggins). They offer two- and four-day combination pack-and-paddle trips on the Main Salmon, five- to seven-day combination trips in Hells Canyon, and seven- to nine-day trips on the Lower Salmon.

Wapiti Meadow Ranch (208-633-3217; www.wapitimeadowranch.com), 1667 Johnson Creek Rd., Cascade. More adventurous riders looking for a deep wilderness pack trip might check out this outfitter, which runs two- to six-day pack trips to breathtaking locations deep within the Salmon River Mountains.

Ya-Hoo Corral (208-634-3360), 2280 Warren Wagon Rd., near McCall. A nice spot for a guided day tour is the network of horseback riding trails cut by J. R. Simplot that meander through state land to the west of Payette Lake.

Hells Canyon Wilderness Area

A slew of outfitters run pack trips in the wilderness area; a couple of them are in Idaho, but the majority are out of Oregon:

Backcountry Outfitters (541-426-5908; www.backcountryoutfittersinc.com), Oregon.

Bigfoot Outfitters (208-628-3539; www.bigfootoutfitters.com), Riggins.

Cornucopia Wilderness Pack Station (888-420-7855 or 541-562-1181; www.cornucopiapackstation.com), Oregon.

Diamond W Outfitters (541-577-3157), Oregon.

Eagle Cap Wilderness Pack Station (541-432-4145; www.eaglecapwilderness packstation.com), Oregon.

Heaven's Gate Outfitters (208-628-3062; www.heavensgateoutfitters.com), Riggins.

Hells Canyon Packers (541-853-2341), Oregon.

Hurricane Creek Llama Treks (866-386-8735 or 541-928-2859; www.hcltrek .com), Oregon.

Millar Pack Station (541-886-4035; www.millarpackstation.com), Oregon.

Steen's Wilderness Adventure (541-432-6545; www.steens-packtrips.com), Oregon.

Wallowa Llamas (541-742-2961; www.wallowallamas.com), Oregon.

HOT SPRINGS

This region of Idaho is hot spring heaven! Idaho has more natural hot springs than any other state, and many of them are located in the Payette, Boise, and Sawtooth national forests. Steaming cauldrons in a variety of shapes and forms—ranging from a collection of old bathtubs sitting side by side on the rocks to cemented rock-walled pools filled with crystal-clear Caribbean-blue water, to secret spots perched aside salmon spawning ground (yes, at the right time of year, you can see them from your soaking spot)—and bearing names including Vulcan Hot Springs, Skinnydipper Hot Springs, Molly's Tubs, and Mile 16 (Sugah!) Hot Spring, dot the landscape. You can easily occupy a week first locating the trailheads to or the hidden mile markers signifying these hidden gems, hiking to them (sometimes easily, sometimes not so easily), soaking, and then eventually dragging yourself out and back to camp somewhere nearby. In fact, some fanatics make a lifestyle out of hot springing, living at or nearby choice hot springs for months on end, trading secrets and building friendships with other hot springers, and taking responsibility for maintaining the pools. For some folks, this is serious stuff. The best way to find these places is to ask around locally. Hot spring protocol varies from pool to pool; at some, bathing suits are expected, at others, anything but skinny-dipping will be scorned. For an easier soak, commercial springs do exist.

Burgdorf Hot Springs (208-636-3036), on Warren Wagon Road outside Warren (30 miles north of McCall). This is one of the notables. Perhaps another Idaho oddity, the place was a former mining outpost, complete with an old, now-defunct hotel, where apparently raging parties were staged. Built by Frederick Burgdorf in the 1890s after his gold prospecting came up short, the site once contained a hotel, cabins, and barns. Burgdorf made his living selling milk and meat to the area's miners and became known for his hospitality and fine dining. Many of the buildings still remain, and today's visitors will find rustic cabins with beds, stoves, outhouses, and pea gravel–floored dressing barns. The pool itself is surrounded by logs and a couple lobster pots. The setting is beautiful, and you might feel as if you just walked on stage for an old western movie. If you are lucky, you'll witness elk coming into the nearby meadow to hang out during a summer's night. The road to Burgdorf is not plowed during the winter, but you can snowmobile or ski in if you are so inclined.

Gold Fork Hot Springs (208-890-8730), near Donnelly. Open year-round. Mineral pools and hydromassage.

Riggins Hot Springs; from Riggins, drive east on a washboard gravel road along south side of Main Salmon River, to just short of Allison Creek. There is a place to camp there as well.

Zim's Hot Springs (208-347-2686), 2995 Zims Rd., New Meadows. Open 9–11 daily in summer, 10–10 Tues.–Sun. in winter. A large swimming pool is filled with 90- to 95-degree F spring water.

Recommended Reading
Pick up a copy of the hot spring bible: Evie Litton's *Hiking: Hot Springs in the Pacific Northwest* (The Globe Pequot Press, 2005).

ICE SKATING
Manchester Ice & Event Center (208-634-3570; www.manchester-icecentre .com), 200 E. Lake St., McCall. This is a great indoor ice rink for free skating, pickup hockey, and broomball. Individual and group ice-skating lessons are also available, and skates can be rented on-site. As the home for the Manchester Mountaineers Hockey Team, the rink is a fun place to check out a local hockey game on Fri. or Sat. night.

MOUNTAIN BIKING
While Sun Valley might be the mecca of mountain biking in Idaho, the McCall and Payette region also offers some good single-track riding.

Easy Rides
Crown Point Rail Trail, at Lake Cascade, has easy riding.

Goose Creek Falls, trailhead behind Last Chance Campground, on ID 55, 6 miles west of McCall. On this mellow ride, you pedal 2.2 miles to the hike up to the falls at the end of the trail.

Lost Valley Reservoir, on FR 89 west of New Meadows. A series of trails are around and near the reservoir.

Ponderosa State Park (208-634-2164; http://parksandrecreation.gov), McCall. A series of mellow trails near Payette Lake are a great place if you just want to spin.

Resort Trails
Brundage Mountain Ski Area (208-634-4151; www.brundage.com), north of McCall. Open July 1–Labor Day. $5 for one ride, $20 for full day. The resort

offers 20 miles of trails that are a bit more demanding aerobically but still of fairly moderate technical difficulty. For adrenaline junkies, you can take the lift to the 7,640-foot summit during the summer months, then ride down.

Little Ski Hill (208-634-5691; www.littleskihill.org), on ID 55, 2.2 miles north of McCall. Easy riding on jeep roads.

Tamarack Resort (208-325-1000; www.tamarackidaho.com), on west side of Lake Cascade. Lifts operate Fri.–Sun. and holidays. $15 for adults, $8 for youth, free for children under six. Tamarack's system of about 25 miles of single- and double-track, lift-accessible trails connects to a much more extensive network (approximately 80 miles' worth) of trails within the contiguous national forest system. Guided tours are available out of Tamarack.

Harder Rides

For more advanced riders looking for hard-core rides, there are plenty to be had. In addition to what's listed below, other popular spots include Victor Creek, Twenty Mile Trail, the Rim Ride, and the Dave Hall–Jughandle Mountain trails.

Ruby Meadows–Loon Lake Loop, 25 miles. This buffed-out ride starts 28 miles north of McCall off Warren Wagon Road. You wind through beautiful alpine forest and broad, flower-strewn meadows, reaching a crystal-blue high-alpine lake. Keep your eyes peeled for wildlife.

Bear Pete Mountain Trail, about 19 miles. This lung-buster of a ride (*not* for novices) takes off 20 miles north of McCall out Warren Wagon Road at Cloochman Saddle. Hot springs await at the end of the trail.

East Fork of Lake Fork, 9.2 miles; from Ponderosa State Park in McCall, head 9 miles out on Lick Creek Road. Ride along a creek, through some beautiful alpine meadows, and check out the stunning alpine vistas.

Silver Creek Summit, 7 miles round trip; take Banks-Lowman Road out of Banks for 8 miles to Crouch turnoff, drive 24 miles to FR 678 (just before Boiling Springs Campground), take a right, and drive 7 miles to trailhead at junction with Silver Creek. This beautiful one- to two-hour ride hugs the headwaters of Silver Creek, winding through stands of spruce and firs and over some steep terrain to a summit lookout, where you can pull out your lunch and take in the scenery.

Rentals

Your best bet is to visit one of the local bike shops and talk to the gearheads. They'll be able to steer you to appropriate rides that match your skill, endurance, and energy levels—as well as set you up with gear and rent you a mountain bike, if need be.

Alpine Sciences (208-634-4707; www.alpinesciences.com), 409 S. Third St., McCall.

Brundage Mountain Resort (208-634-4151) has a shop that also rents mountain bikes.

Gravity Sports (208-634-8530; www.gravitysportsidaho.com), 503 Pine St., McCall; next to Legacy Park.

Pro Peak Sports (208-325-3323; www.propeaksports.com), 412 W. Roseberry Rd., Donnelly.

Recommended Reading

You might also want to check out *Mountain Biking in McCall* by Steve Stuebner and Roger Phillips (Boise Front Adventures, 2003) for detailed maps and descriptions of local rides.

OUTDOOR ADVENTURES

McCall Field Campus (208-885-8981; www.cnrhome.uidaho.edu), next to Ponderosa State Park, McCall. This 11-acre campus perched on the edge of Payette Lake is owned and operated by University of Idaho's College of Natural Resources, and it functions as a residential learning center. It is home to the McCall Outdoor Science School, which offers a series of field courses, including avalanche awareness and wilderness first-aid courses; seminars on topics such as elk bugling, fly-fishing, and animal tracking; graduate courses in environmental education; and three- to five-day residential environmental studies courses for fifth- and sixth-grade students. The facilities are also available to rent for courses, conferences, retreats, and community events. The rustic campus has bunkhouses, yurts for housing or classrooms, cabins, and a main dining lodge that might make you dream of an artistic or academic escape to these idyllic surrounds.

SKIING

With an average of 300 inches of white fluffies annually and a low-key local-ski-town feel, McCall has it going on when it comes to skiing—of all varieties. The second-oldest winter recreation area in Idaho, McCall garnered its recreational stripes when Finnish settlers introduced alpine and Nordic skiing and ski jumping to the area. A rich ski tradition continues here. This funky little town provides a great base, whether for downhill skiing at one of the two alpine resorts in the area—local favorite Brundage Mountain or the new Tamarack Resort, the first four-season ski resort built in the United States in more than two decades—venturing into the backcountry for some killer tele-turns, or Nordic skiing on one of the area's great groomed trail systems.

Rentals

Ski gear, accessories, rentals, and local insight can be found at a number of area ski shops.

Alpine Sciences (208-634-4707; www.alpinesciences.com), 409 S. Third St., McCall.

Gravity Sports (208-634-8530; www.gravitysportsidaho.com), 503 Pine St., McCall; next to Legacy Park.

Home Town Sports (208-634-2302; http://hometownsports.e-siteworks.com/home/), 300 Lenora St., McCall.

Pro Peak Sports (208-325-3323; www.propeaksports.com), 412 W. Roseberry Rd., Donnelly.

Alpine Skiing

Brundage Mountain Resort (800-888-7544; www.brundage.com), off ID 55, 8 miles north of McCall. Open 9:30–4:30. $48 for adults, $34 for seniors and juniors, $22 for youths, free for children under six. If you are looking for freshies, Brundage is the place. With a low-key, old-school lodge, great tree skiing, powder stashes galore, and reasonable lift ticket prices, this is a dirtbag's heaven. While the mountain sports only 1,800 feet of vertical, it has 1,500 acres of lift-access terrain, an impressive 19,000 acres of backcountry snowcat-accessed goods, and a terrain park. What it lacks in vertical it makes up for in powder. It is not entirely uncommon to experience a day of pounding white stuff falling out of the sky and uncountable shots of powder to the face. Plus, you won't feel cheated if you actually buy lunch here. As a tribute to the old days, $15 will get you a Philly cheese steak, the largest pile of fries you can imagine, and a drink. Or check out the Bear's Den yurt at the top of the hill; in a surprising twist, you can order sushi, miso, and beer in this warm little hut. This is a skier's mountain.

Little Ski Hill (208-634-5691; www.littleskihill.org), 3 miles north of McCall. Open for night skiing Fri. (Family Night) and Sat. (Telemark Night). Season

TAMARACK RESORT'S SKI AREA LEADS TO A VAST BACKCOUNTRY.

passes $79.50 for adults, $26.50 for children. True to its name, this little T-bar-and rope-tow-accessed hill has 405 feet of vertical—a great place for kids. Built in 1937, the Little Ski Hill is in good company with Sun Valley Resort and Lookout Pass as the oldest developed ski resorts in Idaho. For most of its history, the hill was the site of the McCall Ski Jump. As with most ski jumps across the country, liability issues have had their way, and the ski jump is no longer.

Tamarack Resort (208-325-1000; www.tamarackidaho.com), on west side of Lake Cascade. Open 9-4. $59 for adults, $30 for youth, $41 for seniors and free for children six and under. Having first opened its lifts in December 2004, Tamarack is the newest show in town, the result of an impressive multidecade and multimillion-dollar (to the tune of $400 million) effort to turn acres upon acres of ranchland and tree-lined slopes into a big-time ski resort and development. Tamarack has caused quite the buzz around Idaho and beyond. The mountain boasts 2,800 feet of vertical, 1,100 acres of lift-accessible terrain, and seven lifts servicing 39 percent expert, 44 percent intermediate, and 17 percent novice terrain on 41 trails. For knuckle-grabbers, they also have one SuperPipe and two terrain parks. While the skiing is fun, experts might be wishing for a few more black-diamond runs. It is definitely a "resort," and you can expect resort prices for food and more. While the enthusiasm exuding from the staff and in the resort's impressive public relations efforts might be warranted by the success of this company's large-scale development coup, Tamarack also possesses a corporate, Disneyland-esque quality that might send free-heelers straight into the nearby hills.

Backcountry Skiing

The McCall area, surrounded by towering peaks in the Payette National Forest—the nearby Salmon River and then the Clearwater Mountains farther northeast and the Seven Devils region to the west—boasts expansive backcountry skiing. The opportunity to get out and climb for some turns is virtually limitless. Popular backcountry destinations include the **Boulder Lake area, Jug Mountain, Lick Creek, and Squaw Peak.**

Experienced skiers looking to explore McCall's backcountry regions are advised to check in with one of the local shops (see Rentals, above) for information about conditions and favored ski locations. Most have powder hounds on staff who will be happy to help. As always in the backcountry, take proper clothing and equipment, plenty of water, and food and know and follow backcountry safety protocol (see Avalanche Safety, below).

Blue Moon Outfitters (208-634-3111), in Ponderosa State Park in McCall. Winter. For a relatively decadent backcountry experience, try swooshing in a mile to the Blue Moon Yurt, nestled among ponderosa pines, for a five-course, gourmet ethnic dinner in a candlelit and prayer flag–adorned Mongolian yurt (reservations required). It is a good way to stretch your legs after a big day in the backcountry, then restoke the fire with mulled cider, hot tea, or cocoa, followed by dishes such as baked Brie with sun-dried tomatoes and basil, grilled salmon in roasted red pepper sauce, leg of lamb or pork tenderloin with all the trimmings, and scrumptious desserts including chocolate torte with raspberry sauce—all washed down, of course, with some great wine. Don't forget your headlamp!

BACKCOUNTRY TRACKS IN PAYETTE NATIONAL FOREST

Brundage Mountain Resort (800-888-7544; www.brundage.com), off ID 55, 8 miles north of McCall. Guided cat-skiing takes you deep into tree-lined glades and steep snowfields. $159 for half day, $259 for full day, $599 for overnight adventure to backcountry yurt. Trip prices per person include guide service, cat transport, food, and skis.

Payette Powder Guides (208-634-4263; www.payettepowderguides.com). If you're looking for some guides to show you where the goods are, check out this outfitter. They own and operate two yurts ($240 and up per person, up to six people) on Lick Creek Summit, providing access to thousands of acres of stunning alpine terrain cloaked in untracked powder. Access to the yurts is via a mellow 11-mile skin up a county road, or via snowmobile or snowcat.

Tamarack Resort (208-325-1000; www.tamarackidaho.com), on west side of Lake Cascade. $200 and up per person for cat-accessed and guided backcountry skiing. This is where Tamarack shines. You can gain access to 5,000 acres of awesome backcountry terrain by hiking, being snowmobile-towed, or hitching a sno-cat ride out the north ridge (to Wildwood Bowl, Half Moon Bowl, and Banana Bowl) or the south ridge (to Grouse Bowl). From there, you can do yo-yos and find fresh powder in the trees, as well as steep drop-offs and great skiing all around. While hitching a ride feels a bit like cheating, and money might be an obstacle, if you can swing it, boy, is it fun!

Avalanche Safety

Friends of the Payette Avalanche Center (www.payette-avalanche.org/calendarofclassesevents.html), in conjunction with **Payette Powder Guides** (208-634-4263; www.payettepowderguides.com), offer avalanche awareness classes.

Payette Avalanche Center (208-634-0409; www.fs.fed.us/r4/payette/avalanche) provides avalanche advisories for this area that are updated three times per week. Since avalanche advisory coverage is limited, it is particularly important to be avalanche safe: tell someone where you are going, know your snow, and bring an avalanche beacon, shovel, and probe—and know how to use them.

Nordic Skiing

Activity Barn (208-634-2222; www.activitybarn.com), on Moonridge Road, outside of McCall. $5 per person. They have miles of dog-friendly groomed trails.

Little Ski Hill (208-634-5691; www.littleskihill.org), 3 miles north of McCall. $145 for season pass. They offer an impressive 50-plus kilometers of groomed skate-skiing and touring trails and a biathlon range.

Ponderosa State Park (208-634-2164; www.idahoparks.org/parks/ponderosa.aspx), McCall. $2 per person per day, $4 per vehicle. Located on a 1,000-acre, pine-loaded peninsula that juts out into Payette Lake, the park is a wonderful place to Nordic ski. Groomed skate-skiing trails, ranging in difficultly from recreational to competition, wind 23 kilometers through stands of towering ponderosa pines, their boughs laden in a blanket of snow, and provide vistas of Payette Lake. The park also has 3.4 miles of **snowshoe trails** through the woods. This United States Ski Association–certified cross-country ski course has been selected to host the 2008 Masters World Cup races.

Tamarack Resort (208-325-1000; www.tamarackidaho.com), on west side of Lake Cascade. $9 for adults, $7 for seniors, $5 for youths, free for kids six and under. Their Nordic center has 25 kilometers of skate-skiing and snowshoeing trails winding through meadows and stands of aspen, pine, fir, and tamarack. Dogs are welcome.

Wapiti Meadow Ranch (208-633-3217; www.wapitimeadowranch.com), 1668 Johnson Creek Rd., Cascade. See Lodging—Guest Ranches for rates. For guests at this beautifully rustic and secluded ranch, mile after mile of isolated groomed trails are available.

WHITE-WATER KAYAKING AND RAFTING

Payette River
The entire Payette River system offers world-class white-water kayaking and rafting. **Payette Boise River Revival Whitewater Event** (PBR—*not* the Pabst Blue Ribbon festival) is a renowned and superfun white-water rodeo event of note (see Special Events—June).

BACKCOUNTRY SKIERS IN THE PAYETTE MOUNTAINS

James Foster

Main Payette has the mellowest running (this still means big features, waves, and holes), with class II–III waters. Day trips on the Main are run out of Banks, where the North and South forks of the Payette join forces to create the Main Payette River. A fun little class II-plus play hole called the "Gutter" can be found on the Payette River about 2 miles south of Horseshoe Bend, at the end of Pioneer Avenue. This park-and-play feature, the result of a diversion for a hydroelectric project, is a fun place to play or spectate.

North Fork of the Payette from just south of Smiths Ferry to Cougar Mountain Lodge just above Banks has bad-ass class IV–V boating. This run is considered one of the finest advanced kayaking runs in the world, with 20 named rapids, coming in quick succession in only 16 river miles due to a precipitous 1,700-foot elevation drop. This boating is no joke, even though the rapids bear a slew of crazy names worth cataloging. Starting with the southernmost rapid, these torrents are called Crunch, Juicer, Otters Run, Hounds Tooth, Jaws, Screaming Left Turn, Golf Course (for the nine holes), Jacobs Ladder, Pectoralis Major, Upper and Lower Bouncer Down the Middle, Upper Chaos, Lower Chaos, Know Where to Run, Bad José, Slide, S-Turn, Disneyland, Nutcracker, and Steepness. If the boiling, churning, crashing water isn't enough to scare away all but the best boaters, the names certainly should. It is not advisable to run the North Fork unless you are an expert boater and are with someone who has run the river before. More than a few strong boaters have died on this section. Please be smart.

South Fork of the Payette is known for a couple solid class III–IV day runs. Out of Crouch, kayakers revel in the Staircase Section, which stretches from the put-in 2 miles west of Crouch to the take-out at the confluence of the South Fork with the North Fork of the Payette at Banks. This section runs right along ID 21, so there is easy access for boaters and spectators alike. Farther east, another popular run goes from a put-in at the confluence with the Deadwood River to a take-out near Danskin Creek. This stretch leaves the highway behind as it plunges into a deep, remote canyon. With the road up to 1,000 feet above, the experience is a deep wilderness one. Both stretches can be floated with local river companies.

Salmon River

Main Salmon River can be floated from Mackay Bar to Vinegar Creek, or another 14 miles on to Riggins. If you take out at Riggins, you might want to camp in the area and check out the Riggins Hot Springs (see Hot Springs).

South Fork of the Salmon River has perhaps a bit more challenging class III–V boating farther north: the East Fork, the Goat Creek section, and the overnight trip down the South Fork to Mackay Bar at the Main Salmon River. From Mackay Bar, you can fly out or continue on the Main Salmon.

Snake River

Hells Canyon stretch of the Snake River is also a popular three- to four-day white-water trip, with two class IV rapids known to eat boating gear for lunch. When it comes to temperature, Hell's Canyon is true to its name. Please be forewarned that you are likely to be searching for shade in this canyon with columnar basalt walls. The beaches along the river are big yet rocky, and what little vegetation exists struggles to provide a bit of shade from the sweltering heat.

Outfitters

A slew of outfitters run trips of various lengths on the area's rivers. If you are running a private trip, some of these shops rent gear as well.

Bear Valley River Co. (208-793-2272; www.bearvalleyrafting.com), Banks. Trips on various sections of the Payette River system.

Brundage Mountain Whitewater Adventures (888-889-8320; www.brundage .com), Riggins. Trips on the Main Salmon.

Canyons Incorporated (208-634-4303), McCall. Trips on the Payette River system.

Cascade Raft & Kayak (208-793-2221; www.cascaderaft.com), Horseshoe Bend. Trips on various sections of the Payette.

Epley's Whitewater Adventure (800-223-1813 or 208-628-3586; www.epleys .com), Riggins. Trips on the Main Salmon.

Exodus River Trips (800-992-3484; www.riverescape.com), Riggins. Trips on the Main Salmon.

Hells Canyon Raft (800-523-6502; www.hellscanyonraft.com), McCall. Trips on the Main Salmon and the Snake.

Idaho Whitewater Unlimited (208-462-1900; www.idahowhitewaterunltd .com), Garden Valley. Trips on various sections of the Payette River.

North Star River Expeditions (208-634-2296 or 877-610-3200), McCall. Trips on the Main Salmon as well as into Hells Canyon on the Snake River.

Payette River Company (208-726-8467; www.payetterivercompany.com), Lowman (and Ketchum). Trips on sections of the Payette River system.

Riverroots, Ltd. (208-850-7637; www.riverrootsltd.com), Boise. Trips on the Payette River.

Salmon River Challenge (www.salmonriverchallenge.com), Riggins. Trips on the Main Salmon.

Salmon River Experience (SRE) (800-892-9223; www.salmonriverexperience .com), Riggins. Trips on the Main Salmon.

Tamarack Resort (208-325-1000; www.tamarackidaho.com), McCall. Trips on sections of the Payette River system.

Wapiti River Guides (800-488-9872; www.wapitiriverguides.com), Riggins. Trips on the Main Salmon.

WILDLIFE VIEWING

Hells Canyon National Recreation Area (see Wilder Places—Nature Preserves). As in much of Idaho, wildlife is abundant in this region; the Hells Canyon sub-basin is thought to provide suitable habitat for 373 species of wildlife for at least some portion of the year. Therefore, explorers who venture

onto a trail here, and particularly the Seven Devils area, might be lucky enough
to spot elk, deer, bighorn sheep, perhaps more elusive mountain lions, bears, or
bobcats. Moose also inhabit this area, and rumor has it that grizzlies, wolves, and
wolverines have been sighted. Birds are abundant; ducks, geese, ospreys, and
bald eagles can been seen cruising the river corridors, while birds of prey,
including falcons, golden eagles, and hawks take to the high country. Peregrine
falcons, which have been reared in captivity and reintroduced to the area, can
sometimes be seen looking for prey. Riparian areas are flush with songbirds such
as thrushes, warblers, and wrens tweeting their sweet melodies, and forested
areas provide refuge for owls, woodpeckers, and jays. Keep your eyes and ears
peeled, stay still and quiet, and be patient; you just might be rewarded with a
vista of one of these beautiful creatures going about its business.

✳ Wilder Places

PARKS

Lake Cascade State Park (208-382-6544; http://parksandrecreation.idaho.gov),
off US 55 in Cascade. This park offers lake access for motorboating, sailing,
windsurfing, and fishing (summer and winter), plus 175 campsites ($9 and up)
and three group yurts ($175 each).

Ponderosa State Park (208-634-2164; http://parksandrecreation.idaho.gov),
next to Payette Lake near McCall. Situated on the beautifully wooded (not surprisingly, full of towering ponderosa pines), 1,000-acre Osprey Point peninsula
that juts into the lake, this parks offers a series of serene hiking and biking trails,
guided walks, and programs with park naturalists. This is a great place to ski in
the winter (see To Do—Nordic Skiing). Canada geese, ospreys, bald eagles,
wood ducks, mallards, songbirds, muskrats, beavers, deer, and the occasional
bear frequent the park. Primitive camping is available in the North Beach Unit
($12 and up).

WILDERNESS AREAS

Hells Canyon National Recreation Area (NRA) and **Hells Canyon Wilderness Area** (208-628-3916; www.fs.fed.us/hellscanyon/), Riggins. The Web site
has a slew of information about camping areas, hiking trails, horseback riding
opportunities, and a map of recreational spots and facilities within the NRA. It
also has information on the Wild and Scenic Snake River, a portion of which
flows through the NRA.

Hells Canyon NRA was created by Congressional mandate in 1975 to encompass 652,488 acres of remote landscape, plunging canyons, and soaring peaks
straddling the border between northeastern Oregon and western Idaho.

Hells Canyon Wilderness Area's designated 215,000 acres are protected within this NRA (83,811 acres of which are within Idaho). Noted for its dramatic
topography, the NRA includes Hells Canyon, North America's deepest gorge
(yes, deeper than the Grand Canyon!), and much of the impressive Seven Devils
Mountain Range. Hells Canyon, sculpted by the great Snake River, plummets
8,043 feet from its eastern canyon rim to the river below; the contrast to the

nearby towering, snowcapped He Devil Peak (elevation 9,400-plus feet) is even more impressive. No roads span the 10-mile-wide Hells Canyon (though there are river crossings to the south at dams).

Historical sites, including Indian pictographs and petroglyphs and ghostly remains of settlers' homes, are scattered about the landscape, providing a window into the history of the region.

Three Wild and Scenic Rivers—the Snake and Rapid rivers in Idaho and the Imnaha River in Oregon—are also part of the NRA. Abundant wildlife, including bobcats, bears, elk, deer, mountain goats, bighorn sheep, and little pikas, make their homes here, and wildflowers in a palette of colors splash themselves across open alpine meadows and mountain flanks in spring and summer. The Hells Canyon portion of the Snake River offers world-class white-water boating with very big waves, soaring canyons, and spectacular alpine scenery (see To Do—White-water Kayaking and Rafting).

Seven Devils Range, which runs for 40 miles along the Idaho side of the border and separates the grand Snake River Canyon from that of the Salmon River, deserves special mention for being one of Idaho's most impressively rugged landscapes. With craggy, snowcapped spires, ramparts, and parapets—of a mismash of geologic heritage that includes volcanism, sediment deposition and subsequent lithification, and metamorphism—plunging into the nation's deepest canyon, the dramatic relief is something to behold. If nothing else, the place names of the Seven Devils holds some allure: the Devils Tooth (elevation about 7,760 feet), the Tower of Babel (elevation 9,269 feet), She Devil (elevation 9,280 feet), He Devil (at 9,393 feet the highest peak in the Seven Devils range), the Goblin (elevation 8,981 feet), Devils Throne (elevation 9,280 feet), and Twin Imps (9,240-plus feet). Local lore suggests that the satanic name of the mountain range derived from a Nez Perce legend in which seven evil child-eating giants were punished by the animals of the forest, who placed them into very deep holes filled with churning, boiling liquid and then turned them into large mountains. A large gash (Hells Canyon) was then placed in the landscape so that the giants could not escape. Individual peak names, consistent with this theme, have been assigned over time by alpinists. Climbing and hiking opportunities into and around the Seven Devils are numerous.

Nearly 900 miles of trails traverse this landscape, providing nearly boundless opportunity for hiking, horseback riding, and mountain biking, plus Nordic skiing during the winter. Nine developed campsites are available within the Idaho portion of the NRA, and dispersed camping is allowed within the wilderness area. Please follow Leave No Trace camping practices.

✳ Lodging

Payette River Mountains Visitor Association (www.payetteriver mountains.com) has more lodging options.

BED & BREAKFASTS

McCall

Hotel McCall (208-634-8105 or 866-800-1183; www.hotelmccall.com), corner of Third and Main, McCall 83638. The historic Hotel McCall, the old salt of the village, has been operating as a charming bed & breakfast–style inn since 1904. In the heart of the downtown action, Hotel McCall's 13 rooms are simply but beautifully appointed with warm antiques and rugs and have a quaint charm that will make you feel at home. Amenities include private baths, wireless Internet access, an indoor pool, and a restaurant. The hotel has beautiful views of Payette Lake, a boccie lawn, and a stately lobby. $135 and up.

CABINS

McCall

Brundage Bungalows (208-634-2344 or 800-643-2009; www.brundage vacations.com), 308 W. Lake St., McCall 83638. If you are looking for a funky place to stay, check out this place just up the road from downtown McCall, which offers cozy individual cabins. $69 and up.

HOTELS AND INNS

For skiers looking more for a bed in which to crash than anything else, McCall has its share of chain-ish hotels and motels too.

Cascade

Ashley Inn (866-382-5621; www.the ashleyinn.com), 500 N. Main St., Cascade 83611. This hotel is fairly large—67 rooms—for this area. Rooms are large and a little on the frilly side. $125 and up.

McCall

AmericInn (208-634-2230 or 800-396-5007; www.americinn.com), 211 S. Third St., McCall 83638. $120 and up.

Brundage Inn (208-634-2344 or 800-643-2009; www.brundage vacations.com) 1005 W. Lake St., McCall 83638. The inn is owned and operated by the same outfit as the Brundage Bungalows a few blocks east. $49 and up.

Holiday Inn Express McCall (aka the Hunt Lodge; 208-634-4700; www .thehuntlodge.com), 210 N. Third St., McCall 83638. $124 and up.

Scandia Inn (888-622-2554; www .thescandiainn.com), 401 N. Third St., McCall 83638. $67 and up.

Super 8 Lodge McCall (208-634-4637; www.mccallsuper8.com), 303 S. Third St., McCall 83638. $89 and up.

Western Mountain Lodge (208-634-6300; www.westernmountain lodge.com), 415 N. Third St., McCall 83638. $84 and up.

LODGES AND GUEST RANCHES

Cascade

Wapiti Meadow Ranch (208-633-3217; www.wapitimeadowranch.com), 1667 Johnson Creek Rd., Cascade 83611. This premier Orvis-endorsed wilderness lodge offers several suites within the lodge and a handful of luxury cabins, each featuring separate bedroom(s), bath, large living room, wood-burning stove, and fully equipped kitchen. All guests share the resort's hot tub, wraparound porch, and gathering room. You'll also have access to all the backcountry activities you could ever want: fly-fishing galore, mountain biking, kayaking, cross-country skiing, horseback riding, and more. The lodge has licensed guides ready to take you on guided fly-fishing, horseback riding, and hiking trips. The lodge is accessible via a scenic backcountry flight or a rugged drive. Cabins $175 per person and up.

Council

Seven Devils Lodge (208-258-4421; www.sevendevilslodge.com), 4043 Council Cuprum Rd., Council 83612. This backcountry lodge offers the classic Idaho ranch vacation. All-inclusive packages provide an escape to a rustic but comfortable lodge with gourmet meals and guided fly-fishing and horseback riding. The lodge can house 10–12 people in western-motif private guest rooms. This quiet retreat is a great place just to relax, write, paint, or think. $349 per person and up for 3 days (winter)–$849 (summer).

McCall

Whitetail Club & Resort (800-657-6464; www.whitetailclub.com), 501 W. Lake St., McCall 83638. This large timber-frame lodge perched on the shore of Payette Lake offers McCall's swankiest digs; it has all you could ask for in an upscale lodging experience. The rooms and suites are large and finely appointed, with plush sofas, huge marble baths, sitting rooms, dining tables, and the like. It feels more like Manhattan than McCall, and guests have joked that you should almost stay in your room for your entire vacation to get your full value's worth! The main lodge itself is grand, built of large timbers and river rock, with a warm sitting area, fireplace, and casual bar. Fine candlelit dining is

provided by the fabulous Narrows Restaurant (see Where to Eat—Dining Out). Don't miss the large, river rock–lined outdoor hot tub perched by the lakeshore. On a snowy winter evening, you can't beat tiptoeing out to the tub in the plush robes provided by the resort, dancing between flakes, and melting into a steaming pool from which to watch the snowfall float onto the lake. The resort also has an incredible full-service inhouse spa—the Mountain Renewal Spa, which offers weekend wellness events, massage, cranial sacral therapy, natural facials, and more. Check it out if you are looking for some true pampering! Rooms $199 and up (summer)–$325 and up (winter).

Smiths Ferry

4D Longhorn Guest Ranch (www.4dranches.com), Ola 83657. This beautiful working ranch provides cozy guest accommodations in Old West–style cabins and offers ranch-style meals. This dude ranch is geared toward horsemen and -women, offering weekly cattle drives, guided trail rides, riding and roping lessons, and more. Rooms $120 and up; $200 and up with horseback riding.

RESORTS

Garden Valley

Terrace Lakes Resort (208-462-3250; www.terracelakes.com), 101 Holiday Dr., Garden Valley 83622. This resort has its own hot-spring swimming pool, an 18-hole golf course, and fine dining. Accommodations range from hotel rooms to cabins and fully equipped condominiums. Rooms $50 and up, cabins $69 and up, condos $125 and up.

Tamarack

Tamarack Resort (866-649-6903; www.tamarackidaho.com), west side of Lake Cascade, Tamarack 83615. A slew of upscale, mountainside accommodations include the Lodge at Osprey Meadows and cottage, chalet, townhome, and estate home rentals. The rustic wood and river rock lodge provides all the amenities of a full-service resort, including comfy rooms with great linens, great service, access to fine dining at Morel's Restaurant (see Where to Eat—Dining Out), a full-service spa, and a workout center, and the like. Packages $110 and up per person.

Warren

Burgdorf Hot Springs (208-636-3036), 30 miles north of McCall on Warren Wagon Road, Burgdorf 83318. This funky old remnant mining outpost has a hot springs pool and cabins for rent (see To Do—Hot Springs). Cabins $27 and up.

A HOT TUB AT TAMARACK RESORT STEAMS IN THE WINTER AIR.

James Foster

✳ Where to Eat

DINING OUT

McCall

Babblefish Restaurant (208-634-8188; www.milehighmarina.com), at the Mile High Marina, 1300 E. Lake St. Open for lunch and dinner daily. This is one of the few waterside dining options in McCall. Plus, it has an outdoor deck! Babblefish has great food, with dishes such as shrimp enchiladas, nori-wrapped ahi on Thai noodles, fresh Pacific oysters, grilled chicken, salads, and an extensive wine list.

Bistro 45 Wine Bar and Cafe (208-634-4515; www.bistro45mccall.com), 1101 N. Third St. Here they serve up some great casual, light bistro fare and have a fine selection of wines from which to choose. There is some great outdoor café seating, and often great local art adorns the walls.

The Narrows at the Whitetail Club (800-657-6464; www.white tailclub.com), 501 W. Lake St. Great service, white linen, and candlelight set the mood for a scrumptious array of fine gourmet fare, including dishes such as garden arugula salad with poached pear, Maytag blue cheese, toasted pine nuts, and balsamic vinaigrette; Idaho rainbow trout stuffed with braised fennel and preserved lemon and served with *pommes Parisian*, green beans Amandine, and caper brown butter. This is definitely a lovely place for a hot date!

Tamarack

Morels Restaurant (208-325-1013; www.tamarackidaho.com), at Tamarack Resort, west side of Lake Cascade. The resort has a handful of restaurants, including the upscale Morels—named for the coveted morel mushrooms found in Idaho forests—which serves scrumptious dishes such as almond-crusted baked Brie, Black Canyon Ranch elk mixed grill, and crème brûlée for dessert. The menu focuses of regional flavors and incorporates native fish and game.

EATING OUT

Donnelly

Buffalo Gal (208-325-8258), 319 N. Main St. Here you can get great New York–style deli food and organic produce.

McCall

Chapala Mexican Restaurant (208-635-3905; www.chapalarestaurants .com), 411 Lenora St. This casual eatery has south-of-the-border flavor.

Crusty's Pizza (208-634-5005; www .crustyspizzamccall.com), 315 Lenora St. Housed in a funky wooden house, this is a great spot to grab some pizza and a beer after skiing. Plus, they have great live entertainment once or more per week.

Lardo's Grill & Saloon (208-634-8191), 600 W. Lake St. Perhaps McCall's longest-standing business, Lardo's offers consistently good food with a fairly wide menu selection, including prime rib, salad, chicken, spaghetti, fettuccine, and the like.

McCall Brewing Company (208-634-3309), 807 N. Third St. This great microbrewery serves up brews with fun local names including Sesech Scotch (after the Secesh River and the Civil War secessionists for which the river was named), Mackinaw Red after the abundant fish that turns up in local waters, and Brundage Brown after the favorite local ski hill. With a great roof deck and an exterior that looks like a true western saloon, this is a fun place to go for happy hour.

Mill Steak & Spirits (208-634-7683; www.themillmccallidaho.com), 324 N. Third St. This old-school tavern has a nice wooden bar, decor that consists of old bikes and other interesting artifacts on the walls, and the largest collection of beer taps in the country. Known for its prime rib, this spot is a local favorite.

Panda Chinese Restaurant (208-634-2266), 317 E. Lake St. If you are looking for some ethnic food, try the Panda, overlooking the lake.

Romano's Italian Restaurant (208-634-4396), 203 E. Lake St. This is another casual eatery with ethnic flavor.

Steamers Steak & Seafood Restaurant (208-634-1411; www.steamersrestaurant.com), 308 Lake St. Try Steamers for steak and seafood.

New Meadows
Sagebrush BBQ Steakhouse and Saloon (208-347-2818), 210 Virginia St. They cook up some serious Texas-style barbecue here, including spicy, tender ribs smoked over a rotisserie-style roaster, charbroiled steaks, and thick hamburgers. Housed in an old western building and filled with ranching memorabilia, this place is an interesting slice of Idaho.

Riggins
Back Eddy Grill (208-628-9233), 533 N. Main St. This is a great little river-rat hangout where, after a good day of fishing or boating, you can kick your feet up on their outdoor patio, share river stories with friends, and enjoy a good burger, fries, and beverage.

Donnelly
Flight of Fancy Bakeshop (208-325-4432 or 800-634-6847; www.dessertjunkies.com), 282 N. Main St. This is a great place to fuel up with coffee and baked goodies on your way to ski at Tamarack.

McCall
Common Ground (208-634-2846), 303 E. Colorado St. Not only can you find great espresso, latte, and organic teas in this funky renovated cabin, but you can also buy a CD from the store's eclectic collection, check your e-mail, or catch some live music here on Fri. nights.

Moxie Java (208-634-3607), 312 W. Lake St. Like any funky little town, McCall has its great java shops, including Moxie, which is an Idaho institution.

✳ Cultural Offerings

THEATER
Starlight Mountain Theatre (208-462-5523; www.starlightmountaintheatre.com), 850 S. Middlefork Rd., Garden Valley. Season runs June–beginning of Sept. Tickets $7–22. This outdoor theater produces a series of summer "Broadway Musicals Under the Stars" that come with rave reviews. Recent productions include *Seven Brides for Seven Brothers*, *The Pirates of Penzance . . . Goes West*, Rodgers and Hammerstein's *State Fair*, and *Big River: The Adventures of Huckleberry Finn*. Nestled in the beautiful Boise Mountains, this is a relaxing venue in which to enjoy some theatrics. Be prepared for cool nighttime temperatures in the mountains.

❋ Selective Shopping

FLEA MARKETS

Cascade Flea Market (208-382-3049 or 208-382-3600), 1455 Main St. (ID 55), Cascade. Open 9–6 Fri.–Sun. Memorial Day–Labor Day; also two weeks starting July 4 weekend. Located by the Cascade Airport, this massive flea market features 25–35 dealers showcasing antiques, collectibles, Indian crafts and jewelry, and the like.

❋ Special Events

January–February: **McCall Winter Carnival** (800-260-5130; www.mccallwintercarnival.com), McCall. In its 40-something year, McCall Winter Carnival is Bacchanalian festivity at its best. Generally more than two dozen snow sculptures (and very impressive ones at that!) adorn the town and compete for the festival crown. A slew of crazy events include dogsledding demonstrations, dances, ice skating, parades, a Beard and Sexy Leg Contest (with categories that include Softest, Longest, Most Colorful, Ugliest, etc.), snowshoe golf, a wine festival, toboggan rides, a series of Idaho winter events, and more. There is more than enough fun to be had during this weeklong party.

June: **PBR Revival** (www.pbrkayak event.com), locations from Horseshoe Bend to Banks and Crouch and various nearby locales along Main, North, and South forks of Payette River. Okay, folks, this is not the Pabst Blue Ribbon festival, but instead a bad-ass weekend of loony kayaking events otherwise known as the Payette Boise River Revival Whitewater Event. Among other events are these: a night disco rodeo, where costumed (and partying) competitors perform river tricks; a series of kayak races for racers of varying abilities, with an Extreme race for expert kayakers on the North Fork Payette; and the Reel Paddling Film Festival, which features top-notch kayaking adventure films from around the globe. This is a great spectator event (or participatory one, if you are so inclined).

Seven Devils Playwrights Conference (www.sevendevils.org), McCall. At this annual invitation-only two-week development conference, selected applicants present fully staged readings and are encouraged to further develop their work.

July: **Brundage Mountain Bike Festival** (www.wildrockies.com), Brundage Mountain Resort. This killer weekend mountain bike event includes the Brundage Bomber Downhill Race and the Brundage Marathon Run. Camping is allowed on-site, and hot springs are nearby.

August: **Brundage Mountain Music Festival** (208-634-4151; www.brundage.com), Brundage Mountain Resort. $20 for adults. This weekend outdoor music event is a treat! With a great mountain venue, awesome bands, and camping on-site, it is a great way to spend a summer weekend. In addition to music, you'll find mountain biking, chairlift rides, kite flying, games, crafts, and food.

Council Mountain Music Festival (http://home.ctcweb.net/~dafisk/festival.html), Council. Lace up your dancing shoes for this weekend of bluegrass, folk, and jam music in the remote mountain setting of Council. There is plenty of camping in the area.

Payette Lake Classic Wooden Boat Show (208-869-3695), Payette Lake. In celebration of Idaho's heritage of boating, the Payette Lakes Chapter of the Antique and Classic Boat Society has started this annual weekend event that promotes the preservation and restoration of classic pleasure craft. Spectators can see more than 50 beautifully restored antique and classic wooden boats tooling around Payette Lake.

Yellow Pine Harmonica Contest (208-633-3300; www.harmonica contest.com), Yellow Pine. Free. Not quite 20 years old, this weekend event has turned sleepy little Yellow Pine into harmonica central, attracted hundreds of harmonica players and thousands of spectators each summer to listen to bluegrass, rock, blues, classical, traditional, and jazz music. Events include open jams, "Crowd Pleaser" competitions, and a street dance, along with plenty of food. Lace up your dancin' shoes, folks. There is plenty of camping nearby.

September: **Payette Lake Writer's Conference and Retreat** (208-315-2124; www.payettelakewriters.org), North Fork Lodge, 200 Scott St., McCall. This five-year-old event provides a weekend of workshops and intensive writing exercises that address topics such as memoir, screenplay writing, and crafting query letters.

BOISE: LIFE IN THE BIG CITY

Boise is not only Idaho's capitol but also the state's largest city (population 514,100), its cultural headquarters, and, like other towns in Idaho, a gateway to outdoor activities. Nestled at the base of the rolling Boise Foothills at the southern end of the Boise National Forest, with enough greenery to have earned it its name (*bois* is French for "forest or wood") and its own "river running through it"—the Boise River—the city itself is a playground, filled with committed backpackers, rafters, hikers, skiers, and anglers. With beautiful, historic neighborhoods such as the North End and Hyde Park; fabulous public parks including Julia Davis, Camel's Back Park, and a greenway running 10 miles along the river; and wonderful museums, Boise is a very walkable and livable city. While its downtown still possesses some architectural reminders of its cow-town past, it continues to evolve into a more bustling, sophisticated community with chic restaurants, art-house movie theaters, a thriving arts scene, and a weekend farmer's market. A symphony orchestra, an opera company, a ballet, and several theater companies bring great performing arts to this corner of Idaho.

Because of these great amenities, plus an active business community, Boise is one of the fastest-growing cities in the nation. In 2007, *Forbes* Magazine rated Boise the number-three metro area in its survey of Best Places for Business and Careers. Several major corporations are headquartered in the city, including Micron Technologies, Albertson's, Boise Cascade Corporation, the J. R. Simplot Company, and Washington Group International.

Just west of Boise, the Caldwell and Nampa area is becoming increasingly well known for its viticulture and award-winning wineries. Other outlying towns include Meridian, Eagle, and Parma—all linked to Boise by the Interstate 84 corridor. Despite Boise's urban flair, it doesn't take much to drive a small distance from downtown Boise and be catapulted back in time.

GUIDANCE

Boise Convention and Visitors Bureau (800-635-5240 or 208-344-7777; www.boise.org) 312 S. Ninth St., Ste. 100, Boise 83702.

Boise Metro Chamber of Commerce (208-472-5200; www.boisechamber .org), 250 S. Fifth St., Boise 83701.

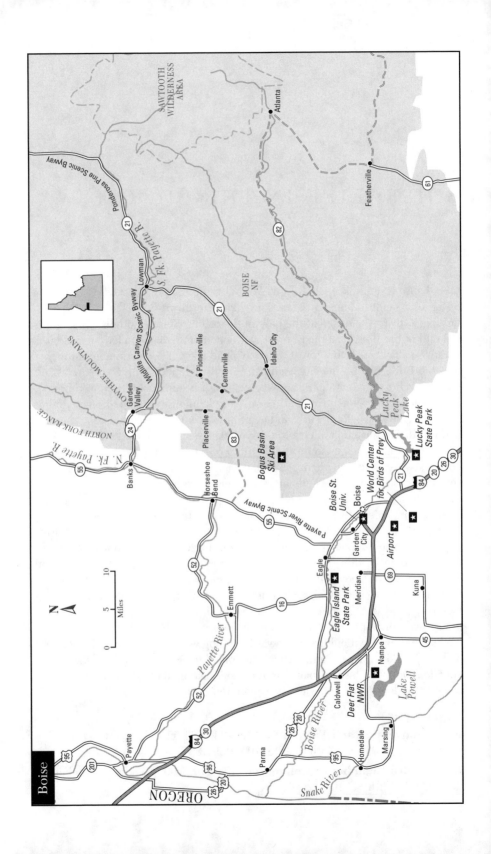

Caldwell Chamber of Commerce (208-459-7493; www.chamber.cityof
caldwell.com), 704 Blaine St., Caldwell 83606.

City of Boise (208-384-4422; www.cityofboise.org), 150 N. Capital Blvd., Boise
83702.

Downtown Boise Association (208-472-5251; www.downtownboise.org).

Meridian Chamber of Commerce (208-888-2817; www.meridianchamber
.com), 215 E. Franklin Rd., Meridian 83680.

Nampa Chamber of Commerce (208-466-4641; www.nampa.com), 312 13th
Ave. S., Nampa 83651.

GETTING THERE

By car
The main thoroughfare running through Boise is **Interstate 84**, which comes
west from just outside Salt Lake City, Utah, and continues on to Portland,
Oregon.

By air
Boise Air Terminal (Gowen Field; 208-383-3110; www.cityofboise.org/
departments/airport/), Boise. A slew or airlines offer service in and out of Boise
(see What's Where in Idaho). Many local hotels offer free shuttle service from
and to the airport. Rental cars companies at the airport include the usual (see
What's Where in Idaho).

By train
Amtrak (800-872-7245; www.amtrak.com) has train service to Salt Lake City,
Utah, and Portland, Oregon, along their Pacific Northwest line, then bus service
from these cities to Boise.

By bus
Greyhound Lines (800-231-2222; www.greyhound.com) provides connecting
service to Boise and a host of other Idaho cities from destinations throughout
the United States.

GETTING AROUND
Commuteride (208-345-7665, www.commuteride.com) is a good resource if
you are looking for information on commuter alternatives, including vanpooling,
carpooling, bus service, biking, and walking.

Taxi companies that can provide transportation to your final destination in
Boise include **A-1 Cab** (208-333-8333), **ABC Taxi** (208-344-4444). **All About
Town** (208-362-4540), **Black & White Cab** (208-371-5662), **Boise City Taxi**
(208-377-3333), and **Yellow Cab** (208-345-5555).

Valley Ride Bus Transportation (208-345-7433; www.valleyride.org) provides
public transportation within Boise.

MEDICAL EMERGENCIES
Intermountain Hospital (800-321-5984 or 208-377-8400; http://intermountain
hospital.com), 303 N. Allumbaugh St., Boise.

St. Alphonsus Regional Medical Center (208-367-2121; www.sarmc.org), 1055 N. Curtis Rd., Boise.

St. Luke's Boise Regional Medical Center (208-381-1200; www.stlukes online.org), 190 E. Bannock St., Boise.

✳ To See

CULTURAL SITES

With some deep roots in the arts—the Boise Arts Museum (see Museums) celebrated its 70th anniversary in 2007—Boise is coming into its own as a cultural mecca, and its art scene is bursting with great galleries, performance art, and outdoor and community art. As a growing and vibrant city, Boise is increasingly attracting an eclectic collection of immigrants seeking adventure, art, good jobs, and a great quality of life. Evidence of this high energy is seen throughout the city—as funky paintings by local artists adorning the walls of coffee shops, as creative flair in store window displays, and in a growing number of high-caliber galleries. In just walking around Boise's downtown core, you'll see plenty of artsy touches that will turn your eye.

IDAHO'S ANNE FRANK HUMAN RIGHTS MEMORIAL, BOISE

Matt Furber

PUBLIC ART ABOUNDS IN DOWNTOWN BOISE.

Boise City Arts Commission (208-433-5670; www.cityofboise.org) offers a free **Public Art Walking Tour** year-round, weather permitting, usually between 8 and 3 by request. Tours begin on the front steps of **Boise City Hall**, 150 N. Capitol Blvd. A map of the tour route is available online. These tours are meant to convey the history, stories, and symbolic meaning of 42 public art installations throughout the city. Public art abounds in Boise, and it can be found in some obscure spots.

Homage to the Pedestrian, on the Grove near Ninth Street. This interactive sculpture produces musical sounds when triggered by passing pedestrians. It is a locals' favorite!

A Ribbon of Hope, Boise Public Library, 715 S. Capitol Blvd. This mixed-media mural graces the library's lobby.

River of Trees, corner of Ninth and Idaho streets. Keep your eyes peeled, and you might see creative expressions in the form of bronze leaves and cast-iron tree grates embedded in the sidewalk.

FARMER'S MARKETS

Capital City Public Market and **Art in the Park,** Capital City Public Market, Eighth Street between Bannock Street and Grove Plaza. Held concurrently

9:30–1:30, Sat., mid-April through end of October. This farmer's and artist's market is truly fabulous. Grab a cup of joe and wander down to buy some great local and organic produce, beautiful flowers, and baked goods for breakfast. Don't be surprised if the *dinero* flows out of your wallet; there are some fabulous arts and crafts, including jewelry that will tempt even the most practical. Performance artists abound as well.

FOR FAMILIES

Discovery Center of Idaho (208-343-9895; www.scidaho.org), in Julia Davis Park, 131 Myrtle St.. Open 9–5 Tues.–Fri., 10–5 Sat., 12–5 Sun. $6.50 for adults, $5.50 for seniors, $4 for children, free for kids under two. This fun science center will entertain and inspire kids (of all ages!) with interactive exhibits and programs. Recent exhibits have included "Contraptions A to Z," which explores the history, art, and science of some of our often black-box but fascinating mechanisms, and "Gyro Rodeo," which offers a full-body experience with a gyroscope.

Zoo Boise (208-384-4260; www.cityofboise.org/Departments/Parks/ZooBoise/ index.aspx), 355 N. Julia Davis Dr. Open 10–5 daily. $6.25 for adults, $4 for seniors, $3.25 for children three years and older, free for children under three. If you like zoos (not all people do), Zoo Boise is home to some interesting critters, including penguins, a red panda, zebras, and ocelots (also known as the painted leopard).

GARDENS

Idaho Botanical Garden (208-343-8649; www.idahobotanicalgarden.com), Main Street and Warm Springs Road. Open 9–5 Mon.–Fri., 12–4 Sat.–Sun. This beautiful garden is spread over 30 acres of the former farm and nursery land for the Idaho State Penitentiary. The penitentiary closed its doors in 1973, leaving this property to lay dormant. In 1985, the Idaho Botanical Garden won a lease on the land and transformed an overgrown, rubble-filled site into the beautiful cultivated gardens that currently grace the property. A series of specialty gardens bursting with full, pink peonies, warm heirloom roses, swathes of yellow and purple herbs, woody species, and water features are a treat to the senses. Particularly soothing are the Meditation Garden and the Labyrinth. The garden hosts several events throughout the year, including summer concerts, Children's Literature Day, Oktoberfest, and Winter Garden Aglow. If this place doesn't inspire you to beef up on your own gardening skills, it will likely provide a relaxing pause in your day.

GHOST TOWNS

Atlanta (www.atlantaidaho.org), just shy of 100 miles east of Boise via 49 miles of rough, winding backcountry road off ID 21 at Idaho City. This tiny town with a boom-to-bust history, established in 1863 as a gold-mining site, was named in honor of the Civil War battle of Atlanta. Part of the townsite itself is on the National Register of Historic Places, and visitors can check out the Old Atlanta Jail, a historic log cabin, old photos of Atlanta and nearby Rocky Bar, a cemetery housing graves dating back to 1870, an old schoolhouse, and a natural hot spring.

MINING RELICS CAN BE FOUND IN MANY IDAHO GHOST TOWNS.

Centerville, Pioneerville, and **Placerville,** north of Idaho City off ID 83. These are other Boise Basin ghost towns.

Idaho City, 45 minutes northeast of Boise off ID 21 (Ponderosa Pine Scenic Byway). This is a living reminder of Idaho's boomtown days. In 1862, gold was discovered in the Boise Basin, and in no time flat, Idaho City became the largest gold-rush town in Idaho Territory, housing more than 250 businesses, including saloons, an opera house, tailors, drugstores, bake shops, and more. Like many of Idaho's boomtowns, Idaho City was replete with gunfights, prostitution, drunkards, and jailbirds. Over time, more than $250 million worth of gold was extracted from the Boise Basin, yet, like all good mining towns, Idaho City and others in the Boise Basin area eventually went bust; in the case of Idaho City, this was not only due to the ebb of mining pioneers leaving for better horizons, but also the result of a string of fires that devastated the community. Today's visitors can see some of the remaining brick buildings from this era, a mercantile, the old jail, an old schoolhouse, Pioneer Cemetery, and the Boise Basin Museum.

HISTORICAL SITES AND HOMES

Geothermal energy. Boise has an interesting history of geothermal use. In 1890, the Boise Water Works Company drilled an exploratory well about 2.5 miles east of Boise and, by 1891, had completed two geothermal wells. Soon thereafter, geothermal waters were used to heat the Boise Natatorium, a beautifully exotic, 15,000-square-foot structure with imposing Moorish towers and arches that enclosed a massive 65-foot-by-125-foot geothermal swimming pool (the structure no longer exists, but historical photos are cool). This water was also used to heat about 200 private residences in the Warm Springs district of Boise.

Boise continues to use its rich geothermal resource. Along with eight other downtown Boise buildings, the state capitol building (see below) is heated primarily by geothermal energy. The State of Idaho Capitol Mall geothermal system went online in 1982 and provides about 90 percent of the heating requirements of these nine buildings, saving the state somewhere on the order of $400,000 per year in averted fuel costs. The system consists of a 3,030-foot-deep production well (capable of flowing at more than 900 gallons per minute) that extracts 155-degree F groundwater, plus heat exchangers and underground delivery and collection pipes that circulate the water to warm the buildings, and a 2,150-foot-deep injection well to return the hot water back into the groundwater system.

This is not the only geothermal system pumping through the city. Other major geothermal users include the City of Boise, the Veterans Administration, and the Boise Warm Springs Water District, which collectively use about three times the resource used by the capitol system.

Fort Boise (208-722-5138), on US 20/26 in Parma, 43 miles west of Boise. Open 1–3 Fri.–Sun. June–Aug. Donations accepted. If you are interested in a little bit of Idaho history, Fort Boise is a good stop. Built by Thomas McKay in 1834 as a Hudson's Bay post, the fort is now on the National Register of Historic Places. It was originally intended as a fur-trading post but quickly changed its focus to serve the emigrants traveling on the Oregon Trail. During the nearly 20 years that it was open, the fort was staffed primarily by the Hawaiian people for whom the Owyhee Mountains and River were named. In 1854 the fort was destroyed by flood. Today, visitors see a replica 5 miles from the original fort in the small town of Parma.

Hyde Park (www.northend.org), N. 13th Street to Camel's Back Park in Boise Foothills. Lovely Hyde Park, in the heart of Boise's North End, is in its entirety on the National Register of Historic Places, both because of its historic structures and its "sub" urban retail character, unusual in a historic district. The area is filled with beautiful Craftsman bungalows, Victorian and Mission Revival homes, great eateries, and specialty shops. Check out the Web site above for more information, maps, and listings of restaurants, shops, and historic sites. A new bus route through Hyde Park is available from **Boise Urban Stage** (www .northend.org/busroute.htm); the Web site has a map of the route.

Idaho Anne Frank Human Rights Memorial (208-345-0304; www.idaho -humanrights.org/Memorial/memorial.html), 777 S. Eighth St. (on Greenbelt). This beautiful, serene tribute to the memory of Anne Frank (who, despite persecution by the Nazis in Germany, prevailed)—an open museum of sorts, built of sandstone and filled with benches, soothing water features, tablets inscribed with more than 60 inspirational quotations, and surrounded by roses and greenery—is a world-class memorial to human rights. In the beautiful words of the founding member of the Idaho Human Rights Education Center, Rev. Nancy S. Taylor, this memorial stands as a tribute to Anne Frank's "memory, as a warning to any who would dare trespass upon the freedom of others, and as an inspiration to all whose lives are devoted to love, respect, understanding, peace, and good will among the totality and diversity of the human family. May this memorial inspire each of us to contemplate the moral implications of our civic responsibilities." This is a contemplative place.

Idaho State Capitol (208-334-5174), 700 W. Jefferson St., Boise. Idaho's capitol is an impressive 201,720-square-foot sandstone building that soars 208 feet to the eagle atop its copper- and bronze-plated dome. The building is surrounded by expansive lawns and shaded by towering trees. Constructed of local sandstone from the Tablerock Quarry in east Boise using convict labor, the capitol building was completed in 1920 and cost taxpayers slightly more than $2 million. The building's interior is decked out with approximately 50,000 square feet of carvings in beautiful red marble from Georgia, gray marble from Alaska, green marble from Vermont, and black marble from Italy. The building is currently enduring an extensive face-lift (estimated at $35 million to 65 million) that is to include an overhaul of the building's heating, air conditioning, plumbing, and electrical systems and repairs to fragile *scagliola* (faux marble) laid by Italian artisans, light fixtures, doorknobs, legislative chamber furnishings, and exterior sandstone. Guided tours have been temporarily suspended until renovations are complete; however, it is still worth sauntering by to see the exterior and the capitol area.

Idaho State Penitentiary (208-334-2844; www.idahohistory.net/oldpen .html), 2445 Old Penitentiary Rd., Boise. Open 12–5 daily. $3–5. Opened as a

Laura Higdon

PEACENIKS GATHER AT THE IDAHO STATE CAPITOL.

single-cell jailhouse in 1870, over time Idaho Territory's penitentiary grew into a multibuilding complex surrounded by an imposing sandstone wall. Over the course of its centurylong history, the jail housed more than 13,000 convicts, including 215 women. After two riots in the early 1970s, the facility was closed in 1973. The site was then placed on the National Register of Historic Places. Visitors to the penitentiary can see a video that conveys the prison's history and provides a look at some of the more notorious prisoners and their daily lives. A tour of the facility takes you through the cellhouses, solitary confinement, death row, and the gallows. Not really a fun place.

North End (www.northend.org), between Boise River and Boise Foothills. Boise. Boise is an extremely walkable and bikable city. If you feel like ambling around, stroll through this charming tree-lined neighborhood filled with renovated Craftsman houses, wraparound porches, and gardens spilling with flowers, as well as funky little blocks with great coffeehouses, little restaurants, and serene green spaces in which to stretch your legs. Filled with historic homes and buildings, many of which are on the National Register of Historic Places, the North End is home to some of Boise's oldest and finest residences.

Boise Art Museum (208-345-8330; boiseartmuseum.org), 670 S. Julia Davis Dr. Open 10–5 Tues.–Sat., 1–8 Thurs., 12–5 Sun.; guided tours by appointment. $8 for adults, $6 for seniors and students, $4 for children grades 1–12; free first Thurs. each month. The Boise Art Museum houses an impressive permanent collection of more than 2,300 works focused on 20th-century American art, particularly art of the Pacific Northwest, American Realism, and ceramics. Museum exhibits include rotations of the permanent collection as well as tours of nationally renowned shows exploring the richness of modern art. The museum has recently expanded its facilities to total 34,800 square feet, much of which is dedicated to serene gallery space.

Idaho Black History Museum (208-433-0017; www.ibhm.org), in Julia Davis Park, 508 Julia Davis Dr. Open 11–4 Sat. and to groups by appointment. Free. Housed in the former Saint Paul Baptist Church building, one of the oldest buildings built by African Americans in Idaho, the Idaho Black History Museum is the only African American history museum in the Pacific Northwest. The museum's vision is to "provide a safe haven to explore the African American experience" and does so by focusing on African American history, art, and culture, with particular emphasis on Idaho.

Idaho State Historical Museum (208-334-2120; www.idahohistory.net/museum .html), 610 N. Julia Davis Dr. Open 9–5 Tues.–Sat. $2 for adults, $1 for children six–18, free for children under six. Founded in 1907, this museum is Idaho's largest and most visited. Museum artifacts provide a window on Idaho's history from prehistoric times through the present day, including instructive exhibits related to the fur trade, Idaho's gold rush, pioneer settlement, and Idaho's Native American, Chinese, and Basque populations.

WILDLIFE VIEWING

Peregrine Fund World Center for Birds of Prey (208-362-8687; www .peregrinefund.org), 5666 W. Flying Hawk La., 7 miles south of Boise. Open 9–5 daily Mar.–Oct.; 10–4 daily Nov.–Feb. $4 for adults, $3 for seniors, $2 for kids ages four–six, free for members and kids under four. Born out of concern that the endangered peregrine falcon might go extinct, the Peregrine Fund was founded in 1970 by Tom Cade, then a professor of ornithology at Cornell University. Over time, the fund has propagated and released peregrine falcons and bald eagles and has helped save the Mauritius kestrel from extinction. Their work with the peregrine falcon was instrumental in its removal from the endangered species List. The Velma Morrison Interpretive Center hosts a suite of innovative interactive exhibits, multimedia shows, original artwork, and, best of all, a slew of resident birds of prey. Exhibits are designed to instruct visitors about raptor biology and conservation science.

WINERY TOURS

Snake River Valley American Viticultural Area (AVA) was recently designated by the U.S. Alcohol and Tobacco Tax and Trade Bureau in recognition of the region's unique grape-growing conditions capable of producing excellent wines. Though the industry is fledgling—Idaho currently has about 18 wineries growing approximately 45 varieties of grape on 1,200 acres of vineyards—new wineries continue to emerge, and the industry continues to garner national and international awards and recognition. Many of these wineries are but a hop, skip, and a jump from Boise: just head southwest on I-84 out of Boise (yes, past the Roaring Springs Water Park and RV sales lots), and you will be on your way to Idaho's Wine Country. The picturesque hills along the Snake River sit on the same latitude as some of the finest vineyards in France. Warm days, cool nights, and fertile soil combine for the perfect recipe for healthy grapes. Visitors to the region enjoy the tours, wine tasting, and relaxation provided by some of the lovely vineyards and wineries that increasingly populate this area.

Idaho Grape Growers and Wine Producers Commission (208-455-8354; www.idahowines.org), 117 Ninth Ave., Ste. 2, Caldwell. Stop here for information on wineries in Caldwell.

Idaho Wineries and Vineyards (www.idahowine.org) is another good source of information for mapping out a wine tour. Wineries in the area include these:

Bitner Vineyards (208-454-0086; www.bitnervineyards.com), 16645 Plum Rd., Caldwell. Open 12–5 Sat.–Sun., Fri. by appointment.

Hells Canyon Winery (208-454-3300 or 800-318-7873; www.hellscanyonwinery .org), 18835 Symms Rd., Caldwell. Tours by appointment.

Indian Creek Winery (208-922-4791; www.indiancreekwinery.com), 1000 N. McDermott Rd., Kuna (on ID 69 east of Nampa). Open 12–5 Fri.–Sun. or by appointment.

Koenig Distillery and Winery (208-455-8386; www.koenigvineyards.com), 20928 Grape La., Caldwell. Open 12–5 Sat.–Sun. Apr.–Dec. or by appointment. At this 100-acre vineyard on the Snake River, Greg and Andy Koenig produce wine, fruit brandy, and potato vodka as part of family tradition. The vineyard's tasting room has a gorgeous view of the valley and surrounding farms.

Ste. Chapelle Winery (208-453-7843 or 877-783-2427; www.stechapelle.com), 19348 Lowell Rd., Caldwell. Open 10–5 Mon.–Sat., 12–5 Sun. Ste. Chapelle has become increasingly well known for its award-winning wines, which are distributed throughout the country. Perched on a hill above the Snake River and rolling wine country, this lovely vineyard is a fabulous spot to listen to the jazz concerts performed here during the summer and to indulge in wine tasting throughout the year.

Sawtooth Winery (208-467-1200; www.sawtoothwinery.com), 13750 Surrey La., Nampa. Open 12–5 Fri.–Sun. or by appointment.

✳ To Do

BOATING

Despite being a desert state, Idaho has more than 2,000 natural lakes and 240,000 acres of reservoirs, providing plenty of water for boating.

Deer Flat National Wildlife Refuge (208-467-9278; www.fws.gov/deerflat), south on ID 55 from Nampa to Lake Lowell exit (30-minute drive from Boise).

One of the oldest in the National Wildlife Refuge system, this is also a popular spot for boating on 9,000-acre Lake Lowell. See also Wildlife Viewing.

Lucky Peak Reservoir, out Warm Springs Road (ID 21), then east on FR 268. This reservoir on the Boise River is a short and pretty drive from downtown Boise. Steep, sheltered canyon walls provide mirror-flat water for great water-skiing and boating. The 2,820-acre reservoir has a Forest Service boat ramp at Mack's Creek at the upstream end of the reservoir. The reservoir has great fishing, but please note that the threatened bull trout, which inhabit these waters, must be released unharmed immediately if they are caught. For more information, contact the **Mountain Home Ranger District** (208-587-7961) or **Idaho Fish and Game Southwest Region** (208-465-8465) in Nampa.

CAMPING

Boise National Forest headquarters (208-373-4100; www.fs.fed.us/r4/boise), 1249 S. Vinnell Wy., Ste. 200, Boise. Within miles of the city proper, there are 2.6 million acres of forest, including more than a half million acres of old-growth forest and 80 developed campgrounds. If you are looking to get out of Dodge, this is a great escape for city dwellers. A diverse landscape of steep mountains, tumbling rivers, dense fir and pine forests, hot springs, and arid sagebrush comprises the Boise National Forest. About 1,300 miles of multiuse trails traverse the forest. Campsites are usually available on arrival, but reserving a site ahead of time is a good idea. Contact headquarters for more information on the forest and camping options.

FISHING

Idaho is renowned for its fishing. Contact **Idaho Fish and Game** (800-554-8685; www.fishandgame.idaho.gov) for information on fishing regulations and required licenses. Some world-famous fishing spots are within reach of Boise:

Boise Greenbelt provides access at several points on the river. Popular fishing areas (from east to west) include Barber Park, the University stretch between Broadway and Capitol boulevards, and Eagle Island. Rainbow trout predominate on the eastern side of town, while the number of brown trout increases as you move west and the river temperature warms.

Boise River, right in downtown Boise, is no exception. You can literally stand in the Boise River, holding a hot latte just purchased at a nearby java shop and catch a brown trout on a fly.

Silver Creek is 2 hours from town (see Central Idaho: An Explorer's Nirvana, Ketchum, Sun Valley, and the Sawtooths: America's Shangri-La).

South Fork and **Henrys Fork of the Snake River** are both about 4.5 hours away, and **Yellowstone National Park** is 6 hours from town (see Southeastern Idaho: The Simple Pleasures, Teton Basin, Swan Valley, and Henrys Fork Country: Gateway to Yellowstone).

Outfitters
Idaho Angler (208-787-9957; www.idahoangler.com), 1682 S. Vista Ave., Boise. This is an incredible resources for flies, advice, and classes.

River Keeper Fly Shop (208-344-3838; www.riverkeeperflyshop.com), 1224 Broadway Ave., Boise. This is another great shop.

GOLF

Crane Creek Country Club (208-344-6529; www.cranecreekcountryclub .com), 500 W. Curling Dr., Boise. This private equity course 2 miles from the center of Boise has 18 holes over 6,594 yards with par 71.

Pierce Park Greens (208-853-3302; www.pierceparkgreens.com), 5812 N. Pierce Park, Boise (4 miles from center of Boise). This public course has nine holes of golf over 900 yards with par 27.

Quail Hollow Golf Club (208-344-7807; www.quailhollowgolfclub.com), 4520 N. 36th St., Boise. This public course is 2 miles from the center of Boise.

Warm Springs Golf Course (208-343-5661), 2495 Warm Springs Ave., Boise. This public course is located 3 miles from the center of Boise.

HIKING

Boise is a haven for outdoorsy urbanites, who find quick access to the expansive Boise foothills for hiking, walking, and romping with their dog. These rolling, tawny hills at the foot of the Boise Mountains rise up along the city's northeastern boundary, providing easy access to miles upon miles of open space and buffed-out trails for hiking and playing. A handful of city parks provide entrée to the hills, each with its own system of trails. **Ridge to Rivers** (www.ridgetorivers

FISHING IS POPULAR IN AND AROUND BOISE.

Chris Pilaro

.org) has a comprehensive map of all the trail systems in the foothills. **Boise Parks and Recreation Department** (208-384-4486; www.cityofboise.org) is also a good resource. Many of these trail systems are shared use, so read the signs and follow the rules. Check out the trails in these areas:

Camel's Back Reserve: see Wilder Places—Nature Preserves.

Castle Rock and Table Rock reserves, 451 N. Quarry View Pl.

Military Reserve, 750 Mountain Cove Rd.

Oregon Trail Reserve, 4500 E. Lake Fork Dr.

For more serious hikes, check out the **Boise National Forest**, home to the Boise Mountains (see Wilder Places—National Forests).

ICE SKATING

Idaho Ice World (208-331-0044), 7072 S. Eisenman Rd. Winters in Boise aren't consistently cold enough to support outdoor rinks, but this indoor ice rink offers public skating sessions and ice-skating lessons.

MOUNTAIN BIKING

Many fanatical mountain bikers call Boise home, and many people use a bike as their main form of transportation. Extensive, buffed-out mountain biking trails throughout the Boise foothills (see Hiking) are renowned for their diversity, extent, and proximity to town, with more than 80 miles of single track spanning elevations from 5,000 feet at the valley floor to 7,600 feet at the summit of Bogus Basin Ski Area.

Schaffer Butte Trail System, Bogus Basin ski resort, on Bogus Basin Road 14 miles northeast of Boise. There is a fairly extensive network of trails in and around the Boise National Forest.

Recommended Reading

For a full listing of trail descriptions, check out *Mountain Biking Boise* by Margin Potucek (FalconGuide, 1998) and *Mountain Biking in Boise* by Stephen Stuebner (Boise Front Adventures, 2002), both of which offer complete driving directions, difficulty ratings, and full trail descriptions for 40 trails in the area.

Rentals

Countless bike shops in Boise can answer questions, give advice (and sell you some gear!).

Idaho Mountain Touring (208-336-3854), 1310 Main St.

Moo Cycles (208-336-5229), in Hyde Park, 1517½ N. 13th St.

Screamin' Toads Cycles (208-367-1899), 3115 N. State St.

World Cycle (208-343-9130), 180 N. Eighth St.

SKIING

Bogus Basin Mountain Resort (208-332-5100; www.bogusbasin.org), 2600 Bogus Basin Rd.; 16 miles from downtown Boise. 10-10 Mon.–Fri., 9–10 weekends and holidays. Full day $46 for adults, $20 for children seven to 11, free for children six and under. Half day $35 for adults, $20 for children. Night only $20.

While this fabulous hometown alpine and Nordic ski resort can be fairly crowded on weekends, weekday skiers can usually ski right onto the lift and do groomer laps or jump into the trees for some great powder skiing. With annual snowfall of about 250 inches, Bogus can get its powder dumps, but it can also be lean. With limited snowmaking capacity, the lack of snow can be an issue at times. The mountain also has night skiing for hard-core Boiseites looking to catch a few turns after work. Nordies enjoy the Frontier Point Nordic Lodge and 23 miles of great groomed cross-country trails winding through evergreen stands and varying terrain. During the summer, Bogus Basin is open for mountain biking and special events. Accommodations are available on-site at Pioneer Condominiums.

WHITE-WATER KAYAKING AND RAFTING

World-class white-water kayaking and rafting can be found not far from Boise; as a result, the city has garnered a formidable collection of weekend white-water warriors.

Payette River, which provides for some serious white-water boating, is an easy drive up ID 55 north of Boise (see McCall and the Payette River Mountain Region: Sun and Fun).

South Fork of the Boise River also provides for a popular class II–III float through a basalt canyon. A popular float, particularly for families, is the 4-hour stretch of the Boise River that starts at Barber Park out Warm Springs Road and ends in Julia Davis Park downtown. This easy run can be floated in an inner tube on a Sat. afternoon. The wooded views along the way are quite soothing.

Outfitters

Boise River Tours (208-333-0003; www.boiserivertours.com). Trips on the Boise River.

Cascade Outfitters (208-322-4411 or 800-223-7238; www.cascadeoutfitters .com), 604 E. 45th St. They can provide information on white-water boating in the area.

Idaho River Sports (208-336-4844; www.idahoriversports.com), 3100 W. Pleasanton Ave.

Inland Surf Company (208-336-3282; www.inlandsurfcompany.com), 4113 W. State St.

WILDLIFE VIEWING

Deer Flat National Wildlife Refuge (208-467-9278; www.fws.gov/deerflat), south on ID 55 from Nampa to Lake Lowell exit (30-minute drive from Boise). Founded by President Theodore Roosevelt in 1909, this refuge is one of the oldest in the National Wildlife Refuge system and a great spot for wildlife watching and boating. With more than 10,000 acres of habitat, it is an important breeding area for birds and mammals and a significant resting and wintering area for birds migrating along the Pacific Flyway. Staggering numbers of Canada geese and mallards can be seen gathered along the shores of the 9,000-acre Lake Lowell. Since 1950, more than 250 bird species have been observed, including loons, pelicans, eagles, hawks, ospreys, cranes, plovers, doves, owls, finches, and more.

NATIONAL FORESTS

Boise National Forest (208-373-4100; www.fs.fed.us/r4/boise), more than 2.6 million acres just north and east of Boise to the Payette National Forest near Lake Cascade. The high-country conifer forest and shrubland encompass the Boise Mountains (elevations to 10,124 feet at the summit of Two Point Mountain), drainages of the Boise and Payette rivers and the South and Middle forks of the Salmon River (totaling more than 7,600 river miles), and more than 250 lakes and reservoirs. Abundant fish, including trout, salmon, and steelhead, inhabit the waters of the forest. More than 1,300 miles of summer trails and 70 campgrounds make this a worthy playground! Most of the area lies within the **Idaho Batholith** (see What's Where in Idaho—Geology). The forest is home to a newly discovered species, the rare Sacajawea's bitterroot (*Lewisia saca-jaweana*), which grows only in central Idaho. About 75 percent of the known two dozen populations of this low-growing succulent, with its delicate snowy-white flowers, are found in the Boise National Forest. Large expanses of summer range attract big-game species such as Rocky Mountain elk and mule deer.

Lucky Peak Nursery (208-343-1977), which grows about 5 million trees on 60 acres for replanting in national forests in southern Idaho, Utah, Nevada, Arizona, New Mexico, and western Wyoming, is located in the Boise National Forest. The nursery offers school tours 10–12 Mon.–Fri. Apr.–June; reservations required.

NATURE PRESERVES

Boise River Greenbelt (www.northend.org/greenbeltmap.htm), 10 miles along Boise River. This great recreational spot connects a series of green spaces along the river. A map of the greenbelt can be found at the Web site.

Camel's Back Reserve, directly behind Camel's Back Park (see Parks). These 63 acres of the rolling Boise Foothills are traversed by a network of about 97 miles worth of hiking and biking trails. This is a great spot to mountain bike, walk your dog, or go for a hike, all within city limits! For a map of the trail system, check out **Ridge to Rivers** (www.ridgetorivers.org).

PARKS

Camel's Back Park, 1200 W. Heron St.; northeast corner of 13th and W. Heron streets. At the far end of Hyde Park lies Boise's playground in the foothills. The park site, acquired by the city in 1932, spans approximately 11 acres. Facilities include green space, a playground, playing fields, tennis courts, and a picnic area. Tennis courts can be reserved by calling **Boise Parks and Recreation** (208-384-4486).

Eagle Island State Park (http://parksandrecreation.idaho.gov), on ID 44 just west of Eagle. This 545-acre day-use park on the Boise River has picnicking, swimming, and fishing about 8 miles west of Boise.

Julia Davis Park, 700 S. Capitol Blvd., near downtown Boise. This nearly 90-acre regional park is a gateway into the heart of the city, housing many of Boise's cultural destinations, such as Boise Art Museum, the lovely Julia Davis Rose Garden, Zoo Boise, the Idaho Black History Museum, the Discovery Center of Idaho, Idaho Anne Frank Human Rights Memorial, and Idaho State Historical Museum. Public art adorns the walkways through this beautiful green space. Visitors also enjoy the riverwalk, bandshell, tennis courts, and playground. Some 43 acres of the park were donated to the city by Thomas Davis in 1907 in memory of his wife, Julia.

Lucky Peak State Park (208-334-2432; http://parksandrecreation.idaho.gov), 10 miles east of Boise off ID 21. Open sunrise–sunset year-round. This park surrounding Lucky Peak Reservoir is a popular spot to picnic, camp, hike, swim, and fish. Lakeside access includes two boat ramps, parking, a full-service marina, on-site boat rentals, and a convenience store. Five **backcountry yurts** (866-634-3246) are available for rent ($75–90 for up to six people).

✳ Lodging

Boise has long been a stopping point for travelers road-tripping west. As a result, the city has nearly 5,000 hotel rooms and a dizzying array of lodging options ranging from mountain inns to hip boutique hotels. There are quite a few lodging options in downtown Boise.

BED & BREAKFASTS
Idaho Heritage Inn (208-342-8055; www.idheritageinn.com), 109 W. Idaho St. 83702. This is one of Boise's cozy bed & breakfast inns, a former governor's mansion.

J. J. Shaw House Bed-and-Breakfast Inn (208-344-8899; www.jjshaw.com), 1411 W. Franklin. 83702. This inn is in the North End.

CONDOS
Pioneer Condominiums (208-332-5200; www.pioneercondos.com), 1770 W. State St., Ste. 394. 83702. About 16 miles from downtown Boise, but feeling much farther away, these condos offer ski-in, ski-out access to Bogus Basin Ski Area and easy access to trails for hikers and mountain bikers.

HOTELS
Grove Hotel (208-333-8000; www.grovehotelboise.com), 245 S. Capitol Blvd. 83702. This large and luxurious hotel is a popular convention venue. It is connected to the Qwest Arena, which hosts Idaho Stampede NBA development league basketball games, concerts, and bizarre monster truck events.

Hotel 43 (208-342-4622; www.hotel43.com), 981 Grove St. 83702. This refurbished boutique hotel in the Linen District is within easy walking distance of the Grove. It has a steakhouse, martini bar, and fashionable modern decor.

Modern Hotel (208-424-8244; www.themodernhotel.com), 1314 W. Grove St. 83702. Once a 1960s TraveLodge, the Modern Hotel now boasts that they are "where style lives." Style aficionados should check it out; hipsters will feel welcomed by the late-century style and the molded-wood martini bar.

Owyhee Plaza Hotel (208-343-4611; www.owyheeplaza.com), 1109 Main St. 83702. Boise's oldest hotel is where performer Will Rogers once set up camp. This 90-year-old hotel offers modern conveniences, including 11 meeting and banquet rooms, while retaining some of its historic charm.

MOTELS

Of course, run-of-the-mill, chainlike hotels abound too. A slew of hotels can be found near Boise Town Square Mall.

AmeriSuites Hotel (208-375-1200 or 800-833-1516), 925 N. Milwaukee St. 83704.

Cavanaughs Parkcenter Suites (208-342-1044), 424 E. Parkcenter Blvd. 83706. Cavanaughs is along the Greenbelt.

Doubletree Club Parkcenter (208-345-2002), 475 W. Parkcenter Blvd. 83706.

Holiday Inn Boise (208-344-8365), 3300 S. Vista Ave. 83705. This is in a fairly bleak but convenient area near the airport. The Holiday Inn boasts the Holidome—a pool, arcade, and fitness center.

Plaza Suite Hotel (208-375-7666), 409 S. Cole Rd. 83709. This hotel is near Boise Town Square Mall.

Shilo Inn Airport (208-343-7662; www.shiloinns.com), 4111 Broadway Ave. 83705. This is also near the airport.

Shilo Inn Riverside (208-344-3521; www.shiloinns.com), 3031 Main St. 83702. This nicer-than-average chain hotel near the Boise River connects to the Greenbelt and boasts an atrium-style indoor pool, spa, and fitness room.

✳ Where to Eat

Boise proper has a wealth of great dining options, and you might be just as happy to go for stroll around the downtown area or Hyde Park, both of which are home to a slew of restaurants, and see what strikes your fancy. However, if you want to know before you go, here is a smattering of your options.

DINING OUT

Boise

Berryhill & Co. Wine Bar and Café (208-387-3553; www.berry hillandco.com), 2170 Broadway Ave. Open for lunch Mon.–Fri., dinner Tues.–Sat. This lovely, fine-dining establishment started as a catering company (which they still are) but has expanded and now has a small restaurant space downtown. They specialize in Northwest cuisine, infused with flavors from around the globe. The ambience is great.

Bungalow (208-331-9855), 1520 N. 13th St. Bungalow has a fabulous menu, filled with creative dishes made of diverse, fresh ingredients, such as wild Alaskan halibut with Gorgonzola risotto cake, roast tomatoes, and confit of leeks; butternut squash ravioli in browned butter with fried sage; and stuffed portobello mushroom sandwich. They also have a full vegetarian menu and a great wine selection.

Chandlers Steakhouse Boise (208-383-4300), 981 W. Grove St. Open for dinner. Located in the lobby of Hotel 43, this well-known fine-dining establishment specializes in innovative American-style cuisine, made with first-class prime steaks, fresh seafood, and other fine ingredients. It also has a great martini bar and wine list.

Milky Way (208-343-4334; www .milkywayboise.com), 205 10th St.

Open for lunch Mon.–Fri., dinner Mon.–Sat. This chic restaurant with a good view of the streetscape serves fancy comfort food and has been ranked the Best of Boise by locals.

Pair (208-343-7034), 601 W. Main St. Open for dinner daily. This newish addition to the Boise bar scene has made quite a splash. With a chic party ambience and plenty of people watching to be done (both in the restaurant and through the looking glass), you might feel like you're in Manhattan. Fab food includes antipasto, Asian salad, chicken with polenta, or lamb. Party drinks run the gamut from the Dame Taylor—a lavender-infused vodka drink—to the Grapefruitini and the Sin Chocolat.

EATING OUT

Boise

Aladdin Traditional Egyptian Cuisine (208-368-0880), 111 Broadway Ave., Ste. 115. Open for lunch Mon.–Thurs., dinner daily. You might not expect great Egyptian cuisine in Boise, but here it is. The menu varies, taking advantage of in-season produce to serve up flavorful cuisine including baba ghanoush, grape leaves stuffed with rice and fresh herbs, and fabulous flatbreads. Occasional belly dancers complete the scene.

Angell's Bar & Grill (208-342-4900; www.angellsbarandgrill.com), Ninth Avenue and Main Street. Open for lunch Tues.–Fri., dinner Mon.–Sun. Angell's is conveniently located downtown. The food is not inexpensive (dinner entrées are all more than $20), but it's the kind of place where almost all eaters, even the pickiest, will find something appetizing.

Bardenay Restaurant and Distillery (208-426-0538; www.bardenay .com), 610 Grove St. Open for lunch and dinner. Located in the Basque area of Boise, this is a great spot for martinis and appetizers. They distill their own vodka, rum, and gin and have a good, diverse menu.

Bar Gernika (208-344-2175), 202 S. Capitol Blvd. Open for lunch and dinner Mon.–Sat. This centerpiece of the Basque Block is a favorite hangout and one of the few places you can get traditional Basque meals. Great grub, super service, and friendly folks.

Bittercreek Ale House (208-345-1213; www.bittercreekalehouse.com), 246 N. Eighth St. Open for lunch and dinner daily. This place is a big bar right downtown that serves up a variety of Northwest microbrewery beers and solid bar food.

Brick Oven Bistro (208-342-3456), 801 Main St. Open for lunch and dinner daily. This authentic, casual restaurant serving great food has been an icon of the Boise culinary landscape for more than 20 years. They serve a range of fabulous deli food, including large, open-faced hot sandwiches with sirloin, wild rice meat loaf, Yankee pot roast, large, fresh specialty salads, and to-die-for desserts.

Cazba (208-381-0222; www.cazba .com), 211 N. Eighth St. Cazba is one of the few places in Idaho to get wonderful Mediterranean food, including shish kebobs, gyros, and wraps. Their pita bread is imported from the country's top pita baker. The restaurant has won acclaim as Best of Boise for ethnic food. The restaurant is connected to **Opas** (213 N. Eighth St.), a sultry cocktail lounge.

Cottonwood Grille (208-333-9800; www.cottonwoodgrille.com), 913 W.

River St. Open for lunch, dinner, and Sun. brunch. Northwest cuisine by the side of the Boise River; this is the perfect place to take your mom for brunch.

Donnie Mac's Trailer Park Cuisine (208-384-9008), 1515 W. Grove St. Open for lunch Mon.–Fri., dinner daily. Yes, the theme of this funky diner is "trailer trash," complete with a bar made of old Ford tailgates, seating for four in a rusty old sedan, privacy shower curtains, fake grass, and a Confederate flag in the window, all evoking the feeling of a "desert roadside café." The place is actually quite fun and serves some great greasy-spoon food, including Couch Potato Fries, a Double Wide Burger, and a Worse Burger. Breakfast includes the hearty Trailer Park Breakfast (two eggs, bacon or sausage, homefries, and toast) or, for the faint of heart (or the smart), a bowl of oatmeal with fruit. The awesome espresso is a twist.

Eighth Street Wine Company (208-426-WINE), 405 S. Eighth St. One of Boise's newest restaurants, the Wine Company offers an eclectic menu of dishes such as ginger melon soup, coco rice, Lebanese salad, chicken pot pie, and Bangkok shrimp noodles. They also have a great selection of cocktails.

Falcon Tavern (208-947-3111), 780 W. Idaho St. This downtown pub serves great tavern food and beer in a friendly pub atmosphere. The salads are definitely a hot item.

Flying Pie Pizzeria (208-345-0000; www.flyingpie.com), 6508 Fairview Ave.; (208-384-0000), 4320 State St. Open for lunch and dinner daily. Flying Pie Pizzeria is a favorite Boise establishment.

Goldy's Breakfast Bistro (208-345-4100), Capitol and Main streets. This Boise institution serves up award-winning breakfast in a funky atmosphere. Menu items such as sweet potato hash browns; heaping piles of tasty, fresh toast stuffed with walnuts, brown sugar, and bananas; and chicken fried steak make this popular spot worth the wait. They also have an espresso bar.

Guido's NY Style Pizzeria (208-345-9011), Fifth Avenue and Idaho Street. This pizza place makes a great slice of pie and might make you think you are in New York.

Happy Fish Sushi and Martini Bar (208-343-4810), Eighth Avenue and Myrtle Street. This part of the city is called BoDo (Boise Downtown—get it?). Despite the silly name, the area has several good restaurants and shops. Happy Fish has a hip bar and serves good sushi.

Highlands Hollow Brewhouse (208-343-6820), 2455 Harrison Hollow La. Here, they serve inexpensive but tasty food and great beer. People rave about the "mess-o-chops."

KB's Burritos (208-336-3390), 405 S. Capitol Blvd. For quick but really solid Mexican food on the fly, check out KBs. Try their R&B Salad and their fish tacos.

Lucky 13 Pizza (208-344-6967), 1609 N. 13th St. In the heart of Hyde Park, this fun local hangout started as a gas station many years ago. With whimsically named pizzas including the Zucchini Meanie, Intergalactic-Super-Fantastic Moon Pie, and Pie Alpha Feta, you are sure to be amused, if nothing else. Don't be surprised if you love the food and the microbrews, too!

Mai Thai (208-344-8424; www
.maithaiboise.com), 750 W. Idaho.
This place serves really good Thai
food in a pretty atmosphere (including running water features). This is a
nice spot for a date.

Proto Pizza (208-331-1400), 345 S.
Eighth St. Open for lunch and dinner
daily. This is one of the few places in
Idaho to get Neapolitan pizza (crispy,
thin crust from a wood-fired oven).

Tablerock Brew Pub (208-342-
0944; www.tablerockbrewpub.com),
705 Fulton St. One of Boise's original
brewpubs, they were voted Boise's
Best Beer seven years in a row. They
offer a diverse and inexpensive menu,
including burgers, salads, steak, and
salmon.

Taste (208-336-5122), 1530 N. 13th
Ave. Open for lunch and dinner daily.
This hip spot serves great sushi made
with high-quality, fresh ingredients
and presented as works of art. Cold
sake and great wine top off a fabulous
meal.

✳ Cultural Offerings

ART GALLERIES

You can easily spend an inspiring day
wandering around Boise's great art
galleries—and making a stop or two
for a latte along the way: many Boise
coffee shops also display art.

First Thursdays, downtown Boise.
Held 5–9 first Thurs. each month.
Throughout the year, downtown Boise
gears up for special events, wine and
cheese, and in-store entertainment at
the shops and art galleries in the area.
Free trolley service is provided. Here
are some of the venues:

Art Source Gallery (208-331-3374;
www.artsourcegallery.com), 1015 W.
Main St. This cooperatively owned
gallery is run by 40 local artists.

Basement Gallery (208-333-0309),
928 W. Main St.

Blue Sky Bagels (208-855-9113),
3161 E. Fairview Ave., Ste. 150. This
java shop often exhibits local art.

Boise Art Glass Studios (208-345-
1825, boiseartglass.com), 530 W. Myrtle St. The studio showcases the work
of creative glassblowers within the
cooperative and also offers classes.

Brown's Gallery (208-342-6661 or
888-342-6661; www.brownsgallery
.com), 1022 W. Main St. One of
Boise's oldest galleries features work
of local and international artists.

Flying M Coffeehouse (208-345-
4320), 500 W. Idaho St. In addition to
providing the best coffee in town, this
coffeehouse is a great supporter of
local artists; the funky gift shop is fun
too.

Gallery at Hyde Park (208-345-
6380), 1613 N. 13th St.

J Crist Gallery (208-336-2671;
www.jcrist.com), 223 S. 17th St. One
of Boise's premier galleries, the J Crist
Gallery is gaining national and international recognition for innovative
exhibits of works produced by contemporary Idaho and Northwest artists.

Lisk Gallery (208-342-3773; www
.liskstudio.com), 850 Main St. The
Photographs and fabulous acrylic on
burnished stainless steel by Jerri and
Mark Lisk are on display here.

Stewart Gallery (208-433-0593;
www.stewartgallery.com), 2212 W.
Main St. This renowned gallery represents contemporary art by nationally
and internationally established and
emerging artists, focusing on painting
and works on paper.

Visual Arts Center (208-426-3994; www.boisestate.edu/art), on Boise State University campus, 1910 University Dr. Here, the work of students, faculty, visiting artists, and more are showcased.

DANCE

Ballet Idaho (208-343-0556; www .balletidaho.com), Ninth and Myrtle. A professional ballet company presents a diverse mix of classical and contemporary performances that have garnered both local and national acclaim.

MUSIC

It would be possible to spend almost every day of the week during the summer enjoying free music and events in Boise.

Alive After Five Summer Concert Series (208-385-7300; www.down townboise.org), Grove Plaza, downtown. Held 5–8 PM Wed. in summer. Free. A summer's worth of fabulous free entertainment is really a great public event that adds to Boise's vibrant downtown scene. Vendor and food booths sell goodies on-site.

Boise Philharmonic (208-344-7849; www.boisephilharmonic.org), 516 S. Ninth St. Sept.–May. Musically Speaking Pre-Concert talks provide historical context to the work, some insight into the lives of the composers, and fun facts about the music.

Great Garden Escape Concerts (208-343-8649; www.idahobotanical garden.com), Idaho Botanical Garden, 2355 N. Penitentiary Rd. Held at 6 or 6:30 PM Thurs. $9 for nonmembers, $7 for members. This fabulous summer concert series features an array of artists and styles, including bluegrass, jazz, country, rock, and

more, all in a serene garden setting. Bring a blanket, a picnic, and friends, and you're all set. Food is also sold on-site.

Opera Idaho (208-345-3531; www .operaidaho.org), Morrison Center, Boise State University campus. Grand opera of the highest possible professional standard includes productions such as *La Bohème* and *Elixir of Love*. The company also produces special events at the Idaho Botanical Garden and the Egyptian Theater.

THEATER

Boise Contemporary Theater (208-331-9224; www.bctheater.org), 854 Fulton St. This company presents a wide variety of edgier off-Broadway and comedy performances.

Idaho Shakespeare Festival (208-429-9908; www.idahoshakespeare .org), 5657 Warm Springs Ave. Attending this Shakespeare festival in a great outdoor amphitheater along the Boise River is a popular summer pastime. Each summer, this theater company presents a handful of classic plays. Recent productions have included *Hay Fever*, *The Little Tempest*, *Arsenic and Old Lace*, *Measure for Measure*, and *Little Shop of Horrors*. Pack a picnic and enjoy the show. Tickets often sell out, so it's worth calling ahead.

✳ Entertainment

FILM

Edwards 21 (208-338-3821; www .boiseonlinemall.com/storeframe .php?ID=61), 760 Broad St.; in BoDo district. Head to this brand-new theater if you're looking to kick back in stadium seating and view a blockbuster.

Egyptian Theater (208-387-1273; www.egyptiantheatre.net), 700 W. Main St. This historic theater often hosts big concerts, film festivals, and other events, but it's also possible to cozy down in the meticulously restored 1920s theater—amid sphinxes and gold-painted mummies—watch a movie, and eat popcorn at one of downtown Boise's two best movie houses.

Flix (208-342-4222; www.theflix boise.com), 646 Fulton St. This art house theater has a great snack bar. They tend to air the newest in alternative films and more eclectic movies, the likes of which you won't find at Blockbuster.

PROFESSIONAL SPORTS

Boise Hawks (208-322-5000; www .boisehawks.com), Memorial Stadium, 5600 Glenwood St. (about 5 miles outside of downtown). During the summer, fans flock to watch Boise's own minor league baseball team, the Boise Hawks.

Bronco Football (208-462-4737; www.broncosports.com), Bronco Stadium, 1400 Bronco La. While Boise State University's Broncos gained national notoriety after winning the Fiesta Bowl, fanaticism was nothing new to the their loyal Idaho fan base. One look at the number of Broncos sweatshirts worn around town will tell you all you need to know. Fans kick off the season with the **Bronco Bodo Block Party** (208-338-5599) in late Aug. and keep tailgating throughout the season.

✳ Selective Shopping

FODD

Boise Coop (208-472-4500; www .boisecoop.com), 888 W. Fort St.

Open 9–6 Mon.–Sat., 9–8 Sun. This funky neighborhood favorite is the quintessential fine market, chock full of tasty organic and wholesome foods. It is the perfect place to pick up a picnic or stock the fridge at your hotel. The friendly service and committed clientele make you feel like a local, and the gelato is worth the trip.

✳ Special Events

Boise has a growing art and cultural scene, and the number of great special events held throughout the city is also growing. For complete listings of local events, check out the Web sites listed under Guidance. The city, local urban organizations, and others are doing a remarkable job of cultivating Boise's cultural scene.

April: **Beaux Arts Wine Festival**. (208-345-8330: www.boiseartmuseum .org), Boise. This fabulous wine auction benefits the even more fabulous Boise Art Museum and includes patron dinners at nearby wineries, wine classes, and wine tasting. The event culminates in a gala evening featuring wine, dinner, dancing, and a silent and live auction.

August: **Caldwell Night Rodeo** (208-459-2060; www.caldwellnight rodeo.com), Rodeo Grounds, 2301 Blaine St., Caldwell. Mid-Aug. Polish your biggest belt buckle and get ready to watch some mean barrel racing at Caldwell's world-class rodeo. Free concerts usually start off the week. If you're into rodeo, this nationally ranked pro-circuit event is worth the drive from downtown Boise. Plus, the people-watching is entertaining too.

Western Idaho Fair (208-287-5650; www.idahofair.com), Expo Idaho, 5610 Glenwood St. If the Caldwell

Rodeo doesn't satisfy your need for Idaho tradition, the Western Idaho Fair should give you a full dose of farm animals, needlework displays, and concerts. You can also check out how many fried food items you can eat just prior to jumping on the Tilt-A-Whirl.

September: **Art in the Park** (208-345-8330), Julia Davis Park. Sponsored by the Boise Art Museum, this weekend-long art festival is the largest in the region, showcasing works from artists in the Northwest. Live entertainment, food, and a "hands-on" area for kids are also part of the program.

City Harvest: A Celebration of Local Arts and Food (208-433-5670), Basque Block and Grove Street. This weekend celebration of all things local includes a seven-course local harvest and wine feast,

public presentations on topics related to sustainability and our local food system, live entertainment, and an art show and sale.

Idaho International Film Festival (208-331-0909; www.idahofilmfestival.com), Egyptian Theatre, Flix, and Edwards 21 (see Entertainment—Film). The festival aims to showcase the best new independent cinema from America and abroad. Other film festival events include parties and workshops.

October: **Fall Brew Fest** (208-887-7880; www.boguscreek.com), Bogus Creek Ranch, 7355 S. Eagle Rd., Meridian. This brew fest is one big Bacchanalian celebration featuring microbrew tasting, a barbecue dinner, music, and dancing.

Oktoberfest (208-343-8649; www.idahobotanicalgarden.com), Idaho

BOISE IS STILL AN AGRICULTURAL TOWN.

Matt Furber

Botanical Garden, 2355 N. Penitentiary Rd. $6 for adults, $4 for children and members. This is perhaps a little more sedate event than the Fall Brew Fest. Food and drink from Tablerock Brewpub and Highlands Hollow Brewhouse are provided, along with German oompah music.

November–January: **Ongoing Winter Garden Aglow at the Idaho Botanical Garden** (208-343-8649; www.idahobotanicalgarden.com), 2355 N. Penitentiary Rd. In winter, the Idaho Botanical Garden is transformed for the holiday season. During the evening, the garden glows with more than 250,000 colorful holiday lights; revelers can enjoy hot cocoa, cookies, carol singing, and blazing bonfires. Santa Claus also makes an appearance.

THE BRUNEAU AND OWYHEE RIVERS: COWBOY COUNTRY

If you look at a map, you'll see that the southwestern corner of Idaho is wide-open country, bisected north–south by only one paved road—ID 51—which stretches from Mountain Home at I-84 south through Grasmere and Riddle to the Nevada state line. ID 78, from Marsing in the west to near Hammett in the east, is the region's east–west route. In between are scattered hamlets, including Melba, Grand View, and Bruneau. Despite its proximity to Boise, this area remains remote, wild country; some call it the wildest part of Idaho. This region is fairly devoid of people, with only 11,000 souls living in Owyhee County's 7,700 square miles.

In contrast to the relief of the Owyhee Mountains (up to 8,403 feet at Hayden Peak) flanking its western edge, the broad, expansive Owyhee desert appears a never-ending sea of shrub-steppe flatness—and a dry, dusty, muted one at that. That is, until you get into its canyons. Over geologic time, the Owyhee, Jarbridge, and Bruneau rivers have sliced deep into this pancake, incising their way down through layers upon layers of rhyolitic ash–flow sheets and black basalt lava flows of the ancient Bruneau-Jarbridge volcano, carving out dramatic vertical-walled canyons that plunge more than 1,000 feet from the canyon walls to the river below. The vast Owyhee Canyonlands encompass about 6 million acres in southwestern Idaho, northern Nevada, and eastern Oregon.

With the exception of a couple specks on the map, southwest Idaho and the Owyhee Canyonlands are owned, almost entirely, by the U.S. Bureau of Land Management (BLM). The BLM offices and their Web sites provide a significant amount of information about public recreational opportunities, including hiking, camping, wildlife viewing, and more, on our public trust lands. Mountain Home, on I-84 between Boise and Twin falls, is one of those specks on the map. If you are looking for a bed or food prior to heading into the desert, check out their chamber's Web site for relevant information. North of Mountain Home via US 20 are a few smaller towns with access to the southern Sawtooths. If you are willing to get out there, this country has an austere beauty that offers serene hiking, white-water boating, mountain biking, and exploring—plus the allure of a ghost town and other relics of the past.

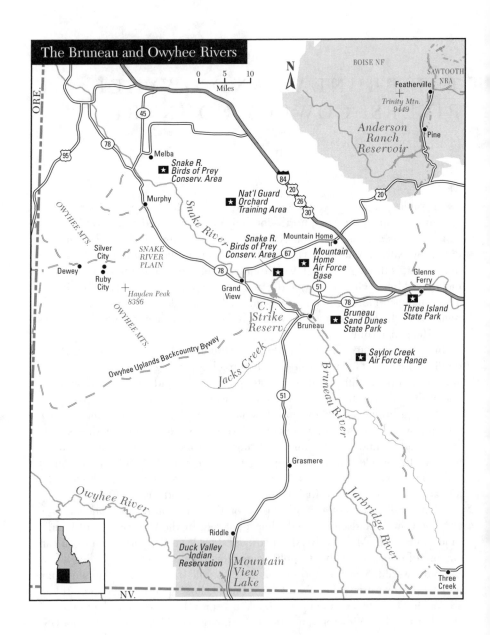

The Bruneau and Owyhee Rivers

0 5 10
Miles

N

ORE.

BOISE NF

SAWTOOTH
NRA

Featherville

Trinity Mtn.
9449

Pine

Anderson
Ranch
Reservoir

45

95

78

Melba

Snake R.
Birds of Prey
Conserv. Area

Murphy

Nat'l Guard
Orchard
Training Area

84

20

26

30

20

OWYHEE MTS.

Silver
City

Dewey

Ruby
City

SNAKE
RIVER
PLAIN

Hayden Peak
8386

Snake River

Snake R.
Birds of Prey
Conserv. Area

Mountain Home

67

Mountain
Home
Air Force
Base

Glenns
Ferry

78

Three Island
State Park

51

78

Grand
View

C. J.
Strike
Reserv.

Bruneau

Bruneau
Sand Dunes
State Park

Saylor Creek
Air Force Range

OWYHEE MTS.

Owyhee Uplands Backcountry Byway

Jacks Creek

51

Bruneau River

Jarbridge River

Grasmere

Owyhee River

Riddle

Duck Valley
Indian
Reservation

Mountain
View
Lake

Three
Creek

NV.

Bureau of Land Management (BLM) Bruneau Field Office (208-384-3300; www.blm.gov), 3948 Development Ave., Boise 83705.

BLM Jarbidge Field Office (208-736-2350; www.blm.gov), 2356 Kimberly Rd., Twin Falls 83301.

BLM Owyhee Field Office (208-896-5912; www.blm.gov), 20 First Ave. W., Marsing 83609 (on ID 78).

Mountain Home Chamber of Commerce (208-587-4334; www.mountain -home.org), 205 N. Third E., Mountain Home 83647.

GETTING THERE

By car

Owyhee country is accessible from Mountain Home on **I-84** to the north via **ID 51**, which becomes NV 225 toward Elko, Nevada south of the stateline. **ID 78** also offers access to the region south of I-84, and **US 20** offers access north of the interstate. Recreational areas within the vast territory are generally accessed via very rugged, desolate jeep roads. If you travel on these, be prepared.

By air

Boise Air Terminal (Gowen Field; 208-383-3110; www.cityofboise.org/ departments/airport/). Most air travelers coming to the Owyhee region fly in and out of Boise, which is less than 100 miles from the center of the region.

MEDICAL EMERGENCIES

The nearest real medical attention you can get is in Boise (see Boise: Life in the Big City). For remote backcountry trips, you might consider purchasing life flight insurance ($50/year). Two companies offer heli-transport to a major medical center for wilderness and other emergencies:

Air St. Luke's (208-706-1000; www.stlukesonline.org/specialties_and_services/ ASL/).

St. Alphonsus Life Flight (208-367-3996; www.sarmc.org/bodysarmc3.cfm ?id=32).

✳ Wandering Around

Bureau of Land Management (BLM, 208-384-3300; www.id.blm.gov) offers two scenic drives that will take you deep into Owyhee country. Maps and further information about both drives are available on their Web site.

Owyhee Uplands Backcountry Byway, 103 miles, partly gravel, partly paved, from near Grand View (60 miles southeast of Boise off ID 78) to Jordan Valley, Oregon (80 miles southwest of Boise). Round-trip drive (suitable for passenger vehicles) from Boise is about 250 miles and takes a full day. Road is usually impassable late Oct.–late May due to snow. Camping at North Fork Campground and dispersed sites on BLM land (see To Do—Camping). The route loops southwest to Mud Flat, then farther west to the North Fork Campground on the rim of the Owyhee Canyon, and north along the border with Oregon, providing access to some stunning high-desert sage-steppe and grassland habitat (wildflower-strewn in the spring); sheer-walled red river canyons, volcanic rhyolitic pinnacles, and other geologic formations; beautiful juniper woodlands filled with gnarled elders (some with 500 years under their belts); irrigated hay meadows; and stands of mountain mahogany. This varied habitat provides homes for more than 180 species of birds and mammals, including bighorn sheep, badgers, and coyotes. With the exception of a restroom at Poison Creek Spring near the start of the drive, there are no services (that means none at all!) along the route, so gas up, travel safely, wear appropriate clothing, and bring plenty of water and food.

Owyhee Watchable Wildlife Loop, 140-mile loop from Marsing to Jordan Valley, Oregon, and back. Camping on BLM lands. This loop provides excellent wildlife-viewing opportunities. Visitors may be lucky enough to spot occasional pronghorn antelopes (the fastest land animal in North America), mule deer, coyotes, sage grouse, golden eagles, and northern harrier, ferruginous, red-tailed, and rough-legged hawks during the winter. Riparian areas are flush with fowl, including ring-necked pheasants, sandhill cranes, white-faced ibis, and geese; other wildlife visitors include red foxes, river otters, beavers, and mink.

✳ To See

GHOST TOWNS

Silver City (www.historicsilvercityidaho.com), via partially improved, partially unimproved road off ID 78 near Murphy or US 95 from Jordan Valley, Oregon; signs point to Silver City from both directions. Abandoned forever in midstep, in the way you might abandon a pile of dishes in your sink (but let's hope you actually return to them), Silver City is truly a frozen-in-time ghost town. Yet another product of Idaho's mining frenzy, Silver City sprung to life after a band of rich silver ore was discovered on nearby War Eagle Mountain in 1865. Within a matter of years, War Eagle Mine and more than 200 other mines in the area produced more than $60 million worth of ore. Silver City grew in lockstep with the mines and in its heyday had 2,500 residents, 300 homes, and 75 businesses. The bustling western town was complete with several saloons, a couple hotels, several churches, six general stores, two lumber yards, its own China Town and—as with all good gold rush towns—houses of ill repute. By all accounts, the scene in Silver City was not always timid, and the graveyards are full of gunshot victims (of the western shoot-out variety) and mining casualties. Today, about 75 structures still remain, only a few of which are (oddly enough) occupied. You can still stay in its hotel (see Lodging).

HISTORICAL SITES

Glenns Ferry (www.glenssferryidaho.org), just off I-84 east of Mountain Home. Tiny Glenns Ferry revels in its role in Idaho's history. Emigrants passed through Glenns Ferry as they headed west from Missouri to Oregon along the Oregon Trail in search of greater opportunity. It is said that some families migrating to Oregon were frontier folks who, after settling for some time, preferred to continue pushing west; others were seeking the promise of a square mile of land

Chris Pilaro

GEOLOGIC WONDERS ABOUND ON THE OWYHEE UPLANDS BACKCOUNTRY BYWAY.

(640 acres)—often with heavily forested lands and productive soils—that the Oregon Country was offering married settlers in the 1840s; more were lured by rumors of gold strikes in the 1850s; others were looking to escape the epidemics that were common in the East. Along the way, travelers faced nearly insurmountable obstacles, not the least of which was the imposing Snake River. Until 1869, when Gus Glenn constructed a ferry about 2 miles from what is now Three Island State Park, emigrants forded the river with their wagons at the Three Island area near Glenns Ferry, in what became known as the most difficult and dramatic crossing along the Oregon Trail.

Oregon Trail History and Education Center (www.idahohistory.net), at Three Island State Park (see Wilder Places—Parks). Open 9–5 year-round. The state park hosts an annual reenactment of the Glenns Ferry crossing each Aug., complete with period costumes, wagons, crafts, and food. The history center offers educational displays focusing on trail lore and history, including the area's Native American history.

WINERY TOURS

Carmela Vineyards (208-366-2313; www.carmelavineyards.com), 795 W. Madison St., Glenns Ferry. This beautiful stone winery has more than 48 acres of grapes and bottles a slew of its own wines, including award-winning Red Meritage, Barrel Select Chardonnay, and Johannisburg Riesling. At this neat stop, they offer tours, wine tasting, and a restaurant.

✳ To Do

BIRD-WATCHING

Owyhee Canyonlands (see Wandering Around) provide fabulous wooded riparian and sagebrush habitat areas that attract a wide variety of songbirds. At least 60 species of birds breed in or migrate through this area, including the yellow warbler, yellow-breasted chat, lazuli bunting, spotted towhee, house wren, robin, song sparrow, and California quail. Brewer's sparrow and sage sparrow frequent higher- and lower-elevation sagebrush, respectively, and lark sparrow, vesper sparrow, horned lark, western meadowlark, and sage thrasher nest in the sagebrush. Approximately 10,000 acres of juniper habitat provides homes for the mountain bluebird, American robin, northern flicker, and yellow-rumped warbler, while steep river canyon walls provide nesting habitat for golden eagles, red-tailed hawks, ferruginous hawks, kestrels, and prairie falcons. Green-winged teals, mallards, common mergansers, spotted sandpiper avocets, black-necked stilts, and white-faced ibis frequent the reservoir and lake areas.

Snake River Birds of Prey National Conservation Area (NCA; 208-384-3300; www.birdsofprey.blm.gov), 81 miles along both sides of Snake River, from just south of Boise near Kuna to Mountain Home area. The Snake River NCA encompasses more than 600,000 acres (about 485,000 of which are public lands) and provides 65,000 acres of critical nesting habitat and 420,000 acres of prey habitat. Access to the northern portion of the preserve is most easily gained via Kuna, on ID 69 just south of Nampa; the western side by Celebration Park, 19 miles from Kuna and 7 miles from Melba; and the eastern part from the towns

of Grand View and Bruneau, both on ID 78 south of Mountain Home. The Web
site provides maps and directions to each access point. Several improved campgrounds and picnic areas are within the NCA, but the best raptor viewing is
gained by hiking or boating into the area. Recreationalists enjoy plentiful opportunities for hiking, rafting, fishing, bird-watching, caving, and historical exploration; archaeological buffs appreciate some of the oldest Native American sites
anywhere, some of the best-preserved sections of the Oregon National Historic
Trail, and several historic gold-mining sites. The NCA was established in 1993 to
protect one of (perhaps *the*) highest population of nesting birds of prey in the
world. This immense tract of chaparral and sagebrush country provides fabulous
nesting and prey habitat. A unique set of environmental conditions, including
great raptor nesting sites in the steep canyon walls of the Snake River (as high as
600 feet), plus deep, windblown soils and dense grasses and shrubs that provide
optimal burrowing and forage for small mammals, have led to a stable and interconnected ecosystem with both abundant predator and prey. Some 24 raptor
species (16 nesting and 8 migratory or wintering species) and more than 700 pairs
of nesting raptors can be found, including bald and golden eagles, several species
of owls, peregrine falcons, prairie falcons, kestrels, and merlins. Burrowing prey
include Piute ground squirrels, black-tailed jackrabbits, pocket gophers, kangaroo
rats, and deer mice, among others.

Outfitters
Birds of Prey Expeditions (208-658-9980; www.birdsofpreyexpeditions.com),
Kuna. This outfitter offers guided field trips within the Birds of Prey NCA.

CAMPING
There are fabulous hiking and camping opportunities throughout this country,
and the BLM encourages the public to visit our own lands. However, they
stress—and so will I—that traveling in this region requires a good deal of self-
sufficiency; road and trails are rough, there are few signs, and poison ivy and rattlesnakes pose some dangers. Please come prepared with a well-functioning
vehicle, water, proper clothing and equipment, water, maps, water, food, water,
and the like. Did I mention you should bring water?

Dispersed camping is allowed in nondesignated areas on BLM property; consult
with one of the BLM offices listed under Guidance for recommended camping
areas. Numerous developed tent sites are also located throughout the area.
Whether you camp in designated or nondesignated areas, please abide by Leave No
Trace practices. Designated BLM camping spots include these (see also Fishing):

Jump Creek Canyon, at the northern end of the region, just southwest of
Marsing. Developed campsites are located near a couple of nice little hikes (0.2
mile or less) to a swimming hole surrounding by lush riparian vegetation, including red osier dogwood trees and water birch and to a spot overlooking Jump
Creek Falls.

North Fork Campground, along Owyhee Uplands Backcountry Byway (see
Wandering Around), about 27 miles southeast of Jordan Valley, Oregon. This
nice option is nestled deep in the Owyhee Canyon.

CAMPING IN OWYHEE CANYONLANDS

Silver City Campground, at historic mining town (see To See—Ghost Towns).

FISHING

For fishing information, contact the **Boise National Forest Headquarters** (208-373-4100; www.fs.fed.us/r4/boise/offices.htm). For fishing regulations and licenses, contact **Idaho Fish and Game** (208-334-3700; http://fishandgame .idaho.gov). In addition to what's listed below, there is great trout fishing on the Duck Valley Indian Reservation (see Wilder Places).

Anderson Ranch Reservoir, via US 20 north from Mountain Home to Anderson Ranch Road or Pine-Featherville Road (latter is paved). This 17-mile-long reservoir is a favorite boating, fishing, and bird-watching area. Camping can be found off either access road, along the Boise River, or at the reservoir.

C. J. Strike Reservoir (www.fishandgame.idaho.gov/fish/anglerguides/cjstrike .cfm), in Snake River Birds of Prey National Conservation Area, south of Mountain Home. Anglers enjoy this reservoir, built in the 1950s to provide water for local communities. The reservoir and the land surrounding it are now maintained by Idaho Fish and Game to maximize habitat for game birds and deer. The reservoir is a popular spot to fish for crappies, bass, rainbow trout, sturgeon, and other species. Developed campsites are available at the Cove Recreation Site, and more primitive camping spots can be found throughout the area.

Trinity Lakes, accessible by Rainbow Lake Trail from Upper Trinity Lake Campground (15 miles up the dirt road beyond Featherville). These hidden gems are Perched above Anderson Ranch Reservoir. Anglers hike to a saddle, which then drops into a basin craddling six fish-filled lakes. The area boasts great hiking and camping as well.

HIKING

Many hikes in this region are undirected and dispersed (i.e., they involve trail-blazing). In all these spots, watch out for ticks, rattlesnakes, and poison ivy. Good camping can also be found in some of these areas. Consult with the BLM (see Guidance) for more detailed trail information. Popular hiking areas include the following (see also Fishing—Trinity Lakes):

Bruneau River, out of Bruneau on ID 51.

Duncan Creek and **Zero Canyon**, about 25 miles south of Bruneau off ID 51.

Indian Hot Springs and **Indian Bathtub**, just outside Bruneau on Hot Springs Road, off ID 51.

Juniper Creek, along the East Fork of the Owyhee River, accessed via ID 51 near the Nevada state line.

Little Jacks Creek, Big Jacks Creek, and **Parker Trail**, just outside Grand-view off ID 78.

HORSEBACK RIDING

Sinker Creek Outfitters (208-863-7960 or 208-834-2237; www.historic silvercityidaho.com/sinkercreekoutfitters.html), Silver City. Guided horseback rides in the area are really cool if you have the time and inclination!

HOT SPRINGS

Givens Hot Springs (208-495-2000; www.givenshotsprings.com), on ID 78, 11 miles south of Marsing. Here, emigrants on the Oregon Trail washed their clothes; a formal bathhouse was built in 1900, and a resort established in 1903. The small resort (which includes cabins and seasonally available camping) was refurbished in the 1990s and is open for business today. While you are in wine country, you might also want to check out these nearby springs. For better or for worse, the pool is now enclosed.

MOUNTAIN BIKING

Southeastern Idaho's cool desert climate provides for an extended mountain bik-ing season—on the order of eight–10 snow-free months. However, this relatively bare high-desert environment is usually broiling in midsummer, with tempera-tures often in the 90s (i.e., you probably don't want to ride here at midday in the dead of summer). The area is very remote, and you are likely to see more cows than people. While this makes for a nice solitary experience, it also means you had best be prepared. Stock up on lots of water and supplies in Boise, Mountain Home, or some other town. Once you get out into the Owyhee Canyonlands, you won't find services anywhere. Also know that you are very far from help if anything goes sideways. Your best bet is to consult with BLM offices (see Guidance) for trail and other relevant information.

WHITE-WATER KAYAKING AND RAFTING

Perhaps the best way to truly see this canyon country is by boating the Bruneau and Jarbidge rivers or the Owyhee River. The experience from a river's surface—gazing hundreds of feet up at red cliffs or shafts of black, columnar hoodoos seemingly leaning in on you, the width of the skyline waxing and waning with the canyon's expansion and contraction as you move downsteam—provides a stark foil to that garnered on a bumpy, dusty road trip on the virtually endless, pancake-flat surface that splays out in all directions from the canyon rim. On these rivers, small beaches provide nice little camping spots, side canyons and drainages offer hiking (or, more often than not, climbing up chimneys and other slots), and ghost remains of settler encampments offer historical diversions along the way. These rivers are generally runnable only in the early season, when there

RIVER RAFTING THE REMOTE OWYHEE RIVER

is enough water. Boating in this region provides a truly serene wilderness experience, but please be clear—these are remote, sparsely visited rivers, and you either need to know what you are doing, go with someone who does, or arrange a guided trip.

Jarbidge-Bruneau River System

The most common trips here are generally one to three days long, depending on where you put in. The shuttle for both the one- and two-day trips requires a drive through the Mountain Home Air Force Base; note the signage warning of possible dangerous objects falling from the sky! It is best to run shuttle early in the morning to avoid the searing desert heat. The one- and two-day trips provide great class II–IV boating and take you through beautiful, narrow canyons. At high water, you definitely need to be on your game to avoid some sizable hydraulic features, and at low water, some of it can be bony. Along the way, you are likely to see wildlife—including bald and golden eagles, badgers, and perhaps a mountain goat if you are lucky—some rickety homestead remains, and a couple hot springs. Be prepared for cold mornings in the early season, and watch out for the abundant poison ivy and poison oak.

One-day trip, from just above Five Mile Rapids (from Bruneau on ID 51, take gravel Clover–Three Creek Road south-southeast to dirt road to west that runs to canyon rim; definitely need a high-clearance, four-wheel-drive vehicle for last mile or so) north to Indian Bathtub (about 12-mile shuttle from put-in). At the put-in's road-end at the canyon rim, you'll hoof all your gear down Roberson Trail to the river's edge, about 25- to 30-minute hike. This short river trip gives you the best of the rapids on the Bruneau, but you miss the most dramatic parts of the canyon.

Two-day trip, from Indian Hot Springs (continue farther down Clover–Three Creek Road to another really rough, nameless road—turn right at Y) to Indian Bathtub. The second put-in on the Bruneau River is about 40 miles south of Bruneau. Once you turn toward the hot springs, the road goes from one on which you might be able to drive 40–50 miles per hour to one on which you might be averaging 5–7 miles per hour. It is enough to jar your fillings loose. The last part of this drive is a daunting descent into the canyon; the road is rugged and boulder strewn, with a precipitous drop on the right. Boaters joke that the toughest part of paddling the Bruneau is the class V drive to the put-in! Most people who run this stretch camp on a nice, tree-sheltered, sandy little beach located just above the put-in for the one-day stretch.

Three-day trip, from Murphy Hot Springs (continue farther down Clover–Three Creek Road to dirt road heading southwest to hot springs, then go a few miles beyond to confluence of a little creek with Jarbidge River) to Indian Bathtub, a 70-mile shuttle. The third section starts even farther upstream, on the Jarbidge River, southwest of its confluence with the Bruneau. On the way to the put-in, you drop down into the canyon and quite suddenly stumble upon a very dry, rugged encampment of hunting and fishing cabins (with perhaps a few year-rounders). There is a cement and wooden hot springs pool here at Murphy, and though the water is nice, the place is a little weird. The put-in is a few miles beyond, where you can camp. The trip is comprised of class III–IV rapids (mostly class III) on a swift, shallow river, with a couple constrictions and a few possible portages, including Jarbidge Falls.

Owyhee River

The Owyhee is even more remote, and if you choose to boat it, it is quite possible that cattle and wildlife will be your only company. Of the handful of trips on the Owyhee, the most common are the 53-mile Three Forks to Rome section and the 250-mile Crutcher's Crossing to Rome section. Lesser traveled are the upstream segments running from Deep Creek to Rickard Crossing (or farther to Crutchers Crossing) and sections of the East and South forks of the Owyhee to Crutchers Crossing. These trips can be tied in to the downstream segments for a seven- to 10-day trip. All trips must be registered with the BLM (see Guidance).

Recommended Reading

To plot out your trip on any or all of these rivers, a great resource is Grant Amaral's *Idaho: The Whitewater State; a Guidebook* (Bookcrafters, 1990), which provides maps and directions to put-ins and take-outs, descriptions of rapids, and other relevant information.

Outfitters

National Outdoor Leadership School (NOLS; 800-710-NOLS; www.nols .edu), Driggs. They run a monthlong backbacking and river trip in the Owyhees.

River Odysseys West (ROW; 208-667-6506; www.rowadventures.com), Coeur d'Alene. They also offer river trips here.

Wilderness River Outfitters (800-252-6581; www.wildernessriver.com), Lemhi. They run trips on these rivers.

WILDLIFE VIEWING

Owyhee Canyonlands (see Wandering Around). The diversity of habitat here—from dry sagebrush plateaus to lush riparian zones, to rolling mahogany savannas, wide grasslands, and salt desert shrub communities—provides for a wide array of wildlife, including pronghorn antelopes, mule deer, California bighorn sheep, pygmy rabbits, chukars, and sage grouse. The region also provides critical habitat for Columbia spotted frogs, loggerhead shrikes, spotted bats, ferruginous hawks, mountain quail, and many other rare and important species. Don't be surprised to see wild horses around; more than 640 feral animals roam the area, the descendants of domesticated horses turned loose or lost to public lands—some by Depression Era farmers and ranchers who couldn't afford to care for them. Numerous rare plant species also thrive on the scattered wetlands and dry, volcanic soils found throughout the Owyhee.

✳ Wilder Places

Duck Valley Indian Reservation (702-757-3161; www.shopaitribes.org), approximately 290,000 acres straddling Idaho–Nevada border about 60 miles south of Bruneau via ID 51. These Tribal Trust lands are owned by the Shoshone-Paiute Tribes; approximately 1,600 members of these tribes live here, in what is their ancestral home. The Owyhee River bisects the reservation, flowing from its southeastern corner in Nevada to its northwestern corner in Idaho, creating a lowland valley at about 5,200 feet nestled between rimrock plateaus and soaring peaks (some nearly 9,000 feet tall) on either side. Agriculture and ranching are the mainstays of the reservation economy, while recreation and tourism are also being cultivated.

The reservation boasts great trout **fishing** in three reservoirs—Sheep Creek, Mountain View, and Lake Billy Shaw reservoirs. The lakes are open to fishing Apr.–Oct., subject only to the fish and game rules of the sovereign Shoshone-Pauite nation. Sheep Creek and Mountain View are catch-and-release, and Billy Shaw has been stocked with 20- to 24-inch rainbow trout. There is a limit of one large trophy fish per day on Billy Shaw. A tribal fishing license ($25 per day) can be purchased on the reservation. A diversity of waterfowl and shorebirds make for good **bird-watching**. **Camping** is available as well.

Owyhee Canyonlands, about 6 million acres in southwestern Idaho, northern Nevada, and eastern Oregon managed by the BLM (see Guidance). The first

OWYHEE CANYONLANDS' RIPARIAN AREAS DRAW WILDLIFE.

white men to explore this region were fur trappers of the 1818 Donald McKenzie expedition. The Owyhee region gained its name after three party members—Hawaiian Islanders—were lost while exploring what is now called the Owyhee River. In a twist of language, the river and the entire region became known as "Owyhee" to honor these men. (The Bruneau River derived its named from French trappers who called it *le brun eau*, or "the brown water.")

Subsequent human visitors to the area were few and far between. Only after the 1863 discovery of gold in the Owyhee Mountains at Jordan Creek did gold miners rush to the area, building towns such as Silver City (see To See—Ghost Towns), Ruby City, and Dewey. Ranchers later saw opportunity on the sage-strewn expanses of the high desert and brought large herds of cattle to the plateau. Both endeavors were fairly short lived, and Silver City and similar ghost towns provide witness to the gold mining frenzy, while the remains of lone homesteading cabins seen at various spots in the area, particularly along the river corridor (and therefore accessible only by boat), are a testament to the lives of these ranching settlers. After the bust of the gold mines, Owyhee country crept

HOMESTEAD CABIN IN OWYHEE CANYON

back into relative obscurity, left to a few resilient cowboys and ranchers.

Fast-forward to present day, and the Owyhee has experienced a resurgence in interest. Ranchers continue to graze (many say overgraze) this land, recreationalists seek solitude, motorized access has meant that four-wheelers are putting pressure on the land, and, since the 1940s, the Mountain Home Air Force Base has conducted military operations here. Yet, because of its wild character, dramatic canyons, and wild, open expanses (it is one of the largest remaining wild, unprotected spaces in the Lower 48), the Owyhee region has long been discussed as a possible wilderness area. Born of these discussions, a diverse group of stakeholders (including county commissioners, conservationists, the Owyhee Cattlemen's Association, motorized interests, outfitters, and others) came together in 2001 to work on a plan hailed as the "Owyhee Initiative," an undertaking aimed at developing a consensus plan to protect both the wild nature of the place and the economic stability of the region (i.e., ranching). To the great surprise of many (in fact, a Sierra Club publication on the Owhyee Initiative shows pigs flying above an Owyhee canyon), the unusual group reached consensus in 2004 on a plan that would protect 517,000 acres of BLM land as the Owyhee-Bruneau Wilderness Area, designate 384 miles of Wild and Scenic Rivers, while also releasing 199,000 acres of Wilderness Study Area (WSA). Release of WSA lands is greatly controversial—WSA designation is a temporary one allowing BLM to protect the land as a wilderness area until Congress decides whether those lands are to be formally designated as such; release means that the lands will be managed for multiple uses (i.e., with much less protection). Senator Crapo (R-Idaho) introduced legislation in 2006 and again in 2007; as of this writing, the bill had just passed out of the Senate Energy and Natural Resources Committee.

Recommended Reading

If you're interested in learning more about the lifestyles of the hardy souls who inhabit this area, check out the beautiful photo-essay book *Gathering Remnants: A Tribute to the Working Cowboy* by Kendall Nelson, Felicitas Funke-Riehle, Clint Eastwood, and Gretel Ehrlich (Prairie Creek Productions, 2001) and the documentary of the same name.

PARKS

Bruneau Sand Dunes State Park (208-366-7919; www.parksandrecreation .idaho.gov), 20 miles south of Boise, near Bruneau; take I-84 east to ID 51 south to ID 78. $4 per vehicle. The Bruneau Sand Dunes are the tallest single-structure sand dunes in North America, rising nearly 500 feet above the desert. Scientists believe eddy-deposited sediment, dropped from a torrent of water that raged across southern Idaho when an ice dam broke during the massive Lake Bonneville Flood 12,000 years ago, provided the seeds for subsequent deposition of aeolian-transported sands to form these massive windblown dunes. A semicircular basin continues to act as a trap for sand transported by prevailing winds from the southeast and northwest. The 4,800-acre state park surrounding the dunes encompasses a variety of desert, prairie, lake, and marsh habitat and the critters that go along with it. Springtime brings luxurious wildflower color to the desert and visitors enjoy Easter lilies, stork's bill, purple prairie clover, Malheur prince's plume, and pale evening primrose.

The park also has one of only two public observatories in Idaho—the **Bruneau Dunes Observatory**—which houses a giant 25-inch Obsession, one of the largest publicly accessible telescopes. Some may find the stargazing in Idaho's dark, wide skies more spectacular than the dunes. Camping is allowed, and wild running and acrobatics on the dunes are encouraged. Facilities include a visitors center, the observatory, and a gift shop. Camping $12–20, cabins $45.

Three Island State Park (208-366-2394, 866-634-3246 reservations; www .parksandrecreation.idaho.gov), off I-84 at Glenns Ferry. The state park hosts an annual reenactment of the Glenns Ferry crossing each Aug. (see To See—Historical Sites), complete with period costumes, wagons, crafts, and food. Campsites $20–33, cabins $45.

✳ Lodging

Most folks heading out into the desert and surrounds plan to camp along with way. If you are looking for a bed on the outskirts of canyon country (or a shower after a backcountry trip), a couple options are listed here. You might also head to Boise or Twin Falls (see those chapters).

HOTELS
Silver City
Idaho Hotel (208-583-4101; www .historicsilvercityidaho.com/idahohotel .html), Silver City 83650. The hotel opened its doors for the first time in 1863, and visitors can still stay at the newly reopened hotel. $45–126.

MOTELS
Glenns Ferry
Redford Motel (208-366-2421), 601 W. First Ave., Glenns Ferry 83623.

Mountain Home
This town on the interstate has a slew of chain hotels.

Best Western Foothills Motor Inn (208-587-8477; www.bestwestern idaho.com), 1080 US 20, Mountain Home 83647.

Hampton Inn & Suites (208-587-7300), 3175 NE Foothills Ave., Mountain Home 83647.

Sleep Inn (800-672-5337), 1180 US 20, Mountain Home 83647.

Thunderbird Motel (208-587-7927; www.thunderbird-motel.com), 910 Sunset Strip, Mountain Home 83647.

✳ Where to Eat

The pickings are slim in this remote region. For longer adventures, your best bet is to bring your own food. When you are near some of the few towns, there are several spots to eat, but don't count on any fine dining.

EATING OUT
Atlanta
Whistle Stop Tavern (208-864-2157), on the main drag. You can buy groceries or eat a meal at this combination restaurant and market.

Glenns Ferry
Carmela Vineyards (208-366-2313; www.carmelavineyards.com), 795 W. Madison St. Open for lunch and dinner. If you're touring wine country, you might check out the restaurant at

this vineyard, which serves steak, seafood, salads, and more.

Homedale
Moxie Java Bistro (208-337-5566; http://cafeleku.com), 404 US 95. This Idaho-grown coffee chain serves up some great brew and café fare and has free wi-fi.

Kuna
El Gallo Giro (208-922-5169), 482 W. Third St. The Mexican food at this spot comes highly recommended.

Marsing
Sandbar River House Restaurant (208-896-4124), 18 First Ave. E.

Open for lunch and dinner Tues.–Sat. This house-cum-restaurant perched along the shores of the Snake River serves sandwiches and burgers at lunch and steak and seafood at dinner.

Mountain Home
Mountain Home has its share of chain restaurants and supermarkets where you can stock up for a trip south. One of the better chains is this:

Smoky Mountain Pizza (208-587-2840; www.smokymountainpizza .com), 1465 American Legion Blvd. Good pizza, sandwiches, and salads.

Central Idaho:
An Explorer's
Nirvana

**SALMON-CHALLIS AND BEYOND:
MOUNTAINS AND RIVERS GALORE**

**KETCHUM, SUN VALLEY, AND
THE SAWTOOTHS: AMERICA'S
SHANGRI-LA**

Chris Pliaro

INTRODUCTION

In a testament to the unthinkable forces of oceanic plate subduction on the West Coast and subsequent continental plate uplift, followed by Basin and Range faulting, Central Idaho is graced by stunning, granitic, northwest-trending mountain ranges, one after another. These mountain ranges come in quick succession, as you move northeast to southwest—from the Beaverhead Range, which forms the Continental Divide with Montana, west to the Lemhi Range, the Lost River Range, then the Pioneers and the Boulder–White Clouds, the Sawtooth Range, and the southernmost Smoky Mountains—each offering a lifetime's worth of adventure. To the northwest of these ranges, forming the heart of Central Idaho, lie the great Salmon River Mountains.

Among the outdoorsy crowd, Central Idaho is well known for its boundless recreational opportunities that include powdery slopes, hundreds of kilometers of impeccably groomed skate-skiing trails, hiking trails galore, and killer mountain-biking terrain. I continue to imagine putting on a backpack and hiking boots, walking straight out my door in Hailey into one of the nearby canyons, and just going, however far and however long—maybe forever.

Sandwiched between these unbelievable mountain ranges are the Lemhi, Big Lost, Big Wood, and Salmon rivers and their valleys—valleys that we generally call home. While the geography and geology make this place as richly spectacular as it is, the people who inhabit the region tend to be independent, creative, and adventurous souls who have brought with them a wealth of mountain music, art, restaurants, and other cultural amenities to complement Mother Nature's offerings.

The best-known towns in the region are Sun Valley and Ketchum, home to the glitzy and world-famous Sun Valley Resort. The ski resort was established in 1936 by Averell Harriman, chairman of the board of Union Pacific Railroad, who had the explicit goal of attracting Hollywood stars and other celebrities to the valley. Sun Valley continues to attract its share of the famous, many of whom own second homes, but they keep fairly quiet, and so do we. If you really need to know who is who, ask a local.

Farther north, Stanley has garnered a quieter reputation as a launch point for some of the country's most bad-ass boating, backcountry skiing, and backpacking. Nestled beneath the jagged and breathtaking Sawtooth Peaks, tiny little

Stanley is said to be one of the most scenic towns in America, and it attracts a
funky, bohemian set in the summer. Stanley remains very, very quiet during the
winter. This is true of most of the towns in this region (or perhaps in most of
Idaho); as you venture farther north toward Challis, Salmon, or North Fork, just
remember that it is all about the country—and stunningly beautiful country it
is!—and amenities are often secondary. However, an explorer in the truest sense
of the word will never be bored in Central Idaho.

SALMON, CHALLIS, AND BEYOND: MOUNTAINS AND RIVERS GALORE

A bird's-eye view to the northeast from Stanley to the Montana border reveals a series of buckles in the earth's crust, like accordion folds in a piece of paper, that form some of the most spectacular mountain chains and verdant valleys you will ever set your eyes upon. Separated from the Pioneer and Boulder–White Cloud mountains by the Lost River Valley, the vast wilderness of the Lost River Range stretches 70 miles from the Salmon River in the northwest to the broad Snake River Plain that opens up to the southwest near Arco. A vast sea of snowcapped peaks, this range is home to Borah Peak (which, at 12,662 feet, is Idaho's highest) and six other 12,000-foot peaks. Next in line are the contiguous Pahsimeroi and Little Lost River valleys and their namesake rivers, followed by more orogeny—the sedimentary Lemhis, which trend northwest–southeast for about 100 miles. Nestled in the Lemhi Range is dramatic Diamond Peak, sometimes referred to as the Lord of the Lemhis, which at 12,197 feet is the fourth-highest peak in Idaho. The Lemhis are perhaps one of the most remote mountain ranges in the Lower 48. Farther northeast are the Lemhi Valley and the Lemhi River, then the Beaverhead Mountains, which form Idaho's border with Montana along the Continental Divide. It was at Lemhi Pass (elevation 7,378 feet) that Lewis and Clark crossed the Continental Divide into Idaho on their historic 1805 expedition.

To the northwest of the Salmon River Valley lies Idaho's jewel: the Frank Church–River of No Return Wilderness Area, which spans 2.3 million acres of pristine wilderness filled with jagged peaks, shining alpine lakes, conifer forests, and broad meadows that provide important habitat to a litany of wildlife species. Within this wilderness area are the Main and the Middle Fork of the Salmon River, both of which are designated Wild and Scenic. All told, this remote and ruggedly beautiful region is an explorer's delight. If you are looking for shopping, fine dining, or lavish accommodations, you are heading in the wrong direction. On the flip side, whether you are looking to hit the trails and hike for days upon days likely without seeing another soul, to recharge your batteries, to experience the white-water adrenaline rush of the crème-de-la-crème of river trips—Idaho's

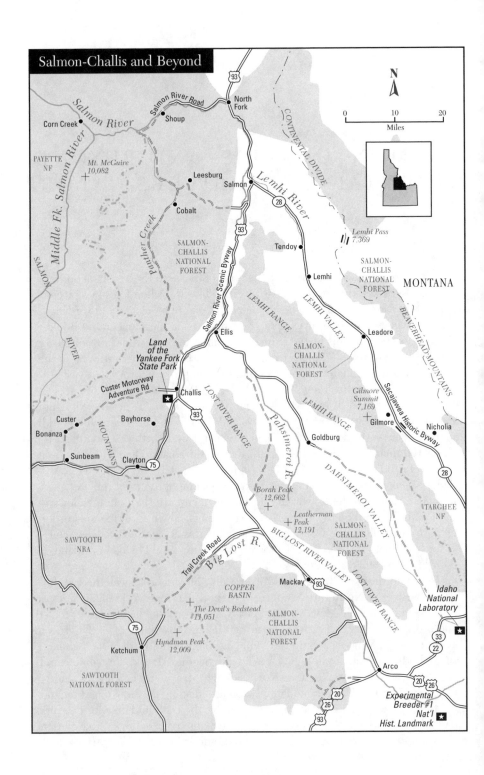

Salmon-Challis and Beyond

grand Middle Fork—or to otherwise soak in the natural beauty of these mountains and rivers, you will not be disappointed.

GUIDANCE

Butte County Chamber of Commerce (208-527-3060 ext. 11; www.cityarco .com/chamber_of_commerce.htm).

Challis Area Chamber of Commerce (208-879-2771; www.challischamber .com), Main Street, Challis.

Lost Rivers Economic Development (208-588-2694; www.mackayidaho.com).

Mackay Chamber of Commerce (208-588-2694).

Salmon Valley Chamber of Commerce (208-756-2100 or 800-727-2540; www .salmonchamber.com).

GETTING THERE

By car

From Stanley, **ID 75** takes you east and then north to Challis, where it meets up with **US 93**, which runs north to Salmon and on to the border crossing with Montana at Lost Trail Pass on the Continental Divide.

From Idaho Falls on I-15, you have several choices: **US 20** and then **US 26** west to Arco, then US 93 north, takes you through Mackay and the Big Lost River Valley to Challis. **I-15** north to **ID 33** takes you west to Mud Lake, where you can catch **ID 28** northwest through Leadore and the Lemhi Valley to Salmon. Gilmore Summit, on ID 28 at 7,186 feet, is not always passable during winter; check with the **Idaho Transportation Department** (www.511.idaho.gov) for road reports on Idaho's mountain passes. More adventurous folks might opt for the path in between these two routes, by taking I-15 north to ID 33 west to Howe, then following an **"improved road"** through the striking Little Lost River and Pahsimeroi valleys northwest to join US 93 partway between Challis and Salmon. (In Idaho-speak, an unimproved road is a *very* long dirt road through wide, uninhabited spaces with no cell-phone coverage and no easy help. As with other remote Idaho roads, if you choose this route, please be prepared to change your own flat tires, camp out if necessary, etc.)

By air

Boise Air Terminal (Gowen Field; 208-383-3110; www.cityofboise.org/ departments/airport/), Boise. Cheaper flights can often be found in and out of Boise, which is a 2.5-hour drive west of ID 75 via US 20 and I-84.

Friedman Memorial Airport (Ketchum–Sun Valley; 208-788-4956; www .flysunairport.com/), Hailey. This air terminal is serviced by Alaska Air/Horizon Air (a Northwest connection) and Delta/Skywest; Frontier Air may add a route to Hailey as well. Flights do not always make it in the winter, and you may find yourself circling the airport, only to be told that the visibility is insufficient and you are being rerouted to Twin Falls, from where you will take a two-hour bus ride up north to Hailey via US 93 and ID 75.

Idaho Falls Regional Airport (www.ci.idaho-falls.id.us), Idaho Falls. If you are looking to road-trip north through the Lost River, Pahsimeroi, or Lemhi Valley (these are remote areas), flying into Idaho Falls is also an option. It is served by Alaska Airlines/Horizon Air, Delta/Skywest, Northwest Airlines, and United Express.

Magic Valley Regional Airport (Joslin Field; 208-733-5215; www.tfid.org/airport/), Twin Falls. Flights are also available into Twin Falls, which is south of this region via US 93 and ID 75. Airport parking is free.

Missoula International Airport (406-7284381; www.msoairport.org), Missoula, Montana. Some may want to fly into Missoula, about 90 miles north of Lost Trail Pass at the border with Idaho. The airport serves several major airlines, including Alaska Airlines/Horizon Air, Delta/Skywest, Northwest/KLM, and United Express.

MEDICAL EMERGENCIES

Steele Memorial Hospital (208-756-5600; www.steelemh.org), 203 S. Daisy St., Salmon. This is the primary medical facility in this region.

Smaller local clinics also exist, including these:

Challis Area Health Center (208-879-4351), 1 Clinic Rd., Challis.

Lost River District Hospital (208-527-8206), 551 Highland Dr., Arco.

For more pressing medical problems, patients might be sent to hospitals in larger towns:

Eastern Idaho Regional Medical Center (208-529-7021; www.eirmc.com), 3100 Channing Wy., Idaho Falls.

St. Luke's Wood River Medical Center (208-727-8800; www.stlukesonline .org/wood_river/), 100 Hospital Dr., Ketchum.

✳ Cities and Villages

Arco, at US 20/26 and US 93, 70 miles northwest of Idaho Falls, at the southeastern end of the Lost River Valley. Arco's town hall, a stone building on Main Street, proclaims it to be the "first city in the world to be lit by atomic power. Elevation 5,320." Arco received electricity generated from nuclear power on July 17, 1955, from nearby Idaho National Laboratory (INL; see To See—Historical Sites). At present, there's not much to the town (population about 1,026), and many of the scientists working for INL now live in Idaho Falls. Inscriptions of high school graduating class years, which have been tattooed on the rock massif towering outside Arco since the 1920s, are an odd sight. This is a good place for a pit stop, but not much more. Craters of the Moon National Monument (see Wilder Places—Nature Preserves) is 18 miles west of Arco.

Challis, junction of ID 75 and US 93 northeast of Stanley. This region of Idaho is particularly rich in mining history. Three years after gold was discovered nearby, Challis was founded as a supply base in 1876 to support the high level of mining and ranching activity that followed. The city quickly became a trading center for mining activities in the region. The community derives it name from Alvah P. Challis, one of the surveyors of the original townsite lots—although at 5,280 feet, it is also aptly referred to as the "Mile High City." When Custer

County was established in 1881, Challis was named the county seat and remains so today. Today, Challis's economy is based on mining, ranching, farming, and tourism, and the city is home to about 1,000 folks. Mining of more than 40 minerals, including gold, silver, and molybdenum, continues today. While it is a sleepy little town, Challis is also a gateway to great outdoor adventures in and around the Frank Church–River of No Return Wilderness and the Salmon River.

Gibbonsville, on US 93 north of North Fork. Gibbonsville, while only a dot on the map (and home to only 120 residents), has quite a history. Lewis and Clark passed through the area in 1805, as they made their way to Montana. In 1877, during the Nez Perce War, Colonel John Gibbons staged his horrific sneak attack on the Nez Perce Indians at Big Hole, Montana, by climbing eastward up the Dahlonega drainage from Gibbonsville and over the Continental Divide at Big Hole Pass and slaughtering between 60 and 90 Nez Perce Indians. (It is lovely that it is Gibbons for whom the town is named.) Later, gold was discovered nearby on Anderson and Dahlonega creeks in 1893, and because the town was on what appeared to be a promising trade route between Utah and Montana, a 30-stamp mill was built in 1895. This spurred yet another Idaho gold rush, during which time the boomtown saw its population grow to 600 people, and 100 buildings, two sawmills, a roller mill, five stamp mills, and eight saloons were

DOWNTOWN CHALLIS

A GIBBONSVILLE HOME

built. Today, visitors can check out the Gibbonsville Museum (See To Do—Museums), the very old town cemetery, and some funky historic structures and mining artifacts. The larger area is beautifully pastoral, and some pretty hikes are nearby.

Lemhi Valley villages, on ID 28. Traveling north through the Lemhi Valley from Idaho Falls to Salmon takes you through the tiny hamlets of Gilmore, Leadore, Lemhi, and Tendoy. This 120-mile stretch is part of Idaho's Sacajawea Historic Byway (see Wandering Around), which provides a series of interpretive stops along the way. A historic mining town in the Birch Creek Valley, today **Gilmore** is a ghost town, containing a collection of dilapidated "Rag Town" cabins, the intact Jagger's Hotel (and about 40 other buildings), and rusted trucks scattered about. **Leadore** (Lead Ore), another mining town, was founded in 1910 with the construction of the Gilmore and Pittsburgh Railroad, which ran from Armstead, Montana, over Bannock Pass into the Lemhi Valley. Repair shops for the railroad were located in Leadore. The headwaters of the Lemhi River are at Leadore. **Tendoy** marks the location of an outpost settled in 1885 by 27 Mormon missionaries who were sent from Salt Lake City to settle among the Bannock and Shoshone Indians to "teach them the principles of citizenship." At this site, the missionaries built a mud-walled fort, the remains of which can be seen today, which they named Limhi after a prominent king in the Book of Mormon. Here in what's now Tendoy (not the town of Lemhi—go figure), the missionaries baptized more than 100 Indians and began to grow a colony. Fearing Mormon secession, President Buchanan sent 2,500 troops to suppress the colony, and Indians then attacked, killing two inhabitants and wounding five others. The missionaries retreated to Utah soon thereafter. In 1805, William Clark (of the Lewis and Clark Expedition) camped 5 miles north of Tendoy. This beautiful region and its abundant wildlife continue to attract fishermen and hunters and provides access to the Lemhi and Beaverhead Mountain ranges. Don't expect many services on this drive.

Mackay, on US 93 about 25 miles north of Arco. Mackay is one of the West's last true ranching communities. This *small* town (population about 566), while lacking in amenities, does provide for some regionally recognized entertainment, including the annual Mackay Rodeo (see Special Events) and a classic Idahoan Independence Day parade. The Lost River Range, a truly majestic backdrop, provides endless hiking, skiing, and snowmobiling opportunities.

North Fork, on US 93 about 20 miles north of Salmon. The tiny hamlet of North Fork is perched at the confluence of the North Fork and Main channel of the Salmon River. While it's not more than a handful of buildings, this funky little enclave is truly an outdoor mecca and the gateway to the Salmon River. The place swarms with river rats in the summer—tanned, relaxed, and water-burnished souls emerging after a week on the Middle Fork or their paler counterparts buzzing about prior to launching on a Main Salmon trip. Fall steelhead season, too, draws a cast of characters that mill around until the river freezes around Thanksgiving each year. The locals are also quite an interesting bunch. Don't let the remote, small nature of this place fool you—the people who choose to live here bring a slew of diverse histories with them. You will find artists, chefs, outdoorsy men and women, intellectuals, and rednecks. Local bar banter might include discussions about biodiesel, national politics, or some scary local lore (apparently this very remote area is a magnet for strange men on the lam, allegedly including murderers). It is a fun spot to hang your hat for a summer's bit (don't expect much in the winter).

Salmon, junction of ID 28 and US 93. This city of approximately 3,059 and the seat of Lemhi County dubs itself "the birthplace of Sacajawea" (the renowned Native American woman who guided Lewis and Clark on their journey to the Pacific Ocean). Located at the confluence of the Salmon and Lemhi rivers, Salmon is where gold miners began to congregate in order to ferry people and supplies across the river to work the gold fields of Leesburg—now a ghost town (see To See—Ghost Towns). In 1867, Colonel George L. Shoup laid out a proper townsite here. Shoup was a prominent businessman who was later appointed as Idaho Territorial Governor in 1889 by President Harrison and subsequently elected as the State of Idaho's first governor in 1890. As in many Idaho mining towns, Chinese miners were prominent, and a section of Salmon was dubbed "Chinatown." Many of the settlers of this region ultimately gave up mining but stayed in the area to ranch. Since that time, lumbering and tourism have also become important components of the local economy. Today, Salmon retains some of that frontier-town flavor, its downtown core dotted with several rustic, western-faced saloons, banks, and restaurants. While it's a little more happening than Challis, still the biggest draw to Salmon is its location—nestled within the Lemhi, Bitterroot, and Salmon mountains and proximate to the Frank Church Wilderness, the city is becoming increasingly known as a launch point for serious outdoor adventures and, as a commercial center, a good place to gear up.

Shoup, on Salmon River Road (see Wandering Around) 18 miles west of North Fork (on US 93). Don't miss this little hamlet named for George L. Shoup, Idaho's first governor, who served less than one year in 1890, after which he was elected senator. Settled as a mining encampment to service the Grunter Mine (the remnants of which can be seen just downstream from the town) and some of the more than 300 other claims in the quartz gold mines of the Mineral Hills District, the settlement was reached only by pack barge or trail. At the time, it was a two-day trail ride to Salmon, but the waterway provided an avenue to haul heavy mining and milling equipment and supplies. In the 1880s, about 200 people lived in Shoup, and the community had several saloons and a school. The mine and the boomtown operated until 1939. Today, the little town—snuggled into the hillside—actively services boaters, fishermen, hunters, and other visitors, many of whom gather at the **Shoup Store** (208-394-2125). While the locals

THE SHOUP STORE

rave about the great milk shakes served up at this favorite spot, I was less than impressed with the disdainful shake server of whom it seemed I asked the world when requesting a milk shake. I never did get that milk shake. Nonetheless, the store's vintage glass gas pump, which delivers gasoline by gravity after it is hand-pumped to an overhead cylinder, is a funky relic to check out. Another fun factoid (or rural legend): the last hand-operated telephone in America (about 1990) was at Shoup, and the relay station was in North Fork; the phone served 27 parties along the length of the Salmon River Road.

Sunbeam and **Clayton,** on ID 75 between Stanley and Challis. These are little outposts along the Salmon River. Sunbeam, 12 miles east of Stanley, marks the start of the Custer Motorway Adventure Road (see Wandering Around). Clayton, another 25 miles east, population 27, drew some recent attention during the ongoing controversy over the gray wolf reintroduction in Idaho (see Ketchum, Sun Valley, and the Sawtooths: America's Shangri La, To Do—Wildlife Viewing). It seems a sign was posted in a storefront window reading "Kill all the GOD-DAMN WOLVES and the people who put them here!"

✳ Wandering Around

Wandering around in Idaho is, perhaps, quite a different experience from exploring the little coastal towns of New England, for example. If you choose to amble about by car, plan on hops and skips that might require a day's worth of driving each. Idaho is remote and covers a very large area. That said, there is a freedom that comes with taking to the road in Idaho, one that is difficult to find in many regions of the United States outside the vast expanses of the West. **Idaho's Scenic Byways** (www.idahobyways.gov) has information.

Custer Motorway Adventure Road, 42 miles of narrow dirt roadway between Sunbeam on ID 75 and Challis on US 93. Road closed in winter, usually late Oct.–May. The Custer Motorway Adventure Road takes explorers past many of the historic markers of the Yankee Fork mining region. The bumpy, unimproved road is not called an "adventure road" for nothing: it should be driven only in a high-clearance vehicle. The Yankee Fork River, which joins the mighty Salmon River at **Sunbeam** (12 miles east of Stanley on ID 75), is one of Idaho's major historic mining districts. A high-grade vein of gold was discovered here in 1875 and by 1879, additional discoveries spurred a gold rush to Yankee Fork, bringing thousands of miners to **Bonanza City**, the ghost remains of which are located 7.5 miles north of Sunbeam on the Custer Motorway (see To See—Ghost Towns). To make large-scale ore production possible, investor Joseph Pfeiffer and his California associates financed a toll road from the Yankee Fork region to Challis. Completed in 1879, the road made it possible to bring in a 30-stamp mill (which crushed material by pounding rather than grinding it) for the mining operation in Custer (2 miles north of Bonanza) so that ore could be processed on-site. Over the next decade, the Custer mine and mill produced about $8 million. The mine operated until 1892, when the parent mining company failed. The toll road was reconstructed in 1933 by the Civilian Conservation Corps (CCC) and designated the Custer Motorway. The Yankee Fork dredge, weighing almost 1,000 tons, 112 feet long, 54 feet wide, and 64 feet tall, was used between

1940 and 1952 to recover gold by washing and separating the gold from rock and dirt. Interpretive signs point out historical sites and ghost-town remains along the way, including the **Sunbeam Store** and **Sunbeam Dam**, constructed in 1910 to generate electrical power for the Sunbeam Mine, dredge tailings, Bonanza City and Custer City (see To See—Ghost Towns), the Yankee Fork dredge, and other remnants of the area's mining history. The road ends in Challis.

Despite the romance and allure of ghost towns and tales of the Wild West, Idaho's mining history comes with a dark side; many mining activities in Idaho, and elsewhere in the West, have been environmentally devastating. For example, modern-day mining activity at the Grouse Creek mine in the Yankee Fork region triggered a massive landslide that buried 100 yards of Jordan Creek (a stream federally designated as critical salmon habitat), produced more than 250 water-quality violations during its short period of operation from 1994 to 1997, and resulted in a catastrophic release of cyanide and heavy metals and a costly taxpayer-funded cleanup (estimated at $53 million), which has left persistent water-quality problems and a site with which the federal government continues to struggle.

Lewis and Clark Back Country Byway, approximately 39-mile mostly single-lane gravel loop east of Tendoy, off ID 28. Closed to cars in winter (but open for

OLD-GROWTH TREE ON THE CUSTER MOTORWAY ADVENTURE ROAD

snowmobiles and skiers). This byway traces the historic steps of Lewis and Clark, who crested Lemhi Pass in 1805 on their famous expedition. Much of the area—with its majestic peaks, towering stands of fir, spectacularly lush high-alpine meadows speckled with wildflowers in spring, and rolling hills—looks much the same today as it did to Lewis and Clark. Along the way, visitors note the site where the U.S. flag was unfurled for the first time west of the Rocky Mountains, climb to Lemhi Pass, and enjoy an interpretive kiosk. Camping (but no potable water) is found at Agency Creek (milepost 33).

Sacajawea Historic Byway (ID 28)**,** 136 miles from I-15 north of Idaho Falls to Salmon. After a short 12-mile stretch on ID 33 between the interstate and Mud Lake, ID 28 takes you north through Birch Creek Valley, over Gilmore Summit, and then into the Lemhi Valley, ultimately landing you in Salmon (see Cities and Villages—Lemhi Valley villages). The absolutely stunning valleys consist of wide-open expanses of ranch- and farmland draped on alluvial sediments and sandwiched between some of the most remotely beautiful mountain ranges in the Lower 48.

Pahsimeroi Valley backroad, 90 miles of paved and unpaved unimproved road from Howe, on ID 22 east of Arco, to US 93 north of Challis; unpaved from Howe to Goldburg, paved from Goldburg north to Ellis. More adventurous explorers (and those with sufficient time on their hands) might choose to drive north on the unimproved road through the Pahsimeroi Valley from the Snake River Plain to the Salmon River. Big skies and sparkling streams, jagged, snow-capped peaks, rolling pastures and abundant wildlife—all will make you think you have died and gone to heaven.

Trail Creek Road, 41 miles from Ketchum to US 93 north of Mackay; four-wheel drive recommended. Road closed in winter; can be pretty dicey in early spring before road crews have cleaned up usual avalanche debris that spreads across roadway. Drive out Sun Valley Road to Trail Creek; 5 miles outside Ketchum, road turns to dirt and winds up a hill-hugging, often bumpy and rock-strewn road to Trail Creek Pass (elevation 7,896 feet). Flattening a tire is not an uncommon experience out here! During the 1880s, ore mined in the Yankee Fork region north of Sunbeam was hauled by horse and ore wagon up and over this pass to the smelters in Ketchum. From the summit of Trail Creek Pass, the road descends into the Challis National Forest, runs along Summit Creek until it joins the Big Lost River, and ultimately empties out at US 93 in the Thousand Springs Valley just west of **Mount Borah**, Idaho's tallest peak (elevation 12,662 feet). Mount Borah is one of nine 12,000-plus-foot peaks (of which there are only 12 in the state) scattered about the Lost River Range (see Wilder Places—Lost River Range). A scarp line visible from the road runs along the base of the mountain range here as evidence of the 7.3 Richter-scale Borah Peak Earthquake that rocked this area in 1983. The earthquake killed two school children and was felt in seven states.

This is, perhaps, one of the most scenic drives in all of Idaho, with spectacular views of the **Pioneer Mountains** to the south, including the Devils Bedstead (11,051 feet) and Hyndman Peak (at 12,009 feet the third-highest peak in Idaho), brilliant red-stemmed willows decorating the riparian zones, and, if you are lucky, glimpses of elk, deer, and other wildlife. If you look carefully, you can see avalanche chutes through the trees on some of the slopes in the Pioneers and indications of freeze-thaw activity on the raw red slopes to the north.

Salmon River Scenic Byway, 161 miles from Stanley to Lost Trail Pass at Montana state line. From Stanley, ID 75 follows alongside the rushing Salmon River through Challis and ultimately to Salmon, a stunning drive. The first part of this solitary byway winds through a relatively narrow canyon lined with stands of blue-green Douglas firs reaching down the hill slopes to the river, which constitutes "the day stretch" of the Salmon River for day rafting trips out of Stanley. As you drive, notice the increasing cant of the river as its plane pitches downgradient and the Salmon picks up steam. The road then takes you through a mosaic of verdant valleys and brilliant, color-splashed canyons that mark the waxing and waning of the river's floodplain. The particularly remote stretch of highway between Challis and Salmon provides a feel for life in the Old West (or even the present-day West), with a smattering of ranches and split-rail fences the only divisions between wide expanses of open space. Driving any piece of this road can be a Zen-like experience, providing room to reconnect with yourself (or mull over your last bad break-up).

Salmon River Road, 46 miles from North Fork on US 93 west to Corn Creek; paved for first 15 miles, then a fairly rugged dirt road. It is not all that uncommon for projectiles emanating from the roadbed to take out oil pans and exhaust systems on this stretch of road. Starting from the North Fork Store, this road heads west along the rugged Salmon River through Shoup to Corn Creek, the put-in for river trips on the Main Salmon River and the take-out for the classic Middle Fork trips. Here, you are in the Frank Church–River of No Return Wilderness, and this road is the only one into this vast wilderness area. The road was constructed as a Civilian Conservation Corp project, originally intended to span 150 miles from North Fork west clear to Riggins on US 95. In 1939, the project was ceased due to demands of World War II; at that point, 46 miles had been constructed from North Fork and another 27 miles east from Riggins. Both roads are still in use today.

Even if you are not planning to run the river, this cool drive will take you through some spectacularly beautiful country and funky little villages along the way. Near the start of the road, the Salmon River opens up into a wide, braided floodplain, stacked with driftwood and frequented by blue heron. Not far down the road, you will see the **Indianola HeliTack base** (for U.S. Forest Service smokejumpers), comprised of a compound of signature white and green U.S. Forest Service buildings. A bronze statue out back commemorates two young firefighters who died fighting the Cramer Fire of 2003. It is this section of the Salmon River (and Pine Creek Rapids in particular), with its steep canyon walls and torrents of water raging through rapid after rapid, where, in 1805, the Lewis and Clark Expedition was forced to retreat from their dream of finding a water route to the Pacific. (That they were to travel in dugout canoes probably didn't help either!) Instead, they voyaged overland northward into Montana, over the Bitterroot Mountains at Lolo Pass, and then across Idaho via the Clearwater River to the Columbia River, which they were able to navigate by canoe to the

SALMON RIVER ROAD OUTSIDE NORTH FORK

Pacific Ocean. Later, pilots in wooden sweep boats navigated this course of the Salmon River—but only in one direction!—selling the wood scraps at the end of the river voyage and completing their round trip back to Salmon overland. Thus, the Salmon River earned the moniker the River of No Return; another version says that the Native Americans told Lewis and Clark that if they went down this river, they would never return.

Other areas of note along the way to Corn Creek include an archaeological site where artifacts, including stone arrows and dart points, and pictographs from the **Sheep Eater Indians** have been excavated. Panther Creek tumbles into the Salmon River from the south, draining the high Big Horn Crags of the Salmon National Forest, and is a coveted fishing and hunting spot for mountain goats, elk, sheep, bears, and other species. (Panther Creek Road/FR 55 runs south through the old mining outpost at Cobalt to Challis.) A series of cabins near Lake Creek are accessible only by a cable and cart across the river. At Colson Creek, you will find renowned backcountry outfitter and guide Stanley Potts selling his books, including *The Potts' Factor versus Murphy's Law* (Stoneydale Press Publishing Co., 2003), *Look Down on the Stars*, and the *Potts Factor's Return* (Stanley Potts, 2006). This area bustles with river-rat activity in the summer, and you are bound to see lots of strong, bronzed, outdoorsy-looking folks buzzing around. In the off-season, however, be prepared to have a much more

PETROGLYPHS ALONG THE SALMON RIVER ROAD

solitary experience—and also, perhaps, to run into some local color (including
bands of somewhat creepy, solemn-faced, camo-ensconced guys on ATVs, rifles
prominently strapped across their chests).

✳ To See

GHOST TOWNS

In this region, ghost towns are scattered about the landscape, buildings dis-
carded like worn shoes, mining equipment left to its own devices, providing a
window into Idaho's frontier days. Some of the more prominent ghost towns
include these:

Bayhorse, in a canyon off ID 75, 14 miles south of Challis. The dilapidated
remains of a silver-lead mine, including a smelter and charcoal kilns, can be
found at this small town, complete with a western-front hotel. The ghost town
itself is on private property but can be viewed from the road. The kilns, however,
are located on U.S. Forest Service property and are open to the public.

Bonanza City and **Custer City**, on Custer Motorway Adventure Road 7.5
miles and 9.5 miles north of Sunbeam, respectively. Located in the Yankee Fork
mining district not far from Stanley, these towns are reached by a narrow dirt
road (see Wandering Around). In 1879, Bonanza City had only one store and
one saloon, but it proceeded to grow as fast as building materials could be
obtained, and for a short time the seasonal population swelled to 7,000 or 8,000
prospectors. It is now a ghost town consisting of a few old buildings and a cemetery. Custer City is a ghost town complete with an old school (now a museum),
stamp mill, tram, and other remnants of frenetic mining activity.

Cobalt, not far from Leesburg (see below); go southwest on Napias Creek Road
and southwest on Panther Creek Road for about 10.5 miles. This ghost mining
town served the Blackbird Cobalt Mine, located to the northwest of Cobalt up
Blackbird Creek from its confluence with Panther Creek. The mine, from which
cobalt and copper have been extracted by both shaft and open-pit methods on
thousands of acres of mining claims from the late 1800s until 1982, is now a federal Superfund site. Acid drainage from the many piles of mining waste at the
headwaters of Bucktrail Creek, a tributary to Big Deer Creek, have leached
arsenic, copper, cobalt, nickel, and other contaminants into many creeks in the
area, resulting in degraded water quality and toxicity threats to endangered
salmon and other wildlife. Signs are posted in the area warning hikers not to
drink from these streams.

Gilmore and **Tendoy**, on ID 28 between ID 22 and Salmon. Historic settle-
ments in the Lemhi Valley also can be seen (see Towns—Lemhi Valley villages).

Leesburg, 13.4 miles northeast of Salmon; go northwest up Williams Creek
Road and then northeast on Napias Creek Road (FR 242). Leesburg was settled
when Frank Barney Sharkey and friends discovered gold, propelling a gold rush
that drew as many as 7,000 residents to Leesburg and that ultimately netted
about $40 million worth of gold.

Nicholia, in Birch Creek Valley off ID 28 southwest of Gilmore Summit. This
little town's general stores, hotels, saloons, and barber shops once bustled with

the activity of up to 1,500 residents working in this mining district. Today, little remains of the town and the mine, except parts of a few log cabins and a rusty ore tram. Remains of the Nicholia Charcoal Kilns, in the form of four clay ovens—oversized beehives perched on the landscape—can be found to the north, on the other side of the valley from the town. The kilns were built in 1885 to smelt lead and silver from the now-defunct Viola Mine, which operated from 1882 to 1890 and produced $2.5 million worth of lead and silver. Today, you can take a self-guided tour through the kilns.

HISTORICAL SITES

Experimental Breeder Reactor-1 (EBR-1) National Historic Landmark, off US 20/26, 18 miles south of Arco. Open daily mid-June–mid-Sept. for self-guided tours. Free. EBR-1, which powered Arco (see Cities and Villages), is located within the **Idaho National Laboratory** (INL Tours Office 208-526-0050 or 208-526-9120; www.inel.gov), north of US 20 between Arco and Idaho Falls. In the middle of an 890-square-mile (about 85 percent the size of Rhode Island!) sea of sagebrush and surrounded by scary-looking signs and barbed wire, the Idaho National Laboratory appears a surreal government enclave, cloaked in secrecy. Seeing this facility from afar for the first time is definitely a bizarre

EXPERIMENTAL BREEDER REACTOR AT IDAHO NATIONAL LABORATORY

Matt Furber

experience; you might find yourself subconsciously on the lookout for UFOs. In 1949, as a spin-off to the World War II Manhattan Project, the Atomic Energy Commission established the National Reactor Testing Station—now the INL— to conduct nuclear energy research for civilian and military purposes. Construction of the facility began in 1950 on land that originally had been used as the Naval Proving Grounds. Chosen because of its remote location, the site was considered ideal for potentially hazardous reactor experiments. The research history of this facility includes the development of an experimental breeder reactor that illuminated lightbulbs with nuclear-generated electric power and successfully converted fertile isotopes to fissile isotopes. In 1955, electricity generated by uranium-fueled nuclear power was fed into power lines and transmitted 20 miles to light up the 1,000-person town of Arco, making Arco the first city in the world to be powered by nuclear energy (albeit only for an hour!). Over time, 52 other reactors were designed and tested here; three still operate today, and one is on standby.

The nuclear activities here have not been without consequence, however. In 1961, a core meltdown and reactor explosion killed three men. In the early 1970s, it was discovered that the INL was routinely injecting liquid radioactive effluent, primarily tritium, into the Snake River Aquifer, Idaho's largest aquifer and one of the largest and most productive aquifers in the world (estimated to hold about as much water as does Lake Erie). This practice began in 1953 and continued until the 1990s. In addition to radioactive contaminants in concentrations exceeding drinking-water standards, contaminants detected in groundwater beneath the site include organic solvents such as acetone, trichloroethylene, and benzene and heavy metals including lead, mercury, and chromium. As a sole-source aquifer (a designation implying that the aquifer provides for more than 50 percent of the drinking water of those who live above the aquifer), the Snake River Aquifer provides domestic water for almost 300,000 people (as well as providing much of the irrigation water for Idaho's agricultural economy) and is particularly vulnerable to contamination. As a result of nuclear contamination emanating from activities at the INL, the area was designated as a Superfund site in 1989. Cleanup activities continue to this day, and concern for the safety of this precious drinking water supply persists. The **Snake River Alliance** (www .snakeriveralliance.org) is an organization that once called itself "Idaho's Nuclear Watchdog."

In addition to conducting nuclear research, INL has more recently expanded its mandate and currently also conducts research related to alternative energy, environmental cleanup technologies (ironically enough), materials science, and biotechnology. The INL is somewhat of an iconic representation of the cultural and political divides that exist in this state—you won't find much support for the INL in the liberal enclave that is the Wood River Valley, while words of protest won't come easily in Pocatello or Idaho Falls, where many of the facility's 8,000 employees live. Tours of other INL facilities can be arranged by calling the INL Tours Office.

Land of the Yankee Fork Historic Area (208-879-5244; www.idahoparks .org/parks/yankeefork.asp), junction of ID 75 and US 93 just south of Challis.

Open 9–5 daily in summer; 9–5 Mon.–Fri. in winter. The Land of the Yankee Fork Historic Area is a federally designated historic area that, through a series of interpretive sites including historic mining equipment, ghost towns, a bison kill site, a state park, and the Yankee Fork dredge, provides a window into Idaho's frontier mining history. The interpretive center in Challis houses museum exhibits, a gold-panning station, and short films on local mining history.

Sacajawea Interpretive, Cultural, and Educational Center (208-756-1188; www.sacajaweacenter.org), 200 Main St., Salmon. Open 9–6 daily Memorial Day–Sept.; 9–5 Sat.–Sun. May and Oct. $4. The facility's 71-acre park, open during daylight hours year-round, is dedicated to the commemoration of Sacajawea, her people the Agaidika, and the Lewis and Clark Expedition; it has an impressive array of facilities. The visitor center showcases interpretive exhibits and artifacts highlighting Sacajawea's role in the Lewis and Clark Expedition, while the Sacajawea Center Research Library houses a collection of resources related to the expedition and to Native American subjects, as well as relevant field guides. Also on-site are the 75-seat Meriwether Theater, housed in a renovated old barn; a primitive camping area; a dogwalk facility; a ropes course; and an amphitheater. The center offers various courses and programs for adults and children. It also sponsors the annual Heritage Day event in Aug. (see Special Events).

MUSEUMS

Lemhi County Historical Museum (208-756-3342; www.sacajaweahome .com), 210 Main St., Salmon. Open 9–5 Mon.–Sat. Apr. 15–Oct. $2. This small museum focuses on the history of the Lemhi Shoshone of the Lemhi and Salmon River valleys and of the gold rush era in this region. The museum houses an extensive collection of Lemhi Shoshone artifacts, including clothing, beadwork, arrowheads, and ceremonial pieces, as well as a collection of mining relics.

North Custer Museum (208-879-2846), 1211 S. Main St., Challis. Open 10–4 Sat.–Sun. and holidays Memorial Day weekend–Sept. or by appointment. Donations appreciated. This museum, also known as the Challis Museum, displays artifacts from early settlers of central Idaho, with a special emphasis on the history of the north Custer County and Challis areas.

WILDLIFE VIEWING

Abundant wildlife inhabits the vast wilds of Central Idaho. Clearly, getting on the trail is the best way to view wildlife, but in this region, there is a good chance you will encounter wildlife while you're driving around. It is not uncommon to see antelope, elk, and mule and white-tailed deer. If you watch the skies, you might be treated to the sight of a bald eagle, osprey, or red-tailed hawk. More elusive critters, including moose, black bears, and mountain goats, can also be seen. See What's Where in Idaho—Wildlife for more resources and field guides to wildlife in the state.

Copper Basin. From Ketchum, drive 22 miles northeast on Trail Creek Road to confluence with East Fork of Big Lost River, turn right, and drive southeast, following signs for Copper Basin, 18 miles to intersection with Copper Basin Loop Road.) This massive, high-elevation (7,000- to 8,000-foot) valley is a wildflower-strewn jewel snuggled between the serrated, oft-snowcapped peaks and hanging glacial valleys of the Pioneer and White Knob mountains. It can be accessed along the East Fork of the Big Lost River, which joins Trail Creek and Trail Creek Road 22 miles east of Ketchum. Spanning about 35 square miles, this triangular basin of earthy, sagebrush steppe provides an oasis for pronghorn antelopes, mule deer, elk, moose, and many other species of wildlife. Animals of prey, including coyotes, cougars, and wolves, are quietly present here as well. Since the 1995 reintroduction of the gray wolf in Idaho (see Ketchum, Sun Valley, and the Sawtooths: America's Shangri-La, To See—Wildlife Viewing), several packs have made their homes in Copper Basin.

✳ To Do

CAMPING

Salmon-Challis National Forest Lost River Ranger District (208-588-3400; www.fs.fed.us/r4/sc/lostriver/) has information on campgrounds, including these listed below.

GIBBONSVILLE RELICS MUSEUM

CAMPING ALONG THE SALMON RIVER

Copper Basin (to get there, see To See—Wildlife Viewing) is a series of kettle-hole ponds, glacial erratics (boulders—often large—that were transported and deposited by a glacier upon bedrock of a different lithology; erratics are indicators of historic ice-flow patterns), and hanging valleys that provide evidence of the massive glaciers that once covered this area. Draining the basin are numerous streams, including Star Hope Creek and the East Fork of the Big Lost River (the headwaters of the Big Lost River), which glint sunbeams and provide verdant riparian and cold-water fish habitat (in other words, excellent trout fishing). The soft purples and reds and elongated shadows that drape the peaks and undulating basin floor are sights earned by those hardy enough to pitch a tent in this fairly remote locale.

Camping options abound in the Copper Basin area, including the **Phi Kappa and Park Creek campgrounds** 23 and 26 miles, respectively, out Trail Creek Road from Sun Valley. **Starhope Campground** is located 9 miles out the Copper Basin Loop Road. **Wildhorse Campground** can be accessed 2 miles down Copper Basin Road, at Wild Horse Creek, by taking a right on Wildhorse Road and driving 5.5 miles to the campground. Dispersed camping is also allowed at **Bellas Canyon** on Copper Basin Loop Road.

Custer Motorway Adventure Road, from Sunbeam on ID 75 to Challis on US 93, has 10 campgrounds along its 42 miles of narrow dirt roadway (see Wandering Around).

Salmon River Road, west of North Fork, has **Deadwater Spring Campground** a few miles west of US 93 and **Corn Creek Campground** at the road's end (see Wandering Around).

US 93, from North Fork to Lost Trail Pass, is entirely in the national forest, with **Wagonhammer Spring Campground** just south of North Fork and **Twin Creek Campground** just south of the pass.

FISHING

Idaho Department of Fish and Game (208-525-7290; www.fishandgame .idaho.gov/cms/fish), Upper Snake River Region, 1515 Lincoln Rd., Idaho Falls. The comprehensive Web site has all the relevant information you will need to plan a fishing excursion in this region (or anywhere else in Idaho), including fishing guides, organized by Idaho region, which include maps locating major fishing

ANGLERS ENJOY FLY-FISHING THE SALMON RIVER.

Matt Furber

spots on lakes, reservoirs, rivers, and streams and tables of species by fishing location; fishing and boating access guides with maps showing points of access for major fisheries and information about camping, boat access, and other services; license information; and fishing regulations.

Lost River Ranger District (208-588-3400), 716 W. Custer, Mackay. They also have information.

Salmon-Challis National Forest (www.fs.fed.us/r4/sc/recreation/fishing/index .shtml) also has information. There are 12 game fish species and nine nongame species known to inhabit the waters of the Salmon-Challis National Forest, including chinook and sockeye salmon (which cannot be fished); rainbow, bull, cutthroat, brook, and golden trout; smallmouth bass; and sculpin.

Many of the spots listed here require some serious hiking to gain access; some have camping facilities. Popular fishing spots include the **Little Lost River–Sawmill Creek area** on the Pahsimeroi Valley backroad (see Wandering Around); **Big, Golden, and Long lakes**, all in the Big Lost River drainage on US 93; and **Hyde Pond, Kids Creek Pond, Hayden Ponds, Lemhi Range mountain lakes,** and **Meadow Lakes** in the Lehmi drainage on ID 28. **Carlson Lake** in the Pahsimeroi Valley, **Blue Mountain Pond** near Challis on US 93, and a slew of lakes in the great Salmon River Mountains northeast of ID 75/US 93, including the **Bighorn Crag mountain lakes, Iron Lake,** and **Wallace Lake**, provide for great trout fishing.

Lemhi, Pahsimeroi, and Salmon rivers are chock full of cold-water fish species, and all have countless fabulous fishing spots. The Upper Salmon River from Stanley to North Fork via ID 75 and US 93 draws fly-fishermen and -women looking for steelhead, while the Middle Fork of the Salmon (accessible via boat, hiking trails, or air) is favored for cutthroat trout fishing.

If you are so inclined, **fishing guides** can be hired for one-day or multiday guided trips; many hunting outfitters (see Hunting, below) also act as fishing guides.

HIKING

Salmon-Challis National Forest (208-756-5100; www.fs.fed.us/r4/sc), 1206 S. Challis St., Salmon. Contact the Salmon office for information on the boundless hiking places (and other recreational activities) in all the mountain areas of the Salmon-Challis National Forest—the Salmon River Mountains, the Lemhis, the Lost River Range, and the Beaverheads. Their web site has a complete listing of trails by ranger district and lots of information about camping opportunities and other recreational activities in the area.

Continental Divide Trail (303-838-3760; www.cdtrail.org). This trail is a work in progress, with plans to span 3,100 miles from Canada to Mexico, tracing the Continental Divide through Montana, Idaho, Wyoming, Colorado, and New Mexico. About 70 percent of the trail is usable today, including several hundred miles of trail along the Idaho–Montana border (running in and out of Idaho), from north of North Fork to outside Island Park near Yellowstone National Park, running through the Bitterroot and Centennial mountains. More than 100 miles of this trail are managed by the Leadore Ranger District (see next page).

Eastern Pioneer Mountains (for access, see Camping). Amazing hiking opportunities lie just outside your car (or tent) door in this area, which offers virtually limitless opportunity to get off the beaten path. Hikers and horseback riders can disappear into this roadless haven via a network of almost 300 maintained trails, covering over 2,600 miles of terrain. Backpackers have been known to take to these hills for months on end without encountering another soul. Hikes include Moose Lake, Boulder Lake, Surprise Valley, Fall Creek, Washington Lake off Wildhorse Road, and Betty, Goat, and Baptie lakes off Copper Basin Loop Road. Serious climbers can find approaches to the Devils Bedstead (elevation 11,051 feet) and Hyndman Peak (12,009 feet) from the Wildhorse Road area.

Leadore Ranger District (208-768-2500; www.fs.fed.us/r4/sc/leadore) has information on the Salmon-Challis National Forest's Leadore District, which manages 33 trails totaling 193 miles into the Lemhi and Beaverhead mountains from the Lemhi Valley on ID 28. These trails access beautiful alpine lakes, streams, and remote wilderness.

Lemhi Range, via the Pahsimeroi Valley (see Wandering Around). Popular recreation spots in the Lemhi Range include Sawmill Canyon, Big Creek Canyon, and Morris Creek. Each of these areas have camping facilities and trailheads into the Lemhis.

Lost River Range. Accessible hiking spots in the Lost River Range via the Pahsimeroi Valley (see Wandering Around) include Doublespring Pass Road, which winds southwest from the Pahsimeroi Valley (north of Goldburg) past Mount Borah (elevation 12,662 feet), Idaho's highest peak, and lands in the Thousand Springs area. Hiking Mount Borah is an annual pilgrimage for many locals. Pass Creek Road also crosses the Lost River Range from Little Lost River Valley into the Big Lost River Valley south of Mackay. Between these two roads is a parallel road that also goes into the Lost Rivers along the Upper Pashimeroi River. Some consider this area to be one of Idaho's most scenic, as the road takes you along the back side of Borah and Leatherman peaks (Idaho's second-highest peak) and Mount Breitenbach (Idaho's fifth-highest peak). The road, however, is really rough and appropriate only for four-wheel-drive vehicles.

Salmon River Range, north of Stanley via Custer Motorway Adventure Road (see Wandering Around). To the northwest of the Salmon River Valley is a vast, untamed wilderness spanning more than 3,800 square miles (nearly the size of Connecticut), much of which falls within the Frank Church–River of No Return Wilderness—at 2.4 million acres, the second-largest roadless area in the Lower 48. Within the Salmon River Range are more than 135 named summits and rock towers, more than 100 nameless peaks, and more than 2,500 miles of trails in the Frank Church. If you were to leave the pavement in Stanley and head due north, your foot wouldn't touch another chunk of asphalt for more than 200 miles. Noteworthy peaks in this region include Mount McGuire, which at 10,082 feet is the highest point in the Bighorn Crags; Cabin Creek Peak near Stanley; Ramskull Peak; Pinnacles Peak; and a series of peaks with graphic names like Knuckle Peak, Snowslide Peak, the Rusty Nail, and Wolf Fang Peak. Because most visitors enter the Frank Church by boat on the Middle Fork, this area offers the most solitary hiking opportunities you'll find anywhere.

A handful of rustic **backcountry ranches**, accessed by small aircraft or Jet Boat, are nestled alongside the Salmon River and can provide perhaps a less arduous entrée to the wilderness area (see Lodging—Backcountry).

Maps

U.S. Geological Survey (www.store.usgs.gov). USGS topos for this area, including "Standhope Peak," "Phi Kappa Mountain," and "Copper Basin," can be purchased directly from the USGS or other maps dealers.

Outfitters

Idaho Outfitters and Guides Association (208-342-1438; www.ioga.org) maintains a complete list of registered guides running trips here and elsewhere in the state. If a guided trip is more your style, scores of outfitters offer guided river, hiking, ski, and horsepacking trips into the Frank Church. Remote regions of the wilderness can also be accessed via about 18 small backcountry airstrips. For private flights, try the following.

Salmon Air (800-448-3413 or 208-756-6211; www.salmonair.com).

Sawtooth Adventure Company (208-774-4644 summer, 801-718-0338 winter, or 866-774-4644; www.sawtoothadventure.com).

Recommended Reading

For a great guide to backcountry hiking in the Salmon River Range, see Margaret Fuller's *Trails of the Frank Church–River of No Return Wilderness* (Trail Guide Books, 2002), a great resource if you are looking to plan a private trip. Other good resources include *Idaho: A Climbing Guide* by Tom Lopez (Mountaineers Books, 2000), *Backpacking Idaho: From Alpine Peaks to Desert Canyons* by Douglas Lorain (Wilderness Press, 2004), and *Hiking Idaho,* second edition, by Ralph and Jackie Maughan (Falcon, 2001).

HORSEBACK RIDING

With its vast expanses of remote, roadless backcountry, this region of Idaho is ideal for horsepack trips. Licensed outfitters can guide you by horseback into some otherwise fairly inaccessible terrain in search of glistening high-alpine lakes secreted away beneath looming spires of metamorphosed rock, ancient Indian trails bearing faint reminders of interdependencies of Native populations and this rugged land, secluded fishing streams in which to catch your dinner, and old mining camps where you might want to drink whiskey and tell stories by an evening fire. Many of these guiding services run fully outfitted pack trips, wherein experienced wranglers tend to the horses, set up your tents, and cook up some hearty meals. Drop camps are also available for hikers and hunters looking to have their gear hauled in by horseback. Outfitters in this region include the following:

Flying Resort Ranches (208-756-6295; www.flyingresortranches.com), Salmon.

Geertson Creek Trail Rides (208-756-2463; www.geertson.com), Salmon.

Horse Creek Outfitters (301-997-0987; www.hcoutfiters.com), Challis.

HISTORIC BATHHOUSE AT SUNBEAM HOT SPRING

Indian Creek Guest Ranch (208-394-2126; www.indiancreekguestranch.com), North Fork.

Mile High Outfitters of Idaho (208-879-4500; www.milehighoutfitters.com), Challis.

100 Acre Wood Bed & Breakfast Resort (208-865-2165; www.100acrewood resort.com), North Fork.

Twin Peaks Ranch (208-894-2429; www.twinpeaksranch.com), Salmon.

White Cloud Outfitters (208-879-4574; www.whitecloudoutfitters.com), Challis.

Wilderness Outfitters (208-879-2203; www.idahowilderness.com), Challis.

HOT SPRINGS

In this region, you can find some great hot springs in which to soak your weary bones. Note that most of Idaho's hot springs are undeveloped and require hiking (and sometimes route-finding) to get to them.

Challis. Near Challis you can find hot springs with entertaining names such as Cronks (Royal Gorge) Hot Spring, Sitz Bath Hot Springs, and Hospital Bar Hot Springs.

Challis Hot Springs (208-879-4442 or 800-479-1295; www.challishotsprings .com) is one of the few developed hot springs in the area, offering year-round swimming in two pools capturing natural hot spring flow. (See also Lodging—B&Bs.)

Salmon. Popular spots out of Salmon include Goldbug Hot Springs, Horse Creek Hot Springs, and Sharkey (Tendoy) Hot Springs. Of course, any river trip on the Middle Fork will dazzle its participants with secluded hot pots amid the wildest of wilds, revered not only for the ambience and medicinal value, but also as a most-welcomed bathing opportunity.

Stanley. Some of the more popular hot pots out of Stanley include Mormon Bend Hot Spring, Sunbeam Hot Spring, the Boat Box (Elkhorn Hot Springs), and Slate Creek (Hoodoo Hot Springs).

Recommended Reading
It would be hard to beat Evie Litton's book *Hiking: Hot Springs in the Pacific Northwest* (The Globe Pequot Press, 1995) for directions, descriptions of individual pools, and hiking routes.

HUNTING
This region is renowned for big-game hunting for elk, deer, bighorn sheep, mountain goats, antelope, black bears, and cougars; bird hunting for Canada geese, ducks, chukar, and grouse is popular.

Idaho Fish and Game (208-334-3700; www.fishandgame.idaho.gov) has information on hunting licenses, fees, and regulations.

Idaho Outfitters and Guides (www.ioga.org) has a complete listing of licensed hunting guides in the area, many of which can arrange single- or multiday trips.

SKIING
Alpine Skiing
Lost Trail Powder Mountain (406-821-3508; www.losttrail.com), on US 93 near Lost Trail Pass, 46 miles north of Salmon. Open Thurs.–Sat. Lift tickets $31 for adults, $21 for kids 6–12, kids 5 and under, free. Perched where US 93 heads up and over the Continental Divide at Lost Trail Pass (elevation 7,014 feet) and into Montana, Lost Trail Powder Mountain is a hidden jewel of an alpine ski resort. While not huge—1,000 acres of skiable terrain, 1,800 vertical feet, and four chairlifts—this place is kicked back, and with an annual snowfall averaging 300 inches, it gets some powpow! Powder hounds with flexible schedules enjoy getting some fresh tracks on Thurs. For more experienced skiers, the resort also offers access to some backcountry terrain.

Nordic Skiing
Chief Joseph Cross-Country Ski Trail System (Sula Ranger Station, 406-821-3201, for information), on US 93 at Lost Trail Pass; from Salmon take US 93

Chris Pilaro

THE FIRST SNOW WHETS SKIERS' ANTICIPATION.

north about 45 miles to Lost Trail Pass, then a right on ID 43 about another mile to parking area on the left. Pit toilets, parking, and trail maps at trailhead. Trails groomed weekly. Dogs discouraged on groomed trails. This trail system includes 8 kilometers of easy trails and another 17 kilometers of more difficult trails winding through beautiful stands of Douglas fir, their boughs lowered toward the ground in acquiescence to blankets of glinting white snow, and quiet, open meadows with stunning alpine vistas along the way.

Willams Creek Summit Cross-Country Ski Complex (Salmon-Challis National Forest, 208-756-5100, for information), on Williams Creek Road, 10 miles southeast of Salmon; from Salmon drive US 93 south 5 miles, turn right at Shoup Bridge across the river, continue about 1 mile to junction of Perreau and Willams creeks, take left fork, and continue to Williams Creek Summit, about 12 miles to parking pullouts just shy of the summit. Generally open mid-Dec.–mid-Mar. Pit toilets at trailhead. This 17-mile trail system was developed jointly by the Salmon National Forest and the Salmon Nordic Ski Association. Ungroomed trails traverse varying terrain and are rated based on difficulty. Surrounding terrain provides for great backcountry skiing.

WHITE-WATER KAYAKING AND RAFTING

Salmon–Challis National Forest (www.fs.fed.us/r4/sc/recreation/whitewater rafting/mainsalmon/index.shtml) has information about access-road conditions, regulations, facilities at put-ins and take-outs, permits, and the like. North Fork, on US 93, is a mecca for white-water adventure. Coveted white-water river trips on the Main and Middle Fork Salmon rivers take explorers deep into the heart of the Frank Church–River of No Return Wilderness Area, providing an unparalleled wilderness experience.

Main Salmon River, 82, 94, or 103 miles from Corn Creek to Carey Creek, Spring Bar, or Riggins; put-in at Corn Creek accessed via Salmon River Road (see Wandering Around), which departs from just near North Fork Store and runs through 46 miles of stunning canyon alongside the river to Corn Creek (the drive is almost as spectacular as the raft trip). Season is Apr.–June. This mellower part of the Salmon River offers an amazing river experience. Six-day river trips (see Outfitters) take adventurers deep into the Frank Church–River of No Return Wilderness, through class III–IV whitewater to magical, white sandy beaches that provide for fabulous camping (and volleyball). Hot springs and abundant wildlife make this trip special. This is a permitted trip, with only four noncommercial launches allowed daily.

Middle Fork Salmon River, about 105 miles, from Salmon River Mountains northwest of Stanley northeastward to Main Salmon near end of Salmon River Road. Season about June 10–Sept. 10, generally regulated by access—Boundary Creek Road closed until snowmelt, but put-ins at Indian Creek and Marsh Creek can still be reached by flying in. Considered Idaho's jewel, the Middle Fork stretches through the vast wilderness chain of the Salmon River Mountains in the Frank Church–River of No Return Wilderness, incising its way further into a V-shape valley of metamorphic and plutonic rock, leaving canyons as high

THE CHURNING SALMON RIVER IS A FAVORITE AMONG WHITE-WATER ENTHUSIASTS.

as 5,000 feet to reach skyward (see Wilder Places—Wilderness Areas). To protect this pristine wilderness, the number of boaters on the Middle Fork is tightly regulated by permit for both commercial trips and private permit trips. The classic Middle Fork trip generally is the crème de la crème of commercial river trips, with gourmet food (outfitters try to outdo each other with the delicacies they provide guests), great service, and an unrivalled wilderness experience that includes a river full of crystal-clear 20-foot pools, phenomenal fishing, luxurious hot springs for lounging (and bathing—*this* is a luxury), stunning scenery, and wildlife galore. Observant boaters may see bighorn sheep, mountain goats, elk, deer, and, perhaps, an elusive mountain lion. If you're looking for a cushier trip, rustic lodges on the Middle Fork (see Lodging) offer warm beds and hot showers to wayward rafters.

Outfitters

There are 17 licensed outfitters running the Middle Fork and 16 on the Main Salmon. A slew of other outfitters out of Salmon can arrange guided trips down the Middle Fork or the Main Salmon. Here's a sampling:

Aggipah River Trips (208-756-4167; www.aggipah.com) offers multiday camping trips on the Middle Fork, the Main Salmon, and the Lower Salmon River, as well as day trips near the town of Salmon and a variety of fishing trips.

Idaho Adventures (208-756-2986 or 800-789-WAVE; www.idahoadventures .com) offers one- to six-day trips on the Middle Fork, as well as fishing and horseback riding trips.

Idaho River Journeys (888-997-8399; www.idahoriverjourneys.com) runs four- to six-day Middle Fork and Main Salmon trips and fly-fishing trips.

Kookaburra Rafting Trips (208-756-4386 or 888-654-4386; www.raft4fun .com) offers one- to three-day white-water adventures on the "Lewis & Clark" stretch of the Salmon River.

Little John's River Rentals (208-756-6477), 1213 Main St., Salmon. Experienced boaters can rent gear here for a permit trip.

North Fork Guides (208-865-2534; www.northforkguides.com), North Fork. Offers half- to six-day white-water trips on the Middle Fork, plus guided fly-fishing expeditions.

Rocky Mountain River Tours (208-345-2400; www.rockymountainrivertours .com), Salmon and Boise. The premier outfitter on the Middle Fork provides a class-act trip with gourmet food. Shiela Mills, one of the group's proprietors, is well known for her book on river cooking (*The Outdoor Dutch Oven Cookbook*, International Marine–Ragged Mountain Press, 1997).

Salmon Air (800-448-3413 and 208-756-6211; www.salmonair.com) offers shuttle service in and out of the Middle Fork and Main Salmon areas and flies in to backcountry put-ins.

Wilderness River Outfitters (800-252-6581; www.wildernessriver.com) runs multiday trips on the Main Salmon and the Middle Fork, as well as hiking, mountain biking, ranch stay, and combination adventures.

Most of this part of Idaho is wild. With miles upon miles of unadulterated landscape—snowcapped peaks stacked one after another, incised by crystal-clear rivers that form dramatic canyons and wide alpine valleys and meadows, and draped by bluebird skies—it is hard to discern the wilder places of Idaho from many others. Belt after belt of orogenically uplifted crust forms an unending list of wilder place names: the Sawtooths, Pioneers, Lost Rivers, Lemhis, Beaverheads, and Salmon River mountains. With about 1.3 million people residing in all of Idaho, and most of those living within valleys, you can imagine how sparsely populated much of this area is. If nothing more than to whet your appetite, I've listed a few of the more renowned wilder places.

Copper Basin, a massive, high-alpine, wildflower-strewn jewel of a valley, spans about 35 square miles at about 7,800 feet in elevation in the Eastern Pioneer Mountains (see To Do—Camping). This triangular basin of earthy, sagebrush steppe provides an oasis for wildlife (see To See—Wildlife Viewing). Draining the basin are numerous streams providing cold-water fish habitat. So beautiful is this basin that it has been likened to the Lamar Valley in Yellowstone National Park, yet despite its raw beauty, this area has not been protected. It has been subject to significant grazing pressure that has both degraded some areas of the basin and stirred heated controversy over the appropriateness of allowing grazing on public lands in such a spectacular and important natural habitat.

PARKS AND PRESERVES

Craters of the Moon National Monument and Preserve (208-527-3257; www.nps.gov/crmo), on US 20/26/93, 20 miles southwest of Arco. Monument and preserve open year-round, except Loop Drive closed mid-Nov.–mid-Apr.; visitor center open 8–4:30 daily in winter except holidays, 8–6 daily Memorial Day–Labor Day. Entrance fee is $8 per vehicle, $4 per person by bike, motorcycle or on foot. Free for children 15 and under. A sea of lava tubes and flows interspersed with cinder cones and isolated oases of sagebrush, called *kipukas*, paint the landscape at Craters of the Moon, creating what seems to be a vast moonscape. This strange landscape appears particularly surreal during winter, when a blanket of snow wraps itself over the earth's tautly stretched crust and pointy lava formations peek through like dark goblins. This is a good spot to stretch your legs if you are on US 93 near Arco.

Land of the Yankee Fork State Park (208-879-5244; www.idahoparks.org/parks/yankeefork.asp), junction of ID 75 and US 93 just south of Challis. Land of the Yankee Fork State Park is part of the larger historic area of the same name, a federally designated historic area with interpretive sites on Idaho's mining history (see To See—Historical Sites).

WILDERNESS AREAS

Frank Church–River of No Return Wilderness, 2.3 million acres in the heart of Idaho. This designated wilderness area, often called "the Frank," is a vast, protected roadless area, the second-largest area of protected wilderness in

CLEAR ALPINE WATERS BECKON IN CENTRAL IDAHO'S INNUMERABLE MOUNTAINS.

the continental United States. Together with the bordering 206,000-acre Gospel Hump Wilderness to the northwest and unprotected Forest Service roadless areas, these areas constitute a 3.3 million-acre roadless area. Created in 1980 by an act of Congress, the area was initially designated the River of No Return Wilderness Area but was renamed the Frank Church–River of No Return Wilderness in 1984 to honor U.S. Senator Frank Church (D-Idaho, 1957–1980), who had been the Senate sponsor for the Wilderness Act of 1964, legislation designed to protect those areas "untrammeled by man."

Containing parts of the Salmon River and Clearwater mountains and encompassing the Bighorn Crags and the Wild and Scenic Middle Fork of the Salmon and Main Salmon rivers, this is a ruggedly beautiful landscape. The jagged summits of the Bighorn Crags tower skyward in contrast to the plunging canyons of the Middle Fork of the Salmon, in spots providing relief of up to 7,000 feet (deeper than the Grand Canyon). The landscape is a patchwork of thick forests of Douglas fir, spruce, and ponderosa and lodgepole pine stretching up dendritic drainages, punctuated by wide meadows filled with lush grass, sun-splashed bald slopes, and glittering, clear, high-alpine lakes. The wilderness is an oasis for wildlife, providing homes for mountain lions, black bears, lynx, coyotes, gray wolves, wolverines, bighorn sheep, mountain goats, elk, moose, mule deer, and white-tailed deer.

✳ Lodging

The allure of much of Idaho, and this region in particular, is the country and the unending opportunity for exploration and adventure. This means your best options are camping, perhaps sleeping in the back of a truck and otherwise dirtbagging it. If you must find a bed and a warm room, some options are listed below, with no endorsement of chic décor or romantic ambience.

For those who can afford it, backcountry lodges are a luxurious way to experience Idaho's wilds. These often rustic, rambling log ranches are, more often than not, situated in some of the most stunning country anywhere—perched next to a raging Wild and Scenic River, nestled beneath towering ridgelines, or hidden in a stand of Douglas fir. They offer relaxed, comfortable accommodations; hearty home-cooked food; and incredible recreational access. Many

of these outfitters can take you fly-fishing, trail riding, hunting, hiking, and the like.

Idaho Outfitters and Guides Association (208-342-1438; www.ioga .com) has a complete listing of backcountry lodges. Secluded lodges on the Middle Fork in the heart of the Frank Church–River of No Return Wilderness are listed below under the town from which they're primarily accessed. Besides these listings, there are also a number of motels in the Challis area.

BED & BREAKFASTS

Challis

Bonanza House Victorian Bed and Breakfast (208-879-4255), corner of 10th and Butte sts., Challis 83226. Several guest rooms are located in a restored log home. $65–120.

Challis Hot Springs (208-879-4442; www.challishotsprings.com), 4.5 miles off US 93, Challis 83226. This resort offers eight bed & breakfast rooms with breakfast and swimming (see also To Do–Hot Springs). Camping is also available. Campsites $19.50; rooms $95.

Creek Side Inn Bed and Breakfast (208-879-5608; www.creeksideinn bandb.com), 638 North Ave., Challis 83226. Single rooms are offered as well as doubles. $65–85.

Rainbow's End (208-879-2267), on US 93, 7 miles north of Challis, 83226. Four guest rooms with breakfast. $165 and up.

River House Resort Bed & Breakfast (208-876-4123; www.riverhouse resort.com), on US 93, 15 miles north of Challis, 83226. Four guest rooms. $65–125.

Salmon

Berrly Inn (208-756-6317 or 208-940-1108; www.berrlyinn.com), 909 Shoup St., Ste. 3, Salmon 83467. This private little cottage-cum-B&B is a cute, homey spot with three bedrooms and two baths. $125 weekdays; $175 weekends and holidays.

Greyhouse Inn Bed and Breakfast (208-756-3968; www.greyhouseinn .com), on US 93, 12 miles south of Salmon, 83467. Bed & breakfast rooms and private cabins. $65–95 in winter; $79–119 in summer.

Solaas Bed and Breakfast (208-756-3903 or 877-507-5741; www .solaasbnb.com), 3 S. Baker Rd., Salmon 83467. This historical B&B is 9 miles east of Salmon. $45–65.

Shoup

Salmon River Bed and Breakfast (208-394-2226; www.salmonriver bb.com), 3175 Salmon River Rd., Shoup 83469. This place is remote,

down Salmon River Road west of North Fork. $40.

LODGES AND GUEST RANCHES

Challis

Flying B Ranch (208-756-6295; www.flyingresortranches.com), on the Middle Fork Salmon, 66 river miles from Boundary Creek launch (38 miles southwest of Salmon). This is one of a few premier lodges on the Middle Fork. The outfit also runs the more rustic **Root Ranch**, located in a high meadow on Whimstick Creek in the wilderness area. These ranches are accessed by small aircraft (each ranch has a private airstrip); rafters can also pull in to the Flying B Ranch (by reservation only). $160 per person per night, including three meals.

Middle Fork Lodge (877-468-6635; www.middleforklodge.com), on the Middle Fork Salmon, 33 river miles from Boundary Creek launch (38 miles southwest of Salmon). This is another classy rustic wilderness lodge accessed only by private flights to Thomas Creek Airstrip. $375 per person per night.

North Fork

Indian Creek Ranch (208-394-2126 or 866-394-2126; www.indiancreek guestranch.com), North Fork 83466. The ranch has four comfortable cabins surrounding a historic lodge with a family-style dining room. It offers a slew of activities including fly-fishing, horseback riding, hiking, and mountain biking. Five-day minimum stay during summer; three-day minimum stay during steelhead fishing season (Oct.). $250 per person per day.

Salmon River Lodge (208-552-2818 or 800-635-4717); www.salmonriver lodge.com), at Corn Creek on the

Salmon River; accessed via Salmon River Road from North Fork and then Jet Boat. $85 and up.

Salmon

While perhaps not quite as romantically remote as places out of Challis or North Fork, numerous guest ranches are speckled about this country.

Syringa Lodge (877-580-6482; www.syringalodge.com), 13 Gott La., Salmon 83467. This large spruce-log lodge 1 mile away from downtown Salmon is located on a bluff overlooking the town with unobstructed panoramic views of the Bitterroot Mountains. The facility, which comes highly recommended, has wireless Internet access, and its six guest rooms come with breakfast. $65–95.

Twin Peaks Ranch (208-894-2290 or 800-659-4899; www.twinpeaksranch .com), 18 miles south of Salmon, 83467. Of note is this place located in a cottonwood canyon. $664 per person for 3-day stay.

RESORTS

North Fork

100 Acre Wood Resort (208-865-2165; www.100acrewoodresort.com), North Fork 83466. This rustic log resort has a gourmet restaurant and rooms that include breakfast. The resort is also a licensed guiding operation, offering fishing and hunting trips, mountain bike and backcountry tours, and the like. $80 and up.

✳ Where to Eat

If you are road-tripping through this region of Idaho, be prepared for vast expanses of open country between towns, with nary a gas stop at which to buy some less-than-desirable junk

food. And even in the widely scattered towns, don't get your hopes up. Gourmet cooking is more likely to be found around your campfire or, if you are lucky enough to meet some locals to take you in, around a friend's dining room table. That said, there are some little finds along the way, some of which are described below.

EATING OUT

Gibbonsville

Ramey's Broken Arrow (208-865-2241), on US 93. Open for dinner Thurs.–Sun. Rose Marie Ramey serves up some killer family-style Mexican food. Since $8–10 will get you a great plate of hot enchiladas and other Mexican tasties here, it's not uncommon for this place to have a line winding out the door. Look for some local color here; it is a good place to people watch. The lace doiley and fake flower décor may just add to the appeal.

Mackay

A handful of casual restaurants serve up some decent food in Mackay, including these:

Amy Lou's Steakhouse (208-588-3185), 503 W. Custer St.

Bear Bottom Inn (208-588-2621), 411 Spruce St.

Burnt Lemon Grill and Custer Coffee and Café (208-588-5282), 119 Main St.

Garden Patch Pizza (208-588-2621), 4243 US 93.

Ken's Club (208-588-9983), 302 Main St.

Spice of Life Coffee House, Bakery, and Gift Shop (208-588-2371), 221 S. Main St.

North Fork

Lewis and Clark Café (208-865-

2440), 2648 US 93. This is one of the only establishments open year-round here, providing a much-welcomed hot meal for hungry steelhead fishermen and hunters in the slower spring and fall seasons. Run by a husband-and-wife team (he serves food and drink, and she cooks some tasty vittles), the café is a local favorite. Not only can you get a good beer and a great burger here, but you are also likely to catch up on local gossip.

North Fork Store and Café (208-865-2412), on US 93. This place doesn't have the best food in the world, but it will feed a hungry crowd. Its general store is a great spot to load up on camping supplies, beer and wine, propane, and the like and to obtain fishing and hunting licenses. The store stocks a great selection of books about the area, many of which are by local authors and difficult to find elsewhere. If you want to know about ghost stories, the history of the Middle Fork area, or some mining lore, you are likely to find something of interest here. The owner and staff are quite knowledgeable and can tell you what's what in and around North Fork and the greater surrounding wilds.

Salmon

Bertram's Salmon Valley Brewery and Restaurant (208-756-3391; www.bertramsbrewery.com), 101 S. Andrews St. The homebrew here draws a good crowd. With award-winning microbrews such as the Mount Borah Brown and Sacajawea Stout, a slew of other tasty suds including the Lost Trail Amber Ale, and tasty vittles, this place is a great spot to quench your thirst on the tail end of a backcountry adventure.

Loryhl's Kitchen (208-756-1641), 205 S. Center St. Open for lunch year-round. Loryhl serves offers wholesome, organic meals of greens, sprouted breads, fresh herbs, salads, juices, buffalo burgers, and vegan and vegetarian dishes.

✳ Special Events

May: **Challis Mountain Lilac Festival** (208-879-5084; www.challislilac festival.com), Challis. In celebration of the historical heritage of Challis, the ranching and mining industries of Custer County, the amazing Frank Church–River of No Return Wilderness Area, and the Salmon River corridor, the local community welcomes visitors to share in a series of events including a Lilac Arts and Crafts Festival, western comedy plays, cowboy poetry, horse show and barrel race, a Lilac Parade, and golf events. At this time of year, Challis is swathed in the sweet fragrance of mature lilacs, which have lined the streets of this small town since the late 1800s.

Mackay Rodeo (208-588-3027), Mackay. People travel from around the state, as if on pilgrimmage, to attend the annual Mackay Rodeo. In this quintessential old-school western town, with the breathtaking Lost River Range as a backdrop, you may feel like you've just stepped into an old western movie set when you pull up to the rodeo grounds. Complete with bull riding, calf roping, and fancy rodeo costumes, this is a serious rodeo. The event has been billed as "Idaho's Wildest Rodeo" (crazy enough that video clips are making it to YouTube!), and for very good reason: it is not for the faint of heart, and you should expect blood and gore and more than a few nail-biter moments. More often than not, it is hot, sunny, and dry. It is wise to bring a wide-brimmed hat, sunscreen, and plenty of water. Following the event is the traditional Rodeo Parade and a mock western shootout on Main Street. If you are lucky, live bands will finish off the evening. This place can be tough; watch out for bar fights.

Salmon River Days (207-756-2100; www.sacajaweacenter.org), Salmon. Held annually since 1958, this four-day festival has been a favorite for communities in the Lemhi and Salmon River valleys. Events held throughout the city of Salmon feature a kids' fishing derby, art shows, cowboy poetry, boat and bike races, a demolition derby, a rodeo, fireworks, and more.

August: **Braun Brothers Reunion** (www.muzziebraun.com), Challis. These guys are local heroes who put on a great weekend of Idaho-grown music every year. Put on your dancing shoes, grab a tent and some beer, and plan to groove all weekend. You'll have a hard time keeping still!

Custer County Fair (208-879-2344), Mackay Rodeo/Fair Grounds, west end of Capitol Avenue, Mackay. Held annually, this is a quintessential old-fashioned county fair, complete with a livestock auction, homemade pies, and fashion shows.

Heritage Days (208-756-1188; www .sacajaweacenter.org), Sacajawea Interpretive Center, Salmon. This commemorative event celebrates Sacajawea's return to her homeland and Lewis and Clark's successful crossing of the Continental Divide. The celebration includes a series of hands-on demonstrations evocative of the times of Sacajawea, including flint-knapping, soapstone carving, dugout canoe building, quilting, wool spinning and dyeing, and more.

Lost Rivers Heritage Days (208-589-3331; www.mackayidaho.com), Mackay. This new event is held in conjunction with the Mackay Barbecue and Annual Cowboy Poetry Reading and features a western film festival, a street dance, and other events.

White Knob Challenge Mountain Bike Race (208-890-3118; www .lostrivercycling.org), Mackay. This 19-mile mountain bike race takes riders from downtown Mackay on a 9-mile ascent with 2,300 feet in elevation gain to the White Knob Mountains and back on a ripping downhill descent. It is the longest-standing mountain bike race in the Northwest. Your heart will pump whether you are riding or watching!

KETCHUM, SUN VALLEY, AND THE SAWTOOTHS: AMERICA'S SHANGRI-LA

The Wood River Valley—along ID 75 from Bellevue to Galena—was settled primarily as a mining center during the late 1800s. Today, it has become known as one of the nation's best small-town art destinations, with more theater, art classes, gallery walks, antiques shows, readings, film festivals, and lectures than even the most cultured inhabitant could soak up.

At the northern end of the valley are Ketchum and Sun Valley, long known as one of America's premier ski resorts. Count Felix Schaffgotsch, a young Austrian sent in 1936 to survey the mountains of the West for possible ski resort sites, had toured some of the best: Mount Hood and Mount Rainier, Yosemite and the San Bernadino mountains, Zion National Park, the Wasatch Mountains, Rocky Mountain National Park, Jackson Hole, Pocatello. Yet upon arriving in the Wood River Valley, Schaffgostch was captivated by the Ketchum area: challenging slopes; light, dry powder; sun, sun, and more sun; the staggeringly beautiful Sawtooth Mountains to the north. This was the place, Schaffgotsch decided.

The opening of Sun Valley Resort was graced by the likes of Gary Cooper, Clark Gable, and Ingrid Bergman. Today's visitors can take a quick promenade down one of the side hallways in the Sun Valley Lodge to see old photographs of some of the valley's more prominent guests. Laying claim as "America's First Destination Ski Resort," Sun Valley boasts 3,400 vertical feet of world-class alpine skiing and more than 200 kilometers of groomed Nordic ski trails. Combined with a full complement of lodging, dining, and entertainment, the area is still a favorite destination for many a skier.

As local lore goes, the residents of the Ketchum and Sun Valley region have mostly fallen prey to the truism "You come for the winter, but if you stay for the summer, you will never leave!" And stay we do: To see an elk poke its head up from its hillside graze as we wander our way, on a crisp October day, through a blazing yellow aspen grove on one of the hundreds of hiking trails meandering though the side canyons of the Big Wood River Valley. To revel in new artwork from nationally and internationally known artists during the monthly Gallery

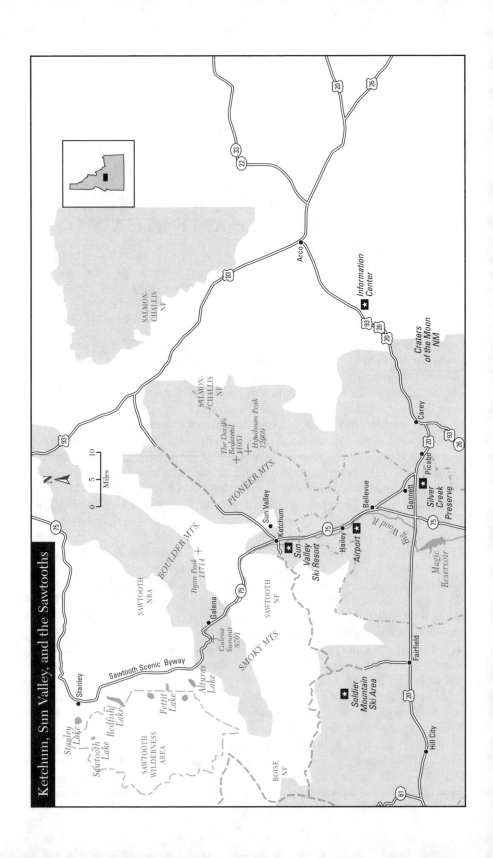

Ketchum, Sun Valley, and the Sawtooths

Walks (not to mention drinking wine and eating cheese with friends!), which continue as a flagship of the valley's thriving art scene. To mountain bike our way over hill and dale on the area's miles and miles of buffed-out trails, all the while trying to maneuver our bikes and simultaneously take in the brilliant, happy colors of the delicate alpine wildflowers—phlox and daisies and asters—that paint our hills during spring. To eat a scrumptious meal of slow-cooked lamb, organically grown vegetables, and Northwest wine in a lovely bistro. To listen to summer jazz or a symphony concert during the outdoor music season from our picnic blankets in the park. Or, simply, after an epic day of skiing, to share a hard-won beer with friends at a favorite watering hole.

Whether it is recreation, fine dining, music, theater, art, or just the history and spirit of the Mountain West that captivates your imagination, you will find it here. Read on to learn more about world-class fly-fishing, an annual wine auction, historic sites and events, and arts festivals. Find out where to play hard, where to hang your hat after a long day of exploring, and where to tempt your palate. Come visit America's Shangri-La and enjoy!

GUIDANCE

Camas Chamber of Commerce (208-764-2222; www.fairfieldidaho.us/chamber.htm), P.O. Box 288, Fairfield 83327.

City of Bellevue (208-788-2128; www.bellevueid.govoffice.com), P.O. Box 825, Bellevue 83313.

Hailey Chamber of Commerce (208-788-2700; www.haileyidaho.com), P.O. Box 100, Hailey 83333.

Stanley-Sawtooth Chamber of Commerce (208-774-3411 or 800-878-7950; www.stanleycc.org), P.O. Box 8, Stanley 83278.

Sun Valley Ketchum Chamber & Visitors Bureau (866-305-0408; www.visitsunvalley.com), P.O. Box 2400, Sun Valley 83353.

GETTING THERE

By car
ID 75 is the main north–south drag through the Wood River Valley, running from Shoshone in the south at US 93 through Bellevue, Hailey, and Ketchum over Galena Summit through Stanley (which connects via ID 21 to McCall and the Payette River Mountain Region) and on to Challis. **US 20,** the southernmost east–west route in this region, runs across southern Blaine County from Hill City and Fairfield in the west (providing a route to Boise) through Picabo and Carey to Arco in the east. From Arco, **US 93** runs north to Challis (on ID 75).

By air
Boise Air Terminal (Gowen Field; 208-383-3110; www.cityofboise.org/departments/airport/), Boise. Cheaper flights can often be found in and out of Boise, which is a 2.5-hour drive west of Ketchum via I-84, US 20, and ID 75.

Friedman Memorial Airport (Ketchum–Sun Valley; 208-788-4956; www.flysunairport.com/), Hailey. Flying into Hailey is by far the most convenient way to arrive in the Wood River Valley. This air terminal is serviced by Alaska

Air/Horizon Air (a Northwest connection) and Delta/Skywest; there is talk that Frontier Air may be adding a route to Hailey as well. Be advised that flights do not always make it in the winter, and you may find yourself circling the airport (with the airstrip, the mountains, and Hailey in full view) only to be told that the visibility is insufficient, and you are being rerouted to Twin Falls, from where you will be subject to a lovely two-hour bus ride back up north via US 93 and ID 75.

Magic Valley Regional Airport (Joslin Field; 208-733-5215; www.tfid.org/airport/), Twin Falls. Flights are also available to Twin Falls, which is about a 1.25-hour drive south of Ketchum via US 93 and ID 75. Airport parking is free.

Sun Valley Express (877-622-8267; www.sunvalleyexpress.com) offers limited shuttle service from Boise to Sun Valley.

Sun Valley Stages (208-733-3921; www.sunvalleystages.com) also offers limited shuttle service between Boise and Sun Valley.

MEDICAL EMERGENCIES

St. Luke's Wood River Medical Center (208-727-8800; www.stlukesonline .org/wood_river/), 100 Hospital Dr., Ketchum. The primary medical facility in the region offers life flights to Boise when necessary.

✳ Cities and Villages

Bellevue, on ID 75 3 miles south of Hailey. Bellevue (population about 1,876) is Idaho's only Chartered City, providing it more autonomy from state regulation than is afforded a General Law City. Founded in 1880, Bellevue's economy was propelled by several silver-lead mines, including the Minnie Moore and Queen of Hills mines. Between 1881 and 1887, the Minnie Moore Mine, located on Broadford Road, produced $7 million worth of silver ore, and adjacent Queen of Hills Mine produced significant quantities of silver, lead, and zinc between 1952 and 1966. In 2005, the Minnie Moore Mine was cleaned up as a U.S. Environmental Protection Agency Superfund site. In Bellevue, the Big Wood River Valley opens up to the fertile Bellevue Triangle lands. Despite the short growing season, the Bellevue Triangle produces significant quantities of malting barley, alfalfa hay, and livestock, among other agricultural products.

Gannett, Picabo, and **Carey,** on US 20 southeast of Bellevue. These little agricultural outposts are charming in their own right, but they are limited in amenities. Gannett, 8.6 miles south of Bellevue off Gannett Road, is but a blip on the map as you drive south through the Bellevue Triangle, the agricultural center of the Wood River Valley. Tiny little Picabo (population 128)—the name of which is derived from the Native American word meaning "shining waters"—is aptly termed: it is the gateway to the gleaming and world-renowned fishing and bird-watching waters of Silver Creek. It is said that Olympic Gold medalist (in downhill skiing) Picabo Street, who grew up farther north in the mining village of Triumph, gained her name from this town. The city of Carey (population 527) was named in 1884 for its first postmaster and was incorporated as the Village of Carey in 1919. With the arrival of the Great Depression and

World War I, government functions in Carey dissolved. In 1995, citizens of
Carey decided to incorporate as a city, only to find that they were already incorporated!

Hailey, on ID 75, 11 miles downvalley from Ketchum and Sun Valley. The city of Hailey (population about 7,000) is the Blaine County seat. As real estate in Ketchum and Sun Valley has become increasingly expensive (sadly catalyzing a transition from funky ski-bum digs, local watering holes, and services for "real people"—i.e., grocery stores, gyms, etc.—to more banks and condos than you can shake a stick at), more and more valley locals are finding a home in Hailey. This little western town was founded in 1881 by John Hailey, an early pioneer who came looking for gold during the Boise Basin Gold Rush and ran the Utah, Idaho, and Oregon Stage Company. The town was the center of the productive Mineral Hill mining district. Hailey and his compatriots laid out the wide, tree-lined streets in the quaint downtown of what is now called "Old Hailey." This hamlet has a vibrant and eclectic community and a sense of place in its own right. It is home to several great restaurants and a small history museum, and it is a launching point for outdoor adventure.

Hill City and **Fairfield,** on US 20 west of Bellevue. Also of note is the tiny town of Hill City, but a blip on the map as you drive east from Boise toward the

BIRD'S-EYE VIEW OF HAILEY

Wood River Valley. This teensy hamlet is worth refraining from; the blink of an eye is long enough to take in the spectacular light show that routinely graces the funky old-time silos and farm buildings of this "town" and the plains and mountains beyond. It is a scene that is worthy of an oil painting—or at least a few strokes in the mind's eye. Fairfield, about 14 miles east on US 20, is home to the fairly local Soldier Mountain Ski Resort and is a good place for a quick pit stop if you are driving from Boise to Sun Valley.

Ketchum and **Sun Valley,** on ID 75 north of Hailey. The primary destination towns in the region have been made famous by the Sun Valley Resort and its world-class skiing, golfing, and glitz. Ketchum, home to Bald Mountain (9,151 feet), was named in 1880 for fur trapper David Ketchum, who discovered a silver nugget and catalyzed a mining boom; Ketchum soon become one of the richest mining districts in the Northwest. The riches didn't last long, and a decade later, Ketchum's economic engines turned to sheep ranching. By 1920, with its fine summer grazing in the Boulder, Pioneer, and Sawtooth mountains and willing Basque sheepherders, Ketchum was second only to Sydney, Australia, as a

OLD FARM BUILDINGS IN HILL CITY

Matt Furber

sheep- and lamb-shipping station. Sheep and their herders (most often Peruvian today) can still be seen migrating north through the valley to verdant green pastures each spring and south each winter to warmer climes. It feels a bit anachronistic (but kind of fun) to be awakened at 5:30 AM as the sheep stampede by your downtown Hailey house. If you happen to spy them from atop a nearby peak, it may take your synapses a brief moment to recognize that the sand-colored mat you are staring at is, in fact, shifting and another moment to comprehend that it is a conglomeration of individuals. Only at that point will you begin discerning the 1-in-100 black sheep. Today's Ketchum is the center of action in the Wood River Valley, offering après-ski beer and vittles, nightlife (of sorts), art galleries, music, occasional theater, and more.

Stanley, on ID 75 about 60 miles north of Ketchum. Located in the Sawtooth Valley, Stanley has been dubbed one of the most picturesque towns in America. A rustic little western town complete with dirt roads, it is nestled in the shadow of the impressively craggy Sawtooth Mountains. With only 101 full-time residents and winter temperatures that are said to have plummeted to minus 59 degrees F, Stanley is a world apart. Stanley is one of several towns in the United States that have claimed title as the "Nation's Icebox" and has, in fact, been the nation's coldest spot outside Alaska more often than any other location, having recorded or tied for the lowest temperature in the contiguous USA for 478 days since April 1995. Stanley is consistently cold because it sits in a bowl-shaped basin surrounded by mountains. At night, cold air sinks down the mountain flanks to fill the valley; the only escape for this cold air is the narrow Salmon River canyon. In its own way, Stanley comes alive in the summer and bustles with river trippers and bohemian spirits. Stanley is the place for a quiet getaway to the gateway of backcountry Sawtooth adventures.

Triumph, off ID 75 between Hailey and Ketchum. This unincorporated village is located 5.6 miles out East Fork Road. The village is the historical site of the Independence Mine, which opened in 1883 and produced lead, zinc, and silver, and then the Triumph Mine, which opened in 1884 and produced millions of dollars of ore. Today, approximately 50 residents live in the funky little community nestled in this drainage. The remains of the mine are still visible. It is a neat spot to visit.

✳ Wandering Around

Central Idaho is a road-tripper's heaven, with miles and miles of blue highway stretching into mountainous horizons, along meandering streams, and between stands of shimmery aspen and red-skinned willows. One of the best is the main north–south thoroughfare in this region:

Sawtooth Scenic Byway (ID 75), 171 miles from Shoshone at US 26/93 through Bellevue, Hailey, Ketchum, Sun Valley, and Stanley to Challis (where it reconnects with US 93). On ID 75, even the most mundane of drives—to get groceries in Ketchum, for instance—provides a series of stunning vistas. A vision that continues to inspire is that of Classford Peak (elevation 11,602 feet), which seems to pop into view out of thin air as you cross over the Big Wood River driving north into Ketchum. This jagged peak can be alternately snowcapped, cloud enshrouded, or dancing in beams of refracted light, but it is always stunning, a sign that you have almost arrived into the alpine wonderland that is Ketchum!

Cold Springs Pegram Truss Railroad Bridge, listed on the National Historic Register, is to your left as you approach Ketchum. Another favorite vista is directly north of Ketchum, heading toward Galena Lodge and then Galena Summit. The Big Wood River stretches out and meanders along the west side of ID 75, its riparian zone lush with willows. Their deep red stems appear like a splash of blood against the whiteness of snow in the winter and provide verdant riparian cover in summer. Farther north, the river winds its way though shimmering aspen groves and then stands of Douglas fir. When driving north on this stretch of highway, watch for road bikers and please give them every courtesy; this is one of the only long rides available to road bikers in the Wood River Valley.

The Galena Lodge marks the north end of the valley, after which the road begins to climb to **Galena Summit**, the gateway to the Sawtooth Valley and the headwaters of the world-famous Salmon River (or River of No Return, as it's also known). Both the valley and the jagged Sawtooth Mountains to the north offer some of the most majestic scenery anywhere.

GALENA SUMMIT ON SAWTOOTH SCENIC BYWAY

Sawtooth Society's (208-387-0852; www.sawtoothsociety.org) hard work has resulted in much of the wide-open expanse, which you see as you crest the summit and begin the descent into the **Sawtooth Valley,** having been preserved as open space via conservation easements. The road ultimately follows the Salmon River as it wends its way north gaining volume and speed; watch for the abundant wildlife. In the winter, it is not uncommon to see herds of elk bedded down in the willows along the river, sometimes just outside Stanley's town center. The highway gradually descends alongside the river into Challis.

✳ To See

FARMER'S MARKETS

Hailey Artist's & Farmer's Market (208-309-2634), Bullion Square, Hailey. Held 2:30–6:30 Thurs. in summer. This great outdoor market provides tasty, locally grown and organic fruit, vegetables, flowers, and baked goodies, along with arts and crafts by local artists and craftsmen and -women.

Ketchum Farmer's Market (208-720-7805), on Fourth Avenue down the street from Atkinsons' Market, Ketchum. Held 2:30–6 Tues., June–Oct. This wonderful farmer's market is bustling with vendors selling great organic produce, food vendors cooking up tasty snacks, and live music.

GARDENS

Sawtooth Botanical Gardens (208-726-9358; www.sbgarden.org), Gimlet Road at ID 75, Ketchum. Open dawn–dusk. Free. Dogs allowed. The Sawtooth Botanical Garden was founded in 1994 by a small local group of passionate gardeners and environmentalists who purchased a 5-acre site, built a community center with a solar greenhouse, and established a public garden. The goal of the garden is to establish a place to build community through the understanding and exploration of both native and cultivated plants and to provide opportunities to "celebrate plants and inspire people." Nestled by the Big Wood River, the garden is a lovely and restful place to meander along the paths, reading the placards describing local ecosystems and individual plants, or simply to sit and think.

The **Garden of Infinite Wisdom**, a new garden built in anticipation of His Holiness the 14th Dalai Lama's visit to Sun Valley in fall 2005, is the permanent site for a beautifully hand-carved Tibetan prayer wheel, the only one in North America to be blessed by the Dalai Lama himself. The prayer wheel forms the centerpiece of this contemplative garden, which was designed by renowned landscape designer Martin Mosko. In this space, giant boulders, a reflective pond, and a quiet, meandering stream form the backdrop for the 3,000 bulbs that have recently been planted here.

The Sawtooth Botanical Garden offers year-round workshops and lectures for adults and camps, festivals, and craft days for children. Popular events at the garden include its Annual Garden Tour, which features private gardens in the Sun Valley area specifically selected for their beauty, creativity, and plant selection; the Annual Plant Sale each June, which highlights native and drought-tolerant plants; and the Fall Bulb Sale, which also focuses on hardy bulbs that grow well here. The garden also orchestrates the valley's popular community-supported agriculture (CSA) program, a share in which (about $25 per week) provides enough organic vegetables to feed a family of four throughout the summer growing season.

HISTORICAL HOMES AND SITES

Ezra Pound House (208-726-9491; www.sunvalleycenter.org), 314 Second Ave. S., Hailey. Open 12–5 Wed.–Fri. Free. Currently owned and operated as a fabulous arts center by the Sun Valley Center for the Arts, this historic home was the birthplace of poet Ezra Loomis Pound (1885–1972). An American poet and critic, Pound was often called the "poet's poet" for his profound impact on the genre, credited with creating Imagism (an Anglo-American poetry movement that used clear, sharp language and precise imagery as a means of meticulous expression) and contributing the name to the Vorticism movement (a short-lived painting style in which artists attempted to capture movement in an image; these paintings tended to portray modern life as an array of bold lines and harsh colors that sought to draw the viewer's eye to the center of the canvas). His major

THE HOME OF POET EZRA POUND IN HAILEY IS NOW AN ARTS CENTER.

Chris Pilaro

ERNEST HEMINGWAY'S MEMORIAL HAS A POEM ABOUT ASPEN TURNING COLORS IN THE FALL.

works include *Cathay* and *The Cantos*. Pound lived abroad in London, Paris, and Rapallo, Italy. In Italy, he grew to sympathize with Mussolini and over time became increasingly politically active, eventually becoming a leading Axis propagandist during World War II. In 1945, Pound was arrested by Italian partisans. He was quickly released but turned himself in to American troops. Pound was incarcerated and, at the conclusion of the war, sent back to the United States to face charges of treason. Under a plea of insanity, he spent 12 years in St. Elizabeth's Hospital in Washington, D.C. After his release, Pound returned to Italy, where he eventually died at age 87 in Venice. A commemorative plaque and a collection of Pound's books are on display at the house.

Hemingway House, off Warm Springs Road, Ketchum. Upon her death in 1986, Ernest Hemingway's wife, Mary Welsh Hemingway, left the couple's home to the Nature Conservancy. The relatively modest cedar house and its 17 acres are currently undergoing renovations. Papa Hemingway was buried in the cemetery north of Ketchum (on the east side of ID 75). Pennies and cigars are often left on his tombstone as tributes to the literary great.

Hemingway Memorial, on Trail Creek Road 1 mile northeast of Sun Valley Lodge, Sun Valley. Ernest Hemingway is an iconic figure in the valley. After completing the Sun Valley Lodge in 1936, Averill Harriman began inviting luminaries to the valley to increase the visibility of his resort. Ernest Hemingway was among the invited, and he spent the fall of 1939 at the lodge. Here he worked on portions of *For Whom the Bell Tolls*. Hemingway spent time in the valley fishing and hunting with Gary Cooper at Silver Creek, frequenting the local watering holes, and living the life that gave color to his novels. This life seemed to agree with him, and he returned again in 1940 and 1941, eventually moving to Ketchum in 1959 after his stint in Cuba was cut short by Fidel Castro's Cuban Revolution. His time in Ketchum was short-lived too; depression, alcoholism, and ailing health preceded Hemingway's suicide in 1961 (though it is said that he killed himself because he was afraid that he would never be able to write again). In tribute to the local hero, a solitary square pillar topped with a bronze bust is nestled in the trees by swirling Trail Creek. The inscription at the base of the monument is one that Hemingway himself wrote as a eulogy for a friend, but which aptly captures his own persona:

Best of all he loved the Fall.
The leaves yellow on the cottonwoods,
Leaves floating on the trout streams and
Above the hills the
High blue windless skies.
Now he will be a part of them forever.

Reinheimer Ranch barn, on ID 75 just south of Ketchum. This historic white structure is one of two iconographic barns around Ketchum (the other is an equally charming red barn on the right as you drive out Sun Valley Road from Ketchum to Sun Valley). The Reinheimer barn is part of a 120-acre working historic ranch property owned and operated by **Idaho Foundation for Parks and Lands** (208-344-7141; www.idaholands.org) that serves as a gateway into

OLD BARN OUT INDIAN CREEK NEAR HAILEY

Ketchum and a legacy for Blaine County. Both barns can be spotted in many a plein air painting.

MUSEUMS

Blaine County Historical Museum (208-788-1801; www.bchistoricalmuseum .org), 218 N. Main St., Hailey. Open 11–5 Mon. and Wed.–Sat., 1–5 Sun. Memorial Day–Labor Day; rest of year by appointment. Free. Housed in an 1883 building, the Blaine County Historical Museum (founded in 1962 to "Discover, procure, and maintain whatever may relate to the history of Blaine County") provides a window on the valley's history through a series of vignettes related to mines, schools, agriculture, transportation, period fashion, western attire, and political memorabilia. The museum is also a great repository of historical papers and maps documenting the history of land use, mining, and genealogy of the area.

Ketchum–Sun Valley Historical Society Heritage and Ski Museum (208-726-8118; www.ksvhistoricalsociety.org), Washington Avenue and First Street, Ketchum. Open 12–5 Mon.–Fri., 1–4 Sat. Free. Established in 1989, the

Ketchum–Sun Valley Historical Society renovated and now operates the Heritage Museum out of two buildings at Forest Service Park, with exhibits detailing the history of the Northern Shoshone–Tukedeka Indians that once inhabited the grassy plains of Salmon country, the early days of skiing, the history of mining and shepherding in the valley, and the life of Ernest Hemingway, among other themes. The grassy lawn surrounding the museum is a great place for a picnic; the Ketch'em Alive concert series is held here during the summer months (see Special Events).

Ore Wagon Museum, corner of East Avenue and Fifth Street, Ketchum. Open year-round. Free. This unstaffed museum houses the original Lewis Ore Wagons that were used to haul silver and lead ore from outlying mines to the smelters in the valley. The wagons are carefully maintained and kept in working order to be pulled by horse teams in Ketchum's Wagon Days Parade each Labor Day (see Special Events). While you can't actually go inside, walk by and give it a peek through the large windows.

SCENIC FLIGHTS

Many a local can tell you about scenic flights over the Sawtooths since, in this region, flights are sometimes required to get to the put-in for a remote rafting trip or a work site or to go on a hot date. Even if you don't have a good reason to hire a pilot to fly you over these stunning peaks, you won't be sorry if you do. From the air, the jagged peaks of the Sawtooth Mountains, their glacial cirques and avalanche chutes made quite obvious from this vantage point, are breathtaking. Chances are good that you will also spot critters—mountain goats, moose, elk, wolves, and even bears.

Salmon Air (800-448-3413 or 208-756-6211; www.salmonair.com), Salmon. They offer scenic flights.

Sawtooth Adventure Company (866-774-4644, 208-774-4644 summer, or 801-718-0338 winter; www.sawtoothadventure.com), Stanley. Scenic flights during the summer months.

WILDLIFE VIEWING

Sawtooth National Recreation Area (SNRA) Headquarters Visitor Center (208-727-5000), 5 North Fork Canyon Rd., on ID 75, 8 miles north of Ketchum; and the **SNRA Stanley Ranger Station** (208-774-3000), on ID 75, 3 miles south of Stanley. With its vast expanses of unadulterated wilderness, Central Idaho has an abundance of wildlife. More than 300 species of wildlife are found in the SNRA, including mule deer, coyotes, foxes, chipmunks, squirrels, Clark's nutcrackers, juncos, and chickadees, as well as more elusive species including black bears, gray wolves, mountain lions, bobcats, beavers, moose, bighorn sheep, elk, sandhill cranes, and golden eagles.

Even for those who are not interested in venturing deep into the wilderness, wildlife often can be viewed from more accessible spots within the SNRA. Beaver ponds can be seen on both sides of ID 75 on the way to Galena Summit, and mountain goats can be spied from the road as they navigate the high peaks of the Boulder Mountains. The meadows of the Sawtooth Valley are rich with deer, elk, coyotes, and sandhill cranes.

Northern Rocky Mountain Grey Wolf Recovery Plan. An interesting wildlife story is that of the wolf reintroduction in Idaho, Wyoming, and Montana. In 1973, the Canadian gray wolf (*Canis lupus*) was listed as an endangered species under the Endangered Species Act. In response to this listing, the federal government developed a reintroduction program, by which gray wolves were reintroduced into Yellowstone National Park and Central Idaho in 1995 and 1996. As a result of this program, by 2003, there were an estimated 1,000 wolves in Idaho, Wyoming, and Montana—approximately 300 in Idaho alone. Due to Idaho's great wolf habitat, the wolves have done extremely well and have been documented in the SNRA and more recently in the Wood River Valley. The reintroduction has not proceeded without problems nor controversy, as wolves have killed livestock, ranchers and hunters have killed wolves, and lawsuits over management practices and lethal and nonlethal control of wolves continue to fly.

Recommended Reading
If you are interested in learning more about these elusive creatures, Jim and Jamie Dutcher's book *Living with Wolves* (The Mountaineers Books, 2005) is a must read. This fabulous book celebrates the lives of wolves by sharing the couple's intimate knowledge of the intelligent, social, and family-oriented wolf, knowledge they gained as they lived for six years among the Sawtooth pack of wolves, ultimately becoming "embedded" members of the pack. For those interested in getting into the backcountry and reading the signs of animals in the wild, a great book to bring along is the pocket-sized *Scats and Tracks of the Rocky Mountains* by James C. Halfpenny, Ph.D. (The Globe Pequot Press, 2001), which provides illustrations of animals native to this region, their prints, and their scat, along with their range and brief descriptions of their habitat, behavior, and other signs. *A Wildlife Viewing Guide* and *Birds of the Sawtooth NRA* are available at the headquarters and ranger station. For other resources on birds in Idaho, see What's Where in Idaho—Birding.

✳ To Do
BICYCLING
While plenty of road bikers make this region home, the lack of roads means road riding is limited. For bike shops that can provide bike rentals, gear, maps, and guidance, see the listings under Mountain Biking.

Sawtooth Scenic Byway (ID 75), 23 miles from Ketchum north to Galena Lodge. Many roadies ride this stretch—and some more dedicated folks make the additional 5-mile grind to Galena Summit (elevation 8,700 feet).

Wood River Trails system, 30 miles of paved bike trails from just south of Bellevue to Hulen Meadows neighborhood north of Ketchum. This thoroughfare provides great riding, with a scenic and mellow pedal through the valley as you wend your way through the funky townsite of Old Bellevue, past some of the remaining farms near city limits, through Old Hailey, and then north to

PEDALING TO GALENA SUMMIT

Ketchum, gaining elevation and mountain views as you go. This trail is well used by bicycle commuters in the valley and is part of the world-class system of groomed skate-skiing trails in the winter (see Skiing). Beware of the katabatic winds in the morning and the anabatic winds of the afternoon that plague those who commute north for work and south for dinner. Free trail maps pointing out historical locations are available along the way.

BOATING

Silver Creek Preserve (208-788-7910; www.nature.org), off US 20 near Picabo. This Nature Conservancy preserve is a beautiful and peaceful place to enjoy a day of canoeing, but you must bring your own. With 883 lush creek and riparian acres under direct ownership and another 9,500 acres in conservation easements, it is a premier bird- and wildlife-watching spot. The spring-fed creek attracts eagles, hawks, waterfowl, songbirds, mountain lions, deer, elk, and bobcats.

Outfitters

Backwoods Mountain Sports (208-726-8818; www.backwoodsmountainsports .com), 711 N. Main St., Ketchum. Kayaks can be rented here.

Lost River Outfitters (208-726-1706; www.lostriveroutfitters.com), 171 N. Main St., Ketchum. They can rent you float tubes.

Silver Creek Outfitters (208-726-5282; www.silver-creek.com), 500 N. Main St., Ketchum. They can also rent you float tubes.

White Otter Outdoor Adventures (208-726-4331; www.whiteotter.com), Ketchum. They rent kayaks.

CAMPING

Camping, a favorite pastime in this region, is abundant off ID 75 and easily accessible in many of the side drainages stretching into the Wood River Valley and along the Salmon River farther north.

Sawtooth National Recreation Area (SNRA; 208-727-5000), **Ketchum Ranger Station** (208-622-5371), and the **SNRA Stanley office** (208-774-3001). The SNRA has 42 developed camping and picnic areas, including individual and group campgrounds and day-use areas; campgrounds have five to seven sites each. These campgrounds are owned by the U.S. Forest Service but operated by concessionaires (see below). Campgrounds are primarily found off ID 75 (all over the place!) and at each of the major lakes in the region, including Alturas, Pettit, Redfish, and Stanley lakes. It never ceases to amaze me how easily one can escape to a serene camp spot just moments from the highway.

Recreation One-Stop (877-444-6777; www.recreation.gov) is the federal government's reservation service. The Web site, however, provides information only on the reservable sites, not the many first-come, first-served sites within the SNRA system. It is better first to obtain a camping map from SNRA Headquarters.

For hikers, camping opportunities are truly boundless. Dispersed camping is allowed within the SNRA, with minimal regulation. In designated wilderness areas, a free camping permit is required for groups of seven or more, and groups cannot have more than 12 people. In the White Clouds, no more than 20 people are allowed in any one group.

FISHING

Fishing abounds in the 1,000-plus alpine lakes nestled in the mountain ranges to the north of the Wood River Valley and in the headwaters of four of Idaho's great rivers: the Salmon, Boise, Payette, and Big Wood rivers. In these lakes and rivers, you can find cutthroat, rainbow, brook, and bull trout, as well as grayling, whitefish, and steelhead. **Idaho Fish & Game** (http://fishandgame.idaho.gov) has fishing rules, permit requirements, and seasons.

Big Wood River, from Galena Summit to Magic Reservoir. In Central Idaho, the Big Wood River is famed for its high-quality, cold-water fishery that supports an excellent population of rainbow trout, some brown trout, and a few brook trout. A snowmelt-driven system, the river runs high generally through June and subsides to leave the water at good fishing levels from mid-June through the fall. Hatches on the Big Wood are prolific, making this a fly-fisher's dream.

Chris Pilaro

FLY-FISHING ON SILVER CREEK

Silver Creek, off US 20 near Picabo. This large, spring-fed creek is well known for its hefty brown and rainbow trout, and it was a favorite spot of Ernest Hemingway.

Outfitters

Walk into one of the valley's fishing outfitters for great local beta, or give a call to one of a number of knowledgeable local guiding operations. These organizations can arrange personalized trips with gear, lunch, and instruction, if desired.

Bill Mason Outfitters (208-622-9305; www.billmasonoutfitters.com), 680 Sun Valley Rd., Ketchum.

Far and Away Fly Fishing Adventures (800-232-8588), Sun Valley.

Idaho Angling Services (208-788-9709; www.anglingservices.com), Bellevue.

Lost River Outfitters (208-726-1706; www.lostriveroutfitters.com), 171 N. Main St., Ketchum.

Silver Creek Outfitters (208-726-5282; www.silver-creek.com), 500 N. Main St., Ketchum.

Sturtevant's Mountain Outfitters (208-726-4501; www.sturtos.com), 340 N. Main St., Ketchum; in Warm Springs Village at Sun Valley Resort; and 201 N. Main St., Hailey.

GOLF

Four premium golf courses in the Wood River Valley offer nine to 26 holes of golf, each with challenging and undulating terrain and breathtaking alpine views. Most courses require that reservations made over 48 hours in advance be pre-paid. Season is Apr. 1–Nov. 1 (or from the time the snow melts until the snow flies, depending upon whom you talk to).

Bigwood Golf Course (208-726-4024), 115 Thunder Trail Rd., Ketchum. Starting times available 7 AM–6 PM daily. This premium nine-hole golf course, designed by Robert Muir Graves and opened in 1971, offers stunning mountain views and an undulating course.

Elkhorn Golf Course (208-622-3309), 100 Badeyana Dr., Sun Valley. An 18-hole, Robert Trent Jones–designed course, the Elkhorn course features 7,214 yards of golf from the longest tees.

Sun Valley Golf Club (208-622-4111; www.sunvalley.com), Sun Valley Rd., Sun Valley. Slated by *Golf Digest* as "one of the best 100 golf courses in the United States and the number-one golf course in Idaho, the 18-hole Sun Valley Golf Club is the valley's premier course. Redesigned by Robert Trent Jones Jr. in 1980, the course is rugged and challenging for every level of player, providing stunning mountain views and an idyllic setting adjacent to Trail Creek.

Valley Club (208-788-5400; www.thevalleyclub.org), 100 Club View Dr. N., Hailey. This course provides 27 holes of championship golf, including 18 holes by Hale Irwin and the new West Nine designed by acclaimed architect Tom Fazio. Dramatic elevation changes and water features provide for a challenging round of golf.

Wood River Valley. With five mountain ranges in the vicinity—the Sawtooth, Boulder, White Cloud, Pioneer, and Smoky mountains—there is literally no end to hiking opportunities (day hiking and longer) in the valley and north. Beginning in Bellevue, you will see one drainage after the next splaying out east–west on both sides of ID 75. Walks and hikes are to be found in almost every one of these gulches; many of them have national forest trail access and parking at the far end. Within easy distances are trails that will take you through conifer forests, aspen groves, sage-covered hills, and alpine meadows strewn with wildflowers.

Sawtooth National Forest (www.fs.fed.us/r4/sawtooth) has maps and information (see also Wilder Places). This region, part of the more than 2.1 million-acre national forest, provides boundless recreational and hiking opportunities. If you are looking to get off the beaten path, Central Idaho is the place to do it.

Public Lands Information Center (505-345-9498 or 877-851-8946; www .publiclands.org) is a great source for information on the Sawtooth National Forest and for identifying and purchasing appropriate maps for areas of interest. Two good maps for hiking and other backcountry adventures are the "Sun Valley, Idaho" and "Sawtooth & White Cloud Mountains Trail Maps" from **Adventure Maps, Inc.** (www.adventuremaps.net).

ALPINE WILDLFLOWER IN THE SAWTOOTHS

Chris Pilaro

HIKING IN THE WHITECLOUD MOUNTAINS

Sawtooth NRA Headquarters Visitor Center (208-727-5000), 5 North Fork Canyon Rd., on ID 75, 8 miles north of Ketchum; and the **SNRA Stanley Ranger Station** (208-774-3000), on ID 75, 3 miles south of Stanley, both have information as well.

The Sawtooth Society (208-387-0852; www.sawtoothsociety.org) has worked hard to protect the wide-open expanses of the Sawtooth Valley and can provide a wealth of information about this area and its history.

Wildflower Viewing

One of the greatest rewards of hiking into this region's high country during spring and early summer is viewing the palette of color splashed across the landscape in the form of wildflowers gone mad. Sometimes it is a subtle play of color—a dash of Indian paintbrush red here, a smudge of lupine purple there—but other times, it is a surprising ambush of color, a full sea of lavender-hued showy penstemon lying in wait to steal the breath of unsuspecting hikers as they round the bend out of the forest and into the meadow of madness. Ask the locals about their favorite wildlife or wildflower hikes. Each of the organizations listed below has, at various times, offered wildflower hikes and talks. See What's Where in Idaho—Wildflowers for a listing of helpful wildflower guidebooks and resources.

Environmental Resource Center (208-726-4333; www.ercsv.org).

Sawtooth Botanical Garden (208-726-9358; www.sbgarden.org); see also To See—Gardens.

Wood River Land Trust (208-788-3947; www.woodriverlandtrust.org).

Outfitters and Shops

Trail maps and hiking guides can be purchased at the first two locations. If you are not very experienced in wilderness travel, you might consider hiring a guide to take you in as well.

Backwoods Mountain Sports (208-726-8818; www.backwoodsmountainsports .com), 711 N. Main St., Ketchum. If you are looking to plan a multiday trip, Backwoods can set you up with gear and guidance. Great local beta (including weather reports, river levels, permit information, etc.) can also be found on their Web site.

The Elephant's Perch (208-726-3497; www.elephantsperch.com), 280 East Ave., Ketchum. Named for the dome-shaped climbing destination of the same moniker near Redfish Lake in the Sawtooth Mountains, this place is full of adventure hounds who are happy to help you get ready to stretch your legs.

Sawtooth Mountain Guides (208-774-3324; www.sawtoothguides.com) offers longer treks, technical mountaineering, and even children's climbing camps.

Sun Valley Trekking (208-788-1966; www.svtrek.com) is a great bet, with very experienced and competent guides who can take you out for half- to full-day trips and tell you all you want to know about the region's natural history (plus a few great adventure tales!).

Recommended Reading

For the bible on day hiking in the area, see *Day Hiking Near Sun Valley* by Gloria Moore (Idaho Conservation League, 2004).

HORSEBACK RIDING

If you want to play out your cowboy or cowgirl fantasies, a multitude of horseback riding outfitters are available to guide you through this region's stunning backcountry. Mountain riding here offers challengingly narrow single-track trails; slanting, mountainous terrain that takes some getting used to; rushing river crossings; and, of course, breathtaking alpine scenery. Many guiding services (see Outfitters) offer half-day, daylong, and multiday treks that will provide you with a true western experience.

Back Country Horsemen of America (www.backcountryhorse.com) is a good source for general information about riding in the backcountry.

Big Wood Backcountry Trails (www.bwbct.org) has information about local trails.

Ketchum Ranger Station (208-622-5371), on Sun Valley Road, Ketchum. Trail maps and advice.

Sawtooth National Recreation Area Headquarters Visitor Center (208-727-5013), on ID 75, 8 miles north of Ketchum. Information on area trails.

Outfitters

A surely incomplete listing of horseback guiding services is provided below:

Diamond D Ranch (208-861-9206 or 800-222-1269; www.diamonddranch -idaho.com), in a valley in Frank Church–River of No Return Wilderness Area between the Salmon River Mountains (see Lodging—Lodges and Guest Ranches). The Diamond D Ranch is a full-service guest ranch that offers daily and a weekly evening ride, riding lessons, and custom pack trips for a minimum of three days. The ranch's Web site boasts that they have horses for every rider: "We have slow horses for those who like to go slow, we have fast horses for those of you who like to go fast, and we have horses that don't like to be ridden for those of you who don't like to ride."

Galena Stage Stop Corrals (208-726-1735), on ID 75 across from Galena Lodge, 23 miles north of Ketchum. Open late June–Labor Day. Run by Mystic Saddle Ranch, this outfit offers a variety of horseback adventures for both novice and experienced equestrians. They offer daily trail rides along historical mining and logging trails that wind deep into evergreen stands and provide wonderful views of the Boulder Mountains.

Mystic Saddle Ranch (208-774-3591 or 888-722-5432; www.mysticsaddleranch .com), HC 64, Stanley. This family has been offering quality wilderness trips for more than 38 years, with catered backcountry trips into the Sawtooth and Frank Church–River of No Return wilderness areas, where you are surrounded by rugged mountain peaks, glacially carved canyons, wildflowers gone crazy, and crystal-blue lakes. Trips of one and a half hours to 10 days can be arranged.

Pioneer Mountain Outfitters (208-774-3737 summer or 208-324-7171 winter; www.pioneermountain.com), Idaho Rocky Mountain Ranch, Stanley. Operating half- and full-day trail rides and multiday pack trips out of the beautifully rustic Idaho Rocky Mountain Ranch, Pioneer Outfitters specializes in custom trips in the White Cloud and Pioneer mountains. All trips offer the opportunity to fish.

Redfish Lake Corrals (208-774-3311), at Redfish Lake, on ID 75 approximately 60 miles north of Ketchum. Open Memorial Day–mid-Sept. The Redfish Lake Corral provides half-hour, half-day, and full-day rides into the spectacular Sawtooth Wilderness, including an Alpine Ride that climbs 3,000 feet to the Sawtooth Divide. Overnight trips pass 11 lakes, two canyons, and a high mountain pass. Pack lunches, route planning, and guides are available.

Sawtooth Adventure Company. (208-774-4644 summer, 801-718-0338 winter, or 866-774-4644; www.sawtoothadventure.com), on ID 75 in Lower Stanley. Sawtooth Adventure Company offers half-hour, half-day, and full-day trips through spectacular high mountain lake terrain. Routes to Redfish, Bench, Sawtooth, Hell Roaring, and Marshall lakes are available with experienced guides and gentle horses.

Sun Valley Stables (208-622-2387 or 208-622-2248), 1 Sun Valley Rd., Sun Valley. The ski resort offers guided one-hour and one and a half-hour rides and wagon rides on Dollar Mountain in the summer and sleigh rides to Trail Creek Cabin for dinner in winter. Longer rides are available by special arrangement.

Super Outfitter Adventures of Sun Valley (208-788-7731), 10731 ID 75, Bellevue. Operates June–Sept. This outfitter offers full-day fishing trips to high-alpine lakes by horseback and half- and full-day trail rides on 20 different trail systems. For groups of 12 or more people, a western barbecue dinner ride is available.

HOT SPRINGS

Idaho is replete with sometimes stunningly beautiful hot springs in which to soak your weary bones (see What's Where in Idaho—Hot Springs). One Central Idaho hot-spring story is worth repeating. It seems that in March 1984, a 20-year-old Hailey man was found soaking in Warfield (French Bend) Hot Springs—located out Warm Springs Road from Ketchum—after having apparently lived there for several weeks. A *Wood River Journal* news article purportedly reported (see "Lean, Green, and Amazingly Serene" by Randy Wayne White in *Outside Magazine*, March 1997) that the man was discovered by two cross-country skiers who observed that some of his skin was peeling and moss was growing on his back. The article quoted the *Journal*:

"The semiconscious victim was taken to Moritz Community Hospital, according to the report. His clothes lay frozen on the ground nearby. A Moritz physician estimated that the victim may have lost 60 pounds while living in the pool. The [victim's sister-in-law] said that the man stood 6 feet 2 inches and weighed 210 pounds prior to leaving for Frenchman's Bend, and that he took a lot of amphetamines. 'His brains are really scrambled,' she said."

Apparently, it was only after soaking for two hours in the hot springs that the young man realized he was fully clothed. He stripped and hung his clothes up to dry, only to find that they quickly froze solid. Rather than hike 10 miles back to Ketchum, sans clothes (or perhaps in stiff, frozen clothes), the victim decided it would be better to wait it out in the thermal water. Waiting it out turned into 28 days. Or so the story goes. He is now a local legend honored by an annual Moss Man Commemoration and Pagan Fun Fest for communing with nature in such a way that he "actually became part human, part plant."

ICE SKATING

Atkinson's Park, Ketchum, has a natural ice rink and collection of skates, helmets, and hockey sticks that you can borrow for a more casual skate or a pick-up game of hockey or broomball.

Sun Valley Ice Rink (208-622-2194; www.sunvalley.com), just outside Sun Valley Lodge, Sun Valley. Open year-round. This outdoor ice rink features world-famous ice shows during the summer and personal ice time year-round. The ice shows have a fairly comical history: when they began in 1937, the performers could barely skate; as the resort says, "Young people employed by Union Pacific to work at the resort in other capacities were given a costume, a pair of skates, and instructions that were often as sketchy as 'just move around'!" Apparently, guests were also involved in some of the productions. The show has evolved to attract some lead figure skaters, and over time the rink has attracted the likes of Peggy Fleming, Dorothy Hamill, Scott Hamilton, and Kitty and Peter Carruthers. Public skating is welcome, and instruction, skate rentals, and a full-service skate shop are available on the premises. For serious skaters, the resort is also home to the **Sun Valley Skating School**, which offers top-notch instruction and training during the summer.

Sun Valley Indoor Ice Arena (208-622-2194; www.sunvalley.com), on Dollar Road, Sun Valley. Open year-round. This rink offers open skating and also is home to an elite men's amateur hockey team, **Sun Valley Suns** (208-788-5377; www.sunvalleysuns.com), which provides for some good, rowdy entertainment during the winter months.

MOUNTAIN BIKING

Central Idaho, with its miles and miles of buffed-out single-track riding through stunning alpine terrain, has become increasingly well known for its killer mountain biking. Riders of all abilities can find challenging routes that serve not only to get the heart pumping (from exertion as well as from adrenaline!) but also to provide a window on the serenity and beauty of Idaho's mountain environment.

The list of fabulous rides in the region is almost endless. The names spill forth: Adams Gulch, Greenhorn Gulch, Slaughterhouse Creek, Corral Creek, Fox Creek, Chocolate Gulch, Oregon Gulch, Curley's Loop, Fourth of July, Fisher Creek. **Rides through these gulches** take you through various ecotones—lush riparian zones stuffed with red-stemmed willows and deep green grasses; dry, sage-covered hills; and alternating stands of Douglas fir and aspen—each with its own distinct smell and feel. Climbing to the top of some of the distant ridges out these gulches is well worth the lung-busting effort; you will be rewarded with panoramic alpine vistas and, if you are lucky, a field bursting with a palette of wildflowers or an isolated, verdant kettle wetland surreptitiously thriving in an otherwise arid landscape. There are rides for bikers of all abilities. Or, for the ultimate multiday mountain biking experience, try biking from Sun Valley Trekking's Coyote Yurt in the Smokey Mountains (see below).

Always be sure to take plenty of water; dehydration happens quickly with altitude and dry mountain heat! Depending upon the time of year and length of ride, it is also often a good idea to take a stash of high-energy food and a thin rain layer. Riders do get lost, and storms do come in.

River Run Lodge (208-622-6133), Sun Valley Resort. Lifts operate June 30–Sept. 3. Single ticket $15, day pass $20. For those looking for a mechanized approach to mountain biking, the resort operates lifts up Baldy Mountain, providing access to 28 miles of trails. Downhill fanatics can get lifted to the top, then catapult down 3,000 feet. Those in it for the grind can pedal (and push) their way to the top and, if desired, take the lift down at no cost. (In some cases, hard work is rewarded!)

MOUNTAIN BIKING IN THE SMOKY MOUNTAINS

Sun Valley Trekking (208-788-1966; www.svtrek.com), P.O. Box 2200, Sun Valley. Coyote Yurt sleeps eight–10; $25 per person per night, $100 minimum. Imagine the feeling: You spend the day pedaling your way through aspen groves, open alpine meadows, and stands of Douglas fir, steadily climbing on your mountain bike toward Sun Valley Trekking's Coyote Yurt in the Smokey Mountains. The sun warms your back and the wind brushes your face. The alpine wildflowers and the smell of pine tantalize your senses. You feel the magic. Depending upon your ability and desires, you can choose either a gradual 12-mile approach on logging roads or a sharper 6-miles on single-track with a 1,400-foot climb to the yurt. The less adventurous can drive an access road to within 0.25 mile of the yurt. Whatever route you choose, the views of the snowcapped Boulder and Pioneer mountains are stunning. After a long day of biking, you and your friends lounge in the sun on Coyote's wooden deck and drink some hard-won beers before setting out to make dinner in the yurt's full kitchen. No need to bring water: a full water system, complete with backpack water bladders (you do need to do *some* work!) and a filtration system are provided. A warm fire in the firepit and a sauna are enough to make a convert out of anyone. Sleep comes early, made easy with bunk beds complete with sleeping pads, allowing you to pack light. The next morning, you set out on your bike, perhaps you go for a hike, or maybe you lie in the grass, reading a book and contemplating the spell of the mountains. Single-track trails near the yurt include Curley's, Fox Peak, Warm Springs Ridge, Adams Gulch, Highline Trail, Rooks Creek, Alden Gulch, Oregon Gulch, Castle Creek, and Lost Shirt Gulch.

Rentals

Bikes can be rented at these shops, which also have good mechanics, gear, maps, and guidance: willing locals who will tell you what's where. If you get them going, you may even get an earful of epic mountain-bike tales.

Backwoods Mountain Sports (208-726-8818; www.backwoodsmountainsports .com), 711 N. Main St., Ketchum.

Durance Cycleworks (208-726-7693), 131 Second St., Ketchum.

Formula Sports (208-726-3194; www.formulasports.com), 460 N. Main St., Ketchum.

Pete Lane's Mountain Sports (208-622-2279), Sun Valley Village, Sun Valley; and (208-622-6144), River Run Plaza, Sun Valley Resort, Ketchum.

The Powerhouse (208-788-9184), 703 North First Ave., Hailey. Elite riders may look to this bike-fitting shop for high-end attention.

Sturtevant's Mountain Outfitters (208-726-4501; www.sturtos.com), 340 N. Main St., Ketchum; Warm Springs Village at Sun Valley Resort, Ketchum; and 201 N. Main St., Hailey.

Sun Summit Ski and Cycle (208-726-0707), 791 Warm Springs Rd., Ketchum.

Recommended Reading

The best way to identify a mountain-bike ride to suit your tastes and abilities is to talk with the locals at the bike shops (see Rentals) or to pick up a copy of *Good Dirt: The Complete Mountain Bike Guide to Sun Valley, Idaho* by Greg

McRoberts (Go Right, LLC, 2003), which provides the dirt on 50 of the most popular mountain bike rides in the Sun Valley and Sawtooth regions; many a local uses this guidebook. If you are interested in camping along the way, *Good Dirt* also provides a list of multiday rides.

SKIING

Alpine Skiing

Soldier Mountain ski area (208-764-2526; www.soldiermountain.com), off US 20, Fairfield. Open Thurs.–Sun. Lift tickets start at $30 for adults. This locally favored mountain some 60-odd miles south of Sun Valley boasts 1,150 acres of inbound skiable terrain, 1,425 feet of vertical, three chairs, and a terrain park. This is a kicked-back and relatively affordable mountain that can get some serious pow. Thurs. can be huge powder days, and the mountain tends to retain its snow.

Sun Valley Resort (208-622-6136 or 800-894-9931; www.sunvalley.com), off River Run and Warm Springs rds., Ketchum. Open every day. Lift tickets $79 for adults, $45 for children. The town of Sun Valley derives its name from this world-famous ski resort, which offers 3,400 vertical feet of world-class alpine skiing on Bald Mountain, one of America's best and largest ski mountains. Consistently rated by *Ski Magazine* as one of the nation's top ski resorts, Sun Valley Resort certainly offers fun in the sun (with an average of 250 sunny days per year). With acres upon acres of buffed-out groomers, thigh-busting runs as long as 3 miles, hidden powder stashes in the trees, wide-open bowls, a superpipe, and bump runs galore, there is terrain to satisfy skiers and snowboarders of all abilities. The resort offers 630 snowmaking acres, 14 lifts, and 65 runs on 2,054 skiable acres. The panoramic view from the top of 9,105-foot Baldy is breathtaking (both literally and, perhaps, physically!). Some say this mountain is not for the faint of heart.

Dollar Mountain, Baldy's sister peak, has gentler, groomed, and treeless slopes that beginner skiers might prefer. With its three chairlifts, 13 runs, a halfpipe, a terrain park, and tubing hill, Dollar Mountain is a great place for kids. Ski instruction can be arranged by contacting the resort; rental gear is available at the hill as well as at many of the ski shops about town.

Sun Valley's lodges—Warm Springs, River Run, and Seattle Ridge—offer all the usual ski-lodge amenities, but they are something to marvel at: tall ceilings adorned with large antler chandeliers, towering river-rock fireplaces, marble in the bathrooms. Yet in this atmosphere, you can feel comfortable kicking up your feet for a $1 PBR and listen to live music after a hard day of skiing.

Backcountry Skiing

Perhaps the best way to experience Central Idaho in winter is to get out into the backcountry on skis. There is nothing quite like the transcendence that occurs when you strap on a pair of telemark skis with skins and start climbing away from the road on a snowy white trail toward the mountains. Were you to venture no further, the experience would still be remarkable: Douglas firs leaning in toward you from the side of the trail, their boughs weighted by a blanket of snow, the subtle sound of the wind as it whistles around phantasmagoric snow sculptures, shaping them toward perfection, the sun's rays warming your face.

Chris Pilaro

SKI-MOUNTAINEERING IN THE SAWTOOTHS

Yet for many adventurers, this is only the start. The real journey begins when you skin up the drainage, swoosh by swoosh, and then up the flanks of the mountains ahead, eventually—perhaps hours and hours and buckets of sweat later—to the top of the ridgeline, where you gain your just reward: a well-earned rest on an improvised seat with a panoramic alpine view, some water, and a hefty lunch. And then, if you are lucky, you get the goods: powder snow in the north-facing trees or silky corn snow on a warm south-facing spring slope. It is for this sensation that Idaho's Sawtooth, Smoky, and Pioneer mountains attract a fair number of adventurous telemark and alpine touring (AT, or randonée) skiers both as visitors and obsessed locals.

Idaho Skiers & Snowshoers Coalition (208-386-9227; www.skiidaho.org) is a great resource for information on backcountry skiing in Idaho.

Nordic and Backcountry Skiers Alliance (www.skiersalliance.net) is a fabulous local organization working hard to preserve Idaho's pristine wilds for non-motorized backcountry activities. A backcountry map of the Wood River Valley is available on their Web site.

Despite the romance of it all, I cannot stress enough how important it is to know what you are doing—to be able to read the snow, to evaluate avalanche conditions, and to bring (and know how to use) the proper gear, including avalanche beacons, probes, shovels, clothing, skis, repair kits, water, food, down layers, etc. Avalanches, cold temperatures, and difficult terrain all pose real hazards. As we say—know before you go! See Avalanche Saftey, below. Here are some great places to go:

Galena Pass, on ID 75, 23 miles north of Ketchum. This is almost always a good place to do some yo-yos: ski down and hitch a ride back up to the top. Check in with some of the local ski shops and ask around about conditions and powder stashes.

Redfish Lake, on ID 75 south of Stanley. In winter, skiing across the frozen, snow-draped surface of this lake—the only noises the swoosh of your skis and, perhaps, the panting of your dog—is truly a Zen-like experience. A skin track is often put in off the road to Redfish Lake for backcountry skiing in to Bench Yurt (see sidebar), which, nestled among the stunning alpine Bench Lakes, provides access to killer backcountry skiing.

Soldier Mountain ski area (see Alpine Skiing) also offers snowcat access to some spectacular backcountry terrain in the Sawtooth National Forest. $250 per person for full day, including lunch.

Wood River Valley, off ID 75 from Bellevue to Galena Summit. More experienced backcountry skiers will find many skiable pitches up and down the valley, but most folks go to a handful of the drainages north of Ketchum, since snow conditions can be sketchy on the slopes farther south. In a great snow year, however, there is killer skiing to be done almost everywhere!

Avalanche Safety
Sawtooth National Forest Avalanche Center 208-622-8027 avalanche hotline; www.avalanche.org/~svavctr/). Be sure to check snow and avalanche condi-

tions either by calling the hotline or checking out the forecast online. The Avalanche Center also offers avalanche education.

Sawtooth Mountain Guides (208-774-3324; www.sawtoothguides.com), Stanley. They routinely offer avalanche education.

Sun Valley Trekking (208-788-1966; www.svtrek.com) also offers avalanche education routinely.

Outfitters and Shops

If you don't know where to go, you are better off arranging a fabulous guided ski tour or sticking to the ski areas. Guided ski tours of one to many days can be arranged for skiers of all abilities, and it is a great way for skiers with any amount of backcountry experience to bone up on their skills safely.

Backwoods Mountain Sports (208-726-8818; www.backwoodsmountainsports .com), 711 N. Main St., Ketchum. They have gear rentals and maps.

Sawtooth Mountain Guides (208-774-3324; www.sawtoothguides.com), Stanley. They ofer guided day trips and longer guided yurt trips.

Sun Valley Trekking (208-788-1966; www.svtrek.com) offers guided hut skiing, courses, catered backcountry dinner tours, and more. Check 'em out! (Also see sidebar.)

Nordic Skiing

This region is a mecca for cross-country skiers, with trails up and down the Wood River Valley, as well as at Sun Valley Resort and north in the Sawtooth Valley. These areas are described below.

YURT TRIPPING

Sun Valley Trekking (208-788-1966; www.svtrek.com) owns and operates six comfy yurts and huts in Idaho's Sawtooth, Smoky, and Pioneer mountains. These Mongolian-style huts are situated in some of the most stunning alpine terrain anywhere, providing access to some killer backcountry skiing—not to mention a warm, comfortable spot to rest your weary bones and a sauna to steam away the day's exertions. For backcountry skiers, a trip to a backcountry yurt is an adventure not to be missed. A yurt trip is not for the faint of heart, perhaps, since it often requires significant effort to ski in and a love of rugged accoutrements, but for those accustomed to backcountry travel and camping, the huts feel like first-class accommodations! Yurt and huts are available for rent, and skiers of all abilities can arrange guided backcountry expeditions from one to many days in length; instruction is also available. Telemark and randonée (alpine touring, or AT) skiers and snowboarders are welcome.

Chris Pilaro

SKI MOUNTAINEERING IN SAWTOOTH NATIONAL RECREATION AREA

Wood River Valley trails. Approximately 210 kilometers of groomed skate-skiing trails from Bellevue to Galena Summit are maintained by **Blaine County Recreation District** (208-788-2117; www.bcrd.org) under a special-use permit from the Sawtooth National Forest and are supported by donations and fees. Day pass $15 for adults, $7 for children, $7 for dogs (doggies need their own passes); weeklong pass $60; season pass $160. Passes can be purchased online; in-season, passes can also be purchased from various outfits around the valley (see Rentals), from Galena Lodge, and from Sawtooth NRA Headquarters (see Hiking). Great trail maps are available online. This is a mecca for Nordies. Trails that are part of this system, described from south to north, include the following:

The bike path, 30 kilometers from Bellevue north to Ketchum. Season generally mid-Nov.–mid-Apr. This becomes a Nordic thoroughfare in winter.

Quigley Canyon, in Hailey, has a spur of the Wood River Valley trail system jutting into it.

North Valley trails. Within the Sawtooth National Recreation Area. Trails wend their way north to Galena Lodge (see below) through a veritable winter wonderland: snow-draped willows, their red stems appearing as splashes of blood against the white backdrop; aspen groves, their tinkling leaves gone for the winter; and a cold river, its hydraulics frozen into beautiful ice sculptures.

Harriman Trail, 30 kilometers at northernmost end of the system. This trail is named for Averill Harriman, the founder of Sun Valley Resort. It is here where top athletes from around the world come to train and the annual preeminent Boulder Mountain Tour (see Special Events) Nordic skiing race takes place.

Smaller trail subsystems along the main Wood River Valley loop into the side drainages that splay out from the valley, including Lake Creek, North Fork, Billy's Bridge, and Prairie Creek.

Galena Lodge (208-726-4010; www.galenalodge.com), on ID 75 at north end of trail system, with more than 120 groomed kilometers. This is the hub of Nordic activity in the valley. This historic day lodge with a cozy atmosphere complete with a crackling fire is a great place to base a day of skiing (or to end one). At its complete ski shop and instruction center, you'll be able to fulfill all your Nordic needs here—plus fill your belly: great baked goodies, espresso, salads, sandwiches, beer, and the works. This fun, social gathering spot is where you'll see both Nordic skiers and local tele-skiers who, after earning their turns up near Galena Pass, might stop in to warm up with hot chocolate (or cool down with a beer) and snuggle up to the fire. The lodge hosts numerous fun events and activities, including snowshoeing, yurt trips, wildlife walks, moonlit dinners, and more.

Sun Valley Resort Nordic Center (208-622-2251; www.sunvalley.com), 40 kilometers of Nordic trails on Trail Creek. The resort operates its own Nordic trails out and along this beautiful creek. Half-, full-day, and season passes are available; Nordic gear can be rented on-site. Ski instruction is also available.

Sawtooth Valley trails. Free. Two more sets of Nordic trails can be found farther north, in the Sawtooth Valley at Alturas Lake and Park Creek. A map (the "Winter Recreation Map for the Sawtooth Valley and Stanley Basin" by the Sawtooth Community Winter Recreation Partnership) detailing these trails, plus the trails at Galena Lodge, is available from the Stanley-Sawtooth Chamber of Commerce.

Rentals

Backwoods Mountain Sports (208-726-8818; www.backwoodsmountainsports .com), 711 N. Main St., Ketchum.

The Elephant's Perch (208-726-3497; www.elephantsperch.com), 280 East Ave., Ketchum.

Galena Lodge (208-726-4010; www.galenalodge.com), on ID 75 24 miles north of Ketchum.

Sturtevants Mountain Outfitters (208-788-7847; www.sturtos.com), 201 N. Main St., Hailey.

WHITE-WATER KAYAKING AND RAFTING

Idaho is *the* white-water state, and Central Idaho certainly has its share of it! With the white-water meccas of the Salmon River to the north and the Snake River to the south, Wood River Valley visitors are often compelled to float at least some portion of these great rivers.

Middle Fork of the Salmon River, 100 miles from Boundary Creek to Cache Bar. Stanley is often the launching point for trips going in to the world-renowned gem of Idaho river trips, the Middle Fork of the Salmon, America's premier wilderness white-water river. Highly coveted trips down the Middle Fork run through stunning canyons, 80 class III–IV-plus rapids—with names such as Dagger Falls, Red Side, Devil's Tooth, and House Rock—and the remote wilds of the Frank Church–River of No Return Wilderness. Along the way, visitors are enchanted by wildflowers, hot pots, crystal waters, and Native American pictographs. See Salmon-Challis and Beyond: Mountains and Rivers Galore.

Outfitters

Many local outfitters can arrange guided trips ranging from a half day to a week for boaters of all abilities. For advanced boaters, these services also rent rafts, inflatable kayaks, and other river gear; food service can also be arranged. Check out **River Connection** (www.riverconnection.com) to arrange river shuttles.

With the usual backcountry mantra of "ounces equal pounds and pounds equal pain" no longer in effect on a river (rafts can carry an astounding amount of food, beer, and toys, on top of all the bare essentials!), a tradition of grand cuisine has evolved, with river outfitters trying to outdo each other for recognition as the best five-star floating resort vacation. The Wood River Valley is home to a handful of top-notch wilderness river outfitters for which the Middle Fork is their playground. A host of other river companies guiding trips on the Middle Fork and other Idaho jewels can be found in Stanley and beyond.

Adventure Guides (208-774-2200 or 888-948-4337), Stanley.

Adventures Wild (208-578-1203), Hailey.

Far & Away Adventures (208-726-8888; www.far-away.com), Sun Valley. Their gourmet chef uses fresh, seasonal, organic ingredients to produce French, Asian, and Pacific Northwest high cuisine served with award-winning wines and beers.

Candlelit dinners on the river are accompanied by linens, chairs, china, and stemmed glassware.

Middle Fork River Expeditions (800-801-5146), Stanley.

Middle Fork River Tours (208-788-6564 or 800-445-9738; www.middlefork .com), Hailey. They have perfected the art of Dutch-oven cooking to present sophisticated bistro entrées and fresh-baked desserts and breads, also served with all the accoutrements of a five-star dining room despite being on the river.

Middle Fork Wilderness Outfitters (208-726-5999; www.idahorapids.com), Boise. They aim for the food to "match the grandeur of the river landscape."

The River Company (208-788-5775), Stanley.

Sawtooth Adventure Company (208-774-4644 or 866-774-4644), Stanley.

Sevy Guide Service (208-774-2200), Stanley.

Triangle C Ranch Whitewater Float Expedition (208-774-2266), Stanley.

White Cloud Rafting Adventures (208-774-7238), Stanley.

White Otter Outdoor Adventures (208-726-4331 or 888-726-4331), Ketchum.

Recommended Reading
Don't forget Grant Amaral's *Idaho—the Whitewater State; a Guidebook* (Bookcrafters, 1990) for all the skinny on boating in Idaho, including information on shuttles, air services (some put-ins are best reached by air), white-water equipment, permits, and the like.

✳ Wilder Places

LAKES
There are few experiences more breathtaking than rounding the corner of a high-alpine trail in the Sawtooth National Recreation Area for your first glimpse of one of more than 1,000 still, cobalt blue, glacially carved lakes that grace this landscape. Within the smaller Sawtooth Wilderness Area, more than 300 lakes provide homes to cutthroat, rainbow, brook, and bull trout, as well as grayling, whitefish, and steelhead. Sockeye and chinook salmon also spawn in these waters, but are becoming increasingly endangered.

The larger lakes in the region—Alturas, Pettit, Redfish, and Stanley lakes—are accessible by car and offer various services, including camping, picnic areas, and restrooms; all except Stanley Lake have boat ramps. As always, please be prepared when venturing into the wilds—bring plenty of food, water, and sunscreen, and wear appropriate clothing. Note that at the wrong time in the summer, the bugs near these lakes can be god-awful. If you are camping, you might need to be prepared to make a panicked dash for your tent and take a short timeout as dusk comes and goes.

Alice Lake, via trail from Pettit Lake. The hike to Alice Lake is not easy but, surrounded by wildflowers and chalky peaks, this lake in the SNRA has gained a reputation as one of the loveliest scenes in all of the Sawtooths.

Alturas Lake, via a road off ID 75 north of Smiley Creek. This is one of the historical rearing lakes for the Snake River sockeye salmon, and it is a great

CLEAR ALPINE LAKES BEJEWEL THE WHITE CLOUD MOUNTAINS.

picnicking, camping, and fishing spot. This lake in the SNRA is the jumping-off point for several great hikes to a handful of other alpine lakes, including Cabin Creek and Alpine lakes.

Magic Reservoir (208-732-7200; www.blm.gov), off ID 75, 5 miles southwest of US 20. This 14,000-acre man-made lake east of Fairfield is a popular spot for fishing (during the summer and winter), boating, water-skiing, and camping. The reservoir has some big fish. The east side of Magic used to be quite a scene, with a serious windsurfing contingent. West Magic now seems to be where the action is. It's a nice place to watch the local color—both the sunset and the characters that hang out here. The local Dam Fools Club sponsors an annual Fourth of July boat parade and a notorious fishing contest. The Bureau of Land Management operates nine semideveloped camping and recreational sites around the reservoir. Bring your own drinking water.

Pettit Lake, off ID 75 just south of Obsidian. This lake in the SNRA also provides access, via the Tin Cup trailhead, to hiking trails that will take you to Alice, Farley, Toxaway, and other lakes.

Redfish Lake, off ID 75 just south of Stanley. At 2.4 square miles, this is the largest lake in the SNRA; it occupies a U-shaped, glacially carved valley. The lake is named for the beautiful sockeye salmon that once migrated some 900 miles from the Pacific Ocean to the lake to spawn in such massive quantities (up to 30,000 per year) that, during spawning season, the lake appeared red. Today, 90 percent of juvenile salmon born in this lake will be killed at four hydroelectric dams on the Columbia, Snake, and Salmon rivers as they make their voyage to the ocean, and only a few fish will make it back to Redfish Lake to spawn. Intense commercial fishing, historic cattle grazing near sensitive habitat, and increased recreational activities have all contributed to the salmon's decline. Redfish Lake is the only lake in Idaho that remains a spawning ground for this endangered species. The lake is a beautiful spot. Its shallows, with their sandy white bottoms, reflect a remarkable Caribbean blue, and the Sawtooth Range to the west forms a backdrop that is truly magical. During the summer, the rustic lakeside Redfish Lake Lodge (see Lodging) bustles with activity. The lodge is a great spot to kick back and listen to free summer concerts.

Stanley Lake, off ID 21 west of Stanley. In the northwest corner of the SNRA is another great beauty. Stanley Lake is watched over by McGowen Peak, which appears to rise directly out of the stillness of the lake. It is a favorite spot for fishing and boating.

Recommended Reading
An explorer looking for gorgeous alpine lakes in this region could spend many moons doing so. Gloria Moore's *Day Hiking Near Sun Valley* (Idaho Conservation League, 2004) outlines numerous hikes that will take you to or near the countless alpine lakes in the region.

NATIONAL RECREATION AREAS
Sawtooth National Recreation Area (SNRA) **Headquarters** (208-272-5000), Star Route (ID 75), Ketchum; and **SNRA Stanley office** (208-774-3001), HC 64, Box 9900, Stanley; 756,000 acres from the SNRA Headquarters, located 8 miles north of Ketchum on ID 75, north to ID 75 just east of Clayton and ID 21 south of Banner Summit. The Sawtooth National Forest, which straddles portions of northern Utah through central Idaho, is named for the stunningly rugged, glacially incised, primarily granite Sawtooth Range, just north of the Wood River Valley. A portion of the 1.7 million-acre forest in Idaho is designated as the playground we call the SNRA, which was created by Congress in 1972 out of public and private lands to protect the natural, historical, and recreational qualities of this grand landscape. The area is widely revered as one of the largest and most magnificent recreation areas in the United States, with 50 peaks higher than 10,000 feet—including 12,009-foot Hyndman Peak, highest in the SNRA and ninth-highest in the state—more than 300 high-alpine lakes with excellent trout fishing, the headwaters of four of Idaho's major rivers—the mighty Salmon, Payette, Boise, and Big Wood rivers—and 250 miles of trails.

In its wildness, the SNRA provides a home for more than 300 species of wildlife, including mule deer, coyotes, foxes, chipmunks, squirrels, Clark's nutcrackers, juncos, and chickadees. More elusive species include black bears, gray wolves,

Chris Pilaro

ROCK CLIMBING IS A FAVORITE ACTIVITY IN THE SAWTOOTHS.

mountain lions, bobcats, beavers, moose, bighorn sheep, elk, sandhill cranes, and golden eagles. The SNRA offers hiking and mountaineering, camping, backcountry and Nordic skiing, mountain biking, horseback riding, hunting, fishing, swimming, and some motorized trial use. The "Sawtooth and White Cloud Mountains Trail Maps" from **Adventure Maps, Inc.** (www.adventuremaps.net) provides a list of suggested hikes and mountain biking routes, along with general information (geology, wildlife, weather, etc.) about the area and rules and etiquette for the backcountry.

WILDERNESS AREAS

Sawtooth Wilderness Area (208-272-5000), 217,000 acres within the western section of the SNRA. Designated as a wilderness area under the Wilderness Act of 1964, and defined among other things as an area "untrammeled by man," this area is afforded the highest level of federal protection of its roadless and remote character.

✳ Lodging

Many property management companies offer condos and homes for vacation rentals, and there are many motels and hotels in the area; www.visitsunvalley.com has a complete listing. Some of the more notable inns, lodges, and B&Bs are listed below.

BED & BREAKFASTS

Hailey

Featherbed Inn (208-578-5227; www.featherbedinnidaho.com), 416 First Ave. N., Hailey 83333. Once the proprietor of Michelin Guide–rated Le Mistral Bed & Breakfast and La Table de Ventabren restaurant in the south of France, Lynn McDonald has introduced a little bit of Provence to historic Old Hailey by way of the Featherbed Inn. This lovely inn is filled with an eclectic mix of antiques, paintings, and flowers, making it a cozy place to relax after a day of recreation in the Wood River Valley, either in the shared living room or the hot tub! Each guest room has a different decorating theme, but all are equipped with plush beds, private bath and deck, TV/DVD/video, coffeemaker, and hair dryer. Lynn's scrumptious homemade breakfasts—the talk of the town—are served outdoors during the summer months. Guests are free to use the bicycles provided by the inn to pedal on the valley's 30-mile-long bike path, which runs just to the east of the property, or wax their skis in the heated garage provided expressly for this purpose. The inn has a return following who seem to find it hard to beat the charm, comfort, and price of this place. $95.

Inn at Ellsworth Estate (208-788-6354; www.ellsworthestate.com), 703 Third Ave. S., Hailey 83333. This rambling old house (built in 1915 as a private residence) with an expansive lawn, impressively massive shade trees, and wraparound porch is a great place to kick your feet up and relax after a busy day. The property has nine charming B&B rooms, furnished with classic antiques and modern decor, each with a private bath. Some rooms have a fireplace and/or hot tub.

A spacious living room provides a place to share a glass of wine at the end of the day, and a three-course gourmet breakfast comes with the room. There is also a tennis court on the property. $110–180.

Povey Pensione Bed & Breakfast (208-788-4682; www.poveypensione .com), 128 W. Bullion St., Hailey 83333. Situated near the Big Wood River and close to downtown Hailey, this historic home is full of antique furnishings and provides comfortable amenities, including a full breakfast. Each of the three guest rooms and a suite has a private bath and a cozy sitting room. The home has a fully equipped country kitchen and laundry facilities for longer stays. The property has high-speed wireless Internet access. $95–135.

INNS

Ketchum

Knob Hill Inn (208-726-8010 or 800-526-8010; www.knobhillinn.com), 960 N. Main St., Ketchum 83340. Located just north of downtown Ketchum, the Knob Hill Inn is one of the posher accommodations in town, and it will keep you warm in high style. The inn has 26 graciously appointed rooms and suites. All accommodations include a wet bar, dressing area, marble-tiled bathroom with tub, and magnificent mountain views. On-site are two restaurants, a fitness room, a sauna, and a pool. $250–500.

LODGES AND GUEST RANCHES

Ketchum

Bald Mountain Lodge (208-726-4776), 100 Picabo St., Ketchum 83340. Located just 100 yards from Warm Springs Ski Lift, this lodge has

you right in the middle of Baldy action. The lodge features elegant studios and suites, complete with fireplaces and Jacuzzi tubs. It also has a fitness center and laundry facilities; some units have cooking facilities. $75–225.

Stanley

Stanley-Sawtooth Chamber of Commerce (www.stanleycc.org) has a complete listing of small log-cabin motels from which to base your Sawtooth adventures. Some of the posher accommodations are listed below.

Diamond D Ranch (208-861-9206 or 800-222-1269; www.diamondd ranch-idaho.com), in Frank Church– River of No Return Wilderness; accessed by a primitive 40-mile road over Loon Creek from Stanley or via chartered airplane. Cabins and lodge rooms. $240 per person per night.

Idaho Rocky Mountain Ranch, (208-774-3544; www.idahorocky.com), Milepost 180 on ID 75, Stanley 83278. Listed on the National Register of Historic Places, the Idaho Rocky Mountain Ranch provides both historic charm and modern comforts. Nestled in the spectacularly beautiful Sawtooth Valley in the heart of the Sawtooth National Recreation Area, beneath snowcapped peaks and along the Salmon River, this 1,000-acre ranch is a western-style delight. An authentic lodge and cabins that house 50 people, natural hot springs, and a kicked-back front porch lull even the most high-wired visitor into relaxation. It provides a great springboard for high-alpine adventure, including hiking, mountain biking, horseback riding, fishing, rafting, and exploring. The ranch has its own excellent horseback riding program. Rooms $330–380; rates decrease for longer stays.

Redfish Lake Lodge (208-774-3536; www.redfishlake.com), Stanley 83278. Partnered with the USDA Forest Service, this rustic lodge on the edge of magical Redfish Lake (see Wilder Places—Lakes) offers 21 cabins, 11 motel rooms, and nine lodge rooms, plus dining, boat rental, lake tours, and a sandy white beach for unlimited recreation and relaxation. Great free acoustic music attracts tourists and locals alike, who laze on the lawn overlooking the lake, often after a big day of hiking or mountain biking, to drink a beer and listen to some strumming. Lodge rooms $70 and up; motel rooms $110 and up; cabins $145 and up.

MOTELS

Ketchum

Like any good ski town, Ketchum offers a slew of ski motels that provide a decent bed after a hard day of skiing.

Best Western Kentwood Lodge (208-726-4114 or 800-805-1001; www.bestwestern.com), 180 S. Main St., Ketchum 83340. 57 rooms. $99–209.

Best Western Tyrolean Lodge (208-726-5336 or 800-333-7912; www.bestwestern.com), 260 Cottonwood St., Ketchum 83340. 56 rooms. $85–134.

Clarion Inn of Sun Valley (208-726-5900 or 800-262-4833), 600 N. Main St., Ketchum 83340. 58 rooms. $79–225.

Lift Tower Lodge (208-726-5163 or 800-462-8646), 703 S. Main St., Ketchum 83340. 14 rooms. $69–95.

Tamarack Lodge (208-726-3344 or 800-521-5379; www.tamaracksun valley.com), 291 Walnut Ave., Ketchum 83340. 26 rooms. $69–159.

Sun Valley

Sun Valley Resort (208-622-4111 or 800-786-8259; www.sunvalley.com), 1 Sun Valley Rd., Sun Valley 83353. There's no getting around it; Sun Valley is a *resort*, with accommodations in 260 rooms and almost every amenity you can think of: full breakfast, lounge area, pool, hot tub, laundry, fitness center. Plus, you are smack in the middle of the activity, which includes access to golf, ice skating shows, live music, and more. $99–1,000.

✳ Where to Eat

The Wood River Valley certainly has its share of tasty vittles, from casual après-ski spots to more upscale fine dining (many with great organic food). It would be hard not to find a great bite to eat here.

DINING OUT

Bellevue

Full Moon Steakhouse & Catering (208-788-5912), 118 S. Main St. Open for dinner Tues.–Sat. Full Moon tops the list as the most upscale restaurant in Bellevue with its cozy, warm atmosphere and menu of grilled prime rib and sirloin, New York, and rib-eye steaks. Red meat is complemented by delicious crab cakes, grilled artichokes served with lemon aioli, and fresh salads, including Caesar, house, spinach, chef, and the popular Full Moon salad, with greens, slivered red onion, and candied almonds tossed in a champagne vinaigrette. Pasta, chicken, and fresh fish entrées are also served.

Hailey

CK's (208-788-1223; www.cksrealfood

.com), 320 Main St. Open for dinner daily. This is another great spot. Slow-cooked, high-quality, local, organic, fresh foods include fresh grilled local Idaho trout rubbed with Cajun-style spices and herbs, served with Carolina tartar sauce and red curry–corn, or Gaucho steak with caramelized shallots, roasted cauliflower, chimichurri, and fries. You won't be disappointed.

DaVinci's (208-788-7699), 17 W. Bullion St. This is the place to go if you are looking for yummy Italian fare and a warm, casual atmosphere.

Di Vine (208-788-4422), 400 S. Main St. Try our local wine bar for a great glass of wine and light fare.

Fresshies (208-788-3621), 122 S. Main St. This is one of the hottest new restaurants in Hailey, with a cozy bistro atmosphere, including exposed brick walls and great paintings. Fresshies serves up scrumptious, light fare and nice wine. A good place to relax.

Zou 75 (208-788-3310), 416 N. Main St. Zou 75 garnered the praise "best sushi in a landlocked state" by *Wine Enthusiast*. And great sushi it is, with mouth-watering Zou-Maki "Locals' Rolls," including the Hailey Roll, stuffed with fresh *hamachi* (tuna) and avocado, topped with orange *tobiko* (flying fish roe), and the Stop, Drop, and Roll, which consists of *ebi* tempura, *unagi* (eel), *shichimi* (seven spice seasoning)–encrusted cream cheese, avocado, and crispy onions topped with layers of fresh ahi tuna and drizzled with *kabayaki* sauce. These and other tasty delights are all served in a eclectic, warm setting complete with a private tatami booth. Your biggest concern here will be to contain your appetite!

Ketchum

Baci Italian Café and Wine Bar (208-726-8384; www.svrestaurant ventures.com/b_main.html), 240 S. Main St. Open for dinner daily. At the southern entrance of Ketchum, this fine spot has great ambience and fabulous northern and southern Italian food, made with the freshest ingredients. The menu includes rustic stone-fired pizzas, homemade pastas, scrumptious seafood, fresh meats, and exquisite desserts. The wine bar, with its impressive selection of delicious wines, is a great place to meet a friend. Voted one of the valley's best restaurants.

Bistro 44 (208-726-2040), 200 E. Sixth St. This is another intimate spot, serving fine French fare with an extensive and eclectic wine list.

Chandler's Restaurant (208-788-1223; www.svrestaurantventures .com/c_main.html), 200 S. Main St., in Trail Creek Village. Open for dinner daily. Housed in a rustic 1940s cabin, with changing art exhibits on the walls, Chandler's is a romantic spot. The menu is also hard to beat, featuring ruby red trout, truffled free-range chicken breast, and Yankee pot roast. The desserts are to-die-for. You won't be disappointed.

Ciro Restaurant and Wine Bar (208-727-1800), 230 Walnut Ave. Open for lunch Mon.–Fri., dinner daily. Relatively new on the scene, Ciro is certainly making its mark for its clean, crisp atmosphere and wood oven–cooked food, grilled meats and fish, and Neopolitan-style pizza with all the fixings. They also have a nice selection of wines by the glass to be sipped with dinner or at the wine bar.

East Avenue Bistro (208-726-9251), 220 East Ave. Fine dining with a

Mediterranean flair in a comfortable atmosphere. A great spot!

Felix's Hillside Restaurant (208-726-1166), 380 First Ave. N. Open for dinner daily. This is one of the valley's more formal restaurants, with white tablecloths, upholstered chairs (a rarity among the generally more casual attitude in the valley), and subtle music. For the full meal-deal, this is a good spot for a romantic date. The restaurant is renowned for its Mediterranean-influenced dishes—such as tasty seafood paella and herb-crusted rack of lamb—and fine wines.

Globus (208-726-1301), 291 Sixth St. Another favorite features classic gourmet Asian cuisine and fine wines. The food is delectable, and the ambience warm and funky. Don't miss the modern paintings that adorn this place.

il Naso Ristorante (208-726-7776), corner of Fifth Avenue and Washington Street. For a gourmet Italian experience, try il Naso. It has a great wine bar, a deck, and scrumptious food.

Ketchum Grill (208-726-4660; www.ketchumgrill.com), 520 East Ave. Open for dinner daily. Reservations recommended. Tucked in one of the area's oldest historic buildings, this charming restaurant is a valley favorite, frequented by celebrities, foodies, and regular folks alike. Its award-winning wine list, local meats, fresh organic vegetables, and scrumptious desserts are prepared with style by husband-and-wife team Scott Mason and Anne Little. The pair have honed their culinary skills through two decades of cooking up and down the West Coast and several apprenticing stints in European kitchens. Offerings include fruitwood-grilled Black Canyon Idaho elk, braised

Idaho lamb shank, oven-roasted chicken with herbs and pan sauces, a daily fish special, and gourmet pizza and pasta dishes. If dessert is in the cards, dare to indulge in the rustic apple tart with cinnamon ice cream and caramel sauce or one of the fruity, house-made ice creams and sorbets. The candlelit tavern warmth makes this a cozy spot to watch the snow fall during winter, and the porch is a great place to enjoy a warm alpine summer evening. Rock shrimp cakes with red pepper remoulade and a warm spinach salad with bacon and grilled chicken breast at the bar is always a good option. Singing their accolades is *Snow Country Magazine*, which chose the Ketchum Grill as one of the eight best ski-town restaurants. This highly recommended place won't disappoint.

Knob Hill Inn Restaurant (208-726-8004), 960 N. Main St. Open for dinner Tues.–Sat. This is another high-end establishment featuring French-influenced delicacies including escargots, sea scallops, roasted duck breast, braised lamb shank, and yellowfin tuna, among others, and an impressive wine list. Dinners are served on fine china with Italian frette linens.

Rasberrys (208-726-0606), 411 E. Fifth St. Open for lunch and dinner daily. By reservation only. In a Parisianesque, intimate atmosphere, the revolving gourmet menu includes such delicacies as wild boar with a red wine reduction sauce, butternut squash chicken salad, curried carrot soup, and Indian spiced chicken and tomato curry. This is the place to bring your date.

Sushi on Second (208-726-5181), 260 Second St. Open for dinner daily.

For great sushi, this place can't be beat. The warm, velvety atmosphere here makes you want to sprawl out in one of the tatami rooms, sipping sake until late in the night. The fish is discernibly fresh, and the nightly specials—such as pan-seared sea scallops with porcini pesto or truffle-oiled arugula and sushi falafel (edamame cake with Vietnamese-style peanut sauce)—are scrumptious.

Sun Valley

The Lodge Dining Room (208-622-2150), second floor of Sun Valley Lodge. This fancy-pants place serves delectables such as pan-seared scallops with coriander-lime sauce and julienne vegetables, apricot- and pine-nut-crusted lamb chops with fingerling potatoes, and grilled prime filet mignon with gratinéed parsnips, braised cipollini onions, and sun-dried cherries.

EATING OUT

Bellevue

Mahoney's Bar and Grill (208-788-4449), 104 S. Main St. Open for lunch and dinner daily. Juicy burgers, chicken burgers, soups, and salads are served up in a fun Irish pub atmosphere.

South Valley Pizzeria (208-788-1456), 108 Elm St. South Valley has been awarded the prize for the Wood River Valley's best pizza for six years running. All pizzas are made with a tasty herb crust and the best ingredients available, making for a variety of tasty gourmet pizzas.

Hailey

More casual spots are perfect for grabbing a bite on your way back from a big day of exploration or a quick lunch.

Big Belly Deli (208-788-2411), 171 N. Main St. Deli fare that will fill your tummy.

Chapala Mexican Restaurant (208-788-5065), 502 N. Main St. Authentic Mexican.

Chester & Jakes (208-788-4722), 116 S. Main St., in the Mint. This casual, family-oriented restaurant offers fresh fish and seafood, including the best fish-and-chips in the valley.

KB's South (208-788-7217), 126 S. Main St. Mexican delights; try the fish tacos!

Lago Azul (208-578-1700), 14 W. Croy St., Ste A. Authentic Mexican.

Sun Valley Brewing Company (208-788-0805), 202 N. Main St. Pub fare.

Taste of Thai (208-578-2488), 106 N. Main St. Great Thai food.

The Wicked Spud (208-788-0009), 305 N. Main St. Pub fare.

Wiseguy Pizza Pie (208-788-8688), 315 S. Main St. Great pies.

Ketchum

For more casual dining, this list provides only a glimpse into the vibrant restaurant scene in the valley. Many other great establishments will satisfy your après-ski (or après–Sun Valley Summer Symphony) hunger in style.

Apple's Bar and Grill (208-726-7067), at Warm Springs base. An easygoing après-ski joint.

Bald Mountain Pizza & Pasta (208-622-2143), at Sun Valley Village. A great pizza and pasta place.

Buffalo Bites (208-726-2833). 491½ N. Leadville Ave. On-the-go lunch all year and dinner during the summer.

Cellar Pub (208-622-3832), 400 Sun Valley Rd. Pub food.

China Panda (208-726-3591), 515 N. East Ave. Chinese food.

Cristina's Restaurant & Bakery (208-726-4499), 520 Second St. E. Open for breakfast, lunch, and take-out daily. Fabulous Tuscan cuisine: steamed artichokes with tomato shallot sauce, piquillo pepper and asiago quiche, and kalamata olive ciabatta—the recipes for which the proprietress, Cristina Cook, has shared in her highly coveted book *Cristina's of Sun Valley* (Gibbs Smith, 2005).

Grumpy's (no phone), 860 Warm Springs Rd. A favorite dive frequented by locals after a hard day of skiing or mountain biking.

KB's Burritos (208-726-2232), corner of Sixth and Washington sts. Mexican food.

The Kneadery (208-726-9462), 260 Leadville Ave. N. Great breakfast and lunch fare.

Lefty's Bar & Grill (208-726-2744), 231 Sixth St. E. Another great divey spot favored by the locals.

McClain's Pizzeria (208-726-8585). 520 N. Washington St. Pies.

No Ho's Hawaiian Café (208-726-8100), corner of Fourth and Washington. Ethnic fare.

Osaka Sushi (208-726-6999), 360 East Ave. N., Ste. 5, in the Courtyard. Ethnic fare.

Papa Hemi's Hideaway (208-726-3773), 310 S. Main St. This place serves up some good pub fare, home-brew, and at times live music and open fires.

Perry's Restaurant (208-726-7703), at Clubhouse Plaza, one block east of post office. Great breakfast and lunch fare.

Pioneer Saloon (208-726-3139), 308 N. Main St. Another standard, with juicy Idaho steaks and the largest spuds you've ever seen; even the heartiest eaters may take home a doggie bag. The classic rustic western decor, complete with racks hanging above your head, make this a cozy spot.

The Rickshaw (208-726-8481; www.eat-at-rickshaw.com), 460 N. Washington Ave. Open for lunch Fri., dinner Tues.–Sat. Fabulous "ethnic street foods" served tapas-style. You'll want to sample more than one item from the tasty menu featuring creative, fresh foods full of organic veggies, meats, and fish inspired by the flavors of Thailand, Vietnam, China, India, and Indonesia.

Rico's Pizza and Pasta (208-726-7426), 200 N. Main St. Pizza and pasta; enough said.

Roosevelt Tavern & Grill (208-726-0051), 280 N. Main St. Open for dinner daily. A menu of classic bistro fare with an Asian and Northwestern flair uses fresh, healthy ingredients. The rooftop deck, with its firepits and gas heaters, is a hit with locals during the summer.

Sawtooth Club (208-726-5233), 231 N. Main St. Open for dinner daily. Voted the valley's best overall restaurant and best bar for four consecutive years, its rustic charm, cozy fireplace and couches, and consistently great mesquite-grilled plates, including Idaho pork tenderloin, breast of duck marinated with warm blackberry port sauce, and ruby red trout, will keep you warm and happy. Try their salads as well.

Strega Bar & Boutique (208-726-6463), 360 First Ave. N. Tea, wine, beer, and international organic cuisine.

Wine Company (208-726-2442), 360 Leadville Ave. Open for lunch and dinner Mon.–Fri. Another favorite gathering spot. For some reason, its friendly atmosphere makes it conducive to mingling with friends and strangers alike. With reportedly the largest wine selection in Idaho and its tasty light menus, this is a great place to wind down the week.

Stanley

Bridge Street Grill (208-774-2208), on the Salmon River in Lower Stanley. Open Apr.–Oct. This is a good spot for a hard-won burger after a killer mountain bike ride. The deck is a great hangout when it's warm outside.

Idaho Rocky Mountain Ranch (208-774-3544; www.idahorocky.com), on ID 75, 9 miles south of Stanley between Mileposts 180 and 181. Fine summer dining and barbecue buffet. The ranch offers spectacular views of the Sawtooth Mountains and live music several nights a week.

Kasino Club (208-774-3516), 21 Ace of Diamonds Ave. American-style dishes include seared prime rib with Cajun spices and Gorgonzola. Locals seem to flock here.

Papa Brunee's (208-774-2536), on Ace of Diamonds Avenue, across from post office. Pizza and beer.

Redfish Lake Lodge (208-774-3536), 2 miles off ID 75 near Milepost 185. Try house-smoked Idaho trout in a rustic dining room, where you can gaze out at Redfish Lake and the Sawtooth Mountains beyond while enjoying tasty vittles.

Stanley Baking Co. (208-774-6573), 14 Wall St. Open for breakfast and lunch daily mid-May–mid-Oct. A real favorite; Wood River folks trek the 60

miles north to get a Sun. breakfast here. This place serves up great home-baked goods, hearty breakfasts, and the best coffee and espresso in the Stanley Basin. The front porch, full of scruffy campers and boaters, is quite a scene on a weekend day.

Sun Valley

Sun Valley Resort offers a slew of dining options catering to the resort set, including the following.

Gretchen's (208-622-2144), first floor of Sun Valley Lodge. Gretchen's serves up a variety of specialty salads, sandwiches, and pasta, plus dinner entrées that include salmon, fresh Idaho lamb, and beef.

The Kontidorei (208-622-2235), Sun Valley Village. Come here for a quick bite and fine pastries and espresso.

The Ram (208-622-2225), Sun Valley Village. The Ram serves Idaho lamb, trout, prime rib, steak, fondue, and the like.

Trail Creek Cabin (208-622-2135), on Sun Valley Road 1.5 miles east of Sun Valley. This cozy restaurant in a historic cabin serves authentic western food, including prime rib, steak, Idaho trout, and barbecued ribs.

COFFEEHOUSES

Hailey

Hailey Coffee Company (208-578-7673), 219 S. Main St.

Zaney's River Street Coffee House (208-788-2062), 208 N. River St.

Ketchum

The valley has a fair number of great java spots, many with wireless Internet connections, so that you can setup a vacation office while you're here.

Coffee Grinder (208-726-8048), 321 E. Fourth St.

Java on Fourth (208-726-2882), 191 Fourth St.

Tully's (208-622-3288), 601 Sun Valley Rd.

✳ Cultural Offerings

Sun Valley Center for the Arts (208-726-9491; www.sunvalleycenter.org), 191 Fifth St. E., Ketchum; and 314 Second Ave., Hailey. This pillar of the local arts community offers first-rate art classes and lectures; sponsors fabulous and sometimes exotic concerts, dance performances, and film series; and curates award-winning visual arts exhibitions. Its Hailey facility is housed in the beautiful and newly renovated Ezra Pound House (see To See—Historical Homes and Sites), birthplace of the famous poet, musician, and critic.

ART GALLERIES
The Wood River Valley has a thriving art scene, with more than 30 galleries in the area and a series of summer art fairs (see Special Events). Many of the galleries listed below display works from nationally and internationally known artists, but a few have more local art.

Sun Valley Gallery Association (208-726-5512; www.svgalleries.org) sponsors almost monthly Gallery Walks, generally on Fri. nights. Gallery Walks, adored by locals and visitors alike, are quite the social scene, providing free wine and cheese and a chance to bump into lots of friends and revel in great art. During holidays, Gallery Walk can be a bit crowded with a few too many pretentious types, and some locals (including me) are known to shy away.

Sun Valley–Ketchum Chamber and Visitors Bureau (www.visit

sunvalley.com) has more information on galleries and the arts.

Anne Reed Gallery (208-726-3036; www.annreedgallery.com), 391 First Ave. N., Ketchum. Works by nationally and internationally recognized contemporary artists and an outdoor sculpture garden.

Broschofsky Galleries (208-726-4950; www.brogallery.com), 360 East Ave. N., Ketchum. Art focused on the West.

David M. Norton Gallery (208-726-3588), lower level of Sheepskin Coat Factory, 511 Sun Valley Rd., Sun Valley. Fine American art and collectibles.

Davies Reid Gallery (208-726-3453; www.daviesreid.com), 131 First Ave. N., Ketchum. Specializes in authentic hand-woven carpets and tribal rugs and, through its Refugee Weaving Project, produces its own line of vegetally-dyed western, traditional, and contemporary rugs.

Dill & Spowze (208-720-0828; www.dillandspowze.com), 291 Washington Ave., Ketchum. Paintings and sculpture by major and emerging artists.

Dream Catcher Gallery (208-726-1305; www.dreamcatchergallery.com), 200 Main St. S., Ketchum. Native American arts and crafts.

Frederic Boloix Fine Arts (208-726-8810; www.boloix.com), 320 First Ave. N., Ketchum. Originals by Picasso, Matisse, Miró, and other famous artists.

Friesen Gallery (208-726-4174; www.friesengallery.com), 320 First Ave. N., Ketchum. Contemporary paintings, glass, and sculpture.

Gail Severn Gallery (208-726-5079; www.gailseverngallery.com), 400 First

Ave. N., Ketchum. This gallery is not to be missed; its revolving collections of contemporary fine art never cease to entrance me.

Gallery DeNovo (208-726-8180; www.gallerydenovo.com), 320 First Ave. N., Ste. 101, Ketchum. Emerging international artists.

Images of Nature (208-727-1836; www.mangelsen.com), 371 Main St. N., Ketchum. Captivating wildlife photography.

Kneeland Gallery (208-726-5512; www.kneelandgallery.com), 271 First Ave. N., Ketchum. Works by artists living and working in the West.

Lynn Toneri R. C. Hink Gallery (208-726-5639 Ketchum and 208-788-3444 Hailey; www.lynntoneri-water colors.com), 360 East Ave. N., Ketchum; and 507 S. Main St., Hailey. Stunning landscape, floral, and wildlife watercolors and fun western-motif wood sculptures.

Stoecklein Photography (208-726-5192; www.stoeckleinphotography .com), on 10th Street East, Ketchum. Stunning western images of renowned photographer David R. Stoecklein.

Will Caldwell Gallery (208-726-3144; www.willcaldwell.com), 400 Sun Valley Rd., Ketchum. Fabulous paintings by a well-known local artist.

Woods Gallery (208-726-5622; www .thewoodsgallery.com), 291 First Ave. N., Ketchum. Signature works by a limited number of master wood-turners.

Zantman Art Gallery (208-727-9099; www.zantmangallery.com), 360 East Ave. N., Ketchum. Paintings, sculpture, and artifacts by acclaimed local and international artists.

DANCE

Sun Valley Ballet School (208-726-2985; www.sunvalleyballet.com), 251 Northwood Wy., Unit J, Ketchum. Its two to three performances each year include the classic *The Nutcracker* each Dec.

MUSIC

Jazz in the Park (208-726-3423; www.visitsunvalley.com), Forest Service Park, First and Washington sts., Ketchum. Sun. nights in summer. Free. This jazz series is a great affair—bring a bottle of wine and a picnic basket, and relax into a starry Sun Valley night.

Ketch'em Alive (208-726-3423), Forest Service Park, First and Washington sts, Ketchum. Held 7–9 Tues. in summer. Free. This evening concert series is a wonderful place to kick back on a blanket, munch on some picnic food, and enjoy great music from the likes of Blue Turtle Seduction, Lamine Sumano, and Kan 'Nal. Beer is sold at the park.

Sun Valley Center for the Arts Summer Concert Series (208-726-9491; www.sunvalleycenter.org), 191 Fifth St. E., Ketchum. Held at various outdoor venues. A wide range of big-name talent comes to the valley each summer for this concert series. You can't beat dancing to a rocking show on a soft, grassy lawn, looking out at an alpine vista!

Sun Valley Summer Symphony (www.visitsunvalley.com), Sun Valley Pavilion on Dollar Road, Sun Valley. Free. This lovely symphony series offers classical performances that will satisfy even the most discerning music aficionado. It is also a great people-watching event!

THEATER

The Wood River Valley is host to live theatrical performances year-round, including plays, musicals, and operas.

Company of Fools (208-788-6520; www.companyoffools.org), Liberty Theatre, 110 N. Main St., Hailey. Performances year-round. This professional, nonprofit theater company offers up some great performance art, including the Summer Fools Festival (see below). Recent performances have included *Doubt, Snowflake, Rabbit Hole,* and *Fools Exposed.* The Liberty Theatre is a really nice, intimate venue, and performances are usually met with high acclaim.

Laughing Stock Theatre Company (208-726-9124; www.sunvalleyarts foundation.org), nexStage Theatre, 120 S. Main St., Ketchum. This community theater company provides a forum for amateur and professional performers to entertain the local community. It generally produces two or three performances per year: a large family musical, a comedy, and a musical revue. The organization also provides education through Camp Little Laugh, a weeklong overnight drama camp during Aug. held at Cathedral Pines Camp north of Ketchum.

Summer Fools Festival (208-788-6520; www.companyoffools.org), Liberty Theatre, 110 N. Main St., Hailey. The Company of Fools (see above) offers this rotating repertory of three distinct works performed over five weeks in the summer. Recent performances have included *The Spitfire Grill, Shirley Valentine,* and *A Body of Water.*

Sun Valley Performing Arts Center (208-726-9124), nexStage Theatre, 120 S. Main St., Ketchum. This organization produces annual Christmas and midsummer shows, including *A Midsummer Night's Dream.*

✷ Entertainment

NIGHTLIFE

The most happening nightlife spots in the Wood River Valley are found in Ketchum. They can be boisterously fun during the peak of the winter and summer seasons and surprisingly quiet during "slack" season, when the locals take over these joints.

Baci Italian Café (208-726-8384), Trail Creek Village, Ketchum. One of the town's nicest wine bars is in this café.

Casino Club (208-726-9901), 220 Main St., Ketchum. Save this for the last stop on your pub crawl. Open the latest, it has that late-night, smoky, dive-bar feel.

Cellar Pub (208-622-3832), 400 Sun Valley Rd., Ketchum. Renowned for its Irish pub feel and its Boston roots, the Cellar boasts pool and shuffleboard, as well as a small outdoor spot for warm summer nights.

Duchin Lounge (208-622-4111), Sun Valley Lodge, 1 Sun Valley Rd., Sun Valley. The Duchin puts on a great music show, with one of our local favorites: Paul Tillotson and his various bands play great, jazzy piano and funk tunes, followed by the Joe Fos Trio.

Grumpy's (no phone—need I say more?), 860 Warm Springs Rd., Ketchum. A dive bar where you'll find hordes of locals.

Ketchum Grill (208-726-4660), 520 East Ave., Ketchum. They have a nice wine bar.

Lefty's Bar & Grill (208-726-2744), 216 Sixth Ave., Ketchum. This is another divey local hangout.

Martini Bar (unlisted phone), on Leadville Avenue, Ketchum. For a more sophisticated evening, try this new bar, where the good bar drinks and the swanky atmosphere, along with the prices, will make you feel like you are in Manhattan.

The Mint (208-788-MINT), on Main Street, Hailey. The Mint has a full bar with live music most weekends. The club has a dance floor on the second floor and pool tables on the first.

Papa Hemi's Hideaway (208-726-3773), 310 S. Main St., Ketchum. This new pub offers home-brewed beer and a casual atmosphere.

River Run Lodge (208-622-2133), Sun Valley Resort, Ketchum. Paul Tillotson and his various bands often play their great, jazzy piano and funk tunes at Sun Valley Resort at the base of Bald Mountain.

Roosevelt Tavern & Grill (208-726-0051), 280 N. Main St., Ketchum. The tavern has a great roof deck for sunny early-evening drinks and food, firepits for when the evenings cool off, and disco nights for the late crowd.

Tapestry Gallery & Wine (208-727-6666), 680 Fourth St. E., Ketchum. Another nice wine bar.

Whiskey Jacques' (208-726-3200), 251 N. Main St., Ketchum. The best music scene in town is found at Whiskey Jacques', which brings in a steady stream of regionally known rockers who are as much fans of Ketchum and the lively dancers on the dance floor as we are of them. Pool tables are found in the rear, and early evening pizza is good.

✳ Special Events

For whatever reason, mountain life seems to include an obsession with costumes. Hawaiian leis are customary on backcountry ski trips, and pink wigs can be seen on river trips. During some of the less formal (and, perhaps, more ridiculous) fun events in this area, locals use any excuse to dress funny: donning a marching-band outfit or full-size flamingo hat to race in the **Hawaiian Nationals** telemark ski race (or drink beer on the sidelines), wearing a way-too-tight hot-pink one-piece for **Unisuit Day** (which often marks the last day of the ski season on Bald Mountain), or putting on tight, false denim biking shorts for a **Giro de Ketchum** (a race around Ketchum on cruisers and old 10-speeds in preparation for a party). Keep your eyes peeled.

Sun Valley Guide (www.svguide .com) has event listings.

Sun Valley–Ketchum Chamber & Visitors' Bureau (www.visitsunvalley .com) has a local calendar of events that is usually up-to-date and fairly inclusive.

Sun Valley Online (www.sunvalley online.com/events/) also has event listings.

This region is special, and there are far too many special events to list them all here. The events listed below represent a good smattering of what goes on. You'll notice fewer Special Events listings during the "slack" season—slang for the spring mud season (just after the ski resort closes until the mud dries up) and late fall (when it is too cold to mountain bike and hike, but too early to ski). This is a quiet time of year here, enjoyed immensely by some as a time to retreat and focus a little more inwardly—on writing, painting, spending time with close friends and family, and just relaxing.

January: **Mountainfilm in Telluride** (www.mountainfilm.org), nexStage Theatre, 120 S. Main St., Ketchum. With its roots in alpine adventure film, Mountainfilm founder's core idea has been that friends, adventure, passion, and powerful ideas are as seductive as ever. Adding this to an evolving mission to display films that educate and inspire audiences "about issues that matter, cultures worth

exploring, environments worth preserving, and conversations worth sustaining" results in a series of entrancing films filled with breathtaking scenery, vibrant personalities, and compelling stories.

February: **Banff Film Festival** (www.banffmountainfestivals.ca), nexStage Theatre, 120 S. Main St., Ketchum. This internationally touring film festival provides the best-of-the-best in armchair adventure, with reels of footage of alpine wonderlands, mountain stories, and adventure hounds. You can't beat it.

HAWAIIAN NATIONALS TELEMARK DAY AT SUN VALLEY

Boulder Mountain Tour (www .bouldermountaintour.com), 32-kilometer Harriman Trail from Galena Lodge south to North Fork. Now in its 33rd running and one of the nation's preeminent Nordic ski races, this is a centerpiece of the winter season in the Wood River Valley. With about 1,000 entrants, the race attracts talent from across the country. The groomed racecourse undulates along the Big Wood River corridor and drops 1,100 feet in elevation along the way. Cold temperatures notwithstanding, this is a great spectator event!

March: **Paw n' Pole Race** (www .animalshelterwrv.org), Sun Valley Gun Club on Sun Valley Road, or Galena Lodge on ID 75. This annual race, which benefits the Animal Shelter of the Wood River Valley, is often called the last remaining crazy Ketchum tradition. The Nordic and showshoe race requires that your leashed dog (or borrowed shelter dog) accompany you, and you are encouraged to wear a costume. Recent themes have been "The Chinese Year of the Dog" and "Paws-itively Magic." A Silly Pet Trick contest follows the race. Be prepared for some laughs whether you join in as a skier or spectator!

Sawtooth Ski and Snowshoe Festival (www.stanleycc.org), Park Creek Ski Area, off ID 21, 7 miles northwest of Stanley. This fund-raising event provides for a weekend of cross-county ski fun, including a ski and snowshoe "Poker Run" event with a short course and five poker card stops, a chili-fest, a fund-raising enchilada dinner, and a wildlife tracking workshop. Proceeds benefit the Sawtooth Ski Club, which grooms and maintains the Sawtooth Ski Trails.

April: **April First Spring Prom** (www.visitsunvalley.com), Sun Valley Inn, Sun Valley. $20. Created in the late 1970s, the Spring Prom was initially founded as a fictitious prom for the fictitious "University of Ketchum." The event recently has been resurrected; prom-goers sport prom attire from all decades and compete for the titles of King and Queen of the Prom.

May: **Sun Valley Wellness Festival** (208-726-2777; www.sunvalley wellness.org), Sun Valley Inn, Sun Valley. This great conference, which celebrated its 10th anniversary in 2007, focuses on wellness of body, mind, and spirit and is increasingly dedicated to bringing science-based knowledge to this conversation. From hands-on workshops on life-optimizing strategies, medical intuition, and relationship-building to seminars and presentations by world-renowned spiritual leaders, this is a worthy event.

June: **Sawtooth Relay** (www.saw toothrelay.com), 62 miles from Stanley to Ketchum. This burly running and walking relay event boasts a course that winds south along the Salmon River and over Galena Pass. Despite the arduous course, you couldn't ask for more spectacular scenery, including views of the Sawtooth Mountains at sunrise, the chalky White Cloud Mountains to the east, the panoramic vistas from Galena Summit, the lush riparian vegetation of the Big Wood River drainage, and views of the Pioneer and Boulder Mountain ranges. A post-relay party, complete with a live band, honors participants; the event benefits charities.

Sun Valley Food and Wine Festival (866-305-9798), various restaurants and galleries, Ketchum. Weekend passes $250 and up per person, Epicurious VIP passes $350. This weekend extravaganza features guest chef speakers, wine-pairing dinners, and themed culinary cooking classes and seminars. The culmination is a grand tasting event at the Elkhorn Resort in Ketchum that will please even the most sophisticated gourmand. A limited number of participants can attend a VIP reception with keynote speakers.

July: **Fly-Fishing Film Festival** (208-726-5280; www.silver-creek .com), NexStage Theatre, 120 S. Main St., Ketchum. A nascent annual event, this festival features some of the finest fly-fishing films from around the country and provides a window into the psyche of the crazed angler. Proceeds from the event are donated to the Nature Conservancy to support its Silver Creek Preserve (see To Do—Fishing) and its blue-ribbon fishery.

Ketchum Arts Festival (208-309-1960; www.mountainangels.com/ kaf.html), Festival Meadows on Sun Valley Road, Sun Valley. Free. This festival is one of the few that showcases the works of local artists and provides a weekend chock full of stunning art, live music, entertainment, and food and brew. The 2007 roster had more than 90 artists, musicians, culinary chefs, and brewmeisters. The lovely event site provides lush green grass, shade trees, and stunning mountain vistas. This event is a locals' favorite.

Mountain Mamas' Arts & Crafts Show (www.stanleycc.com), off ID 21, Stanley. This two-day event is full of handcrafted arts and crafts designed by more than 130 artists

working throughout the Northwest. Food is also available. Live entertainment occurs throughout the weekend, and Sun. morning holds a great pancake breakfast.

Sawtooth Music Festival (www .sawtoothmusicfestival.com), outskirts of Stanley. Held as a benefit for the Parents' Association of the Stanley Community School, this fabulous outdoor event is hard to beat. With the gorgeous, snowcapped Sawtooth Mountain Range as a backdrop, this event has a great lineup of acoustic, folk rock, and indie music that will keep you grooving all day and night. Camp on-site for the full experience!

Sun Valley Center for the Arts Wine Auction (208-726-9491; www .sunvalleycenter.org), various venues throughout Ketchum and Sun Valley. Individual events $35 and up; packages $2,000. Named by *Wine Spectator* as one of the Top Ten U.S. Charity Auctions, the Sun Valley Center for the Arts Wine Auction supports educational arts programming and community outreach by hosting an auction, vintner dinners, wine tastings, and a golf-course picnic that attract wine buffs from near and far. This event is a chance to see Sun Valley at its glitziest and during its summer prime.

August: **Northern Rockies Folk Festival** (www.nrff.net), Hop Porter Park, Hailey. For 30 years running, this festival has been a valley favorite. Over two days, a slew of great bluegrass, R&B, and rock performers charm the locals. Bring a blanket, a picnic, and your dancing shoes (or your bare feet!).

Sun Valley Arts and Crafts Festival (208-726-9491; www.sunvalley center.org), Atkinson Park, Ketchum. Free. This wonderful festival is ranked among the top 100 arts and craft shows in the country by the *Art Fair Source Book* and among the top 20 in the Pacific Northwest and California by the Harris List of the Nation's Best Arts and Crafts Shows. This weekend affair widely anticipated by artists, locals, and visitors is chock full of fine arts and crafts, entertainment, and educational programs displayed beneath a mountain vista. You are likely to leave this event either with artwork in tow or inspired to create your own!

Sun Valley Renaissance Faire
(www.nexstage.org), Festival Meadows on Sun Valley Road, Sun Valley. $8 for adults, $5 for seniors and children, free for children under 14. In its fourth year, this event offers a weekend of medieval pageantry, music, drama, comedy, and dance, including performances by equestrian troupes, actors, jugglers, fire eaters, bagpipers, Celtic dancers, medieval combat groups, and more. Artisan and food vendors sell medieval wares and vittles, and costumes are encouraged.

SAWTOOTH MUSIC FESTIVAL IN STANLEY

This event is produced as part of the Sun Valley Performing Arts–nexStage Theatre's Sun Valley Shakespeare Festival (see below).

Sun Valley Shakespeare Festival (208-726-4TKS; www.nexstage.org), Festival Meadows on Sun Valley Road, Sun Valley. Held generally end of Aug. $20 for adults, discounts for seniors and students. This celebration of the life and times of William Shakespeare includes highly professional outdoor productions of a Shakespeare play nightly. Bleacher and picnic seating.

Sun Valley Writers' Conference (208-672-8660; www.svwc.org), near Sun Valley Lodge, Sun Valley. $600 for four days. This coveted four-day annual event celebrates the art of prose and poetry and features talks, panels, readings, and small workshops on contemporary issues in fiction, nonfiction, and journalism. Its list of presenters and attendees reads like a veritable catalog of who's who in contemporary literature and culture, including more than a few Pulitzer Prize winners. For those interested in literature, writing, and publishing, this event is not to be missed.

September: **Ernest Hemingway Festival** (www.visitsunvalley.org), most events at Carol's Dollar Mountain Lodge, on Dollar Road, Sun Valley. This event honors the life and heritage of Ernest Hemingway and his connection with the Wood River Valley and Idaho. The four-day event features notable academic speakers, slide presentations, short-story contests, and a guided tour of Hemingway haunts.

Sun Valley Spiritual Film Festival (www.svspiritualfilmfestival.org), at Liberty Theatre (208-788-3300), 110 N. Main St., Hailey; and Sun Valley Opera House (208-622-2244), Sun Valley Village, Sun Valley. This celebration of human spirituality presents an annual collection of films that explore spiritual traditions around the world, cherish the human spirit, encourage the production of new films and documentaries, and promote discussion among recognized leaders in the fields of arts and spirituality. Many of these films feature breathtaking alpine scenery and allure. With the number of free-spirited mountain adventurers living in this valley, it is no surprise that this film festival is so popular.

Sun Valley Sustainability Conference (www.sunvalleysustainability .org), Sun Valley Inn, Sun Valley. This two-and-a-half-day professional conference focuses on green building, renewable energy, and smart growth, featuring seminars and workshops with leading practitioners and academics in the field, a public fair showcasing sustainable products and services, and tours of sustainable homes, gardens, and businesses. The target audience for this event includes elected officials and planners, architects, realtors and developers, builders, attorneys, landscape architects, educators, homeowners, and other interested citizens.

Wagon Days Celebration (866-305-9899; www.visitsunvalley.com), Ketchum. Labor Day weekend. Free. Since 1958, this celebration has honored Ketchum's mining heritage through a series of Old West activities that include a shoot-out on Main Street, a kiddie carnival, barbecues, pancake breakfasts, western dances,

IN OCTOBER, SHEEP HERDS ARE BROUGHT DOWN TO LOWER ELEVATIONS FROM THEIR
SUMMER GRAZING SPOTS IN THE MOUNTAINS.

antique shows, live entertainment, food, a rodeo, and an old-fashioned fiddlers' contest. The big deal of the weekend is the Big Hitch Parade, the largest nonmotorized parade in the Pacific Northwest, featuring more than 100 museum-quality wagons, buggies, carriages, tacks, carts, and buckboards. The parade culminates with the arrival of the Big Hitch, Ketchum's massive historic ore wagon, powered by an authentic 16–draft mule jerkline. Kids (and big kids) love this event.

October: **Sun Valley Swing 'n' Dixie Jazz Jamboree** (877-478-5277; www.sunvalleyjazz.com), various locations throughout Sun Valley Resort, Ketchum, and Sun Valley. This weeklong marathon of Dixieland fun is considered one of the nation's premier musical events, offering 300 live performances by more than 40 trios, octets, and big bands.

The event attracts 6,000–7,000 jazz aficionados (many of whom RV it here) each year.

Trailing of the Sheep Festival. (www.trailingofthesheep.org), Main Street, Ketchum. In keeping with a century of tradition, this annual festival celebrates the region's rich sheep-ranching heritage and marks the shepherding of flocks upon flocks of sheep—numbering in the thousands—by traditional Basque sheepherders from high mountain summer pastures north of Ketchum and Sun Valley, south through the Wood River Valley, to winter desert grazing areas. A sea of sheep in downtown Ketchum is a sight to be seen. This parade is complemented by a weekend of Basque dance, music, and food.

Southeastern Idaho: The Simple Pleasures

TETON BASIN, SWAN VALLEY, AND
HENRYS FORK COUNTRY: GATEWAY
TO YELLOWSTONE

EASTERN SNAKE RIVER PLAIN:
IDAHO'S BREADBASKET

TETON BASIN, SWAN VALLEY, AND HENRYS FORK COUNTRY: GATEWAY TO YELLOWSTONE

This corner of Idaho is a little jewel. Yet one more diamond in a glittering array of gems, Idaho's gateway to Yellowstone National Park is characterized by several wide-open, grassy valleys—Swan Valley and Teton Basin among them—and punctuated by a series of soaring, jagged mountain ranges that are evidence of episodes of dramatic crustal uplift: from the Caribou Range, and the Big Holes Mountains to the south, to the spectacularly iconic Teton Range to the east, and the Centennial Mountains along the continental divide at the Montana border. Long in the shadow of its glitzy neighbor to the west—Jackson, Wyoming—in recent years Teton Basin and its funky little towns of Victor, Driggs, and Tetonia are coming into their own. Driven by soaring real estate prices, more than a few hard-core Jacksonites have abandoned the swank for a quieter and more manageable lifestyle on the Idaho side of the Tetons. With the influx of outdoorsy types, progressive change is a-coming to these historically conservative agricultural communities. These places are definitely experiencing growing pains, but visitors might enjoy some of the spoils: a couple funky coffee shops and drive-up latte stands, a brewery, live outdoor summer concerts, and more. Yet it still is quiet here, and the real reason to visit is to get out into the great outdoors—there's lots of it to be had here. With about 500 inches of light, powdery snow each year, the Tetons are a skiers' paradise.

To the south, the South Fork of the Snake River has carved out another high-alpine basin: the pastoral Swan Valley, named for the graceful endangered trumpeter swans that frequent the basin between the Big Hole Range to the north and the Caribou Mountains to the south. The South Fork of the Snake, which flows northwest out of the 20-mile-long Palisades Reservoir at the Idaho-Wyoming border, is a renowned fly-fishery, boasting 4,000 fish per mile. The amazing riparian zone surrounding the river is the largest cottonwood ecosystem in the state, providing habitat to bald eagles, ospreys, and other magnificent birds of prey.

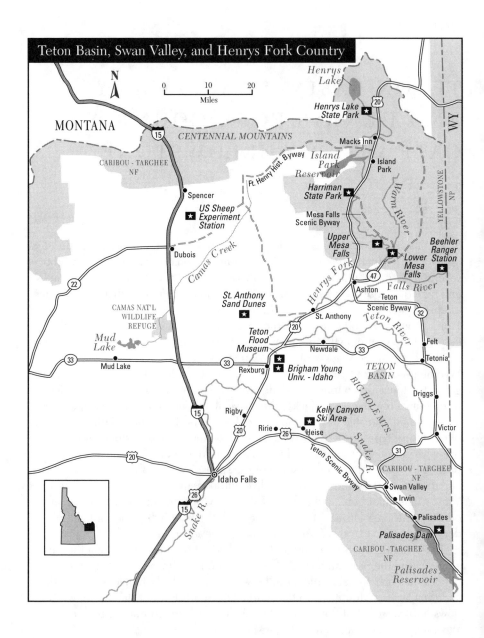

Teton Basin, Swan Valley, and Henrys Fork Country

N

0   10   20
Miles

MONTANA

CENTENNIAL MOUNTAINS

Henrys Lake

Henrys Lake State Park ★

Macks Inn

CARIBOU - TARGHEE NF

Ft. Henry Hist. Byway

Island Park Reservoir

Island Park

Spencer

Harriman State Park ★

US Sheep Experiment Station ★

Mesa Falls Scenic Byway

Warm River

Beehler Ranger Station ★

Dubois

Camas Creek

Upper Mesa Falls ★

Lower Mesa Falls ★

YELLOWSTONE NP

WY

22

Henrys Fork

47

Ashton
Teton

St. Anthony Sand Dunes ★

Falls River

CAMAS NAT'L WILDLIFE REFUGE

Scenic Byway

Teton River

32

Mud Lake

Teton Flood Museum

St. Anthony

20

Felt

33

Mud Lake

33

Newdale

33

Tetonia

TETON BASIN

Rexburg

Brigham Young Univ. - Idaho ★

BIG HOLE MTS.

Driggs

15

Rigby

Kelly Canyon Ski Area ★

20

Ririe

26

Heise

Snake R.

Victor

31

Teton Scenic Byway

20

CARIBOU - TARGHEE NF

Idaho Falls

26

Swan Valley

Irwin

15

Snake R.

Palisades

Palisades Dam ★

CARIBOU - TARGHEE NF

Palisades Reservoir

Farther north, the world-class Henrys Fork of the Snake River and its head-waters at Henrys Lake are tucked up into the three-corner area where Idaho, Montana, and Wyoming share borders. From here the Henrys Fork runs nearly 100 miles southwest to its confluence with the Snake River near Rexburg. Along the way, it courses through the beautiful alpine terrain of the Caribou-Targhee National Forest, part of the 18 million-acre Greater Yellowstone Ecosystem—one of the largest remaining intact temperate-zone ecosystems in the world. Anglers from near and far are drawn to what is touted as one of the best and most varied fly-fishing spots in the world. Winter turns this landscape into a shimmer of white, and while Nordic and backcountry ski opportunities abound, this region has become known for its throngs of snowmobilers, who seem to travel in packs, leaving a haze of exhaust behind them. You'll see them not only on trails but parked in packs along city streets. While you might find interesting activities in some of the towns in this region—from south to north, Idaho Falls, Rexburg, St. Anthony, Ashton, Island Park, and Macks Inn—most visitors are passing through to Yellowstone National Park or other outdoor destinations.

GUIDANCE

Ashton Area Chamber of Commerce (208-652-3355; www.ashtonidaho.com), P.O. Box 351, 714 Main St., Ashton 83420.

Greater Idaho Falls Chamber of Commerce (208-523-1010 or 866-365-6943; www.idahofallschamber.com), 630 W. Broadway, P.O. Box 50498, Idaho Falls 83405-0498.

Greater St. Anthony Chamber of Commerce (www.stanthonychamber.com), St. Anthony 83445.

Island Park Area Chamber of Commerce (208-558-7755; www.islandpark chamber.org), P.O. Box 83, Island Park 83429.

Rexburg Chamber of Commerce (208-356-5700; www.rexcc.com), in the CottonTree Conference Center, 420 W. Fourth South, Rexburg 83440.

Teton Valley Chamber of Commerce (208-354-2500; www.tetonvalley chamber.com), P.O. Box 250, Driggs 83422.

GETTING THERE

By car

I-15 forms the western border of this region, running from the Continental Divide at Idaho's border with Montana south through Spencer, Dubois, and Roberts on its way to Idaho Falls. From Idaho Falls, **US 20** heads northeast into the heart of this region through Rexburg, St. Anthony, Island Park, and Macks Inn, continuing over Targhee Pass to West Yellowstone in Montana. Also from Idaho Falls, **US 26** heads east-southeast along the South Fork of the Snake to the Wyoming border. Between the two US highways are several state routes— **ID 31, ID 33**, and **ID 32**—that connect Swan Valley in the south to Ashton in the north.

Driggs, the center of Teton Valley, is about 75 minutes east of Idaho Falls and a scenic 45-minute drive west from Jackson Hole. Victor, Driggs, and Tetonia can be reached from I-15 at Idaho Falls by taking US 20 east to Rexburg and ID 33 east. From the Jackson, Wyoming area, WY 22 takes you up over Teton Pass (elevation 8,431 feet), becoming ID 33 on the Idaho side. This road, particularly treacherous during winter conditions, can be avalanche prone. Check the **Wyoming Road Report** (888-WYO-ROAD; www.dot.state.wy.us/Index.jsp) or the **Idaho Department of Transportation** (www.511.idaho.gov) for road reports. Travelers from Montana and points east can access the region by taking I-90 to Bozeman then following US 191 south, connecting with US 20 at West Yellowstone and traveling over Targhee Pass (elevation 7,072 feet) to Macks Inn and points south.

By air

Idaho Falls Regional Airport (Fanning Field; 208-612-8221; www.ci.idaho -falls.id.us) is serviced by Alaska Airlines/Horizon Air, Delta/SkyWest, Northwest, and United Airlines; most visitors to this region fly into Idaho Falls or Jackson, Wyoming.

Jackson Hole Airport (307-733-5454; www.jacksonholeairport.com), 1250 E. Airport Rd., Jackson, Wyoming. Served by American Airlines, Delta/SkyWest, and United Airlines/United Express.

MEDICAL EMERGENCIES

Eastern Idaho Regional Medical Center (208-529-6111; www.eirmc.org), 3100 Channing Wy., Idaho Falls. The largest medical facility in the region that serves Jackson Hole, Yellowstone, and Idaho Falls. The center has a helicopter ambulance—Air Idaho Rescue—for transporting trauma patients within a 150-mile radius.

Madison Memorial Hospital (208-356-3691; www.madisonhospital.org), 450 E. Main, Rexburg. Offers 24-hour emergency care.

Mountain View Hospital (208-557-2700; www.mountainviewhospital.org), 2325 Coronado St., Idaho Falls. This is also a full-service hospital providing urgent care services; however, it doesn't have an emergency room.

Teton Valley Hospital (208-354-2383; www.tetonvalleyhospital.com), 120 E. Howard Ave., Driggs. Physicians here are on call 24 hours.

✳ Cities and Villages

Ashton, on US 20 north of Rexburg. Despite a growing season lasting about 86 days, Ashton proudly claims the title of the seed potato capital of the world; it has been producing certified seed stock for nearly 100 years. A sleepy little town of 1,100 (although the second largest in Fremont County), over its history Ashton does have a tradition of tourism. For decades, a railroad spur took visitors from Ashton to West Yellowstone to visit the nation's first national park. Today, however, it is remarkably quiet.

Driggs, Victor, and Tetonia, on ID 33 between Swan Valley and Ashton. Nestled between the majestic Teton Mountains to the east, the rolling Big Hole Mountains to the west, and the looming Palisades Range to the south, these little

towns are located in the 6,000-foot-high Teton Basin, a long, narrow—about 20
miles long by 2 miles wide—mountain oasis. Once covered primarily by deep
alpine meadow grasses, the area was a favored hunting ground and an annual
(and raucous) rendezvous point for hundreds of mountain men, Indians, and fur
trappers and traders, who met to trade furs and supplies. The basin was originally called "Pierre's Hole" after "le grande Pierre" Tevanitagon, an Iroquois trapper with the North West Company of Montreal. After the fur trade declined
around 1840, the trappers and traders left the area, to be replaced in 1888 by
the settlement of a sizable Mormon community. Though the population has
diversified in recent years, the influence of these early settlers remains. Today, as
property prices continue to soar in Jackson, Wyoming, millionaires (Jackson's bil-
lionaires are the new millionaires), ski bums, and service industry employees
increasingly seek refuge on the Idaho side of the range. As a result, the little
enclaves in the Teton Basin—Driggs (particularly), Victor, and Tetonia—are
becoming increasingly well known as outdoor adventure meccas: places where
those who truly love the mountains come to live and play. While a latte is little
easier to come by than it once was, the place still maintains it rural charm and
quirkiness. Keep on the lookout for the locally iconic giant potato perched on a

HYDRO DAM IN SOUTHEASTERN IDAHO

Matt Furber

flatbed truck in front of the drive-in movie theater south of Driggs and the big buffalo that peers out from a perch overlooking Driggs' only traffic light.

Idaho Falls, on I-15 at US 20 and US 26 along the Snake River. This is the seat of Bonneville County and the commercial center of eastern Idaho. With almost 53,000 residents, Idaho Falls is the state's fifth-largest city—and has the accompanying amenities. Like many of Idaho's towns and cities, Idaho Falls's history is steeped in the stories of miners, trappers, fur traders, pioneers, and early settlers. During the gold-boom years of the mid-1800s, the region served as a trade center, and a number of bridges were built and ferry services developed to transport goods across the Snake River. In 1864, the enterprising Harry Rickets began running a ferry across the river 9 miles north of present-day Idaho Falls. The ferry was soon followed by an impressive timber-frame toll bridge built downstream by J. M. Taylor; the town was first known as Taylor's Bridge in his honor. The honor was short-lived, and the town was renamed Eagle Rock, denoting an isolated, dark basalt rock in the middle of the river. In 1891, the town was again renamed for the rapids beneath Taylor's Bridge. Today, the falls are created by a hydroelectric diversion that produces power for the city and surrounding communities. The area is currently the state's highest producer of potatoes, grain, and other crops, as well as home to many employees of the Idaho National Laboratory, located 35 miles to the west.

Island Park, on US 20 north of Ashton. This town was named for the "islands" of open land dotting an otherwise forested landscape; these islands were coveted as resting spots for explorers traversing this region. The community, situated in an ancient caldera 14 miles from Yellowstone National Park's West Entrance, claims to have the longest "main street" in America. Incorporated in 1947, only after state law required all businesses selling alcohol to be located within incorporated towns, the city's boundaries were drawn in such a way—extending nearly 39 miles along ID 20 toward Montana—to include all businesses in the vicinity that either were selling or seeking to sell alcohol. This town's true draw is its surrounds and the recreational activities—fishing, hunting, boating, hiking, and snowmobiling—it begets. This area has become a popular place for second homes.

Rexburg, on US 20, 32 miles northeast of Idaho Falls. A result of prototypical Mormon group colonization and town planning, Rexburg is ultimately organized with gridded streets, an old-fashioned downtown, and abundantly green. Settled by Mormon pioneers in 1883, Rexburg is the home of Brigham Young University's branch campus in Idaho (BYU-Idaho). In 2006, a 57,000-square-foot Mormon temple—the Rexburg Idaho Temple—was completed, the third to be built in Idaho. If the town weren't already clean enough, in 1976, the newly completed Teton dam, 20 miles east of town, collapsed, unleashing a torrent of water (about 80 billion gallons) to ravage 300 square miles of countryside, including downtown Rexburg, and causing $800 million in damage. Much of lower Rexburg had to be completely rebuilt. A high-water mark can still be seen today on the outside of the Rexburg Tabernacle (home to the Teton Dam Museum), but the town seems to have recovered.

Swan Valley, on US 26 on the South Fork of the Snake River at the base of Pine Creek Pass. With a population of about 200, this tiny settlement is still quite clearly a ranching enclave with a strong Mormon influence (the local Mormon church is the largest structure in the basin). Swan Valley doesn't offer much in the way of amenities (nor do its neighboring towns, Irwin and Palisades), but its proximity to world-class fishing and boating on the South Fork of the Snake River and Palisades Reservoir, and spectacular hiking in the surrounding drainages, draws a healthy number of recreationalists to the area. There are a handful of stunning (and pricey) fly-fishing lodges in the vicinity.

✳ Wandering Around

Fort Henry Historic Byway (www.idahobyways.gov), 81 paved miles on back roads from Rexburg to Island Park. Best traveled mid-Apr.–mid-Nov.; road becomes a snowmobile trail in winter. The route starts at the North Rexburg exit off US 20, following the Salem Highway north over the Egin Bench, where the highway becomes Red Road, to the junction with A2, then northeast along A2 back to US 20 at Island Park. History buffs might enjoy this flatland driving tour that starts at the Henrys Fork of the Snake River—one of the most famous and diverse fly-fishing rivers in the world—and winds through some classically western terrain, providing glimpses of pioneer history. Along the way you'll see the **Fort Henry Monument**, which marks the site of the first white settlement in Idaho; several historic ranches and the relict town site of **Idmon**; the spectacular waves of aeolian-deposited sand comprising the **St. Anthony Sand Dunes**; the **Camas National Wildlife Refuge**; and, to the north, the towering stands of Douglas fir and the high-alpine peaks of the Targhee-Caribou National Forest. At the northern end of the route, watch for the **Camas Meadow**. In the spring, the meadow is awash in the purplish blue tinge of camas lilies, the roots of which were a staple food for the Nez Perce. The meadow is also a landing ground for scores of migrating sandhill cranes. The area is the site of the historical **Camas Meadows Battleground**, where the Nez Perce Indians won a tactical victory over the U.S. military.

Lost Gold Trails Loop (www.idahobyways.gov), 48 paved miles on A-2 from Red Road to Dubois, on Old Highway 91 to Spencer, and on Idmon Road back to A-2. Best traveled spring through fall—it is converted to a snowmobile trail during winter. From the junction of Red Road and A-2 on the Fort Henry Historic Byway, the loop heads southwest on A-2 to Dubois, where it runs north on Old Highway 91 to Spencer and then east on Idmon Road to rejoin A-2, again on the Fort Henry Historic Byway. Today, mining of high-grade opals has replaced gold mining in the region. Most of the opal mines are located about 6 miles northeast of Spencer, and several **opal shops** can be found in town. Other points of interest include the historic **Dubois Hotel**—now a visitor center; the **Heritage Hall Museum** in Dubois, which houses a collection of early pioneer memorabilia; and the U.S. Sheep Experiment Station, where three breeds of sheep have been developed since its inception in 1915.

Mesa Falls Scenic Byway (www.idahobyways.gov), 29 paved miles on ID 47 and FS 294 from Ashton to US 20. Open only during the snow-free months; in winter it becomes one of the many snowmobile trails in the area (providing beautiful snowmobile and cross-country ski access). Beginning at the junction of

IDAHO'S FAMOUS POTATOES ARE GROWN IN THE UPPER SNAKE RIVER VALLEY ALONG MESA FALLS AND TETON SCENIC BYWAYS.

ID 40 and US 20 in Ashton (at the northern end of the Teton Scenic Byway), this route wanders along ID 47 through the verdant farmlands of the **Upper Snake River Valley**—its fertile volcanic soil making it one of Idaho's richest farmlands. Homesteaded in the 1890s by pioneers who prized this productive plain, today the region is the largest seed-potato producer in the world. The route continues north on FS 294 to the spectacularly plunging Upper (114 feet tall) and Lower (65 feet tall) **Mesa Falls**. These falls are the only major ones in Idaho that remain unbridled; all others have been exploited for irrigation or hydroelectric power. Admission to the Upper Falls is $3 per car; facilities include trails, restrooms, and boardwalks. The panoramic vista along the way—with the Tetons towering to the east, the Centennial Mountains hovering north, and the St. Anthony Sand Dunes visible on the western horizon—makes this drive worth the effort.

Teton Scenic Byway (www.idahobyways.gov), 69 paved miles on ID 31, ID 33, and ID 32 from Swan Valley to Ashton. Open year-round. This route climbs over

Chris Pilaro

ALPINE WILDFLOWER IN THE TETONS

Pine Creek Pass in the Big Hole Mountains into the Teton Basin, continuing on through the **Teton Valley** towns of Victor, Driggs, Tetonia, and Felt to meet up with the Mesa Falls Scenic Byway in Ashton. Skirting the western edge of the Teton Range, this drive offers spectacular views of the jagged Teton peaks from the quieter Idaho side. Sheltered by the rolling Big Hole Mountains that flank the valley to the southwest and the stunning Tetons that rise up to the northeast, the Teton Basin is a sprawling, fertile valley producing tons upon tons of seed potatoes annually. Potato-storing Quonset huts speckle the valley. Sadly, in a sign of the times, these notable structures are increasingly being displaced by McMansions. Many visitors come for spectacular wildflower blooms in spring-time or the subtle display of color and form that defines autumn.

✳ To See

BREWERY TOURS

Grand Teton Brewing Company (208-787-9000; www.grandtetonbrewing .com), 430 Old Jackson Hwy., Victor. Founded in 1988 by Charlie and Ernie Otto as Otto Brothers' Brewing Company, the first modern microbrewery in Wyoming, the company eventually expanded into Idaho. The brewery produces 10,000 bar-rels of fine brew, including Teton Ale, Old Faithful Ale, Moose Juice Stout, and

THE ICONIC TETON RANGE AT DUSK

James Foster

Bitch Creek ESB, winning seven medals at a recent North American Brewers
Awards. Visitors are invited to taste beer and check out the brewery's retail space.

FARMER'S MARKETS
Idaho Falls Saturday Market, in the Key Bank parking lot, just off Broadway, Idaho Falls. Open 9–1 Sat. Memorial Day–Labor Day. Handmade crafts, soaps and lotions, fruit and vegetables, plants, and more.

FOR FAMILIES
Tautphaus Park Zoo (208-612-8552; www.idahofallszoo.org), 2725 Carnival Wy., Idaho Falls. Open 9–5 Tues.–Sun., 9–8 Mon. Memorial Day–Labor Day; 9–4 daily May and Sept.; 9–4 Sat.–Sun. only Apr. and Oct.; gates close one hour after last admission. $5 for adults, $3.50 for seniors 62 and over, $2.50 for children four–12, free for children three and under. Visit more than 350 animal species from around the world, including Asia, Patagonia, Australia and New Guinea, Africa, and North America.

MUSEUMS
Hess Heritage Museum (208-652-7353), 3409 E. 1200 N., Ashton. Open by appointment only Mon.–Wed. and Fri.–Sat. mid-Apr.–mid-Oct. $5 for adults, $3 for children under 12. This 250-acre restored pioneer farm is dotted with authentic farm buildings, including a carriage house, one-room schoolhouse, blacksmith shop, a Pioneer Home restored with 19th-century-vintage furnishings, a historic barn full of farm implements and with a mural depicting early agricultural activities, a hangar exhibition on the history of land, snow, and air travel, and a Village Green with Revolutionary and Civil War artifacts.

Museum of Idaho (208-522-1400; www.museumofidaho.org), 200 N. Eastern Ave., Idaho Falls. Open 9–8 Mon.–Tues., 9–5 Wed.–Sat. $6 for adults, $5 for seniors and youths, free for children under four. Nationally acclaimed exhibits and a permanent collection are augmented by educational programs and presentations and a reading and reference library. Dedicated to preserving and showcasing the national and cultural history of Idaho and the Intermountain West, this year's exhibits include "World of the Pharaohs," "Hot Type, Hard Times," "Children's Discovery Room," "Lewis & Clark in Idaho," "Race for Atomic Energy," and "Eagle Rock."

Teton Flood Museum (208-359-3063), 51 N. Center St. (former LDS Tabernacle), Rexburg. Open 10–3 Mon.–Fri. Oct.–May; 9–4 Mon.–Sat. June and Aug. $1 for adults, $0.50 for children 12 and under. The museum chronicles the 1976 Teton Dam collapse that unleashed 80 billion gallons of water through the valley, driving more than 25,000 people from their homes and resulting in $800 million in damages. The museum collection includes video, photos, and artifacts pertaining to the flood, as well as pioneer relics and an opal and agate collection. The building itself is listed on the National Register of Historic Places. The grounds have public picnic tables.

Teton Valley Museum (208-354-6000), 137 N. ID 33, Driggs. Open 12–5 Tues.–Wed., 10–6 Thurs.–Sat. end of May–end of Sept.; in winter by appointment.

$5 for adults, $1 for children six–12, free for children under six. This museum maintains a series of collections celebrating the rich pioneer, mining, and agricultural history of the Teton Basin and has an extensive collection of historical artifacts, newspapers, and photographs.

SCENIC FLIGHTS

Soar the Tetons (208-354-3100 or 800-472-6382), 675 Airport Rd., Driggs. Scenic airplane and glider rides are offered at Teton Aviation Center.

SLEIGH, WAGON, AND DOGSLED TOURS

Bagley's Teton Mountain Ranch (208-787-9005; www.elkadventures.com), 269 W. 200 S. St., Victor. Sleigh rides during winter and wagon rides in summer and fall take you to watch grazing, bugling, and running elk.

Grand Targhee Resort (307-353-2300 or 800-827-4433; www.grandtarghee .com), on Ski Hill Road, outside Driggs. Take a horse-drawn sleigh ride to a high-altitude yurt for a western-style dinner (reservations required); $35 for adults, $15 for children 14 and under. They also offer one- to one and a half-hour backcountry dogsled tours at 9:45 AM and 1 PM; $115 for adults, $65 for children 12 and under.

✳ To Do

BALLOONING

Grand Teton Balloon Flights (208-787-5500 or 866-533-6404; www.teton ballooning.com), Driggs. Scenic flights aboard a nine-story balloon take you over the spectacular Teton landscape.

BOATING

Upper Snake River Basin—which includes Henrys Fork and its tributaries: Bitch Creek, the Teton River, and others, plus the upper Snake and the Blackfoot rivers—has its fair share of boating, with runs that range from the lazy class II Cutthroat Run on the Blackfoot River and the Lower Mesa Run of Henrys Fork to hair-raising class IV–V runs on the Teton River, Bitch Creek Canyon, and Canyon Creek.

Outfitters

Three Rivers Ranch (208-652-3750; www.threeriversranch.com), Ashton. Check them out for guided river trips on the Henrys Fork and Teton rivers.

Recommended Reading

Consult Grant Amaral's bible, *Idaho: The Whitewater State* (BookCrafters, 1990), for detailed descriptions of these and other runs.

FISHING

The South Fork and Henrys Fork of the Snake River are both world-renowned trout fisheries.

Henrys Fork wanders about 150 miles through varied scenery, boasting churning water, prolific hatches, and large, wild rainbow trout that attract dry-fly-

FLY-FISHING IS POPULAR THROUGHOUT IDAHO.

fishermen and -women from near and far.

South Fork is known as an outstanding tail-water fishery, with quality fry hatches and abundant cutthroat, brown, and rainbow trout. The river corridor, quite beautiful, is frequented by bald eagles.

Teton River is another favorite spot.

Smaller streams by the hundreds also traverse the region, providing limitless opportunity to angle for native Yellowstone cutthroat trout and introduced populations of brook, brown, and rainbow trout.

Natural lake fishing in this region is found primarily in the Teton Basin and north in the Ashton–Island Park area. Numerous reservoirs, including Island Park, Ashton, and Palisades, also offer flatwater and ice fishing.

Outfitters
In addition to the listings below, several top-notch fly-fishing lodges also provide visitors with high-end guided services and accommodations (see Lodging—Lodges and Guest Ranches).

Halo Ranch Outfitters (208-558-7077), 3489 Green Canyon Rd., Island Park.

Heise Expeditions (208-538-7453; www.heiseexpeditions.com), Ririe. They float the South Fork.

Henry's Fork Anglers (208-558-7525 or 800-788-4479; www.henrysforkanglers .com), 3340 US 20, Island Park.

Hyde Outfitters (208-558-7068), 3350 US 20, Island Park.

South Fork Outfitters (800-483-2110; www.southforkoutfitters.com), on Conant Valley Road, Swan Valley.

Teton Valley Lodge (800-455-1182; www.tetonvalleylodge.com), 379 Adams Rd., Driggs. First-class fly-fishing guides can be found here.

Three Rivers Ranch (208-652-3750; www.threeriversranch.com), Ashton. They also provide guide services.

Victor Emporium Sporting Goods (208-787-2221), 45 N. Main St., Victor. Tackle can be found here.

WorldCast Anglers (800-654-0676; www.worldcastanglers.com), offices in Victor and in Jackson, Wyoming. First-class fly-fishing guides can be found here.

Recommended Reading
For good reading on the nuances of fly-fishing and specific guidance to fishing the rivers of eastern Idaho, see Mike Lawson and Gary LaFontaine's *Fly Fishing the Henry's Fork* (Greycliff Publishing Co., 2000), Ken Retallic's *Greater Yellowstone Fly Fisher's Stream Guide* (GBH ink, 1996), and *Spring Creeks* by Mike Lawson (Stackpole Books, 2003).

HIKING
With the largest of the iconic granite spires of the Teton Range—Grand Teton, stretching nearly 14,000 feet toward the heavens—and nestled between the Big Hole Mountains and the Palisades Range, this region abounds in hiking opportunities.

Alaska Basin is a favored backpacking and hiking area.

Caribou-Targhee National Forest (www.fs.fed.us/r4/caribou-targhee/) encompasses this part of Idaho in its entirety; the Web site is a great resource for picking hikes in this region. Detailed, printable ranger district topographic maps that include hiking trails into the Jedediah Wilderness, eastern parts of Grand Teton National Park, the Palisades, and the Dubois District (northwest of Ashton and home to Diamond Peak, elevation 12,197 feet, the third-highest peak in Idaho) are available on this site.

Swan Valley has spectacular trails in Palisades, Indian, Fall, and Bear creeks.

Teton Basin environs include Darby, Fox, and Moose canyons, as well as Horseshoe and Cabin creeks, all of which offer trails through stunning alpine forest and meadows littered with wildflowers.

HORSEBACK RIDING
A few outfitters offer day and pack trips through stunning alpine terrain in the Targhee National Forest and the 124,000-acre Jedediah Smith Wilderness just east of Teton Valley in Wyoming. Trips often allow opportunity for fly-fishing and camping. Check out these outfitters:

Dry Ridge Outfitter (208-354-2284; www.dryridge.com), 160 N. Fourth St. E.,
Driggs.

Halo Ranch Outfitters (406-646-7246; www.yellowstonehorses.com), on
Targhee Pass Highway in West Yellowstone, Montana.

Three Rivers Ranch (208-652-3750; www.threeriversranch.com), Ashton.

HOT SPRINGS

Bear Creek Hot Springs is reached via a demanding 15-mile round-trip hike
on FR 58 from the Palisades Dam at Palisades Reservoir.

Green Canyon Hot Springs (208-458-4454; www.greencanyonhotspring.com),
on ID 33, Newdale (northeast of Rexburg). Open Mon.–Sat. Apr.–Sept.;
Sat.–Sun. rest of the year. $4.50 for single entry for anyone two years old and
older, $5.75 for day pass. This commercial hot springs offers indoor and outdoor
pools.

Heise Hot Springs (208-538-7453; www.heiseexpeditions.com), on ID 20, 3
miles northeast of Ririe. Open Dec.–Oct. $8 for adults, $7 for seniors, $4.50 for
children under 12. This commercial hot springs overlooking the Snake River
near Idaho Falls has three swimming pools and a 350-foot water slide.

HORSES AND MULES WAITING TO TAKE RIDERS INTO THE BACKCOUNTRY

SKIING IN TO YELLOWSTONE NATIONAL PARK'S STEAMING HOT SPRINGS IS A WINTER DELIGHT.

Recommended Reading

See Evie Litton's *Hiking: Hot Springs in the Pacific Northwest* (Globe Pequot Press, 1995) for details.

MOUNTAIN BIKING

This area has some fantastic mountain biking. Many of the same drainages listed in Hiking offer great riding.

Outfitters

Teton Mountain Bike Tours (800-733-0788; www.tetonmtbike.com), Jackson, Wyoming. They offer guided mountain biking tours in Targhee National Forest on the Idaho side as well as tours into Yellowstone and Grand Teton national parks and other destinations in Wyoming.

Western Spirit Cycling Adventures (435-259-8732 or 800-845-2453; www.westernspirit.com), Island Park. They offer multiday trips through spectacular terrain near Grand Teton National Park as well as trips into Yellowstone National Park.

Local bike stores are the best way to get beta on nearby trails. Try the following:

Big Hole Mountain Bikes (208-354-2828), 12 E. Little Ave., Driggs.

Habitat High Altitude Provisions (208-787-7669; www.ridethetetons.com), 170 N. Main St., Victor.

Peaked Sports (208-354-2354), 70 E. Little Ave., Driggs.

Recommended Reading

Stephen Steubner's *Mountain Biking Idaho* (Falcon Publishing, 1999) offers some suggestions for riding around Idaho Falls.

SKIING

Alpine Skiing

Grand Targhee Resort (307-353-2300 or 800-827-4433; www.grandtarghee .com), on Ski Hill Road, outside Driggs (a 20-minute drive). Lift tickets $59 for adults, $36 for kids. With 2,000 feet of vertical, legendary powder, killer views, and a more kicked-back attitude than its Wyoming counterpart, Grand Targhee is a local's favorite. The resort has almost 2,000 acres of skiable terrain and another 1,000 spectacular acres accessible by snowcat ($349 per person per day, $259 per person per half day). A terrain park, Nordic skiing, snowshoeing, dogsledding, snowmobile tours, and sleigh-ride dinners are also available. The resort is increasingly being recognized for its efforts in sustainable energy and water and resource use.

Jackson Hole Mountain Resort (307-733-2292; www.jacksonhole.com), 3395 W. Village Dr., Teton Village, Wyoming. Lift tickets $77 for adults, $63 for young adults, $39 for seniors and children 14 and under. Just across the state line is world-famous Jackson Hole, home of the steeps (the legendary Corbet's Couloir among them), an elevation drop (4,139 feet) unmatched in the United States, and lots of bad boys. The town of Jackson is known for its glitzy visitors, but the locals have their own brand of grit.

Kelly Canyon Ski Area (208-538-7700; www.skikelly.com), 5488 E. Kelly Canyon Rd., Ririe (25 miles northeast of Idaho Falls). Lift tickets $30 for adults, $22 for kids. For mom-and-pop skiing, check out this resort, which offers four lifts serving 640 skiable acres, 1,000 feet of vertical, and night skiing.

Backcountry Skiing

With lots of open-bowl skiing and deep champagne powder, this region is renowned for its backcountry ski opportunities—and its hard-core local backcountry skiers.

Teton Pass (on ID 33 east of Victor) and **Togwotee Pass** (on US 287/US 26 about one hour east of Jackson, Wyoming) are frequented by locals.

Avalanche Safety

Bridger-Teton National Forest Backcountry Avalanche Hazard & Weather Forecast (307-733-2664; www.jhavalanche.org) has avalanche advisories.

Jackson Hole Snow Observations (www.jhsnowobs.org) has other avalanche tidbits.

Outfitters

A good option is always to hire a guide, and guides extraordinaire seem to be relatively plentiful here.

Exum Mountain Guides (307-733-2297; www.exumguides.com), out of Grand Teton National Park, Wyoming.

National Outdoor Leadership Schools (NOLS) Teton Valley (208-354-8443; www.nols.edu), Driggs. NOLS offers two- and three-week backcountry ski or snowboarding courses.

Rendezvous Backcountry Tours (307-353-2900 or 877-754-4887; www.skithe tetons.com), 1110 Alta Rd. N., Alta, Wyoming. Rendezvous also rents yurts.

Yellowstone Expeditions (406-646-9333 or 800-728-9333; www.yellowstone expeditions.com), West Yellowstone, Montana.

Rentals

There are also several shops in the Jackson, Wyoming, area.

BACKCOUNTRY SKIER IN A WINTER CAMP IN YELLOWSTONE NATIONAL PARK

Habitat High Altitude Provisions (208-787-7669; www.ridethetetons.com), 170 N. Main St., Victor. Check out this place for gear.

Peaked Sports (208-354-2354), 70 E. Little Ave., Driggs. They also have gear.

Recommended Reading

For detailed guides to skiing the Tetons (including routes and approaches), see *Teton Skiing: A History & Guide to the Teton Range* by Thomas Turiano (Homestead Publishing, 1995) and *50 Ski Tours in Jackson Hole and Yellowstone* by Richard DuMais (High Peak Books, 1990).

Nordic Skiing

Numerous fabulous Nordic ski centers pepper the Teton Basin region, including these:

Grand Targhee Resort (307-353-2300 or 800-827-4433; www.grandtarghee .com) on Ski Hill Road, outside Driggs. Daily passes $10 for adults, $5 for kids. The Targhee Nordic Trail System has 15 kilometers of groomed tracks for both classic and skate skiing that wind through wooded glades and scenic meadows.

Harriman State Park Nordic Ski Trails (208-558-7368; www.idahoparks.org), Island Park. Park entrance fee $2 per person per day, $25 for Idaho State Park annual passport (for entry to any of numerous Idaho state parks). In the north of this region, this state park offers 30 miles of trails (half of which are groomed) and two yurts for rent.

Island Park Area Nordic Ski Trails (208-652-7442), Island Park. $7.50 for three-day permit, $25 for annual permit. This park (and others in the system) offers additional trails on varying terrain as part of Idaho's Park N' Ski Program. The **Bear Gulch–Mesa Falls Park N' Ski area**, on Mesa Falls Forest Highway 47, 7 miles northeast of Ashton, offers 9 miles of intermediate and advanced ski trails. The **Fall River Ridge Park N' Ski area**, on Cave Falls Road 10 miles east of Ashton, offers 7 miles of beginner and intermediate trails.

Island Park Ranger Station (208-558-7301) has information on other Nordic ski areas around Island Park: The **Brimstone Trail** has another 9 miles of scenic trails overlooking a reservoir and river. The 2.6-mile **Buffalo River Trail** winds through a lodgepole pine forest along the Buffalo River.

Kelly Mountain Nordic Ski Trails (Palisades Ranger District, 208-523-1412), adjacent to Kelly Canyon Ski Resort, Ririe (25 miles northeast of Idaho Falls). The Targhee National Forest offers 24 miles of cross-country trails through heavily wooded, varied terrain.

Teton Ridge Ranch (208-201-1622; www.tetonridge.com), Tetonia. Ski more than 30 kilometers of groomed trails.

Teton Valley Trails and Pathways (208-201-1622; www.tvtap.org) grooms about 50 kilometers of classic and skate skiing trails throughout Teton Valley: **Alta Ski Trails**, **Teton Canyon Ski Trails**, and **Teton Springs Ski Trails** (208-787-3600; www.tetonsprings.com). Trail maps for each of these areas are available on TVTAP's Web site.

Countless ungroomed trails also await your cross-country skis. As with any backcountry travel, you should be **avalanche aware** (see Avalanche Safety, above).

Guides are also a good bet for helping you find the goods (see Outfitters, above).

Grand Teton National Park (www.nps.gov/grte/), Wyoming. This renowned park just across the border in Wyoming is particularly rich in Nordic skiing options.

Swan Valley has spectacular trails in Palisades, Indian, Fall, and Bear creek drainages.

Teton Valley's favorite spots include Darby, Fox, and Moose canyons and Cabin Creek.

Rentals

Local shops can provide recommendations for cross-country skiing and equipment for rent or sale.

Skinny Skis (307-733-6094; www.skinnyskis.com), 65 W. Deloney Ave., Jackson, Wyoming.

Teton Mountaineering (800-850-3595; www.tetonmtn.com), 170 N. Cache St., Jackson, Wyoming.

Yöstmark Equipment (208-354-2828; www.yostmark.com), 12 E. Little Ave., Driggs.

WILDLIFE VIEWING

Camas National Wildlife Refuge (208-662-5423), 2150 E. 2350 N., Hamer; off I-15 north of Idaho Falls. This 10,578-acre protected area, with its expansive marshes, meadows, and uplands, provides resting, nesting, and feeding habitat for songbirds and migrating waterfowl, including ducks, geese, trumpeter swans, herons, egrets, and cranes. Moose, antelope, elk, mule and white-tailed deer, muskrats, and beavers also frequent the sanctuary. Peak migrations occur in Mar. and Apr. and again in Oct., when the refuge is teeming with about 3,000 geese and swans and up to 50,000 ducks.

✳ Wilder Places

LAKES

Henrys Lake, at the intersection of US 20 and ID 87 north of Macks Inn. This small lake (4 miles by 2 miles), nestled beneath the Henrys Lake Mountains and Targhee Pass near the Montana border, forms the headwaters of Henrys Fork and is a favored fly-fishing spot. In 1978 a brook trout pulled from the lake broke the Idaho state record. With the lake's maximum depth only 20 feet, the fishing is best near springs and creeks that bring colder water to the lake. The lake and mountains are named for Andrew Henry (1775ish to 1833), a fur trapper and explorer who, as the founder of the St. Louis Missouri Fur Company, explored this area. Henrys Lake State Park is perched at the southeastern corner of the lake (see Parks).

Island Park Reservoir (208-652-7442), off US 20, 30 miles north of Ashton. The area between Island Park and Ashton to the south comprises one of the world's largest calderas (18 miles long by 23 miles wide), left in the wake of a volcanic eruption about 1.3 million years ago. The northern slope of this caldera forms the southern bank of the 7,794-acre Island Park Reservoir, which was formed by impoundment of Henrys Fork at the Island Park Dam in 1939. The dam today also houses a 4,700-kilowatt hydroelectric facility, built in 1994 and operated by Fall River Rural Electric. The reservoir, which lies entirely within the Targhee National Forest, is a popular recreational spot. Rainbow, brook, and cutthroat trout, whitefish, and kokanee salmon draw anglers; bird-watchers enjoy thousands of birds that stop here on their spring and fall migrations. Developed camping is found at Buttermilk Campground on the northeastern end of the reservoir and at the West End Campground on the southwestern shore; both have boat ramps.

Palisades Reservoir, alongside US 26 southeast of Swan Valley to Alpine, Wyoming. Nestled between the high, forested ridges of the Snake River and Caribou ranges in the Caribou-Targhee National Forest, the Palisades Reservoir is an impressive 18-mile-long, 16,000-acre, high-altitude reservoir formed by Palisades Dam on the Snake River. Completed in 1957 and standing 260 feet tall, the dam is one of the largest earthen dams ever constructed by the Bureau of Reclamation. The project required more than 13.5 million yards of material and took four years to build. With 70 miles of limited-access shoreline, the reservoir is a favorite spot for boaters, picnickers, campers, and anglers chasing cutthroat and brown trout, kokanee, and mackinaw lake trout. The **Palisades Ranger District** (208-523-1412; www.fs.fed.us/r4/caribou-targhee/caribou -targhee/palisades) of the Targhee National Forest maintains a series of campgrounds around the reservoir with nearly 200 campsites.

PARKS

Grand Teton National Park (307-739-3300; www.nps.gov/grte), Wyoming—the Web site is a fantastic resource. Just over the state line is the iconic Teton Mountain Range, with its granitic spires reaching 7,000 feet skyward from the valley floor, one of the most breathtaking vistas anywhere. Comprised of some of the oldest rock in North America—2,500 million-year-old metamorphic rock of marine origin, interspersed with volcanic intrusions—the range itself is one of the youngest orogenies, a mere 9 million years old. Subsequently exposed by weather and sculpted by glaciers, the present-day configuration is characterized by U-shaped hanging valleys, morainal lakes, and classic spires. The range's three distinctive peaks have drawn their fair share of attention—prior to 1820, Native Americans referred to the peaks as the Hoary Brothers; later explorers called them the Pilot Knob; but the name that stuck was that provided by French Canadian trappers, who called the peaks Les Trois Tetons, or "the Three Breasts." Today the three peaks are called the South, Middle, and Grand Teton. At 13,770 feet, Grand Teton is clearly the grandest of them all.

Even today, the etymological games continue. In recent years, in response to complaints from blanching tourists, Grand Targhee Resort shortened the name of one of its off-piste peaks from (hold your breath) Mary's Nipple to the more proper Mary's. While the move may have appeased some visitors, it provoked the ire of the locals, who chastised the resort for being a corporate sellout, saying things such as, "What is a Teton without a nipple?" The etymology of the name became a hotly contested topic, with Mary alternatively being described as a ski patroler, local waitress, and/or streaker. For many, the identity of the peak's namesake still remains a mystery.

History aside, not only are the peaks a geologic marvel, but the park's diverse habitat—which includes alpine, sagebrush, forest, and aquatic systems—is home to abundant wildlife. Look for marmots, pikas, bighorn sheep, pronghorns, coyotes, bison, elk, badgers, Uinta ground squirrels, mule deer, black bears, martens, muskrats, moose, river otters, and more.

Harriman State Park (208-558-7368; http://parksandrecreation.idaho.gov), 3489 Green Canyon Rd., Island Park; on US 20, 18 miles north of Ashton. Originally owned and run as a cattle ranch and private retreat by the Harriman and Guggenheim families—investors in Union Pacific Railroad—today, Harriman State Park is a 11,000-acre wildlife refuge. With its numerous ponds and lakes and 8 miles of the meandering Henrys Fork, the park provides great habitat for elk, deer, moose, and abundant waterfowl, including sandhill cranes, trumpeter swans, buffleheads, grebes, Canada geese, and loons. Visitors enjoy 20 miles of trails for hiking, biking, horseback riding, and Nordic skiing, as well as regular summer tours of the Railroad Ranch buildings and spectacular views of the Teton Range. The spring wildflowers are brilliant. Several yurts ($45) and ranch houses ($140 and up) are available.

Henrys Lake State Park (208-558-7532; http://parksandrecreation.idaho.gov), 3917 E. 5100 N., Island Park; on US 20, 45 miles north of Ashton. Open May–Oct. Providing access to Henrys Lake (see Lakes) and its fine trout fishery, this park offers a modern fish-cleaning station, a boat ramp, and campfire programs. The park runs 44 campsites ($12 standard, $20 serviced); several cabins are also available ($45).

Yellowstone National Park (307-344-7381; www.nps.gov/yell/), a very small sliver in southeast Idaho. Despite claiming only a little bit of the national park, this corner of Idaho is a primary gateway to Yellowstone. Inspired by the steaming cauldrons and exploding geysers (including Old Faithful), abundant wildlife, and stunning scenic vistas, in 1872 Congress established our national park system with Yellowstone as the inaugural park. As one of the largest geothermal anomalies in the world, the Yellowstone Hotspot—and its resultant fumaroles, mud pots, geysers, and hot springs—is both breathtaking and scientifically intriguing. Since its inception, the park has stimulated a long history of scientific inquiry into the region's geothermal and seismic activity, the collection of odd and brilliantly colored thermophilic bacteria that thrive in the steaming waters (as hot as 170 degrees F in some pools), and its prolific wildlife, including grizzlies, bison, elk, and wolves.

During high summer, Yellowstone is more often than not overrun with tourists, particularly on the standard Yellowstone Loop Road. However, if it is solitude you seek, you need only step on a trail, and within moments, all traffic will vanish (in fact, you may, more quickly than you'd like, find yourself a Goldilocks in the grizzlies' forest). Visiting Yellowstone in the off-season is spectacular, and with a little more footwork (i.e., arranging to take a course, assist with research, or enter under your own locomotion), your experience might be much more rewarding. For information on research activities conducted within the park, check out the **Yellowstone Volcanic Observatory** (http://volcanoes.usgs.gov/ yvo/), **Greater Yellowstone Science Learning Center** (www.greateryellow stonescience.org), and **Yellowstone Association** (303-344-2293; www.yellow stoneassociation.org). The latter also offers short natural history, geology, writing, painting, and other courses. For information on management and conservation issues, check out **Greater Yellowstone Ecosystem** (www.greateryellowstone .org) and **Yellowstone to Yukon Conservation Initiative** (www.y2y.net).

Most visitors from the Idaho side enter the park via West Yellowstone, in Montana, 10 miles north of the Idaho border (take ID 20 to the Montana border).

BECHLER FALLS, IN IDAHO'S SLIVER OF YELLOWSTONE NATIONAL PARK

For the road less traveled, check out the park's southwest "**Cascade Corner**"—where half the park's waterfalls are located—accessible only via car from Idaho. Take Cave Falls Road east of Ashton about 25 miles to the **Bechler Ranger Station** (307-344-2160 backcountry office), which provides access to a vast network of trails. The ranger station provides maps, information, and permits. This remote spot is a favorite backcountry ski trek for some hardy western folks.

WILDERNESS AREAS

Caribou-Targhee National Forest (208-524-7500; www.fs.fed.us/r4/caribou -targhee/), more than 3 million acres, primarily in southeastern Idaho, stretching from the state's borders with Montana, Wyoming, and Utah. This national forest supports a variety of ecosystem types, including semiarid desert, sagebrush and grass steppe, and alpine forests of lodgepole pine, Douglas fir, and spruce beneath towering peaks. The national forest also claims precious water resources, including Big Springs, the headwaters of the renowned Henrys Fork of the Snake River. This diversity of habitat provides homes for grizzlies, black bears, moose, elk, wolves, mule deer, pronghorns, bison, mountain lions, peregrine falcons, and numerous other species. As part of the 20 million-acre Greater Yellowstone Ecosystem, the Caribou-Targhee National Forest abuts Yellowstone National Park, Grand Teton National Park, and Bridger-Teton National Forest to the east. The Continental Divide forms much of the forest's northern boundary.

Jedediah Smith Wilderness Area and the **Winegar Hole Wilderness Area** (both entirely within Wyoming) are two spectacular wilderness areas within the national forest boundaries. Scores of campgrounds and nearly 3,000 miles of trails provide access to much of the forest. The national forest Web site and office are great resources for planning hiking, wildlife viewing, skiing, camping, fishing, and other expeditions. Individual ranger districts are often quite helpful as well:

Ashton Ranger District (208-652-7442), 46 ID 20, Ashton.

Dubois Ranger District (208-374-5422), 127 W. Main St., Dubois.

Island Park Ranger District (208-558-7301), 3726 ID 20, Island Park.

Palisades Ranger District (208-523-1412), 3659 E. Ririe Hwy., Idaho Falls.

Teton Basin Ranger District (208-354-2312), 515 S. Main St., Driggs.

St. Anthony Sand Dunes (for information: Bureau of Land Management's Idaho Falls Visitor Center, 208-523-1012; www.blm.gov), 50 miles northeast of Idaho Falls; from US 20 in Rexburg, take North Rexburg exit, travel 6.3 miles north to second flashing light, turn left, and continue 2.9 miles to Egin Lakes Access. The St. Anthony Sand Dunes are a spectacular example of aoelian (wind) transport, which has heaped grain upon grain of silica sand into dunes ranging 50–400 feet tall. This impressively sculpted field of dunes stretches 35 miles long and covers nearly 175 square miles. At the end of the last Ice Age, when the sandy shorelines of shrinking lakes were exposed to the air, the dried sand began to blow and collect as dunes. The classic barchan (Arabic for "ram's horn," denoting the dunes' sharply crescent shape, which ends in a pair of horns facing the direction of sand movement) dunes march forward nearly 10 feet per year through cycles of wind loading at the crest of the dune, followed by avalanching on the leeward side. The dunes comprise a Wilderness Study Area, and in some bizarre contradiction, BLM has allowed this impressive natural treasure to become a raceway for off-road vehicles. If you're looking for a little tranquility, it might be best to visit in the off-season when vehicle traffic is likely to be more limited.

✳ Lodging

If you are merely looking for a bed, all the major cities and towns in this region—Ashton, Island Park, Rexburg, and Idaho Falls—have countless motels. Lodging is a little tougher to come by in Victor and Driggs, but even these little towns have a motel or two. Some less-expensive ranches and bed & breakfasts also provide great access to fishing, horseback riding, hiking, and more: The world-class fishing of the South Fork and Henrys Fork is matched with first-class accommodations.

BED & BREAKFASTS

Driggs

Locanda di Fiori (208-456-0909; www.inntetonia.com), on Valeview Road, Driggs 83422. The Inn of Flowers (as this Italian name translates) is a lovely little spot. With only two guest rooms, beautiful flowers, a lovely full breakfast, a hot tub, and spectacular views, this is the quintessential B&B experience. $150.

GUEST RANCHES

Ashton

Squirrel Creek Guest Ranch and Inn (208-652-3972; www.idahoranch .com), on Flagg Ranch Road, Ashton 83420. This ranch house with guest rooms, a four-bedroom guest lodge,

cabins, and tent and RV spots provides lots of options. Campsites $7.50; RV sites $20 and up; cabins $75 and up; ranch-house rooms $85 and up; guest lodge $465.

Ririe

Granite Creek Guest Ranch (208-538-7140, 208-483-3175 in summer; www.granitecreekranch.com), Ririe 83443. This working cattle ranch is situated on 4,000 acres in the Rocky Mountains. Guests enjoy trail rides, cattle drives, boating, and fishing. $220 per person and up.

Swan Valley

Hansen Guest Ranch (800-277-9041; www.hansenguestranch.com), 956 Rainey Creek Rd., Swan Valley 83449. This 17.5-acre property on the banks of Rainey Creek has easy access to the South Fork. The ranch has a riding arena and corrals (for those who bring their own horses) and access to trail guides, fishing, hiking, and hunting. $125 and up in summer; $90 and up in winter.

Victor

Moose Creek Ranch (208-787-2871 or 208-313-4840; www.moosecreek ranch.com), 219 E. Moose Creek Rd., Victor 83455. This ranch trains wild mustangs and offers daily trail riding and a riding program. Simple cabins are available. $119 and up in summer (two-night minimum); $89 and up off-season.

INNS

Rigby

Blue Heron Inn (208-745-9922; www.idahoblueheron.com), 4175 E. Menan Lorenzo Hwy. (just off US 20), Rigby 83442. Rooms here are perched on the banks of the Snake River. $99 and up.

LODGES

Southeast Idaho certainly has its fair share of elegant fly-fishing lodges for the discriminating traveler. Some of the more spectacular lodges include the following.

Driggs

Teton Valley Lodge (208-354-2386; www.tetonvalleylodge.com), 379 Adams Rd., 7 miles west of Driggs 83422. On the banks of the Teton River is this full-service fly-fishing lodge providing meals, lodging, and guide services. $1,485 and up for two nights.

Irwin

The Lodge at Palisades Creek (208-483-2222 or 866-393-1613; www.tlapc.com), 3720 US 26, Irwin 83428. June 8–Sept. 27. Sitting above the confluence of Palisades Creek and the Snake River, this fine fishing lodge offers rustic but luxurious cottage accommodations, barbecue dinners, world-class fishing, and spectacular views. $275 and up (four-night minimum).

Island Park

Henry's Fork Lodge (208-558-7953; www.henrysforklodge.com), 2794 S. Pinehaven Dr., Island Park 83429. This beautiful, rustic fly-fishing lodge with fabulous views of Henrys Fork was nominated for national architecture awards for its elegance and comfort. All meals are included; guide services are available. $350 and up (three-night minimum).

Hyde Lodge (208-558-7068; www.hydeoutdoors.com), 3350 US 20, Island Park 83429. Guests can enjoy lodging and meals with or without guided fly-fishing packages. $105 and up; packages $405 and up for one or two anglers.

A River Runs By It Lodge (208-558-2245; www.ariverrunsbyitlodge.com), 4026 Tygee La., Island Park 83429. Lodge rooms are the draw here. $95 and up.

Swan Valley

South Fork Lodge (208-483-2112; www.southforklodge.com), on Conant Valley Road, Swan Valley 83449. This classic, finely appointed, rustic western fly-fishing lodge is perched on a dramatic bend in the South Fork. Room rates include meals; guided fly-fishing packages are available. $305 and up; packages $460 and up for two anglers.

Tetonia

Teton Ridge Ranch (208-456-2650 or 800-926-3579; www.tetonridge.com), 200 Valley View Rd., Tetonia 83452. This rustic but grand (10,000-square-foot) alpine lodge is situated on 4,000 acres of private land, providing spectacular views of the Tetons. Guests enjoy a full complement of outdoor activities, including horseback riding, bird hunting, fishing, sporting clays, rafting, mountain biking, cross-country skiing, snowmobiling, sleigh rides, snowshoeing, and dogsledding. Rates include all meals (and the dining is fine). $474 and up per person.

☀ Where to Eat

While Teton Valley is not known for its limitless fine-dining experiences, the influx of new blood here is bringing an exciting change to the restaurant scene, with a few new upscale restaurants and plenty of good little spots that will fuel you up for your next adventure. A couple good restaurants have popped up in Idaho Falls as well.

DINING OUT

Driggs

Grand Targhee Resort (307-353-2300 or 800-827-4433; www.grand targhee.com), on Ski Hill Road, outside Driggs. The ski resort also has a couple eateries, including the après-ski **Trapbar**, which features a large outdoor deck and frequent live music, and the **Targhee Steakhouse**, serving local and imported game, steaks, pasta, and other upscale dishes.

Idaho Falls

The Cellar (208-525-9300; www .thecellar.biz), 3520 E. 17th St., Ammon (just east of Idaho Falls). This fine-dining establishment serves tasty dishes that include sesame seared ahi, Cambodian grouper, filet mignon with Gorgonzola butter, and fresh salads and soup, plus live music on Fri. and Sat. nights.

Collage (208-524-0875; www.collage finedining.com), 445 A St. This award-winning, high-end restaurant features international three-course meals made with ingredients and techniques from around the world. The menu includes pancetta-wrapped sea scallops, Greek-style escargot, house-made lobster bisque, rosemary-breaded New Zealand rack of lamb, and other delectables.

Rutabagas (208-529-3990; www .rutabagasidahofalls.com), 415 River Pkwy. (on Idaho Falls Greenbelt). This is one of Idaho Falls' favorites. The globally influenced, changing menu features dishes such as miso-marinated sea bass, Thai roasted rack of lamb, and New Orleans fish.

Whitewater Grill (208-529-3990), 415 River Pkwy. (on Idaho Falls Greenbelt). This great fusion restaurant serves authentic Japanese, European, and Mediterranean fare. It's another local favorite.

Victor

Lucatelli Café (208-787-3463), 6 Main St. Open for lunch and dinner Tues.–Sun. This place is widely considered to have the best Italian food in Teton Valley, serving very authentic panini, antipasto, grilled trout, and cheese ravioli, all made with the freshest ingredients. Fabulous desserts and espresso top off the experience.

Sun Dog Deli & Café (208-787-3354), 57 S. Main St. Open for lunch and dinner Sun.–Wed. While relatively new, this spot is garnering attention for its great menu, which includes sirloin, sockeye salmon, risotto, juicy burgers, gourmet salads, and fancy desserts. Dishes are made from local ingredients to the extent possible. An impressive array of wines and German and Belgian beers make this place a go.

EATING OUT

Driggs

Bunk House Bistro (208-354-3770), 285 N. Main St. Open for breakfast and lunch. Hearty cowboy cuisine (i.e., greasy spoon).

Daily Buzz (208-354-2899), Broulims Shopping Plaza. For a quick pick-me-up on your way to the woods, try their espresso, coffee, smoothies, bagels, bagel sandwiches, and more.

Guadalajara Mexican Restaurant (208-354-9000), 355 N. Main St. For authentic Mexican cuisine, try steak ranchero, chicken fajitas, margaritas, and more.

Miso Hungry Café (208-354-8015), 165 N. Main St. Open for lunch and dinner Mon.–Sat. This woman-owned café serves wholesome, global cuisine. A hip spot with fabulous artwork, live music, and an occasional slow-cooking course or two, the café is a hit with locals.

Northern Lights Take & Bake Pizza (208-354-0200), 65 S. Main St. They make it; you take it and bake it (in your own oven)—pizzas with healthy heaps of toppings.

O'Rourke's (208-354-8115), 42 E. Little Ave. Long a local's bar and restaurant, O'Rourke's serves great burgers, pizzas, sandwiches, fish-and-chips, and pub food.

Pendl's Bakery & Café (208-354-5623; www.pendlspastries.com), 40 W. Depot Rd. Open from 7 AM daily. Fabulous Austrian pastries, espresso, and sandwiches.

Royal Wolf (208-354-8365), 63 Depot St. Open for dinner daily. This pub offers a great selection of regional microbrews, a full bar, and solid burgers, sandwiches, salads, and appetizers.

Tony's Pizza and Pasta (208-354-8829), 364 N. Main St. For pizza, try this spot.

Victor

Knotty Pine (208-787-2866), 58 S. Main St. Open for dinner daily. Kansas City–style barbecue and tasty Idaho beef burgers are washed down with microbrew beer. A good live music lineup, often featuring touring bands, makes this a festive place.

Timberline Bar & Grill (208-787-2608), 31 W. Center St. Open for breakfast, lunch, and dinner. This bistro serves up tasty burgers, sandwiches, and homemade soups and salads. Winter brings a warm fire for après ski, while summer is full of live music.

Victor Emporium (208-787-2221), 45 N. Main St. Open for breakfast and lunch daily. This fly shop has a soda fountain famous for its huckleberry milk shakes. They also serve light lunches and espresso.

Wildlife Brewing & Pizza (208-787-2623), 145 S. Main St. Open for dinner Tues.–Sun. This cozy pizza joint serves award-winning home brews, including Mighty Bison Brown Ale, Might Point It! Pale Ale, and Porcupine Porter. Locals dig this place.

✳ Cultural Offerings

Idaho Falls Arts Council (208-522-0471; www.idahofallsarts.org), 498 A St., Idaho Falls. Operating the **Carr Gallery/Willard Arts Center** and the **Colonial Theater**, this organization provides high-quality programming in performing and visual arts. They also offers art classes and summer concerts and are supporters of the **Idaho Falls Cultural District**, which offers art walks and other events.

Teton Arts Council (208-354-4278; www.tetonartscouncil.com), 8 Rodeo Rd., Driggs. They organize performances, workshops, and community events throughout Teton Valley. The Council offers ceramic and dance classes at the **Community Art Center** and has periodic gallery showings of high-quality local art.

MUSIC

EIRMC Summer River Concerts (208-522-0471; www.idahofallsarts .org/river_concerts.html), on east side of Idaho Falls Greenbelt between D and E streets, Idaho Falls. Held at 7 PM. Tues. Free. The concert series includes an ecclectic mix of jazz, rock, blues, big band, folk, and more.

THEATER

Pierre's Playhouse (208-787-2249), just north of the stoplight in Victor. This lively theater showcases local talent. The playhouse produces a variety of events, including classic melodramas full of dastardly villains, dashing heroes, and lovely heroines.

✳ Special Events

February: **American Dog Derby** (www.americandogderby.org), from Ashton to Yellowstone National Park and back. First run in 1917, this historic dogsled race takes mushers and their dogs 100 miles. Four other races, ranging from 20 to 60 miles, plus a juniors' race, along with a celebrity race, a snowshoe race, and a weight pull, are held over this weekend. This is quite an event, drawing mushers from as far as Alaska!

SpudFest Take 1 (208-354-3221 or 208-237-6365; www.idahofilminstitute .org/spudfest), Pierre's Playhouse, Victor, and Spud Drive In, Driggs. Founded by Dawn Wells (Mary Ann from *Gilligan's Island*) in 2004 to find, develop, and nurture new and established film artists, this winter film fes-

tival is geared exclusively to showcase the work of high school students.

July: **Liberty Festival on the Falls** (www.idahofallschamber.com), Idaho Falls. July Fourth. This celebration is bound to entertain, with what is said to be the largest fireworks display west of the Mississippi River, a traditional parade, live music, food, and some entertainment oddities, including the Biggest Liar Contest, in which contestants are asked to spin the most outrageous tales possible.

Targhee Fest (307-353-2300 or 800-827-4433; www.grandtarghee.com), Grand Targhee Resort, on Ski Hill Road, outside Driggs. While only entering its fourth season, this annual three-day music festival features an amazing lineup of acoustic musicians (including some headliners) playing Americana, folk, blues, and roots music. Camping and food are available on-site. Bring your tent, a chair, a hat, plenty of sunscreen, and water— and be prepared to rock!

Teton Valley Summer Festival (208-354-2500; www.tetonvalley chamber.com), locations throughout Teton Valley. July Fourth. Hot-air balloons rise up to color the sky during this week of festivities centered around a traditional Fourth of July celebration. Festival activities include arts and crafts, an Old Time Fiddlers' Contest, food, and more.

July–August: **SpudFest Take 2** (208-354-3221 or 208-237-6365; www .idahofilminstitute.org/spudfest), Pierre's Playhouse, Victor, and Spud Drive In, Driggs. Like SpudFest Take 1 (see February, above), this annual film festival is aimed at finding, developing, and nurturing new and established film artists.

August: **Bluegrass Festival** (307-353-2300 or 800-827-4433; www.grandtarghee.com), Grand Targhee Resort, on Ski Hill Road, outside Driggs. The three-day festival is grandfather of bluegrass festivals in the Northern Rockies, attracting a great lineup and a lively crowd. Camping and food are available on-site.

Madison County Fair (208-356-3020), Madison County Fairgrounds, 203 N. 5 W. Ave., Rexburg. Yet another traditional Idaho county fair features a rodeo, car show, livestock exhibits, home arts, crops, art and crafts, photography, and more.

Mesa Falls Marathon (www.mesafallsmarathon.com), Ashton. Held annually, this is a fabulous way to see Idaho country. The course begins on gravel roads in Targhee National Forest near the spectacular Upper Mesa Falls and winds through the forest, providing breathtaking views of the forest, the Tetons, Lower Mesa Falls, and Warm River. Wildlife sightings are not uncommon. Course elevation is at around 6,000 feet.

BLACKFOOT, POCATELLO
AND TWIN FALLS REGION:
IDAHO'S BREADBASKET

T he Snake River Plain can be seen quite dramatically in satellite images, cutting a broad arc across southern Idaho. Along this corridor lie the southeastern enclaves of Idaho Falls, Blackfoot, Pocatello, American Falls, and Twin Falls. The presence of water coursing through the great Snake and other rivers (combined with fertile volcanic soils) has made possible the transformation of an extremely arid landscape—naturally covered in sagebrush and receiving 8–12 inches of precipitation annually (not enough water to support crops)—into highly productive agricultural lands.

In 1837, early Mormon settlers began digging ditches and diverting water for irrigation, starting what became a major transformation of the Idaho landscape and economy, encouraged by two acts of Congress some 50 years later: The Desert Land Act of 1877 promoted the economic development of the arid and semiarid public lands of the West by allowing individuals to apply for a desert-land entry to reclaim, irrigate, and cultivate up to 640 acres in return for a promise to irrigate within three years. The Carey Act of 1894 allowed private companies to erect irrigation systems in the semiarid western states and to profit from the sale of water; it also allowed farmers to purchase land for irrigation at $0.25 per acre. The result is that today, Idaho supports tens of thousands of acres of potatoes, wheat, hay, alfalfa, hops, corn, mint, beets, and other crops and enjoys a $4.5 billion agricultural economy. Much of this can be seen as lush green fields stretching out in all directions in southern Idaho's Snake River Plain. Idaho grows more of its famous spuds than any other region in the United States, producing almost 30 percent of all potatoes grown domestically—worth $721 million in 2007. Wheat pulls a close second, with 2007 sales totaling $511 million. With this concentration in agricultural activities comes a (relative) density in population and the largest number of agricultural and food-processing jobs in the state.

Typically, this region is not regarded as a destination, nor are its cities and villages known for their highfalutin' amenities. However, some say this is the "real"

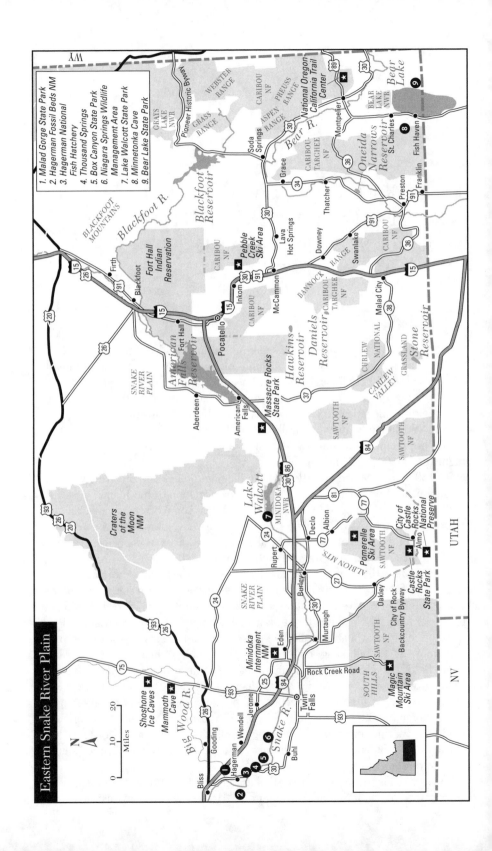

Eastern Snake River Plain

Idaho. Despite being overshadowed by the glitzier resort towns of Ketchum, McCall, and Coeur d'Alene, southeastern Idaho offers a chance to explore Idaho's pioneer history and some profoundly interesting geologic sites—Craters of the Moon National Monument, Hagerman Fossil Beds National Monument, and City of Rocks National Reserve, among them. The far southeastern corner of the state contains scenic byways, Minnetonka Cave, and Bear Lake, which straddles the border with Utah. While this region is not quite as dramatic as the great wilds of central and northern Idaho, there is also plenty of open space in which to stretch your wings.

GUIDANCE

American Falls Chamber of Commerce (208- 226-7214; www.american fallschamber.org), P.O. Box 207, Soda Springs 83211.

Greater Bear Lake Valley Chamber of Commerce (208-847-0067; www .bearlakechamber.org), 915 Washington St., Montpelier 83254.

Greater Blackfoot Area Chamber of Commerce (208-785-0510; www .blackfootchamber.org), in Potato Expo Building, 130 NW Main St., Blackfoot 83221.

Greater Pocatello Chamber of Commerce (208-233-1525; www.pocatello idaho.com), 324 S. Main St., Pocatello 83204.

Malad Chamber of Commerce (208-317-1827; www.maladidaho.org), 59 Bannock St., Malad City 83252.

Preston Area Chamber of Commerce (208-852-2703; www.prestonidaho .org), 49 N. State St., Ste. A, Preston 83263.

Soda Springs Chamber of Commerce (208-547-4964; www.sodachamber .com), 9 W. Second S., Soda Springs 83276.

Twin Falls Chamber of Commerce (208-733-3974; www.twinfallschamber .com), 858 Blue Lakes Blvd. N., Twin Falls 83301.

GETTING THERE

By car

I-84 runs from Portland, Oregon, through southern Idaho to Salt Lake City, Utah; in this region, it passes near Twin Falls, Jerome, Burley, and Rupert. Just east of Rupert, I-84 intersects with **I-86,** which heads northeast through American Falls to Pocatello at I-15. From Pocatello, **I-15** heads both north—through Chubbuck and Blackfoot on its way to Idaho Falls and the Montana state line— and south, through McCammon and Malad City to the Utah state line.

East of I-15, smaller highways thread the state's far southeastern corner. **US 30** heads west from the Wyoming state line through Montpelier, Soda Springs, and McCammon, where it picks up I-15 to Pocatello, then I-86 and I-84 to Burley; here it continues west, paralleling I-84, through Buhl and Hagerman to Bliss. **US 91** heads southeast from I-15 at Virginia, passing through Downey, Swanlake, and Preston before heading into Utah. **US 89** enters Idaho from Utah at the Bear Lake town of Fish Haven, then heads north to Montpelier and east into Wyoming. Between these highways, two smaller state highways connect little burgs: **ID 34** goes from Preston north through Soda Springs to Wyoming, and **ID 36** heads from Malad City east through Preston to Montpelier.

By air

Pocatello Regional Airport (www.pocatello.us/Airport/Airport.htm) is serviced by Delta/SkyWest from Salt Lake City. The airport offers free parking.

Magic Valley Regional Airport (Joslin Field; 208-733-5215; www.tfid.org/airport/), Twin Falls, is also serviced by Delta/SkyWest from Salt Lake City. The airport offers free parking.

Rental cars are available from **Avis** (208-733-5527 Twin Falls or 208-232-3244 Pocatello; www.avis.com), **Budget** (208-734-4067 Twin Falls or 208-233-0600 Pocatello; www.budget.com), **Enterprise** (208-736-6281 Twin Falls or 208-232-1444 Pocatello; www.enterprise.com), and **Hertz** (208-733-2668 Twin Falls or 208-233-2970 Pocatello; www.hertz.com).

MEDICAL EMERGENCIES

Bear Lake Memorial Hospital (208-847-1630; www.blmhospital.com), 164 S. Fifth Ave., Montpelier.

Bingham Memorial Hospital (208-785-4100; www.binghammemorial.org), 98 Poplar St., Blackfoot.

Caribou Memorial Hospital (208-547-3341; www.cariboumemorial.org), 300 S. Third W., Soda Springs.

Franklin County Medical Center (208-852-0137; www.fcmc.org), 22 N. 100 E., Preston.

Gooding County Memorial Hospital (208-934-4433; www.goodinghospital .org), 1120 Montana St., Gooding.

Harms Memorial Hospital (208-226-3200; www.harmsmemorial.org), 510 Roosevelt Ave., American Falls.

Magic Valley Regional Medical Center (208-737-2000 or 800-947-4825; www.stlukesonline.org/magic_valley), 650 Addison Ave. W., Twin Falls. One of two primary medical centers in this area, Magic Valley Regional Medical Center is a full-service hospital with 213 acute-care beds.

Minidoka Memorial Hospital (208-436-0481; www.minidokamemorial.com), 1224 Eighth St., Rupert.

Portneuf Medical Center (208-239-1000; www.portmed.org), 651 Memorial Dr. and 777 Hospital Wy., Pocatello. Portneuf Medical Center, the other primary medical center in this region, is a Level III Trauma Center, with life-flight capabilities and 24-hour care.

St. Benedicts Medical Center (208-324-4301; www.stbenshospital.com), 709 N. Lincoln St., Jerome.

✳ Cities and Villages

With a higher population density than much of the state, southeastern Idaho has numerous small towns dotting the landscape. The two largest cities in the region

are Pocatello, with an astounding 54,000 people, and Twin Falls, with about
40,000.

American Falls on I-86 southwest of Pocatello. This town was named for the impressive falls on the Snake River.

Blackfoot on I-15 between Pocatello and Idaho Falls. Originally called Grove City, the county seat for Bingham County is the self-proclaimed Potato Capital of the World.

Montpelier, at the junction of US 89 and US 30, in the state's far southeastern corner. Famed for Butch Cassidy's 1896 Montpelier Bank robbery and present-day home of the Oregon Trail Center, Montpelier is largely Mormon.

Pocatello, junction of I-15 and I-86. Nestled in the foothills of the Portneuf Range at 4,448 feet and home to Idaho State University, Pocatello feels like small-town America. Founded in 1889 and named for the Shoshone chief who granted a right-of-way for the railroad, Pocatello, like many other Idaho cities, experienced a boom during the gold rush years of the mid- to late 1800s. Pocatello quickly became a railroad and stage hub for the Union Pacific Railroad as it provided goods and services to Idaho's booming mine towns. With the demise of the gold mining industry, Pocatello, like much of this region, turned to agriculture. Today, the city has a growing high-tech sector, and its green spaces (with 32 parks and a greenbelt along the Portneuf River) and proximity to great skiing, biking, hiking, and climbing—not to mention its cultural resources—continues to attract new blood.

DOWNTOWN BLACKFOOT

Matt Furber

IDAHO'S STATE SYMBOL, THE TRACTOR—PART OF POCATELLO'S AGRICULTURAL HERITAGE

Preston, on US 91 and ID 36 near the Utah state line. This is where Napoleon Dynamite found his groove.

Soda Springs, junction of US 30 and ID 34. Renowned for its remarkable natural springs and pioneer history, Soda Springs is more recently, and less fortunately, known for a catastrophic accident at a fertilizer plant chronicled by Joseph Hilldorfer and Robert Dugoni in the *Cyanide Canary* (Free Press, 2004).

Twin Falls, on I 74 alongside the impressive Snake River Canyon and Perrine Bridge—at one time the world's highest cantilever bridge of its length. Twin Falls is the county seat, home to College of Southern Idaho, and an agricultural and cultural hub. First settled by the Shoshone, the area was heavily traveled by pioneers traversing the Oregon Trail and was founded as a city in 1904. The city offers museums, fairs, galleries, music, antiques stores, and other urban amenities, along with proximity to recreational green spaces. Its Old Town is particularly quaint. However, Twin, or "Twinkie Town," is definitely plagued by box-store sprawl around its margins. Smaller cities in its orbit include Jerome, Gooding, and Shoshone.

City of Rocks Backcountry Byway (208-824-5519; www.idahobyways.gov), 49 paved and gravel miles on ID 77 from Albion to Elba-Almo Highway at Connor through Almo to City of Rocks Road, then north on Birch Creek Road to Oakley. Best driven Apr.–Nov. This route winds its way around the Albion Mountain Range to the City of Rocks National Reserve (see Wilder Places). With spires of 2.5 billion-year-old granite rising incongruously out of a gentle pastoral landscape, the "city" is a geologic oddity. Here, thousands of emigrants traveling the California Trail from 1843 to 1869 took respite and left their names inscribed on the rocks using axle grease. Today the preserve is a rock-climbing mecca (see To Do—Rock Climbing) that continues to gain popularity as a desert climbing and camping spot. Other points of interest along the route include the alpine scenery of Howell Canyon Pomerelle Recreation Area, **Pomerelle Ski Area** (see To Do—Skiing), and the town of **Oakley**, which is listed, in its entirety, on the National Register of Historic Places and is home to Idaho's largest concentration of historic wood-frame and stone buildings (see To See—Museums).

Oregon Trail Bear Lake Scenic Byway (866-847-3800; www.idahobyways .gov), 110 paved miles on US 89 and US 30 from Fish Haven to McCammon. Open year-round. This historic byway traces a portion of the nearly 2,000-mile-long Oregon–California Trail, along which, starting in 1843, perhaps as many as

AS AGRICULTURAL HUBS LIKE TWIN FALLS GAIN AN URBAN ECONOMY, OUTLYING FARM TOWNS PUT THEIR TRUCKS OUT TO PASTURE.

500,000 emigrants traveled from Missouri to California, the Pacific Northwest, and Utah, marking the largest voluntary migration in U.S. history. The route starts on US 89 at the Utah border and follows north along beautiful, alpine Bear Lake (elevation 5,900 feet)—sometimes called the Caribbean of the Rockies for its stunning turquoise hue; the lake is a popular recreational destination. The route continues north to US 30 at Montpelier through Soda Springs to McCammon at I-15. Sites along the way include several historic towns; the **Gutzon Borglum Monument** in St. Charles, which honors the prolific American sculptor best known for his carvings at Mount Rushmore, South Dakota; the 320 million-year-old **Minnetonka Cave** and its spectacular array of stalactites, stalagmites, and banded travertine (see To See—Cave Tours); the **National Oregon–California Trail Center** in Montpelier, which showcases the history of the trail (see To See—Museums), and a series of hot springs, including **Sulphur Springs**, which smells as good as the name suggests; **Lava Hot Springs**, now a well-known commercial hot spring with and Olympic-size pool; and the **Soda Springs geyser** (see Pioneer Historic Byway).

Pioneer Historic Byway (208-852-2703; www.idahobyways.gov), 127 paved miles on US 91 and ID 34 from Utah border at Franklin (Idaho's oldest town) to Wyoming border at Freedom. Easternmost part is tough going in winter and

CAVES CAN BE EXPLORED ON THE OREGON TRAIL BEAR LAKE AND PIONEER SCENIC BYWAYS.

may be closed occasionally. The route follows US 91 north to Preston at ID 34, then ID 34 north through Soda Springs to Grays Lake, where it heads east to the Wyoming border. This corridor meanders north along the historic pathway taken by early pioneers and later visitors to Yellowstone National Park. The route follows a portion of the historic Oregon–California Trail (see Oregon Trail Bear Lake Scenic Byway), along which several placards commemorate pioneer history, and wagon ruts are still visible in spots. Points of note along the way include **Niter Ice Cave**, a basalt lava tube used by early pioneers for refrigerated food storage and as a refuge from unfriendly Native Americans; the site of the **Bear River Massacre**, where almost 300 Shoshone were killed by U.S. soldiers in the largest massacre of Native Americans in U.S. history; the restored ghost remains of the town of **Chesterfield** (now on the National Register of Historic Places), which after being settled by Mormons in 1879 went into disrepair; and the 19,000-acre **Grays Lake National Wildlife Refuge** (see Wilder Places). The route also passes through **Soda Springs**, which among other attractions boasts a cold-water geyser born of an ill-fated attempt to drill a hot-water source for a swimming pool. The geyser, controlled by a timer, erupts hourly on the hour.

Thousand Springs Scenic Byway (208-837-4505; www.idahobyways.gov), 68 paved miles on US 30 near Blissthrough Twin Falls to ID 50 to I-84 east of Twin Falls, parallelling the Snake River. Open year-round. Idaho's Snake River Aquifer is one of the world's largest, thought to contain as much as 1 billion acre-feet of water. In the Hagerman area, cold artesian water from this aquifer pours out of the basalt walls of the Snake River Canyon in a series of impressive cascades, some with velocities of as much as 250 cubic feet per second. These springs are thought to be the reemergence of the Lost and the Little Lost rivers, which disappear into highly porous lava fields near Arco, about 100 miles to the northeast, and flow through fractured subterranean basalt. The area provides refuge for wildlife, including bald eagles, ospreys, waterfowl, foxes, deer, raccoons, and more. A substantial trout-farming industry has grown up around these springs and now accounts for about 77 percent of the trout eaten in the United States. The springs are also used for hydro power. Other attractions along the route include the **Hagerman Fossil Beds National Monument** (see To See—Historical Sites); the **Hagerman National and State fish hatcheries**, which produces millions of trout and steelhead each year; and the **Twin Falls County Historical Museum** (see To See—Museums).

✳ To See

CAVE TOURS

Mammoth Cave (www.idahosmammothcave.com), on ID 75, 8 miles north of Shoshone. Open 9–6 daily in summer. $8 for adults, $4 for children, free for kids six and under. If you are up for a more bizarre Idaho moment, visit the Mammoth Cave, touted as the "largest volcanic cave in the world open to the public." As you approach the cave site on the dirt access road, the facility appears in the distance as a spaceship-esque vision rising out of a relatively flat lava field. Near the encampment, which houses a "natural history museum" and other buildings, you will likely be greeted by a cacophony of calls—from caged emus, battling

SPACESHIP-ESQUE MUSEUM AT MAMMOTH CAVES

turkeys, and prancing peacocks—all running amok amid a sea of relic farm implements, machinery, and buildings. Enter the visitor center, and you might be bowled over by a strange smell (formaldehyde and arsenic?), pay your dues, and tour the natural history museum (aka road kill café). Take a couple of the lanterns provided by the staff (lest one go out) and enter the cave. You can walk about 0.25 mile to the end, beneath soaring chapel ceilings, to see stalactites, stalagmites, ice pools, and slick walls dancing with muted color. The cave itself is actually quite interesting; as for the rest, be prepared to get your kitsch fix.

Minnetonka Cave (435-245-4422), in St. Charles Canyon northwest of Bear Lake; fromMontpelier, take US 89 south to FR 412 (St. Charles Creek Road) and turn west. Open 10–5:30 daily around Memorial Day (weather-dependent)–Labor Day. $5 for adults, $4 for kids six–15, free for kids five and under. Administered by the Forest Service, this beautiful cavern is the largest developed limestone cave in Idaho, with nine expansive chambers and 0.5 mile of sacred stalactites, stalagmites, and banded travertine. The air temperature in the cave is a constant 40 degrees F year-round, so bring warm clothes. There are several campgrounds nearby in St. Charles Canyon.

Shoshone Ice Cave (208-886-2058), 1561 N. ID 75, 16 miles north of Shoshone. Open 8–8 daily May–Sept. $6 for adults, $5.50 for seniors and children five–14, free for kids four and under. Known by the Shoshone Indians as "the Cave of Mystery," the Shoshone Ice Cave reportedly was rediscovered in the early 1880s by a young boy from a nearby sheep-ranching family. Of the many lava tubes in the area, this particular one possesses just the right geometry to set up a low-pressure wind tunnel that, under vacuum, draws in ambient air and, by evaporative cooling, cools it to temperatures just below freezing year-round. When first discovered, the tunnel was entirely plugged with ice, which quickly became a prized commodity—spawning 22 saloons and three restaurants in Shoshone to serve patrons passing through on the Oregon Short Line Railroad. Around 1930, in order to make ice-gathering easier, a group of men blasted a rock overhang from the entrance, unknowingly disturbing the delicate airflow. In subsequent years, the ice began to recede and the cave was abandoned. Around 1960, the current owners restored the entrance to the cave, reestablishing the circulation system. Ice has been accumulating since and today stretches 1,000 feet long, 60–80 feet wide, and 8–30 feet deep. Today, visitors can tour the cave and surrounding lava fields, with tour guides possessing a wealth of knowledge about the area, its history, and geology. Only slightly odd are the large cement sculptures that adorn the property, including a replica of a dinosaur with an odd fellow sitting on its head, a squaw and her man (who wears a very bad wig), and a mountain lion guarding the entrance to the cave.

RELICS AT THE SHOSHONE ICE CAVES

IDAHO ODDITIES AT THE SHOSHONE ICE CAVES

FARMER'S MARKETS

Given the agricultural bounty of this region, it is no surprise that there are quite a few farmer's markets around. Check out these.

Blackfoot Farmers' Market (208-681-2231), Idaho Potato Museum parking lot, 130 NW Main St., Blackfoot. Open 9–1 Sat.

Buhl Farmers' Market (208-543-4577) at Main Street and Broadway, Buhl (on US 30 southwest of Twin Falls). Open 4:30–6:30 Wed.

Gooding Farmers' Market (208-934-8904) at Idaho School for the Deaf and Blind, 1450 Main St., Gooding (on ID 46 west of Shoshone). Open 3–6 Tues.

Soda Springs Farmers' Market (208-241-6396), at Soda Springs City Park. Held 4–7 Wed.

Southeast Idaho Farmers' Market (www.pocatellofarmersmarket.com), at the 400 block of Union Pacific Avenue, Pocatello. Held 9–1 Sat.

Twin Falls Farmers' Market (208-543-4582), on North College Road across from CSI Expo Building, Twin Falls. Held 9–1 Sat.

FARM TOURS

Valley View Lavender Farm (208-543-4283; www.valleyviewlavenderfarm .com), 4297 Carter Pack Rd., Buhl. Open 10–5 Tues.–Sat. Free. This working lavender farm grows 15 varieties of lavender and more than 15,000 lavender plants; the gently undulating fields of purple are quite a sight! The farm welcomes visitors to learn about growing, caring for, and even cooking with lavender. Lavender plants and products are sold on-site.

HISTORICAL SITES

Hagerman Fossil Beds National Monument (208-837-4793 ext. 5227; www .nps.gov/hafo), on US 30 in Hagerman (about 25 miles west of Twin Falls). Open 9–6 daily Memorial Day weekend–Aug. 25; 9–5 Thurs.–Mon. rest of the year. Free. Here, erosion of a series of outcropped sedimentary bluffs on the Snake River has revealed the largest concentration of the extinct Hagerman Horse (*Equus simplicidens*) fossils in North America, making it a highly significant geologic site. Fossils from 30 complete horses, and parts of 200 more, plus more than 220 species of plants, have been found in this deposit. The deposit was excavated over several years after its discovery in 1928, and many of the specimens were analyzed by the Smithsonian Institution. The high concentration of fossils is unusual; it is hypothesized that an entire herd of horses drowned while attempting to cross a swelled river, and their bodies were quickly buried by sand. The area was established as a national monument in 1988.

SPRING FLOOD ON CAMAS PRAIRIE

Minidoka Internment National Monument (208-837-4793; www.nps.gov/archive/miin/home.htm), in Hunt (17 miles northeast of Twin Falls); take US 93 north from Twin Falls 5 miles to Eden exit, take ID 25 east 9.5 miles to Hunt Road exit, turn right, and continue 2.2 miles. This national monument was established in 2001 to commemorate the hardship endured by more than 120,000 people of Japanese ancestry (Nikkei), forced during World War II by President Roosevelt's Executive Order 9066 to leave their lives behind and relocate to one of 10 internment camps, as a "precautionary measure." Minidoka Relocation Center was a 33,000-acre site, and between August 1942 and October 1945, it housed about 13,000 Japanese Americans, primarily from Washington, Oregon, and Alaska. This hastily constructed facility contained approximately 600 buildings—many of them poorly insulated—including administration and warehouse buildings, 44 residential blocks, schools, fire stations, a hospital, a post office, a cemetery, and various stores. Surrounded by barbed wire and unsuitable for the dramatic temperature extremes of southern Idaho, the facility was essentially a prison. Today, visitors can view the remains of the entry guard station, waiting room, rock gardens, and a monument. As of yet, there are no facilities on-site.

MUSEUMS

This region is proud of its history, and it seems that almost every little village sports a museum of sorts—some quite bizarre, but offering a taste of Idaho not found in the glamorous towns.

Bannock County Historical Museum (208-233-0434), 3000 Alvord Loop, Pocatello. Open 10–6 daily Memorial Day–Labor Day; 10–2 Tues.–Sat. in winter. $1 for adults, $0.50 for children six–12, free for kids under six. This museum houses a collection of Shoshone-Bannock Indian artifacts and exhibits detailing Pocatello's railroad history.

Bingham County Historical Museum (208-785-8065), 190 N. Shilling Ave., Blackfoot. Open 10–3 Thurs.–Sat. Donations requested. Residing in a restored Southern plantation-esque home, this museum houses a collection of historic dolls and Native American artifacts.

Cassia County Historical Society Museum (208-678-7172), East Main and Hiland streets, Burley (on US 30 just south of I-84). Open 10–5 Tues.–Sat. Apr.–Oct.; other times by appointment. Donations welcome. Displays include a collection of Indian artifacts, fossils, farm tools and equipment, clothing, and two train cars.

Fort Hall Replica (208-234-1795; www.forthall.net), 911 N. Seventh St., Pocatello. Open 10–2 Tues.–Sat. mid-Apr.–Memorial Day; 10–7 Mon.–Sun. Memorial Day–Labor Day; 10–2 Tues.–Sat. in Sept. $2.25 for adults, $1.75 for seniors and children six–11, $1 for children three–four, free for kids under three. This is a reproduction of the building built by Nathaniel Wyeth in 1834 as a trading post but that ultimately served as a refuge for pioneers migrating west along the Oregon Trail. The hall showcases a series of mock frontier rooms and a covered wagon and tepee.

Hagerman Valley Historical Museum (208-837-6288), 100 S. State St., Hagerman (on US 30 west of Twin Falls). Open 1–4 Tues.–Sun. mid-Mar.–Nov.

Free. This museum displays fossils from the Hagerman Fossil Beds National Monument (see Historical Sites), a full-cast replica of the fossilized Hagerman Horse, and regional historical displays.

Herrett Center for Arts and Science (208-732-6655; http://herrett.csi.edu), 315 Falls Ave., on College of Southern Idaho campus, Twin Falls. Open 9:30–9 Tues. and Fri., 9:30–4:30 Wed.–Thurs., 1–9 Sat. Admission and lectures free; fees for planetarium vary. This is another top-notch museum, with its collections and exhibits of anthropological artifacts, including pre-Inca textiles, Peruvian pottery, Mayan jade, and natural history specimens from the ancient Americas. The museum is also home to Faulkner Planetarium, the Jean B. King Gallery, and a gift shop.

Idaho Heritage Museum (208-655-4444), 2390 US 93, Twin Falls. Open 10–4 daily Mar.–Dec. $4 for adults, $3.50 for seniors, $2.50 for children six–16. Here you'll find one of the West's largest private collections of Native American artifacts, including lance points, bone needles and awls, arrowheads, and an antique gun collection, as well as and mounted indigenous wildlife, including a 15,000-year-old bison skull.

Idaho Museum of Natural History (208-282-3317; http://imnh.isu.edu), 921 S. Eighth Ave., Pocatello. Open 10–5 Tues.–Sat. $5 for adults, $4 for seniors, $3 for students, $2 for children four–11, free for children under four. Idaho's official state museum of natural history (run by Idaho State University), and among the larger, more popular museums, it houses extensive anthropological, earth and life science, and vertebrate paleontological exhibits and document and photography archives. The museum's collections are used in scholarly research. The museum offers lectures, tours, and classes.

Idaho Potato Museum (208-785-2517; www.potatoexpo.com), 130 NW Main St., Blackfoot. Open 9:30–5 Mon.–Sat. Apr.–Sept.; 9:30–3 Mon.–Fri. Oct.–Mar. $3 for adults, $2.50 for seniors, $1 for children six–12. This place is all about the infamous Idaho spud, featuring the world's largest potato chip, old farming equipment, historical artifacts (including ancient Peruvian vessels), and the Spud Cellar Gift Shop, where you can buy potato lotion, potato fudge, and other strange concoctions.

Jerome County Historical Museum and **Idaho Farm and Ranch Museum** (208-324-5641; www.historicaljeromecounty.com), 220 N. Lincoln St., Jerome (on I-84 northwest of Twin Falls). Open 1–5 Tues.–Fri., 1–4:30 Sat. Donations welcome. The museum houses a collection of old newspapers, pictures, and artifacts documenting the Japanese internment, farming practices, and other area history. The Farm and Ranch Museum (open by appointment year-round; donations welcome) is being developed on a 100-acre site to help preserve the agricultural heritage of the region. On display are historic farm implements and machinery, buildings, a windmill, and a Japanese internment barrack.

Minidoka County Historical Society Museum (208-436-0336; www.minidoka .id.us), 99 E. Baseline Rd., Rupert (north of I-84 just north of Burley). Open 1–5 Mon.–Sat. Donations accepted. This museum houses a collection of railroad relics, including a depot, caboose, steam engine, and wooden fire carts, plus a marble soda fountain, horse-drawn farming equipment, and items from the historic Minidoka Dam and power plant.

National Oregon-California Trail Center (208-847-3800; www.oregontrail center.org), 320 N. Fourth St., Montpelier. Open 10–5 daily May–Sept.; by appointment for groups of 15 or more. $8 for adults, $7 for seniors and children five–12. This spot provides an interpretive computer-simulated wagon ride along the Oregon Trail, complete with live actors, as well as a museum of pioneer and railroad artifacts.

Oakley Valley Historical Museum (208-862-7890), 140 W. Main St., Oakley (on ID 27 south of Burley). Open 1–5 Fri.–Sat. or by appointment. Donations welcome. Founded in 1878 by ranchers and Mormon immigrants, the entire town of Oakley, and its old stone and brick buildings, is now on the National Register of Historic Places. The museum chronicles the history of Oakley and its surrounds.

Oneida Pioneer Museum (208-766-9247; www.maladidaho.org/museum/ museum.htm), 27 Bannock St., Malad City. Open 1–5 Tues.–Sat. or by appointment. Donations accepted. Examine the early pioneer days of Oneida County with this small collection of furnishings, clothing, and artifacts housed in an old drug store.

Shoshone-Bannock Tribal Museum (208-237-9791; www.sho-ban.com), on Simplot Road in Fort Hall (on US 91 just north of Pocatello). Open 9:30–5 daily June–Aug.; 9:30–5 Mon.–Fri. Sept.–May. $2.50 for adults, $1 for children six–18. This place houses a collection of Shoshone-Bannock tribal artifacts, beadwork, and photographs.

South Bannock County Historical Museum (208-776-5254; www.lavahot springs.com/museum.htm), 110 E. Main St., Lava Hot Springs (on US 30 just east of I-15). Open 12–5 daily. Donations welcome. Permanent and rotating exhibits depict the history of the healing waters of the Lava Hot Springs, which were first used by the Shoshone Indians.

Twin Falls County Historical Museum (208-733-3974; www.twinfalls chamber.com), 858 Blue Lakes Blvd. N., Twin Falls. Open 10–5 Tues.–Sat. or by appointment. Donations welcome. This collection of pioneer artifacts includes farm machinery, butter churns, vintage clothing, photographs, and other household items in a historic schoolhouse.

WATERFALLS

Shoshone Falls (208-733-3974), off US 93 in Twin Falls; take US 93 across Snake River into Twin Falls, proceed 1.8 miles to Falls Avenue, take a left, and drive 3 miles to signed park entrance. $3 per car. Shoshone Falls are both the most powerful cascade in the Northwest, plunging 212 feet—higher than Niagara Falls—and the most well-known falls in Idaho, in no small part due to Evil Knievel's 1974 attempt to jump the Snake River Canyon nearby on motorcycle. The failed attempt left Knievel with only minor injuries but propelled him into great fame: the ABC *Wide World of Sports* showing of the event remains one of the series' top-watched events of all time. The falls are largely controlled by Milner Dam, where irrigation diversions in the summer result in decreased flows to the falls; viewing is best during spring melt. The park has hiking trails, picnic areas, a boat ramp, a swimming area, and restrooms.

WINERY TOURS

The Twin Falls area, on the eastern flank of Idaho's wine region (see Southwestern Idaho: Class V Adventure, the Bruneau and Owyhee Rivers: Cowboy Country), offers several wineries.

Blue Rock Vineyard and Winery (208-543-6938), 4060 N. 1200 E., Buhl. Tasting room open 12–dusk Fri.–Sun. Apr.–Dec. and by appointment. This recent addition to the winery scene is perched on a hill overlooking lovely grounds and the vineyard, providing expansive views of the Snake River Canyon and the stunning mountains of Central Idaho to the north. The winery offers jazz and blues dinners and lunches during the summer.

Hegy's South Hills Winery (208-734-6369), 3099 W. 3400 N., Twin Falls. Tours and wine-tasting by appointment. This family-run operation opened in 1989, and all phases of wine-making—from crushing to bottling and labeling—are undertaken by family members.

RELICT POTATO HARVESTER

Matt Furber

Thousand Springs Winery (208-837-4001), 18852 US 30, Buhl. Tours by appointment.

✳ To Do

FISHING

While this region is not a destination fishing spot, if you feel the need to sink a line in the water, there is plenty of fishing (and ice fishing) to be done here. Contact **BLM Upper Snake River District** (208-478-6340) for information on fishing and camping in all these areas. Some of the more popular areas are these:

Blackfoot River on the north side of Blackfoot Reservoir (11 miles north of Soda Springs on ID 34), **Hawkins Reservoir** (west of I-15 just south of McCammon), and **Oneida Narrows Reservoir** (between ID 34 and ID 36 north of Preston) all have campgrounds.

Chesterfield Reservoir (off US 30 north of Lava Hot Springs), **Daniels Reservoir** (west of I-15 north of Malad City), **Stone Reservoir** (off I-84 just north of the Utah border), **Alexander Reservoir** (on US 30 at Soda Springs), and **Bear River** are also good fishing holes.

Lake Walcott Reservoir (208-334-4180) in the Minidoka Wildlife Refuge (northeast of Rupert off ID 24) is also popular, as are **Bear Lake National Wildlife Refuge, Caribou National Forest**, and **Curlew National Grassland** (see Wilder Places). You might also try **Hagerman Fossil Beds National Monument** (see To See—Historical Sites).

GOLF

The sometimes-balmy high-desert clime (dramatically contrasted by bone-chilling snow- and windstorms in the winter) of southern Idaho has attracted a number of golf courses, including these:

American Falls Golf Club (208-226-5827), 610 N. Oregon Trail, American Falls. Nine holes.

Bear Lake West Golf Course (208-945-2744), 155 US 89, Fish Haven. Nine holes.

Blackfoot Municipal Golf Course (208-785-9960), at 3115 Teeples Dr., Blackfoot. 18 holes.

Burley Municipal Golf Course (208-878-9807), 131 ID 81, Burley. 18 holes.

Canyon Springs Golf Course (208-734-7609; www.canyonspringsgolf.com), 199 Canyon Springs Rd., Twin Falls. 18 holes.

Central Links Golf Course (208-425-3585; www.centrallinksgolf.com), 1750 Gibson La., Grace (on ID 34 south of Soda Springs). Nine holes.

Clear Lake Country Club (208-543-4849), 1575 F Clear Lakes Grade, Buhl. 18 holes.

Gooding Country Club (208-934-9977), 1951 US 26, Gooding (north of Twin Falls). Nine holes.

Hazard Creek Golf Course (208-397-5308), 419 E. Bingham Ave., Aberdeen (on ID 39 north of American Falls). Nine holes.

Highland Golf Course (208-237-9922), 201 Van Elm La., Pocatello. 18 holes.

Montpelier Municipal Golf Course (208-847-1981), 210 Boise St., Montpelier. Nine holes.

Oregon Trail Country Club Golf Course (208-547-2204), 2525 US 30, Soda Springs. Nine holes.

Pleasant Valley Golf Course (208-423-5800), 3504 E. 3195 N., Kimberly (on US 30 just east of Twin Falls). Nine holes.

Ponderosa Golf Course (208-679-5730), 320 Minidoka Ave., Burley. Nine holes.

Preston Golf and Country Club (208-852-2408 or 877-852-2408), 1215 N. 800 E., Preston. Nine holes.

Riverside Golf Course (208-232-9515), 3500 Bannock Hwy., Pocatello. 18 holes.

Thunder Canyon Golf Course (208-776-5048; www.golflava.com), 9898 E. Merrick Rd., Lava Hot Springs. Nine holes.

HIKING

Travelers in southeastern Idaho who are looking for a way to stretch their legs will find that many of the areas listed in Wilder Places have hiking trails. If you are looking for a deep wilderness experience, the **Caribou-Targhee National Forest** (see Wilder Places) provides countless opportunities to hike along mountain streams, in to alpine lakes, and through subalpine terrain. Your best bet is to contact individual ranger district offices for detailed information about recreational activities in the region of interest within the forest. Hiking opportunities are particularly good in the Pocatello region's **Westside Ranger District** (208-236-7500). Many of the areas mentioned under Rock Climbing, Skiing (see Backcountry Skiing), and Mountain Biking are also great hiking spots.

HOT SPRINGS

The abundance of rhyolite, basalt, and ash blanketing much of southern Idaho is a testament to the region's volcanic past. Consistent with this history, all of the Snake River Plain falls within the Cordillerian Thermotectonic Anomaly, which contains 70 percent of the identified hydrothermal convection systems greater than 194 degrees F (90 degrees C) in the continental United States. One of the benefits of such geothermal activity is a plethora of hot springs! If you're looking for a soak, you might try one of several commercial hot springs in the region.

Aura Soma Lava (208-776-5800 or 800-757-1233; www.aurasomalava.com), 196 E. Main St., Lava Hot Springs.

Banbury Hot Springs (208-543-4098; www.banburyhotsprings.com), off US 30, 10 miles west of Buhl.

Bear Lake Hot Springs (208-945-4545), on north end of Bear Lake, just outside St. Charles. Open 10–10 Tues.–Sun.

Downata Hot Springs (208-897-5736; www.downatahotsprings.com), 25900 Downata Rd., Downey (on US 91 just south of I-15).

Lava Hot Springs (208-776-5221 or 800-423-8597; www.lavahotsprings.com), 430 E. Main St., Lava Hot Springs. Open 8 AM–11 PM Apr. 1–Sept. 30; 9 AM– 10 PM Mon.–Fri., 9 AM–11 PM Fri.–Sat. Oct. 1–Mar. 31. $5 and up per day. Lava Hot Springs, with its Olympic-size pool and waterslide, is much more commercial, but in some cases, soaking is soaking!

Maple Grove Hot Springs (208-851-1137; www.maplegrovehotsprings.com), 11386 N. Oneida Narrows Rd., Thatcher (on ID 34 south of Grace). Open 10–10 daily. $7 for adults, $3 for kids three–12, free for kids under three. This lovely, quiet natural hot springs is perched along the Bear River at the north end of Oneida Narrows Reservoir.

Miracle Hot Springs (208-543-6002; www.mhsprings.com), 19073 US 30, 9 miles south of Hagerman. Open 8 AM–11 PM Mon.–Sat. $9 for adults, $7 for seniors, $4 for kids four–13, $1 for kids under four. Zen-like Miracle Hot Springs, which offers a hot swimming pool, several private pools, therapeutic massage, and tranquil geodesic dome accommodations ($39 and up), is a favorite and reasonably priced.

Nat-Soo-Pah Hot Springs (208-655-4337; www.natsoopah.com), 2738 E. 2400 N., Twin Falls.

Riverdale Resort Hot Springs (208-852-0266; www.riverdaleresort.com), 3696 N. 1600 E. St., Preston.

MOUNTAIN BIKING

Portneuf Mountains near Pocatello offer great riding that vary from trails on steep, angular alpine slopes to buffed-out single track that winds though meadows, aspen stands, and thickly wooded areas.

South Hills, about 30 miles southeast of Twin Falls in the Minidoka District of the **Sawtooth National Forest** (208-737-3200; www.fs.fed.us/r4/sawtooth), is a popular riding spot. The area offers a 50-mile network of trails and a couple burly rides, including **Third Fork–Heart Attack Loop**, a 13.7-mile moderate to strenuous loop that runs along the South Fork of Rock Creek, and **South Hills Singletrack Nirvana**, a 26.8-mile strenuous and fairly technical loop through a varied landscape of open meadows, thick forest, and rushing streams.

Recommended Reading
For a guide to the six major riding areas around Pocatello, check out Bruce Blacks' *A Guide to Pocatello Mountain Bike Trails* (www.isu.edu/outdoor/mtbike .htm). Stephen Stuebner's *Mountain Biking Idaho* (Falcon, 1999) also provides details on rides in both the South Hills and the Portneuf Mountains.

ROCK CLIMBING
Castle Rocks State Park (208-824-5519; http://parksandrecreation.idaho.gov), 2 miles north of Almo on Elba-Almo Road, then west 1.4 miles on 2800 S. (Big Cove Ranch) Road. Open 7–10 year-round. $4 per vehicle per day. Part of the Almo Pluton, these 400-foot quartz monzonite spires have long drawn climbers, but only recently has the area been transformed from private property to a

1,440-acre state park. The majority of this land was formerly a ranch, and ranch structures and irrigated pasture are still present.

City of Rocks National Reserve (208-824-5519; http://home.nps.gov/ciro), off ID 77 just west of Almo (about 45 miles south of Burley); from I-84, take exit 216/Declo to ID 77 south to Connor Creek, then southwest on Elba-Almo Road to park entrance and visitor center. Open 8–4:30 year-round; it is hot, hot, hot here in mid-Aug.—climbing is best Apr.–Oct. Seemingly rising up from nowhere, like goblins, these towering granite pinnacles—some reaching as high as 70 stories—appear one after another on the horizon, marking the City of Rocks. Some as old as 2.5 billion years, these outstanding massive columns of the Green River Complex—with names such as Twin Sisters, Morning Glory Spire (aka Incisor), and Lost Arrow Spire—are among the oldest formations in North America. Interspersed among these ancient spires are some younger (25 million-year-old) intrusions of the Almo Pluton, notably the lighter of the two Twin Sisters. First dubbed the "Silent City of Rocks" by James F. Wilkins in 1849, the City became a beacon on the landscape for pioneers traveling west on the California Trail. Using axle grease, explorers left inscriptions on the spires; many remain today as a testament to this pioneer history. Set aside in 1988 as a 14,407-acre national reserve, the raw beauty of the granite city is complemented by a high-desert landscape of sagebrush steppe, 55-foot pinyon pines, and gnarled juniper. Spring and summer boast spectacular wildflower blooms.

Today the City of Rocks is an increasingly popular (and highly regarded) climbing destination, with more than 750 identified routes sporting names such as Wheat Thin, Rye Crisp, Private Idaho, Funky Bolt, and Tow Away Zone, on protruding plates, crags, and cracks of varying difficulty. About 75 designated camping spots ($7) and three group sites are scattered throughout the reserve; reservations are highly recommended, since, at times, the place can be a scene.

Idaho Falls, Firth (on US 91 north of Blackfoot), and **Kelly Canyon Ski Area** have climbs; **Southeast Idaho Climbing** (www.seiclimbing.com) has information.

Massacre Rocks State Park (208-548-2672; http://parksandrecreation.idaho .gov), off I-86 southwest of American Falls. Said to be the "best basalt climbing in the world," with more than 20 basalt walls, this is a favored climbing area in the Pocatello area.

Pocatello also has several bouldering spots around town. For climbing guides to Pocatello spots, check out **Idaho State University's Outdoor Program** (www .isu.edu/outdoor/climbing).

Outfitters
Several outfitters offer guided climbs and climbing instruction including these:

Exum Mountain Guides (307-733-2297; www.exumguides.com), Moose Wyoming.

Jackson Hole Mountain Guides (307-733-4979; www.jhmg.com), Jackson, Wyoming.

Sawtooth Mountain Guides (208-774-3324; www.sawtoothguides.com), Stanley.

Recommended Reading

Several hard-core climbers have written climbing guides to the City. A local favorite is *City of Rocks Idaho, 7th: A Climber's Guide* by Dave Bingham (Falcon, 2004); you might also try *Classic Rock Climbs No. 15 City of Rocks National Reserve* by Laird David (Falcon, 1996). For Castle Rocks climbing routes, check out Dave Bingham's *Castle Rocks Idaho* (Falcon, 2004).

SKIING

Alpine Skiing

Magic Mountain Ski Resort (208-734-5979; www.magicmountainresort.com), on Rock Creek Road 28 miles south of Hansen (southeast of Twin Falls). Lift tickets $25 for adults, $20 for seniors, $17 for youths, free for children six and under. This beginners' slope has 700 feet of vertical, 20 runs on 120 skiable acres, and one lift (plus a Poma and a rope tow).

Pebble Creek Ski Area (208-775-4452; www.pebblecreekskiarea.com), 3340 E. Green Canyon Rd., Inkom (on I-15 south of Pocatello). Lift tickets $35 for adults, $22 for seniors and children six–12, $3 for kids five and under. This is a well-kept secret with reasonable prices. Its mom-and-pop atmosphere (with only three lifts) doesn't easily reveal its 2,200 lift-serve vertical (2,911 feet of vertical within the permitted area) and advanced terrain (53 percent advanced runs). The resort has 54 runs on 1,100 skiable acres. Local lore says that Averill Harriman considered Mount Bonneville (on which Pebble Creek resides) as a site for Sun Valley, but found road access to the east slopes too difficult (we in Sun Valley might claim differently!). You can access backcountry terrain in the Caribou-Targhee National Forest from the top of Pebble Creek.

Pomerelle Mountain Resort (208-673-5599; www.pomerelle-mtn.com), off ID 77 outside of Albion (25 miles off I-84 via exit 216/Declo-Albion). Lift tickets $32 for adults, $20 for seniors and kids. While it doesn't have much in the way of challenging slopes, Pomerelle often seems to be collecting snow as its more glitzy neighbors in Central Idaho bide their time. A small, family mountain with only two chairs, 24 runs, and 1,000 feet of vertical, it does have some sweet little glades and often some hidden (or not-so-hidden) powder stashes.

Backcountry Skiing

Between wide-expanses of windswept snow blanketing nothing but sage, there are some high-alpine backcountry ski experiences to be had in southeastern Idaho. An abundance of snowmobilers in this region can be of concern, and it would be wise to inquire about the tendency for off-trail snowmobiling around your route of interest.

Bannock Range's Elkhorn and Oxford peaks can be accessed via I-15 north of Malad City.

Bear River Range's favored peaks can be accessed via ID 36 between Montpelier and Preston, as the road passes over a saddle between Emigration Canyon to the west and Strawberry Canyon to the east.

Preuss Range's Meade Peak is east of Montpelier.

Caribou-Targhee National Forest (208-524-7500; www.fs.fed.us/r4/caribou -targhee) district offices in the region may be helpful in planning a backcountry route:

Montpelier Ranger District (208-847-0375), 322 N. Fourth St., Montpelier.

Soda Springs Ranger District (208-547-4356), 410 Hooper Ave., Soda Springs.

Westside Ranger District, Malad Office (208-766-5900), 195 S. 300 St., Malad City.

Westside Ranger District, Pocatello Office (208-236-7500), 4350 Cliffs Dr., Pocatello.

Idaho State University's Outdoor Program (208-282-3912; www.isu.edu/ outdoor/yurtinfo.html) runs a system of five yurts in the Portneuf Range east of Downey and a sixth yurt in Bloomington Canyon, northwest of Bear Lake. Organized tours to the huts are available and encouraged, but more experienced skiers may be able to take responsibility for their own routefinding.

Recommended Reading
See *Winter Tales and Trails: Skiing Snowshoeing and Snowboarding in Idaho, the Grand Tetons and Yellowstone National Park* (Great Rift Press, 1997) by Ron Watters for more information.

Nordic Skiing
As in much of Idaho, wide-open spaces here mean plenty of opportunity for Nordic skiing in this region. There is great cross-country skiing in many of the open spaces and wild places listed throughout this section, including **Bear Lake National Wildlife Refuge** (see Wilder Places), **City of Rocks National Reserve** (see Rock Climbing), and **Craters of the Moon National Monument** (see Parks). Areas with Nordic tracks include these:

Bear Lake–Cub River Nordic Ski & Snowshoe Trails (208-852-2124; www .cubriverguestranch.com), 1942 N. Deer Cliff Rd., Preston.

Kelly Park Nordic Ski Area (208-547-2600), near Soda Springs.

Magic Mountain Ski Resort (see Alpine Skiing).

Mink Creek Nordic Ski Area (208-236-7500), near Pocatello.

North Fork Inman Nordic Ski Trail (208-236-7500), near Pocatello.

Penstemon Nordic Ski Trail (208-678-0430), outside Twin Falls.

Pomerelle Ski Resort (see Alpine Skiing).

Rock Creek Canyon Trails (208-678-0430), outside Twin Falls.

Trail Canyon Nordic Ski Trail (208-547-4356), near Soda Springs.

Recommended Reading
For other cross-country ski routes in southeast Idaho, check out *Winter Tales and Trails: Skiing Snowshoeing and Snowboarding in Idaho, the Grand Tetons and Yellowstone National Park* (Great Rift Press, 1997) by Ron Watters.

Malad River, above its confluence with the Snake at Malad Gorge State Park, has a couple miles that are raftable.

Snake River, which sweeps through southeastern Idaho in an arching crescent, is known for its big surf waves. While the Snake is not a big boating destination, several of its sections are favored by boaters. These include the following:

Milner Gorge, class V, is a favorite destination.

Murtaugh Canyon sports some big class III–V rapids—Let's Make a Deal and Pair-A-Dice among them.

Wiley Reach (aka the Bliss Run) is one of the few stretches boatable year-round. It's a fairly mellow (although it does have some class II–III rapids) 6-mile run.

Outfitters
For guided trips on this portion of the Snake, check out **Idaho Guide Service** (208-734-4998 or 888-73IDAHO; www.idahoguideservice.com).

Recommended Reading
For detailed information on these stretches, consult Grant Amaral's *Idaho: The Whitewater State* (BookCrafters, 1990).

✳ Wilder Places

Caribou-Targhee National Forest (208-524-7500; www.fs.fed.us/r4/caribou -targhee), more than 3 million acres of southeastern Idaho, from its borders with Montana, Wyoming, and Utah. This immense forest stretching across southeastern Idaho encompasses a series of northwest–southeast-trending, rugged mountain ranges, including the Bannock, Porneuf, Wasatch, Aspen, and Caribou ranges, as well as the Curlew Valley and its Curlew National Grassland (see Parks and Monuments), and crystalline rivers and creeks. About 300 species of nesting birds and 85 species of mammals, amphibians, and reptiles make their homes in the Caribou-Targhee. Among them are elk, deer, bighorn sheep, black bears, coyotes, mountain lions, trumpeter swans, prairie falcons, ferruginous hawks, bald and golden eagles, and ospreys. Approximately 1,200 miles of trails traverse the forest, providing fabulous hiking, backpacking, and camping. Contact individual ranger districts for more information about specific areas of the forest and recreational opportunities (see To Do—Skiing—Backcountry Skiing).

PARKS AND PRESERVES
Bear Lake State Park (208-847-1045; http://parksandrecreation.idaho.gov), east of US 89 near St. Charles (20 miles south of Montpelier). Stretching 966 acres along the east shore of Bear Lake (see Lakes), the park offers boating, water-skiing, swimming, fishing, and two sandy beaches: a 2-mile-long beach at the north end and a 1.5-mile-long beach on the eastern shore. Some 47 individual campsites ($12 standard, $16 serviced) and three group sites ($75 and $100) are available.

Box Canyon State Park (208-334-4199), off I-84 west of Wendell (20 miles northwest of Twin Falls); take exit 155 off I-84 in Wendell, go west 3 miles to

CR 1500 E., turn left, and go 3.2 miles to signed parking lot on the right. Recently transferred to the state by the Nature Conservancy, Box Canyon is a unique geologic feature. The 11th-largest spring in the United States, its crystalline blue artesian waters emerge after traveling subterraneously through fractured lava formations for nearly a century. The spectacular springs are home to endangered Shoshone sculpin, and the cliffs that line the mile-long canyon provide habitat for eagles, owls, hawks, and falcons. The U.S. Department of Energy has used infiltration data from this site to calibrate some of their groundwater flow models for the Snake River aquifer. Visitors to the park enjoy hiking, birdwatching, and wildlife viewing. Restrooms are available.

Castle Rocks State Park: see To Do—Rock Climbing.

Craters of the Moon National Monument (208-527-3257; www.nps.gov/crmo), off US 93, 18 miles southwest of Arco. Open 8–4:40 most of the year; 8–6 in summer. Free. With more than 70 percent of the area designated in 1970 as a wilderness area, Craters of the Moon is aptly named. This windswept lavascape—the signature of repeated volcanic eruptions along the Great Rift some 15,000–2,100 years ago, with its cinder cones and spatter cones, lava tubes and ice caves—certainly possesses a lunar quality. In fact, in 1969 *Apollo* astronauts Joe Engle, Alan Shepard, Eugen Cernan, and Edgar Mitchell visited Craters of the Moon to study its varied volcanic features, helping them learn to discern

NORDIC SKIING AT CRATERS OF THE MOON NATIONAL MONUMENT

meteor craters from volcanic craters. With splashes of wildflower color in spring and a wind-whipped meringue layer of snow blanketing the ragged earth in winter, it is at once surreal and starkly beautiful. Of particular interest is the **Tree Molds** area, where more than 100 tree impressions have been mapped—as lava enveloped the trees, they began to burn, releasing water and other vapors, which quickly cooled the surrounding lava and left sometimes quite-detailed impressions of the tree branches and bark. Over time, the trees themselves decomposed, leaving only images in the lava. The **Devil's Orchard**, with its collection of small, gnarled trees, is also intriguing. The 43,243-acre wilderness area is accessed by trails that allow for hiking, Nordic skiing, and camping. It is very dry and hot here during the summer, so please bring plenty of water and sunscreen.

Curlew National Grassland (208-766-4743), off ID 37 near Holbrook; from I-15 at Malad City, go west on ID 38 and south on Stone Road, about 31 miles total. Open 6–10 Apr. 15–Oct. 15. $8 per vehicle. The only national grassland in the intermountain West (representing the Great Basin Ecosystem), the Curlew National Grassland was established in 1960 and spans more than 47,000 acres of non-native seeded grasses and sagebrush. First inhabited by the Bannock and Shoshone Indians, the area was eventually settled by Mormon pioneers and used extensively for cattle ranching, with a ranch on every 160 acres. Plagued by overgrazing, the drought of the late 1920s and early 1930s, and the Depression, many of the ranches fell into disuse, leaving the land barren and desiccated. As a relief measure, the federal government purchased much of the land between 1934 and 1942 and worked to restore the soils and vegetation. Today, the expansive grasslands are administered by the U.S. Forest Service and managed to promote grassland agriculture and sustainable yields of forage, fish, and wildlife. The grassland provides habitat for a diversity of wildlife, upland game, and waterfowl, including the threatened sage grouse, and sustains more than 21,000 animal months of grazing.

Hagerman Fossil Beds National Monument: see To See—Historical Sites.

Lake Walcott State Park (208-436-1258; http://parksandrecreation.idaho.gov), 11 miles northeast of Rupert off ID 24. With more than 20,000 acres, over half of which is open water and marsh, this park offers great water access for windsurfing, sailing, water-skiing, boating, swimming, and bird-watching. Visitors can also check out the Minidoka Dam, and grassy picnic areas and camping spots ($12) are available.

Malad Gorge State Park (208-837-4505), 1074 E. 2350 S., Hagerman; take exit 147 off I-84. Open 7–10 year-round. $4 per vehicle. Here, the spectacular Malad River Canyon crashes down staircase cascades into the Devil's Washbowl and then slices 250 feet into the underlying basalt of the Snake River Canyon rim, running 2.5 miles to its confluence with the Snake River. The river gained its name when a French trapping party fell ill after eating beavers from the river, dubbing it "Malade." A slender bridge arcs over the canyon at the 652-acre park, providing fabulous views (not for the faint of heart) of the cascades and the columnar basalt walls. With its amazing light play, this is a favored spot for photographers. Today the river is a mere ghost of its former grandeur, having fallen prey to copious irrigation diversions upgradient. Camping ($12) and a reserve shelter ($30) are available.

Massacre Rocks State Park: see To Do—Rock Climbing.

WILDLIFE REFUGES

Bear Lake National Wildlife Refuge (208-847-1757; www.fws.gov/refuges), off US 89 between Montpelier and Ovid; from Montpelier, take US 89 west to marked turnoff for a gravel road running south midway between Montpelier and Ovid, then head south for about 5 miles. Bear Lake has an interesting geologic past, with benchlike shoreline terraces demarking earlier and higher shorelines, which many moons (130,000–600,000 years) ago may have reached as much as 75 feet above present-day levels. At high water, the lake may have reached 50 miles long (in contrast to 18 miles today). Only in recent geologic history has the Bear River been directed into Bear Lake to maintain it as a reservoir. Prior to this, only springwater and runoff fed the lake, resulting in fairly unique water chemistry derived from the mineral contribution of the springs. As a result, the lake has a high rate of endemism, with at least four species—the Bonneville cisco, Bonneville whitefish, Bear Lake whitefish, and Bear Lake sculpin—found nowhere else. The dilution of the lake with river water is a threat to these species and may have caused extinction of at least several endemic ostracodes identified in the paleologic record. Artifacts found within the marsh suggest that the Shoshone used Bear Lake Valley for grazing horses and hunting, and Bannock tribes may also have visited. With 19,000 acres of bulrush marsh, open water and flooded sedge, rushes, and grasslands nestled in a long graben valley between the Bear River Range to the west and the Aspen Range to the east, this refuge is an important nesting, resting, and feeding spot for 161 bird species, including greater sandhill cranes (seen by the hundreds), redhead ducks, the rare white-faced ibis, Canada geese, and other waterfowl. Among those drawn to the bulrush habitat are snowy egrets, great blue herons, Caspian terns, and black-crowned night-herons. Four-legged critters, including mule deer, moose, muskrats, cottontail rabbits, skunks, coyotes, beavers, mink, and weasels, can also been seen. The vista here is particularly breathtaking in winter, when the white of rounded, snow-draped hills rises up from the gleaming blue of the lake to again meet the brilliant blue of our wide sky, all grounded by a swath of reddish-umber reed.

Grays Lake National Wildlife Refuge (208-574-2755; www.fws.gov/Refuges), off ID 34 about 27 miles north of Soda Springs. This spectacular, 19,400-acre refuge managed by the U.S. Fish and Wildlife Service contains the largest montane, hardstem bulrush marsh in North America. Located in a high-altitude valley (elevation 6,400 feet), the large, open bulrush and cattail marsh is surrounded by wet meadows and grasslands, providing habitat to more than 200 species of mammals, amphibians, fish, and birds. Encircled by mountains—the Caribou Range to the northeast, the Webster Range to the southeast, and Gray's Range to the south—and bursting with the colors of wildflowers during the spring and changing foliage in the fall, the refuge is quite spectacular. Visitors enjoy watching the nesting populations of graceful trumpeter swans and greater sandhill cranes. During migration and staging seasons, it is not uncommon to see more than 1,000 cranes throughout the valley. Sadly, the marsh is facing increased pressure from development.

Hagerman Wildlife Management Area (208-324-4359; http://fishandgame .idaho.gov/cms/wildlife/wma/hag), off US 30 south of Hagerman; drive US 30 12.5 miles south of Hagerman to just past turnoff for Hagerman National Fish Hatchery, then turn east at WMA sign onto a gravel road. Open year-round. Established in 1940, this was Idaho's first wildlife management area, set aside to provide habitat for waterfowl and upland game birds. Much of the 880-acre area is devoted to wildlife habitat and is filled with marshes, ponds, and open waterways, attracting as many as 55,000 ducks and 4,000 Canada geese during winter. Abundant resident waterfowl include ruddy ducks, mallards, gadwalls, Canada geese, and redheads; migratory species include northern pintails, cinnamon- and green-winged teals, ring-necked ducks, trumpeter and tundra swans, and American wigeons. Visitors might also spy graceful great blue herons, black-crowned night herons, Virginia rails, spotted sandpipers, California quail, ring-necked pheasants, ospreys, bald eagles, and peregrine falcons. Mammals include mule deer, red foxes, badgers, cottontail rabbits, coyotes, yellow-bellied marmots, river otters, beavers, and muskrats. Amphibians and reptiles include western rat-

LAVA FIELDS NEAR SHOSHONE ON THE SNAKE RIVER PLAIN

tlesnakes, gopher snakes, western and Great Basin spadefoot toads, and bull-
frogs. A portion of the area is also used as a fish hatchery.

Minidoka National Wildlife Refuge (208-436-3589; www.fws.gov/pacific/
refuges/field/ID_minidoka.htm), off ID 24, 5.5 miles northeast of Rupert; turn right
on Minidoka Dam road to the refuge. This 20,721-acre refuge runs 25 miles along
the Snake River and includes 11,000-acre Lake Walcott (created by Minidoka
Dam), with its abundant aquatic and marshy vegetation, and surrounding sagebrush
and grassland uplands. Several islands dot the reservoir. This combined habitat supports up to 100,000 ducks and geese as they migrate along the Pacific Flyway during spring and fall. The lucky visitor might also glimpse flocks of migrating tundra
swans and bald and golden eagles, owls, and hawks, as well as beavers, muskrats,
coyotes, Nutall's cottontails, mule deer, and pronghorn antelope.

Niagara Springs Wildlife Management Area (208-677-6641; www.blm.gov),
off I-84 south of Wendell; take exit 157 and head south 7 miles to signed
entrance road. This wildlife area spans 957 acres along the Snake River, encompassing eight islands and the Niagara Springs Ranch. The well-developed riparian ecosystem and the steep walls of the Snake River Canyon provide habitat for
canyon wrens, Say's phoebes, Bullock's orioles, common yellowthroats, yellow-
breasted chats, American white pelicans, great blue herons, golden eagles,
Caspian terns, and double-crested cormorants. Mule deer and various small
mammals also abound.

✴ Lodging

Southeastern Idaho is not known for
its tasteful accommodations, and
many of the more upscale spots that
do exist tend to be of baroque,
themed décor—go figure. It's all a little much, but certainly interesting.

BED & BREAKFASTS

Blackfoot
Stout Street Bed and Breakfast
(208-785-0282 or 866-735-2901; www
.stoutst-bedandbreakfast.com), 87 N.
Stout St., Blackfoot 83221. This 1905
Victorian mansion hosts four themed
guest rooms, an entertainment room
and theater, a reception hall, and an
elaborate dining room and lounge
area with a fireplace. Rooms include
breakfast. $75.

Fish Haven
Bear Lake Bed & Breakfast (208-
945-2688; www.bearlakebedand

breakfast.com), 500 Loveland La.,
Fish Haven 83287. Five themed guest
rooms—including the Bear, Cowboy,
and Country rooms—are augmented
by a hot tub, recreation room, and
deck. Rooms include a hearty breakfast. $70 and up.

Bluebird Inn (208-945-2571 or 800-
797-6448; www.thebluebirdinn.com),
423 US 89, Fish Haven 83287. Overlooking Bear Lake, this is yet another
themed B&B, with Bear, Beehive, and
Bluebird rooms. Rooms come with a
gourmet breakfast. $140–150.

Gooding
Gooding Hotel Bed & Breakfast
(208-934-43740, 112 Main St., Gooding 83330. Listed on the National
Register of Historic Places, the Gooding Hotel was built in the late 1880s,
with an addition in 1906, to provide
rooms for railroad workers and rail

travelers. At one time owned by Frank R. Gooding—the city's namesake and a former governor and Idaho state senator, the property is currently owned by his descendents. The B&B has 10 guest rooms, breakfast included. $69–95.

Hagerman

Ein Tisch Inn Bed & Breakfast (208-837-9099; www.eintischinn.com), 165 W. Valley Rd., Hagerman 83332. Two little cottages come with continental breakfast; dining and cooking classes are also offered here. $65 and $90.

Lava Hot Springs

Lion's Gate Manor Bed and Breakfast (208-776-5118; www .lionsgatemanor.com), 10376 Dempsey Creek Rd., Lava Hot Springs 83246. The themed rooms in this B&B, which run from the Medieval Chamber and Touch of Spain to Roman Bath and Persian Dream, include breakfast. $109 and up.

Swanlake

Smithland Bed and Breakfast (208-897-5148; www.smithland.cc), 10286 E. Red Rock Rd., Swanlake (on US 91 north of Preston) 83281. Situated on 480 acres of homesteaded land, this B&B began as a post–World War I log cabin. The current owners expanded the home with an addition. The property now has four guest rooms with private baths, handpeeled logs, solar electricity, and a collection of kerosene lamps. Rooms include a full breakfast. $70 and up.

CABINS

U.S. Forest Service (www.fs.fed .us/r4/caribou-targhee/recreation/ cabins/index.shtml) has a handful of rustic cabins throughout the Caribou-Targhee National Forest. $25–45.

Downey

Downata Hot Springs (208-897-5736; www.downatahotsprings.com), 25900 S. Downata Rd., Downey 83234. Yurts and cabins are available at this developed hot springs. $75 and up.

Pocatello

Buckskin Outpost (208-232-9456; www.buckskinoutpost.com), 5430 W. Skyview Rd., Pocatello 83201. This place is an oddity in that it provides laid-back, quaint accommodations in a beautiful, rustic cabin and tepee nestled in a wooded alpine setting just east of Pocatello. This is a really nice spot. $95.

INNS & MOTELS

American Falls

Fairview Inn (208-226-2060), 2998 Fairview La., American Falls 83211. Nestled in the hills of Southeastern Idaho, this 100-year-old Victorian-era country inn provides a pleasurable, pastoral sojourn. $69–100.

Inkom

Jackson Creek Inn (208-241-9089; www.jacksoncreekinn.com), 1005 E. Jackson Creek Rd., Inkom 83245. A two-bedroom barn has a full kitchen. $99.

Pocatello

Black Swan Inn (208-233-3051; www.blackswaninn.com), 746 E. Center St., Pocatello 83201. This unique English Tudor built in 1933 originally featured 10 two-story apartments. Recently renovated and luxuriously appointed with sculptures and murals, each room in the inn has a unique theme—including the Egyptian, Black Swan, Arabian Nights, and Caveman suites. $99 and up.

Twin Falls

Blue Lakes Boulevard has an abundance of chain hotels (in addition to being a box-store hell) if you need a place to crash on your way to and from the Twin Falls airport.

LODGES AND GUEST RANCHES

Lava Hot Springs

Andrus Ranch (208-776-5113; www.andrusranch.com), 6948 E. Old Oregon Trail, Lava Hot Springs 83246. At this rustic working ranch at the foot of the Caribou-Targhee National Forest, guests can participate in trail rides, cattle roundups, sheep shearing, roping, fishing, and other daily ranch activities. The area also offers hiking and mountain biking trails. $85 and up.

Preston

Cub River Lodge & Guest Ranch (208-852-2124; www.cubriverguest ranch.com), 1942 N. Deer Cliff Rd., Preston 83263. Rooms in the guest lodge can accommodate large groups. $49 and up.

Soda Springs

Bar H Bar Ranch (208-547-3082; www.BarHBar.com), 1501 Eight Mile Creek Rd., Soda Springs 83276. This 10,000-acre working ranch lies deep in the Bear River Valley. Visitors may expect to see calving, branding, and cattle roundups. Activities including horseback riding, hiking, and fishing. Bunkhouse lodging includes all home-cooked meals. $900 for five nights.

RESORTS

Hagerman

Miracle Hot Springs (208-543-6002;

www.mhsprings.com), 19073 US 30, Buhl (9 miles south of Hagerman) 83316. Tranquil geodesic dome accommodations, a hot swimming pool, several private pools, and therapeutic massage are found at this resort. $39 and up.

✳ Where to Eat

DINING OUT

As a friend said, "Southeastern Idaho fine dining is an oxymoron." Nevertheless, there are a couple gems in Pocatello.

Pocatello

Continental Bistro (208-233-4433), 140 S. Main St. With a diverse menu of fine fusion food augmented by 16 microbrews on tap and an impressive wine selection, this is a local favorite. Outdoor seating and live music on Wed. nights make this place a go.

Senang Wine Bar and Tapas Bistro (208-478-6732; www.senang tapas.com), 815 S. First Ave. This fabulous, intimate place with exposed-brick walls has a classy wine bar and tasty fresh tapas, including ceviche with shrimp, shark, and mango or perhaps slow-roasted baby beets and Humbolt Fog goat cheese, as well as bruschetta, all made with as many regional ingredients as possible. A special find in this neck of the woods.

✳ Cultural Offerings

Magic Valley Arts Council (208-734-ARTS; www.magicvalleyarts council.org), 132 Main Ave. S., Twin Falls. The most vibrant cultural scene in this region is found in and around Twin Falls. The arts council runs two galleries, produces plays, promotes outdoor art in the region, and hosts gallery openings and gallery walks.

Davis Art Gallery (208-282-2361; www.isu.edu/art), lower level of Fine Arts Building, on Idaho State University campus, Pocatello. Open 10–4. This gallery hosts student and touring art shows.

Full Moon Gallery of Fine Art and Contemporary Craft (208-734-ARTS; www.magicvalleyartscouncil .org), Twin Falls. This local cooperative gallery run by the Magic Valley Arts Council features sculpture, ceramics, painting, photography, and prints.

Galeria Pequena (208-734-ARTS; www.magicvalleyartscouncil.org), Twin Falls. Single-artist shows are held for emerging and established artists with small inventories of work and working in a variety of media. This gallery is also operated by the Magic Valley Arts Council.

Transitional Gallery (208-282-3451; www.isu.edu/stunion/gallery), lower level of Earl R. Pond Student Union, Idaho State University campus, Pocatello. Most of this region is not known for its highfalutin' arts scene, but this gallery hosts student and touring art shows.

DANCE AND THEATER

College of Southern Idaho Fine Arts Center (208-732-6288; http://fineartscenter.csi.edu), 315 Falls Ave., Twin Falls. CSI hosts an impressive array of ongoing performances by local theater and dance troops, plus concerts and lectures. The center serves as the permanent home of the **Arts on Tour** performance series and **Dilettantes of the Magic Valley**, the oldest theater group in the region.

Iron Door Playhouse (208-766-4705), 59 N. Main St., Malad City.

The playhouse showcases local talent in plays and cowboy poetry.

Nuart Theater (208-785-5344; www .nuarttheatre.org), 195 N. Broadway St., Blackfoot. $7 per person. Home to the **Blackfoot Community Players**, whose recent theatrical productions have included *The Music Man* and *Mousetrap*, this funky brick theater building is listed on the National Register of Historic Places.

Oakley Valley Arts Council (208-677-ARTS; www.oakleyvalleyarts .com), Oakley. Plays are performed at Howells Opera House, opened in 1907 and said to be the oldest-running theater in Idaho. It is replete with crystal chandeliers, velvet curtains, and a domed ceiling.

Worm Creek Opera House (208-852-0088), 70 S. State St., Preston. Plays and melodramas by the **Northern Cache Valley Theatre Guild** and other groups are hosted here during the summer. Movies, school productions, theater guild performances, and other community activities are offered year-round.

MUSIC

College of Southern Idaho Fine Arts Center (208-732-6288; http:// fineartscenter.csi.edu), 315 Falls Ave., Twin Falls. CSI hosts concerts and lectures; the center serves as the permanent home of the **Magic Valley Symphony**, the **Magic Valley Chorale**, and the **MagiChords**.

Twin Falls Tonight Concert Series (208-734-2113; www.twinfallsid.org), near fountain on Main Street, Twin Falls. Held 6–9 PM Wed. in summer. This concert series cosponsored by Historic Old Towne Twin Falls and the Magic Valley Arts Council features blues, bluegrass, rhythm and blues, rock, and world beat music. Food and drink are available from local vendors.

✳ Entertainment

FILM

Lamphouse Theater (208-736-8600), 223 Fifth Ave. S., Twin Falls. They show foreign and independent films and also host various plays, poetry readings, and midnight showings of *Rocky Horror Picture Show*.

✳ Special Events

February: **Fire and Ice Winter Festival** (208-776-5500; www.lavahotsprings.org), Lava Hot Springs. Idahoans are known for their robust celebrations of winter. This winter festival includes Idaho wine tasting, best barista, bartender, and chili contests, a Polar Bear race down the Portneuf River, and a Running of the Bulls (i.e., scantily clad contestants running down Main Street to plunge into Lava Hot Springs).

Simplot Games (208-235-5604; www.simplotgames.com), Holt Arena at Idaho State University, Pocatello. Third weekend in Feb. This is the nation's premier indoor track and field event for high school athletes. The facility boasts a 200-meter banked-board track that is one of the fastest in the nation; records are broken each year. Athletes come from across the United States and Canada to compete.

March: **Dodge National Circuit Finals Rodeo** (208-233-1546; www.dncfr.org), Idaho State University Holt Arena, Pocatello. This popular, weeklong rodeo promises lots of excitement, including bucking chutes, slalom and barrel racing, concerts, a

Cowboy Expo, a Rodeo Queen contest, and a horse sale.

May: **Hagerman Fossil Days** (208-837-9131; www.hagermanchamber.com), Hagerman. Memorial Day weekend. This family event offers music, live entertainment, dancing, craft vendors, games for kids, and food.

June–July: **Biggest Show in Idaho Fireworks Extravaganza** (208-237-1340), Bannock County Fairgrounds, Pocatello. Held 2 PM–dusk July 4. This lively event features entertainment, music, food, games, and, of course, impressive fireworks.

Blackfoot Pride Days (www.blackfootpridedays.org), various locations, Blackfoot. This weekend event features down-home fun—a triathlon, basketball tournament, snow machine racing, car show, battle of the bands, skateboard rally, dog show, and potato feed.

Idaho Music & Wildflower Festival (208-775-4452; www.pebblecreekskiarea.com/wildflower.html), at Pebble Creek Ski Area, Inkom. $5 in advance, $7 at the door. What better way to check out the mountain scene than by relaxing on the grassy slopes listening to fabulous alternative, blues, and rock music while lounging on a picnic blanket and drinking microbrewed beer from Portneuf Brewing Company? Guided wildflower hikes are offered before the concert. Proceeds support the National Ski Patrol.

Jazz in the Canyon (208-734-ARTS; www.magicvalleyartscouncil.org), Centennial Park and downtown Twin Falls. Mid-June. This annual weekendlong jazz celebration features an evening of jazz and wine tasting, jazz concerts in historic downtown Twin Falls, and a day of jazz nestled in the Snake River Canyon at Centennial Park.

Lavender Festival (208-543-4283; www.valleyviewlavenderfarm.com), Valley View Lavender Farm, 4297 Carter Pack Rd., Buhl. Weekend after July 4. This event features a Lavender Luncheon with lavender-roasted chicken, lavender sweet tea, lavender margaritas, and lavender ice cream. Local artisans sell homemade goods, and visitors are invited to pick lavender, listen to music, enjoy pony cart rides through aromatic lavender fields, and watch lavender-oil-distilling demonstrations.

Live History Day (208-324-5641; www.historicaljeromecounty.com), Idaho Farm and Ranch Museum, 220 N. Lincoln St., Jerome. Second Sat. of June. This annual event provides a window into pioneer life.

Malad Valley Welsh Festival (208-766-4010; www.welshfestival.com), Malad City. In celebration of their Welsh history, the people of Malad Valley come together in an *eisteddfod* (a Welsh translation of literature, music and performance) to share a weekend of arts. Welsh pioneers of the 1860s were the first settlers of Malad Valley; today, this area boasts the largest per capita concentration of people of Welsh ancestry outside Wales.

SPUD ART

Matt Furber

Portneuf Greenway RiverFest

(208-234-GWAY; www.pgfweb.com), Taysom Rotary Park, Pocatello. Since 1992, Pocatello has been celebrating its Greenway trail system with a RiverFest featuring live outdoor music, a fund-raiser raffle, hands-on activities, and food and beverages.

Portneuf Mountain Man Rendezvous

(208-237-4475; www.pocatellocvb.com), just outside McCammon (3.5 miles west of I-15 at McCammon exit 44). Yup, this is Idaho. This crazy reenactment weekend by rugged mountain men offers plenty of fun with guns—with trade-gun, cartridge, and long-range black-powder cartridge shoots. Also offered is a "special shoot for a man's, woman's, and kid's rifle." Bring the whole family! You can also learn how to start a fire with flint and steel and purchase pre-1840s goods at a trader's circle.

Western Days

(208-733-3974; www.twinfallschamber.com), City Park, Twin Falls. This is Twin Falls' big party, where "everyone's a cowboy," with opening ceremonies, Queen of the Magic Valley contest, a full western parade—complete with beautifully restored horsedrawn wagons, big Shriners in their little cars, and old-fashioned trolleys—dancing, and rocking music (sometimes even the Braun Brothers gang). The event attracts about 30,000 people.

August: **Bannock County Bluegrass Festival** (www.bannockcountyblue grassfestival.com), Bannock County Fairgrounds, Pocatello. $35 for weekend pass. This three-day bluegrass jam-fest includes numerous bands, free music workshops, beginners and advanced bluegrass jam sessions, and good food. Camping is available on-site.

September: **Eastern Idaho State Fair** (208-785-2480; www.idaho-state-fair.com), Eastern Idaho State Fairgrounds, 97 Park St., Blackfoot. $5 for adults, $1 for children, free for kids five and under. This weeklong event features traditional fair fare—farm animals and produce exhibits, a rodeo, bull riding, a carnival, concerts, a demolition derby, a horse show, and food—attracting more than 30,000 people each year.

Sagebrush Arts Fest (208-232-0970; http://pocatelloartctr.org), Pocatello Art Center on Idaho State University campus, Pocatello. This weekend arts and crafts fair showcases regional art and provides live music and dance, food, and free art activities for children.

Thousand Springs Festival (www.thousandspringsfestival.org), Thousand Springs Preserve, near Hagerman. This weekend event features great juried art, music, and environmental education in a lovely setting. Magicians, storytellers, and horserides entertain kids (and adults).

October: **Oktoberfest** (208-734-2113; www.twinfallid.org), historic downtown Twin Falls. Held in the beginning of the month, this festival features a chalk walk, live entertainment, and music. At the same time, various beer-tasting events can be found at pubs around town.

November: **Preston Festival of Lights** (208-852-2703; www.preston idaho.org), Preston. At the end of the month, this annual festival kicks off the holiday season with a city-wide light display, parade, and live entertainment.

INDEX